The Promises of Liberty

The Promises of Liberty

THE HISTORY AND CONTEMPORARY RELEVANCE
OF THE THIRTEENTH AMENDMENT

Edited by Alexander Tsesis

COLUMBIA UNIVERSITY PRESS

NEW YORK

Columbia University Press
Publishers Since 1893
New York   Chichester, West Sussex

Library of Congress Cataloging-in-Publication Data

The promises of liberty : the history and contemporary relevance of the Thirteenth
Amendment / edited by Alexander Tsesis.

    p.   cm.

Includes bibliographical references and index.

ISBN 978-0-231-14144-4 (cloth : alk. paper)—ISBN 978-0-231-52013-3 (e-book)

    1. Slavery—Law and legislation—United States.   2. United States. Constitution. 13th
Amendment.   I. Tsesis, Alexander.   II. Title.

KF4545.S5P76   2010

342.7308'7—dc22   2010003026

Columbia University Press books are printed on permanent and durable acid-free paper.
This book is printed on paper with recycled content.
Printed in the United States of America
c 10 9 8 7 6 5 4 3

References to Internet Web sites (URLs) were accurate at the time of writing. Neither the author
nor Columbia University Press is responsible for URLs that may have expired or changed since
the manuscript was prepared.

In memory of Charles Sumner and Thaddeus Stevens

CONTENTS

Foreword: The Rocky Road to Freedom

CRUCIAL BARRIERS TO ABOLITION IN THE ANTEBELLUM YEARS

David Brion Davis

The Thirteenth Amendment, finally approved by Congress on January 31, 1865, and ratified on December 6, 1865, almost eight months after the Confederate surrender at Appomattox, outlawed slavery and involuntary servitude, except as punishment for crime, in the United States and its territories. The amendment repeated the words of the Northwest Ordinance (1787), which drew in turn on Thomas Jefferson's rejected words in the Ordinance of 1784, banning slavery after the year 1800 in all the western territories. It was Jefferson who chose the phrase "neither slavery nor involuntary servitude," followed by the significant exception that sanctioned even slavery as a punishment for someone duly convicted of crime (there is a certain irony in the fact that African rulers regarded many of the slaves sold to European traders as guilty of some kind of crime).

The word "slave," derived in western European languages from the Latin word for Slav, due to the large number of so-called Slavic peoples who were enslaved from the tenth to the mid-fifteenth centuries and sold in Mediterranean markets, had long carried negative and wildly metaphoric meanings even for the vast majorities who accepted the actual, millennia-old institution of chattel bondage (hence the tendency to find substitutes for the words "slaves" and "slavery" from the King James Bible to the U.S. Constitution). Thus one could be enslaved to love, sex, alcohol, work, and daily routines, and any threat of encroaching authority could be viewed as impending "enslavement," as dramatized by American colonists in response to British taxation and other measures following the Seven Years' War. In short, slavery and enslavement loomed as any perceived infringement on *freedom*, and the meanings and importance of freedom expanded dramatically as Western societies moved from the late Middle Ages to the nineteenth century. Given this linguistic background, and the fact that the second section of the Thirteenth Amendment gives Congress seemingly unlimited power to enforce the prohibition of slavery or involuntary servitude by appropriate legislation, it is hardly surprising that interpreters of the amendment could find the so-called remaining incidents and badges of slavery to include such matters as violations of civil rights, racial profiling and discrimination in housing, assaults on labor unions, and many other subjects covered in this collection of essays, though the jurisprudence contains little mention of the slavelike exploitation of women.

Nevertheless, following Lincoln's highly specific Emancipation Proclamation, which freed African American slaves only in particular parts of the United States, it would have been possible, as in other nations' emancipation edicts, to avoid the terms "involuntary servitude" and "punishment for crime" and limit the effects of the article to the specific institution of chattel slavery, as it had been defined since Aristotle. That would mean a supposedly dehumanized person who is owned like a domestic animal and can be sold, traded, bartered, and inherited like other property; a person who has no legal rights and is in effect socially dead; a person over whom an owner or master has almost unlimited authority but who, because of his or her value as property, may have protections that penal and indentured workers would lack. Since the slave lived as human property under the near-absolute control of an owner, it is not surprising that the first important philosophical challenge to the institution came from a defender of absolutist government, Jean Bodin, who, in the 1570s, objected to the slaveholder's semisovereignty and freedom from full governmental control, which insulated the slave from the true sovereign's authority. Bodin's insight pointed to the later difficulty of governmental emancipation, especially in a nation whose states-rights Constitution had been framed largely by slaveholders. Ironically, it would be the Southern slaveholders' rare judicial defense of exceptional governmental power, in retrieving fugitive slaves in the North, that would provide a key precedent for the Thirteenth Amendment's power in enforcing emancipation.

It is my purpose here to describe some of the often ignored obstacles to slave emancipation in America, which help to account for the long failure of the Thirteenth Amendment to achieve its framers' objectives. While one is always impressed by the *success* of the radical Republicans in securing the Civil Rights Act of 1866 as well as the following Reconstruction measures, including the Fourteenth and Fifteenth amendments, it becomes increasingly difficult, as we now move forward with a black American president, to come to terms with the dismal century of post-Reconstruction Jim Crow. I think especially of David Oshinsky's appalling details in his accounts of Southern penal servitude, which really was in many respects "worse than slavery." There were, of course, many specific and fortuitous reasons for the failure of Reconstruction, but we can also put the subject in perspective by examining, first, the economic vitality and importance of slavery before the Civil War and, second, the continuing repugnance and even dread, on the part of the vast majority of white Americans, regarding any massive slave emancipation.

Despite the prolonged antiblack racism that helped people deny or marginalize any black contributions to our history, it can now hardly be denied—especially in view of the long economic dominance of the colonial Caribbean and the essential nineteenth-century cotton exports of the American South—that African slaves and their descendants became indispensable in creating the prosperous New World that, by the mid-nineteenth century, began attracting millions of voluntary European immigrants. In a very real sense, it was coerced black labor that created Europe's image of a shimmering New World Arcadia, as well as the so-called American Dream.

Even in its first centuries, the Atlantic slave system foreshadowed many features of our modern global economy. For example, one sees international investment of capital in distant colonial regions, where the slave trade resulted in extremely low labor costs (or what we today might call "outsourcing") to produce commodities for a transatlantic market. This point leads me to some fundamental observations on the global economic importance of New World slavery. Fundamentals are especially needed since our culture still contains much mythological residue based on the assumption that an immoral and flagrantly unjust system of labor could not possibly be congruent with long-term economic and material progress. This long-dominant mythology concerning a supposedly backward, semifeudal, and obsolete institution seemed to draw some confirmation from the fact that slavery was often associated with soil exhaustion, indebtedness, and low levels of literacy, urban growth, industry, and immigration. Drawing on Adam Smith's arguments on the superiority of free labor, or on racist views that slavery, while an anachronism, helped to civilize so-called African savages and would have soon died out on its own without a needless Civil War, countless historians, novelists, politicians, and others totally misrepresented an institution that served as the crucial basis for New World settlement and expansion for over three centuries and that anticipated the efficiency and productivity of factory assembly lines while also leading the way to the first stage of a globalized economy.

In recent decades historians and economists have reached a broad consensus that while the profitability of single export crops like cotton could discourage a more diversified economy, slave labor could still be efficient, productive, and adaptable to a variety of trades and occupations ranging from mining and factory work to the technologically modernized, steam-powered Cuban sugar mills. The research of Robert Fogel, Stanley Engerman, David Eltis, Seymour Drescher, Rebecca Scott, Herbert Klein, and many others has moved even beyond the now conventional view that black slave labor provided the foundation for the wealthiest and most dynamic New World economies from 1580 to 1800, a long period during which every white transatlantic immigrant was matched by nearly five involuntarily migrant African slaves.

There is now impressive evidence that the economic importance of slavery *increased* in the nineteenth century along with the soaring global demand for such consumer goods as sugar, coffee, tobacco, and cotton textiles. The slave trade hit its all-time peak toward the end of the 1700s and was certainly not declining in 1807 and 1808 when outlawed by Britain and the United States. Some 3 million Africans, or about one-fourth of the grand total exported, were shipped off to the Americas *after* 1807, despite the militant efforts of the British navy to suppress this mostly illegal commerce. As David Eltis has insightfully observed, one can easily imagine the increasingly powerful British and American steam-driven merchant fleets' *expanding*, by the 1850s, the flow of African slaves not only to Cuba and Brazil but also to the American South, where a vigorous movement to reopen the slave trade rightly claimed that the lowering of slave prices would make such labor more affordable and the institution more democratic. This Anglo-American expansion of the slave trade was prevented not by market forces but by a major transformation in Anglo-American public moral perception, spearheaded by a small group of abolitionist reformers (and, as we will see, most Americans were not eager to increase the black population).

Contrary to traditional dogma, and as many Anglo-American economists came to realize even by the 1820s, under most circumstances free labor was *not* cheaper or more productive than slave labor. In any event, a sufficient supply of free labor was never available. And as the British learned to their dismay after fully emancipating some 800,000 colonial slaves in 1838, free laborers were unwilling to accept the coercive plantation discipline and working conditions that made sugar production a highly profitable investment. One unexpected result of this emancipation was that Britain found it necessary to transport hundreds of thousands of hardly free East Asian indentured workers, who eventually replaced many of the emancipated West Indian blacks in such colonies as Trinidad and Guiana.

Britain's suicidal or, as Drescher terms it, "econocidal" destruction of its own slave trade and slave colonies, which had been the world's leading producers of sugar and coffee, provided an extra and enormous stimulus to the plantations of Cuba and Brazil and thus to the then illegal slave trade that supplied them with labor. In mid-nineteenth-century Brazil, black slavery proved to be highly compatible with urban life and virtually every urban trade and skill. In mid-nineteenth-century Cuba, black slaves were profitably employed in the most capital-intensive and highly mechanized sugar production. In both Cuba and Brazil, as Herbert Klein notes, slaves were "most heavily concentrated in the most *dynamic* regions of their respective societies on the eve of emancipation" (i.e., in the 1880s). I should add that in the American South slaveholders effectively applied slave labor to the cultivation of corn, grain, and hemp (for making rope and twine), to both mining and lumbering, to building canals and railroads, and even to the manufacturing of textiles, iron, and other industrial products. But of course slave labor was concentrated mainly on the production of cotton, which, by 1840, constituted 59 percent of all U.S. exports, enabling the country not only to buy manufactured goods from Europe but also to pay interest on its foreign debt and continue to import more capital to invest in transportation and industry.

Moreover, there was a strong symbiotic relationship between New World slavery and industrial capitalism. Slave labor produced most of the first luxury goods that reached a mass consumer market, particularly in England, and that therefore contributed to the labor *incentives* needed for English industrial work discipline. Britain's preeminent textile industry, the core of the Industrial Revolution, was wholly dependent on an expanding supply of cotton. Thanks largely to the invention of the cotton gin, in 1793, American slaves produced most of Britain's cotton until the end of the American Civil War. Further, the dramatic drop in price for British manufactured goods reduced the cost of buying slaves on the African coast. While the price of slaves in Africa remained low and relatively stable during much of the nineteenth century—and virtually all the slaves taken to the Americas were purchased with European, Asian, and American commodities—the price of slaves continued to rise in the New World, in part because of the strong negative slave-population growth rates except in the United States, where even though the slave population doubled, tripled, and quadrupled by natural means, the price of slaves soared in the 1840s and 1850s.

The symbiosis between slavery and industrial capitalism is perhaps most vividly illustrated by the fact that the illicit Atlantic slave trade to Cuba and Brazil depended on *British* capital, credit, insurance, and the manufactured goods, including firearms, that were exchanged in Africa for slaves. As David Eltis convincingly argues, "for the Americas as well as for Britain at the outset of industrialization there was a profound incompatibility between economic self-interest and antislavery policy." This point was well understood by most American politicians, even Northerners like President Martin Van Buren. There is a subtle irony in the way Eltis's neoclassical economic analysis exposes the possible pathological consequences of a worldview subordinating all human relationships to free-market choices and the supreme goal of achieving the largest national product. And here I should mention that the value of Southern slaves in 1860 equaled 80 percent of the gross national product, or what today would be equivalent to $9.75 trillion. There were good reasons why, in 1860, two-thirds of the richest Americans lived in the slaveholding South. And there were good reasons why any constitutional amendment annihilating that crucial property, which was worth three times the cost of constructing the nation's railroads or three times the combined capital invested nationally in business and industrial property, would have seemed utterly inconceivable.

It is true, of course, that in America the abolitionists were able to indict the entire nation for what appeared to be one of the most hypocritical contradictions in all human history: a nation conceived in liberty and dedicated to equal rights happened also to be the nation, by the mid-nineteenth century, with the largest number of slaves in the Western Hemisphere. And after 1807, when Britain outlawed the world's largest slave trade, Americans could no longer cast the blame on the British crown, as Jefferson did in 1776 in a clause to the draft of the Declaration of Independence that the Continental Congress refused to adopt, for waging "cruel war against human nature itself, violating the most sacred rights of life and liberty in the persons of a distant people who never offended him, captivating and carrying them into slavery in another hemisphere, or to incur miserable death in their transportation thither." Let me also note, before I turn to the next barrier to emancipation, that thanks to the rapid natural increase of the American slave population—North America imported less than 4 percent of the Africans transported across the Atlantic—Americans like Jefferson had the moral luxury of condemning the slave trade and sharply differentiating it from the domestic institution.

Even apart from the momentous importance of racial slavery in the Atlantic and New World economies, white Americans, unlike the British, French, and Dutch, who lived thousands of miles away from their colonial slaves, faced the challenge of living together with millions of black people who were seen either as primitive and savage Africans or as being degraded and dehumanized by generations of bondage, and thus incapable of the freedom and equality embodied in American ideals. Many liberal-minded people today simply assume that antebellum whites should have ideally overcome their racist prejudices, immediately freed the slaves, and then welcomed the blacks as free and equal members of society, an outcome that definitely failed to occur even in the more racially integrated Latin America.

But it is almost impossible to imagine the cultural and psychological gulf that then separated American blacks from whites and that perplexed even most sincere opponents of human bondage when they contemplated the sudden release into society of from 1 to 4 million supposedly "dehumanized" human beings who, it was assumed, lacked the skills, knowledge, frugality, and self-discipline needed for responsible participation in society. How would the existing free white population respond to and interact with such "liberated" people? Wholly apart from shocking racist stereotypes, which were nearly universal, it was hardly irrational to assume that a sudden emancipation, without considerable preparation, would inflict heavy burdens on society, greatly lowering the wages of white workers and escalating crime and insecurity of many kinds.

One can see a white aversion and opposition to living with blacks from the early and continuing attempts to restrict slave imports, to the nineteenth-century debates in virtually every Northern state over prohibiting even the entry of free blacks, and on to the growing interest in colonizing freed slaves outside the regions of white settlement.

Looking first at the slave trade, one of the reasons North Americans imported so few Africans was a fear, expressed even in South Carolina as early as the late 1600s, that a higher percentage of blacks would be dangerous as well as highly repugnant and undesirable. Jefferson was quite right when he claimed, in 1776, that Virginia had tried to restrict or even ban the import of African slaves. In 1807 the central issue faced by Congress was not slave-trade abolition—the final vote in the House of Representatives was 113 to 5! The most-debated issue concerned the fear of free blacks and what to *do* with the illegally imported slaves once they were seized. In a close decision, Southern states were allowed to sell such supposedly liberated people like other contraband goods. Few representatives supported outright emancipation, for as Josiah Quincy, of Massachusetts, pointed out, the slaves were as "helpless, ignorant, and incompetent as poor children," and "to release them would be inhumane and condemn them to live as vagabonds." Furthermore, he stressed, "the first duty of the Southern states, self-preservation, forbids it."

Given such views, it is not surprising that, in 1790, Congress limited the right of national citizenship to incoming whites or that new and Northern states began to prohibit the entry of free Negroes, exemplified by the great Missouri Crisis (1819–1822). As a sign of the diminishing possibilities for any major slave emancipation, what began as a moderate proposal for the very gradual ending of slavery in the new state of Missouri ended with the state constitution's legalizing slavery *in perpetuity* and prohibiting free Negroes and mulattoes from coming to and settling in the state. While the latter action raised the constitutional issue of "privileges and immunities," since a very few Northern blacks were citizens of states like Massachusetts, by 1847 Missouri felt secure in totally banning all free black settlers. Indeed, in 1822 even the Massachusetts legislature considered such a measure. The states of the Old Northwest, which bordered slaveholding states like Kentucky and Missouri, expressed particular fear of being inundated by freed blacks from the south. In Illinois a constitutional convention of 1847 adopted a provision, ratified by a popular vote margin of over two to one, instructing the legislature to prohibit the immigration of all colored persons. Once enacted, this measure provided that any Negro who violated the law and could not pay a large fine could be sold into service at a public auction. Indiana, Iowa, and even Oregon adopted similar measures, though in 1849 reformers in Ohio achieved partial repeal of so-called Black Laws compelling Negroes to post a large bond in order to settle in the state.

Ohio's Black Laws bring to mind the harassment and mob violence free blacks in the North experienced throughout the antebellum years. In 1829, after Cincinnati authorities insisted on the better enforcement of such Black Laws, white mobs succeeded in driving out from 1,100 to 2,200 of the city's Negroes, many of whom fled to Canada. Other antiblack riots erupted in New York, Philadelphia, and Providence. Moreover, from the admission of Maine, in 1819, to the end of the Civil War, the constitution of every new state denied blacks the right to vote. Connecticut's citizens did the same as late as the fall of 1865. Except in Massachusetts, blacks were excluded from juries, and Illinois, Ohio, Indiana, Iowa, and California all prohibited Negro testimony in legal cases involving a white man.

As Alexis de Tocqueville put it, following his extensive tour of the United States in 1831: "The Negro is free, but he can share neither the rights, nor the pleasures, nor the labor, nor the afflictions, nor the tomb of him whose equal he has been declared to be." Tocqueville concluded that racial prejudice was strongest in the Northern states that had abolished slavery; that blacks and whites could never live in the same country on an equal footing; and that the oppressed race ultimately faced extinction or expulsion.

The idea of deporting or colonizing emancipated blacks outside the North American states or colonies long preceded the Haitian Revolution (1791–1804). But in the United States the specter of Haiti, with its gory images of rape and extermination of whites, reinforced by the Virginia slave conspiracies of 1800 and 1802 and the massive Barbadian insurrection of 1816, all of which were influenced by the Haitian Revolution, gave an enormous impetus to the colonization movement. Some advocates understood colonization as a way of making slavery more secure by removing the dangerous (as Haiti had shown) free black and colored population. But colonization was more commonly seen as the first and indispensable step toward the *very* gradual abolition of slavery. In effect, it would reverse and undo the nearly two-century flow of the Atlantic slave ships, and, by transporting the freed slaves back to Africa, it would gradually and peacefully redeem America from what James Madison called "the dreadful fruitfulness of the original sin of the African trade."

The very thought of shipping from 1.5 to more than 4 million black Americans to an inhospitable Africa has seemed so preposterous and even criminal that many historians have tended to dismiss the subject of colonization out of hand (despite the British deportation of criminals to Australia and the success of white Americans in "removing" Indians to the West and ultimately to "reservations"). This means, however, that historians have never really explained why the coupling of emancipation and colonization appealed to leading American statesmen from Jefferson to Lincoln, why this formula won the endorsement, by 1832, of nine state legislatures, and why William Lloyd Garrison, Theodore Weld, the Tappan brothers, Gerrit Smith, James G. Birney, and virtually all the other prominent and radical abolitionists of their generation *had* accepted colonization before finally embracing the doctrine of "immediate emancipation." Colonizationists warned that emancipation without some kind of emigration would create a huge idle, disgruntled population, escalating the economic burden of poor relief and leading to cruel and drastic punishments to counteract the soaring rate of crime. Southerners rejoiced over the continuing flow of statistics, including the highly distorted census of 1840, claiming that an immensely disproportionate number of free blacks in the North were living in poverty or were confined in jails, prisons, and asylums for the insane.

Blacks in Pennsylvania were reported to make up one-thirty-fourth of the state's population but one-third of the state's prisoners. According to a Pennsylvania state committee report of 1836: "The disparity of crime between the whites and blacks, which is at present so distressing to every friend of humanity and virtue, and so burdensome to the community, will become absolutely intolerable in a few years: and the danger to be apprehended is, that if not removed, they will be exterminated." As Thomas Jefferson aptly described the dilemma, "We have the wolf by the ears, and we can neither hold him, nor safely let him go. Justice is in one scale and self-preservation in the other."

Leading colonizationists like Connecticut's Reverend Leonard Bacon argued, in assessing the slaves' alleged incapacity for freedom, that whites could only faintly imagine how generations of oppression had degraded the black slave, "whose mind has scarcely been enlightened by one ray of knowledge, whose soul has never been expanded by one adequate conception of his moral dignity and moral relations, and in whose heart hardly one of those affections that soften our character, or those hopes that animate and bless our being, has been allowed to germinate."

According to Bacon, who saw slavery as an intolerable national evil, the African American could never be raised "from the abyss of his degradation." Not in the United States, that is, where the force of racial prejudice was understandably magnified by the fear of a black biblical Samson "thirsting for vengeance" and bursting his chains asunder. With Haiti obviously in mind, Bacon warned that "the moment you raise this degraded community to an intellectual existence, their chains will burst asunder like the fetters of Sampson [*sic*], and they will stand forth in the might and dignity of manhood, and in all the terrors of a long injured people, thirsting for vengeance."

In this example, having raised blacks from their "abyss" of degradation to the "dignity of manhood," Bacon clearly rejected any thought of inherent inferiority. Nevertheless, his major argument tied degradation with an incapacity for peaceful coexistence. And the dismal history of black Haiti, whose freed people had no way of migrating to Canaanite "free soil," seemed to underscore their incapacity for economic success and genuine freedom. Haiti was cut off by America, shunned by much of the rest of the world, and soon almost bankrupted by reparation payments to France for even the act of national recognition. Hardly less discouraging was the fate of thousands of freed slaves in the northern United States, who, being mostly barred from white schools and respectable employment, quickly sank into an underclass—the first of many generations of African Americans who privately struggled, in a world dominated by whites, with the central psychological issue of self-esteem.

In short, it was the new possibility of eradicating slavery—which became meaningful only in the late eighteenth century, with the beginning of gradual emancipation in the northern United States, followed by the Haitian Revolution and France's revolutionary emancipation act of 1794—that greatly magnified the importance of race. And a belief in a people's dehumanization had become the key to race. I have no space here to discuss the spectrum from scientific racism, which acquired semiofficial sanction in the Western world by the 1850s, to the biblical Curse of Ham, and on to the cartoons and caricatures of blacks that gave a popular cultural sanction to the racist discriminatory laws and behavior that probably reached their most extreme level in the United States.

Suffice it to say that by March 2, 1861, when Congress passed a proposed but never-ratified Thirteenth Amendment that would have prohibited the federal government even by constitutional amendment to interfere with slavery in the existing states, a copy of which Lincoln sent on March 16 to the governors of even the seceded states, the barriers to any immediate slave emancipation seemed to be insuperable. As I have tried to show, the extraordinary economic value of American slavery was reinforced by a profound racism and antipathy toward so-called free Negroes. Moreover, by the 1850s there was a growing consensus, even in England, that Britain's "Mighty Experiment" of slave emancipation in the 1830s had been an economic disaster. It was only the wholly unexpected nature of the American Civil War, leading to the Emancipation Proclamation and Thirteenth Amendment, that finally transformed common perceptions of Britain's actions into a bold, pioneering moral achievement that then teleologically led to the outlawing of human bondage in most of the world.

The only foreign emancipation decree that was really comparable to the Thirteenth Amendment was the proclamation, of February 4, 1794, made by the French National Convention. We don't think of the somewhat conservative Abraham Lincoln as endorsing something similar to a radical declaration of the French Reign of Terror. While Lincoln hated slavery, he long favored gradual and compensated emancipation as well as colonization. His political success had depended on a brilliant synthesis that merged an appeal to Northern anti-slavery sentiment with a dedication to the interests of white free labor, acknowledging the pervasive aversion to black social or political equality. Lincoln revealed his deep understanding of the barriers to emancipation in 1858 when he affirmed that "I do not suppose that in the most peaceful way ultimate extinction [of slavery] would occur in less than a hundred years at the least." In other words, without a devastating civil war, he was thinking of ultimate slave emancipation in what we now term the civil rights period. Yet Lincoln drew above all on the American Revolutionary heritage and worshipped the Declaration of Independence much as the excited members of the French Convention worshipped and cited the Declaration of the Rights of Man.

The French emancipation decree, like the Thirteenth Amendment, was the result of a major war in which slaves themselves had helped win their freedom. Indeed, by February 1794 the French agents Sonthonax and Polverel had already issued emancipation edicts in Saint Domingue, and the slaves had overthrown their masters and were fighting English and Spanish invaders. If Lincoln and the Republicans knew that slave emancipation would win praise and support abroad, Danton could exclaim: "We are working for future generations, let us launch liberty into the colonies; the English are dead—today [applause] . . . France will regain the rank and influence that its energy, its soil, and its population merit." The French deputies hailed the act as a much-belated reparation of one of the worst French examples of inequality and specifically proclaimed, unlike the Thirteenth Amendment, "that all men living in the colonies, without distinction of color, are French citizens and enjoy all the rights guaranteed by the constitution." Unfortunately, even French radicals like Victor Hugues, who months later sought to liberate slaves while invading Guadeloupe, found it necessary to force blacks to work on the plantations. And as a sign of international obstacles to successful emancipation, in 1802 Napoléon restored both slavery and the slave trade! It would take forty-six more years before another revolution enabled France to free all colonial slaves, this time paying indemnity to their owners.

Most of the other acts of slave emancipation involved compensation to the owners and focused on attempts to implant in the freed slaves motivations to work and to avoid the alleged idleness that outraged critics of the freed slaves in the larger British colonies following the end of four years of coercive apprenticeship. Little attention was given to measures that might ensure the blacks' continuing freedom, as in America's Civil Rights Act of 1866 and the next two constitutional amendments.

For example, the celebrated British Emancipation Act, of 1833, awarded a huge 20 million pounds sterling of taxpayers' money to the colonial owners or their creditors and first called for six years of uncompensated labor, which in effect required blacks to subsidize a large share of their own emancipation. Even when apprenticeship was reduced to four years, the act in effect rewarded owners with approximately the market value of their slaves. While the law prevented colonial governments from extending the time of apprenticeship, it allowed them to punish "willful absence from work" on the part of delinquent blacks with up to seven years of labor after the termination of apprenticeship. Despite the national celebrations, many abolitionists privately saw the emancipation law as a disastrous failure.

Nevertheless, most British abolitionists recognized the supreme need for creating what they termed "habits of diligence and self-discipline" among freed people, and in France, Spain, Cuba, and Brazil the proponents of emancipation would have agreed with Sir James Stephen, a member of a prominent abolitionist family and a framer of the British Emancipation Act, that "measures must be adopted, tending more directly to counteract the disposition to sloth which may be expected to manifest itself, so soon as the coercive force of the Owners' Authority shall have been withdrawn. The manumitted Slaves must be stimulated to Industry by positive Laws which shall enhance the difficulty of obtaining a mere subsistence." Cubans, for example, feared that without their imposed period of slavelike apprenticeship, the blacks "would run off to the woods and live like savages."

The architects of emancipation in Cuba and Brazil hoped to learn from the mistakes of the British, French, and Americans. In Brazil the Rio Branco Law, of 1871, gave recognition to the owners' rights in human property as well as the need to slowly prepare the children of slaves for freedom. When the technically freed child of a slave turned eight, the mother's owner could choose between getting 600 milreis in compensation, and turning the child over to the state, or retaining the child's slavelike service until age twenty-one. Slaves could also purchase their freedom, but they then came under state control and were obliged to hire themselves out under pain of compulsion. The law was poorly enforced, and, in 1888, following some years of intense abolitionist agitation and the flight of thousands of slaves from their owners, the emancipation edict of Princess Regent Isabel contained only two brief provisions, like the Thirteenth Amendment, but led to the downfall of the monarchy. And according to the historian Robert Edgar Conrad, the law did not end the "de facto servitude that survived chattel slavery in much of rural Brazil."

To conclude, emancipation embodied the paradox of breaking the chains of a grateful slave, symbolized by the kneeling black in the abolitionist icon "Am I Not a Man and a Brother," but then trying to ensure that he would continue to work as hard as he had when driven and whipped by a plantation overseer. Given the enormous obstacles to slave emancipation, no law succeeded in the New World in moving easily or rapidly from chattel bondage to anything like true freedom—despite the growing public condemnation of chattel slavery as an institution. On the other hand, America's Thirteenth Amendment did lay the groundwork for destroying what had been a highly profitable and thriving system of labor and racial control. No less important, by including the phrase "involuntary servitude" and giving Congress the power to enforce the article by appropriate legislation, it implanted in the Constitution ideal goals and values that created new meanings of freedom even for the twentieth and twenty-first centuries.

The Promises of Liberty

1. Introduction

THE THIRTEENTH AMENDMENT'S
REVOLUTIONARY AIMS

Alexander Tsesis

The origins of the Thirteenth Amendment are found as much in the American Revolution as they are in the period of Reconstruction, when the American people ratified it into the Constitution. During both eras Americans emphasized the human value of liberty.

This chapter explores the dominant understanding of liberty that informed congressional debates on the proposed amendment. It first reflects on Revolutionary notions of liberty and then demonstrates how abolitionists relied on them. The chapter next turns to the principles that animated House and Senate debates about the proposed Thirteenth Amendment. I argue that with the ratification of the amendment the federal government gained a tremendous nationwide power to protect civil rights against individual and governmental abuses.

The first part of this introductory chapter concludes with an explanation of why the amendment proved to be inadequate to achieve Radical Reconstruction. The second part of the introduction sketches the developing interpretations of the Thirteenth Amendment following ratification. Supreme Court decisions as well as scholarly writings molded its meaning. A road map of the essays in this collection appears at the end.

REVOLUTIONARY FERVOR

Before the Thirteenth Amendment's ratification, for many Americans the national purpose of protecting life, liberty, and property was only an unfulfilled ideal in a culture that sanctioned slavery in its Constitution. The nation's statements of purpose, the Declaration of Independence and the Preamble to the Constitution, lacked any governmental grant of enforcement. Many voices in the Revolutionary generation recognized the contrast between the colonies' plaints against their British rulers and a national constitution containing the three-fifths, the slave importation, and the fugitive slave clauses. The framers' preference for property rights and colonial order over the universal ideals they professed led to decades of exploitation. After the Revolution, few of the framers retained the zeal for liberty they had expressed in their battle for the rights of free citizenship. Only decades after the Revolution, following the Civil War, was an enforcement provision added to the Constitution, in the second section of the Thirteenth Amendment, to provide the federal government with nearly plenary power over civil rights.

Political and religious leaders regarded the American Revolution as a struggle to secure natural liberties. Their ideology was inconsistent with the colonies' legal recognition of slavery. Alexander Hamilton was one of the framers who denounced this incongruity between aspirations and practices, writing that "no reason can be assigned why one man should exercise any power, or preeminence over his fellow creatures more than another." In an article that has long been attributed to Thomas Paine, the author drew attention to the inconsistency of arguing that the British were enslaving the colonists through oppressive laws while holding "so many hundred thousands in slavery."[1]

Colonial pamphleteers used "slavery" to express their sense of political impotence in the face of British parliamentary tariffs. In later years, members of the Reconstruction Congress would often refer to the Revolutionary generation's devotion to liberty, while renouncing the founders' decision to include slave-protecting provisions in the Constitution. Radical Republican notions of the Revolution informed their understanding of the Thirteenth Amendment's grant of federal enforcement power to secure liberty.

Radical Reconstruction was rooted in Revolutionary demands for a participatory government of equally free individuals. Revolutionaries often likened their civil and political circumstances under British rule to slavery. They demanded to exercise their will and not be "wholly under the power and controul of" others.[2] Despite the widespread distinction between natural liberty and the arbitrary exploitation of power, which as early as the 1740s appeared in colonial writings, many colonists exploited African and Native American slaves to an extent that paled the duties imposed by the British government. Political and religious polemicists commonly ignored chattel slavery, while they decried the oppressiveness of such laws as the Stamp Act (1765) and the Townshend Revenue Act (1767).

The parliamentary subjugation of the colonies to a levy of unwanted taxes, Hamilton remarked, amounted to colonial slavery. The Tea Act (1773), which spurred the Boston Tea Party, was regarded as an "ensign of their arbitrary Dominion [and] of your Slavery." Dramatically, Josiah Quincy declared, "We Are Slaves!" A slave, in the broad sense, meant anyone unable to exercise rights common to all citizens. John Dickinson, in 1768, wrote that by imposing taxes without colonial representation, Parliament had subjected colonists to "a state of the most abject slavery." Governor Thomas Hutchinson reported the anxiety in Massachusetts, where minds were filled "with Apprehensions of the total Extinctions of . . . Liberties" binding the people to "a State of abject Slavery." The notion of political slavery was widespread; an army private, on July 4, 1777, wrote his parents that only courage would "determine whether Americans are to be free men or slaves."[3]

While chattel slavery was an unmistakable form of oppression, it was not until 1865, with the ratification of the Thirteenth Amendment, that the Revolutionary demand to end slavery became an explicit part of the Constitution. Yet, the conceptual seeds of the amendment had been planted in 1776. Soon after the Revolution, beginning with the July 2, 1777, Vermont Constitution, Northern states immediately or gradually abolished slavery.

Pamphlets drew attention to the inconsistency of fighting for the Rights of Man and maintaining slavery. Benjamin Rush, a physician who was a delegate of the Continental Congress, wrote of how contradictory it was to denounce "the servitude to which the *Parliament of Great Britain* wishes to reduce us, while we continue to keep our fellow creatures in slavery just because their color is different from ours." England would never accept the Revolution, exclaimed another apologist, unless Americans desisted from enslaving others. John Allen, who lacked Rush's political ambitions and could therefore be more frank, called slaveholders "trifling patriots" who advocated on behalf of "the liberties of mankind" while they ignored Africans' natural rights and privileges.[4]

Natural law principles pervaded literature decrying the legal concessions to slave owners. James Otis, for instance, spoke of the natural right of freedom that all people, black and white, shared in common. He considered slavery to be the despoiler of civilization since it placed demagogy in the way of universal liberty. Chattel servitude rendered masters "hereditary tyrants," asserted an anonymous pamphlet in 1784, by aggrandizing whites to the faux pedestal of divinity and disparaging the humanity of Africans. The rights to which Revolutionaries were committed, maintained Abraham Booth, are innate to all humanity. Everyone has an "equal claim to personal liberty with any man upon earth."[5]

To many living during the Revolution, it appeared as if the demise of slavery was at hand. The historian Winthrop D. Jordan's evaluation of contemporary sources revealed a widespread recognition that slavery was a "communal sin."[6] In 1774, Rush was optimistic enough about the cause of freedom to predict slavery's demise in forty years.[7] He had misgauged the South's commitment to slavery, and it took ninety years, a Civil War, and the ratification of the Thirteenth Amendment to end the peculiar institution.

Black contemporaries who joined colonial liberation efforts anticipated that all races would benefit: "Freedom is an inherent right of the human species," wrote black New Hampshire petitioners, and private tyranny, just as its public counterpart, violates natural rights. A racially mixed minister, Lemuel Haynes, defended blacks' "undeniable right" to be free. Massachusetts black petitioners, in 1773, expressed the hope that white colonists seeking to liberate themselves from British oppression would do the same on behalf of black slaves. Their petition denounced New England slavery, as did a 1777 petition to the Massachusetts Assembly of a large number of enslaved blacks. They implored legislators to desist from their inconsistency and to restore them to "the Natural Right of all men."[8]

The call for civil reform came from religious leaders as well. Samuel Hopkins encouraged Americans to respect the rights of Africans, who "have as good a right to liberty as ourselves." Clergyman Nathaniel Appleton recognized that the slave trade violated the ideals of the "sons of liberty," and Reverend Nathaniel Niles, of Newbury, Massachusetts, drew attention to the shamefulness of enslaving fellow men. Anthony Benezet, who was arguably the most influential religious abolitionist of the eighteenth century, both called for abolition and spoke in some detail about meeting the needs of liberated slaves. He counseled that freed children and adults be educated to be productive members of society. Writing about the effects of universal liberty on general welfare, Benezet explained that it would reduce the tax burden and increase the cultivation of vacant land.[9]

Several Southern slave owners, likewise, understood the incompatibility of slavery with both the terms of equality in the Declaration of Independence and the contractarian notions of property to which colonists were committed. Patrick Henry, after reading one of Benezet's antislavery tracts, expressed his angst that a people committed to liberty and the "rights of humanity" would persist with the institution. Despite his self-conscious realization, Henry refused to emancipate his own slaves: "Would any one believe that I am Master of Slaves of my own purchase! I am drawn along by ye general Inconvenience of living without them; I will not, I cannot justify it."[10]

Thomas Jefferson, a Virginian like Henry, not only realized the incongruity of slavery with the age of revolution but also foresaw the making of a national catastrophe. Jefferson knew from personal experience the ill effects of slavery on personal morals. Yet he typified the disconnect between liberal ideals and the personal selfishness of slave ownership. In his youthful ambition for liberty, Jefferson had included a passage in the drafted Declaration of Independence accusing King George III of acting "against human nature" by maintaining an international slave trade. That passage, which was not adopted into the final version of the Declaration of Independence, accused the British monarch of violating the lives and freedoms of distant peoples. Jefferson had not only opposed the slave trade but had wanted to abolish domestic slavery as well. Also in 1776, Jefferson had included a provision in his second and third drafts of the Virginia Constitution proving that "no persons hereafter coming into this country shall be held in slavery under any pretext whatever."[11]

With the passage of time and the political stability of the new nation, which had, after all, been established after a constitutional compromise with slave interests, Jefferson became jaded. Thirty-eight years after independence, Jefferson wrote Edward Coles, who later became an antislavery governor of Illinois, with nostalgia of the "flame of liberty" that Jefferson had hoped would spark a popular movement against slavery. The younger generation of Americans had not taken to that notion, and, with the passage of years, Jefferson also became complacent. He counseled the younger Coles not to liberate his slaves.[12]

In 1776, with the many slavery-related controversies still ahead, even without Jefferson's condemnation of slave importation, the Declaration of Independence established equal liberty as a key national aspiration. The document created an unenforceable policy that conflicted sharply with proslavery commitments. The founding generation was left with the political dilemma of justifying the Revolution while denying rights to persons of African descent.

In practical terms, the expansive notion of liberty applied only to propertied white men. The limits slave codes set on fundamental rights, from conjugal stability to individual leisure, were the most extreme example of state-approved autocracy practiced in the colonies and coexisting alongside the sincere remonstrance and desire for a free society.

Slavery had been legal in all thirteen colonies before the Revolution. Yet even then a movement was afoot to put words into action, beginning with the Continental Congress's requirement that the slave trade be ended after December 1, 1775. The limitations that the colonies had placed on the Continental Congress's authority made the decree unenforceable. After independence but before the ratification of the Constitution, the Northwest Ordinance (1787) was another effort to end the spread of slavery.

The determination of several states to outlaw slavery is a testament that freedom was not a hollow concept to all. In 1774, Rhode Island and Connecticut began the Northern antislavery effort. In June, a Rhode Island statute restricted the slave trade because, as the preface succinctly explained, "those who are desirous of enjoying all the advantages of liberty themselves, should be willing to extend personal liberty to others." That same year, Connecticut prohibited the importation of "Indian, Negro or Molatto Slaves." Then, in 1777, Vermont directly outlawed slavery. The New Hampshire Bill of Rights (1784) seems to have been the primary means by which slavery was eliminated there. The Massachusetts Superior Court, in an opinion that Chief Justice William Cushing drafted, determined that slavery was unconstitutional because it violated the natural right of all men to be born free and equal. A gradualist approach to abolition was taken in Pennsylvania in 1780, Rhode Island and Connecticut in 1784, New York in 1799, and New Jersey in 1804.[13]

The effect of these state-by-state efforts did not extend to the nation as a whole. Laws such as the Fugitive Slave acts of 1793 and 1850, facilitating the return of runaways, stood in sharp relief from the nation's stated purpose.

The Declaration of Independence sparked the hope that America would be committed to liberal equality, but only the ratification of the Thirteenth Amendment made that hope applicable to blacks. There were, of course, positive signs during and immediately after the Revolution. The antislavery disposition of the Revolutionary age was not enough to translate into universal or national prohibitions against the institution. To the contrary, several clauses in the Constitution either explicitly or implicitly recognized slavery and gave it federal legitimacy.[14]

While constitutional concession to slavery made union possible in 1787, it set the nation on a course culminating in Southern secession and later the ratification of the Thirteenth Amendment. The amendment nullified clauses specifically related to slavery and altered the meaning of others, such as the Commerce Clause and Insurrection Clause, to transform their original design. The framers of the amendment relied not only on Revolutionary ideology, as it appeared in the Declaration of Independence and preamble, but also on the abolitionist interpretations of liberty.

ABOLITIONIST INTERPRETATION OF LIBERTY

Nineteenth-century abolitionists adopted natural rights principles from the Revolutionary generation but decried its willingness to accept inequality for the sake of national unity. From the American Anti-Slavery Society's earliest days, it professed its zeal for the framers' convictions while renouncing their political capitulations. Abolitionists, in turn, influenced Radical Republican supporters of the Thirteenth Amendment to provide Congress power needed for promulgating substantive civil rights reforms.

Early abolitionists regarded the struggle against slavery to be the logical outgrowth of the War of Independence. William Lloyd Garrison traced his radical abolitionism to the Declaration of Independence. He thought the document to be a substantive commitment of national government; otherwise, its "self-evident truths" would be "self-evident lies." For him, as for many abolitionists, the Declaration of Independence mandated Congress to protect natural rights against exploitation. Natural rights were the innate birthright of everyone born in the United States. Civil societies, as Unitarian abolitionist William E. Channing explained, were established to protect divinely granted human rights. The American Anti-Slavery Society was committed to the principle that inalienable rights were common to all persons. The nation's identification with those rights, in Theodore Parker's opinion, derived from the centrality of the Declaration of Independence and the preamble to the Constitution. These two statements of governmental purpose obligated the federal government to pass laws achieving real equality in "civil and political rights and privileges."[15]

The equal protection of civil rights was quintessential to the abolitionist theory of national governance. The cornerstone of civic order was the Declaration of Independence that inspired "three millions of people" to rise up "as from the sleep of death" and rush "to the strife of blood; deeming it more glorious to die instantly as freemen, than desirable to live an hour as slaves." Since the Revolution was fought in protest of Great Britain's violations against the colonists' natural rights, wrote abolitionist attorney Joel Tiffany, the new nation was precluded from tolerating or supporting slavery.[16]

As with the Declaration of Independence, the preamble to the Constitution was a statement of governance. Garrisonians regarded it Congress's duty under the General Welfare Clause to prevent the exploitation of slaves. Using utilitarian terms, Charles Olcott pointed out that slavery violates the "whole spirit" of the Preamble to the Constitution because it detracts from the general welfare and the blessings of liberty. Radical constitutional abolitionists recognized that the nation's founders had "separated from the mother country" and had declared independence in order to resist "the attempt of Great Britain to impose on them a political slavery." The national government breached its duty by countenancing the exploitation of hundreds of thousands of laborers.[17]

In the debates leading to the ratification of the Thirteenth Amendment, Radical Republicans drew from the work of abolitionists, thereby espousing the natural rights ideals of the founding generation. Radicals realized that only a constitutional amendment could provide the federal government with the added authority to translate the principles of the Declaration of Independence and the Preamble into enforceable laws.

DEBATES ON THE PROPOSED AMENDMENT

From its inception the Republican Party officially opposed the western spread of slavery, but not the institution itself. However, for a brief time at the end of the Civil War, before President Andrew Johnson put the brakes on radicalism and a moderate congressional leadership took the reins of power, Radical Republicans sought to achieve constitutional abolitionism and an expansion of federal civil rights authority.

ABOLITIONIST INFLUENCES ON THE RECONSTRUCTION CONGRESS

The recognition that slavery had led the country into war helped committed abolitionists gain influential political offices. Many congressional Radical Republicans based their support of the Thirteenth Amendment on American natural rights tradition. For them, the amendment offered the opportunity to put principles into law that they had unsuccessfully supported since the 1840s. "Slavery," Charles Sumner said during a representative speech against the Kansas-Nebraska bill, "is an infraction of the immutable law of nature, and, as such, cannot be considered a natural incident to any sovereignty, especially in a country which has solemnly declared, in its Declaration of Independence, the inalienable right of all men to life, *liberty*, and the pursuit of happiness."[18]

Sumner accepted some aspects of radical constitutionalism before the Civil War, arguing that the original Constitution, even without amendment, allowed Congress to prohibit slavery in the District of Columbia, the territories, and on the high seas.[19] Not until the war did he and other Republicans begin to assert the need for drastic constitutional change. The Thirteenth Amendment's grant of power to act against civil rights discriminations broke with the more strict antebellum dichotomy between federal and state powers.

Angered by secession, voters in the 1864 election opted for a federalist-minded group of legislators, many of whom had participated in that year's debates on the Thirteenth Amendment. During the Civil War, a substantial number of Republicans adopted radical abolitionist principles about the federal government's obligation to eradicate slavery. As the war came to take a toll on lives, moderates began to join the ranks of congressmen seeking radical constitutional change. President Abraham Lincoln, although never a radical, abandoned gradualism by 1863 and soon became instrumental in gaining votes for the Thirteenth Amendment. His speeches often relied on natural rights language, stating that the Declaration of Independence guaranteed equality to whites and blacks.

Schuyler Colfax, the incoming Speaker of the House for the Thirty-ninth Congress, opened the session soon after the amendment was ratified in 1865 with a statement on Congress's power: "It is yours to mature and enact legislation which . . . shall establish [state governments] anew on such a basis of enduring justice as will guarantee all necessary safeguards to the people, and afford what our Magna Carta, the Declaration of Independence, proclaims is the chief object of government—protection of all men in their inalienable rights."[20] His statement reflected the dominant congressional view on the Thirteenth Amendment's scope, before the beginning of debates on the proposed Fourteenth Amendment.

The concept of freedom had rarely been so well parsed as it was during the debates on the Thirteenth Amendment. Statements were general enough to leave it to future generations to evaluate and enact statutes for ending specific infringements against civil rights. Soon after Representative James M. Ashley of Ohio introduced the proposed Thirteenth Amendment in Congress,[21] at an April 18, 1864, speech in Baltimore, Lincoln articulated the ambiguous meaning of "liberty": "We all declare for liberty; but in using the same word we do not all mean the same thing. With some the word liberty may mean for each man to do as he pleases with himself, and the product of his labor; while with others the same word may mean for some men to do as they please with other men, and the product of other men's labor. Here are two, not only different, but incompatible things, called by the same name, liberty."[22] Members of the Thirty-eighth Congress, who debated on passing the proposed Thirteenth Amendment, did much to dispel this paradoxical vagueness about liberty and to elevate the principle of equality. The amendment was also critical for permanently ending slavery, something that the Emancipation Proclamation alone was unable to achieve since it was grounded on presidential commander in chief powers.[23]

The "self-evident" truth that "all men are created equal" influenced those congressmen who played the pivotal role in the advancement of freedom. They considered slavery to be inimical to a wide range of freedoms, and the breadth of their views derived from the far-reaching perspective of Revolutionary founders. One representative, advocating passage of the amendment, reminded Congress that the framers had made inalienable the rights of a person "to himself, to his wife and children, to his liberty, and to the fruits of his own industry." Another Republican understood that the founders had acceded to the demands of slavery but thought they considered the institution to be a tolerable evil that was "temporary in its character."[24]

In 1864, a congressman recognized that the majesty of the Declaration of Independence did not relieve the framers of their "errors" on slavery, which had been "expiated by blood and agony and death."[25] Passage of the Thirteenth

Amendment was meant to break down the discrepancy between the nation's commitments and its practices. The original Constitution, as Representative Thaddeus Stevens pointed out, did not endow the nation with the authority to end slavery.[26]

The Thirteenth Amendment's enforcement provision, found in its second section, made the federal government responsible for protecting rights that had previously been subject to the states' sole discretion. The amendment's framers intended to grant Congress the power to achieve the founding fathers' normative objective of protecting individual liberty and providing for the general welfare. According to Representative Godlove S. Orth and other radicals, the Thirteenth Amendment would grant legislators the authority to achieve the "practical application of that self-evident truth," of the Declaration of Independence. In their minds, that truth was also linked to the preamble's charge to the national government that it promote the general welfare and secure equal liberty.[27]

For constitutional power to be more than merely symbolic, congressional action was required to protect basic rights. Ebon C. Ingersoll, who was elected to the Thirty-eighth Congress to represent the House district of recently deceased abolitionist Owen Lovejoy, regarded the profits of personal labor and conjugal happiness to be intrinsic to complete civil freedom. Congressman M. Russell Thayer, of Pennsylvania, wondered incredulously whether a constitutionally granted freedom could be "confined simply to the exemption of the freedom from sale and barter? Do you give freedom to a man when you allow him to be deprived of those great natural rights to which every man is entitled?"[28]

The Thirteenth Amendment altered federalism by increasing congressional power over civil rights. The Enforcement Clause would remain the linchpin for the exercise of that power. The clause provided Congress with an innovative means both to evaluate and to act upon any remaining vestige or incident of servitude.

Representative Isaac N. Arnold, who was President Lincoln's confidant, asserted that the Thirteenth Amendment would establish *"equality before the law . . . to be the great cornerstone"* of the United States government. Such a grand design would provide for the betterment of all economic strata. Unspecific as this ideal may have seemed, it contained an undeniable determination to protect the inalienable rights of all persons, irrespective of their class or race. Congressmen, whether they were on the radical or moderate side of the political spectrum, realized that such a civil transformation could be achieved only if the national government were granted constitutional power to pass laws necessary to make meaningful changes in the lives of newly freed slaves. Liberty would be no more than "a bitter mockery" and "a cruel delusion," the representative and future president James A. Garfield pointed out in 1865, if it were merely the loosening of shackles. Without protections for "great natural rights," said Congressman Thayer, freedom would be chimerical.[29]

Radicals developed the Enforcement Clause of the Thirteenth Amendment from their commitment to individual liberties and overall welfare. Freedom could be universal only where civil rights were predicated on federal rather than state citizenship. Senator John Sherman, of Ohio, who had his hand on the pulse of federal power, later becoming secretary of the treasury and then secretary of state, asserted that the enforcement provision was "an express grant of power to Congress to secure . . . liberty by appropriate legislation." He regarded the congressional grant of authority to be necessary for interstate comity, maintaining that friction between states was avoidable only where national government determined citizenship rights.[30]

The Thirteenth Amendment was to end more than de jure slavery; it was to allow Congress to identify and address any de facto public or private practices associated with it. Among the de facto practices that would need to end, as many members of the Thirty-eighth Congress saw it, were private discriminations, which were often initiated through gentlemen's agreements or vigilante violence, that prevented blacks and, to a lesser degree, white laborers from engaging in business, entering into contracts, and becoming educated.[31]

The three debates surrounding passage of the Thirteenth Amendment, one in the Senate and two in the House, reacted to both these private violations and to legally sanctioned discrimination. The debates demonstrated that both supporters and opponents of the amendment expected the constitutional change to provide sweeping power to protect civil rights. Section 2, as the congressmen understood it and the Supreme Court later interpreted it, provided the authority to end all manner of subjugation, not only chattel slavery. In the course of a contentious debate, a consensus developed that the Thirteenth Amendment would empower Congress to end arbitrary practices connected to the incidents of involuntary servitude.

Few explications of rights were as visionary as the analysis of Senator James Harlan, of Iowa. It was he who first referred to the disabilities that the Thirteenth Amendment would address as the "incidents of servitude." The Supreme Court would later adopt that terminology. Slavery, according to Harlan, was an institution infecting many of the privileges of citizenship. The amendment would, therefore, enable the federal government to prevent human rights violations analogous to slavery, such as interference with marriage, intrusion of parental decision making, prohibition against property ownership and alienation, restriction against participation in equitable trials, penalty for teaching or learning how to read and write, and similar degradations.[32] After the amendment's ratification, Senator Jacob M. Howard, who was a member of the Senate

Judiciary Committee, which reported the language of the Thirteenth Amendment, remembered that its purpose was to secure "the ordinary rights of a freeman."[33] Essential to the radicals' aims was providing necessary protections for free people who desired to be educated and raise their families.[34]

Opponents of the proposed amendment understood that the profound change radicals had initiated went far beyond ending forced labor. Several Democratic representatives, such as Chilton A. White, of Ohio, cautioned that the amendment would enable Congress to fashion a government of equals, where blacks would be treated the same as other citizens in voting, holding political office, and serving on juries. The concern that the Thirteenth Amendment could be used to achieve equal citizenship was raised in a debate between two Pennsylvania congressmen, William D. Kelley and John D. Stiles. To the latter's inquiry whether the amendment's supporters meant for it to help achieve racial equality, Kelley replied that blacks should not be barred from equal participation because of racism. Given these indications of radical purposes, the amendment's opponents regarded it as an impermissible assertion of federal power since the amendment would materially alter the structure of government.[35] The opponents' fears were born out when the Thirty-ninth Congress began relying on its enforcement power to provide relief against private and public discriminations.

LEGISLATIVE EFFORTS

During the Radical Republicans' brief hold on power, they passed legislation guaranteeing equal access to courts, the right to purchase and convey real and personal property, and the power to enter and enforce contracts. Of the statutes they passed using Thirteenth Amendment authority, the Civil Rights Act of 1866 had the most sustaining impact.[36]

Debates leading up to the act's passage, just as those before the Thirteenth Amendment's ratification, demonstrated the resilience of Revolutionary and abolitionist notions of fundamental rights. Radicals had not yet lost control of Congress, as they would during debates on the Fourteenth Amendment. In 1866, supporters of the Civil Rights Act regarded one of the national government's primary roles to be the protection of civil rights. The act was a determined effort to use the Thirteenth Amendment for more than simply freeing slaves. It explicitly prohibited violations against civil rights, such as the right to contract.[37]

The act was to have universal force; its applicability was not limited to any race or locality. During debates on the bill, Senator Sherman demanded that Congress protect free citizens' rights to testify at trial, to own property, to profit from labor, to raise a family, to pursue an education, and to travel.[38] The newly created federal power to act in those areas of law could have been derived only from the Enforcement Clause of the Thirteenth Amendment. Civil rights authority, according to Senator Henry Wilson, a long-committed abolitionist, "is the true office of Government."[39] Sherman was even more explicit about authority under the Thirteenth Amendment, arguing that it "is not only a guarantee of liberty to every inhabitant of the United States, but an express grant of power to Congress to secure this liberty by appropriate legislation."[40]

For the first time since independence, the national government had a constitutional mechanism for guaranteeing the fundamental rights of life, liberty, and property to its citizenry.

CONCLUSION

The Thirteenth Amendment granted Congress the power to assess and define forms of subordination that were incidental to slavery. The eventual legislative neglect of the Thirteenth Amendment went hand in hand with the abandonment of Radical Reconstruction. And that was the product of President Andrew Johnson's intransigence, Congress's eventual indifference, and the Waite and Fuller Courts' calculated deference to states' rights principles. Radicals first realized the Thirteenth Amendment was too unspecific to withstand the resilience of racism when Johnson vetoed the Civil Rights Act of 1866. They then began debating the Fourteenth Amendment to fill the missed opportunity of including equal protection language in the Thirteenth Amendment, which Senator Sumner had proposed but failed to gain support for back in April 1864.[41]

After Reconstruction, especially following the Compromise of 1877, Congress turned away from radicalism. Even before 1877, the moderate representative John A. Bingham, who was the primary House proponent of section 1 of the Fourteenth Amendment, abandoned the more positive equal protection formulation—"Congress shall have power to make all laws which shall be necessary and proper to secure all persons in every state full protection in the enjoyment of life, liberty and property; and to all citizens of the United States in any state the same immunities and also equal political rights and privileges"—for the current, negatively formulated Equal Protection Clause, "No State shall . . . deny to any person within its jurisdiction the equal protection of the laws." Later Congresses, through the leadership of Republican congressmen such as Roscoe Conkling and James G. Blaine, turned away from civil rights to other priorities, such as tariff schedules, currency, and the local concerns of their constituencies.[42]

Finally, the Supreme Court stunted the remaining potential for Congress's sweeping use of the Thirteenth Amendment. In the *Civil Rights Cases*, the Court found that even though the Thirteenth Amendment prohibited state and private badges of servitude, it did not provide Congress with the power to pro-hibit public accommodation discrimination.[43] Putting another nail in the mori-bund Enforcement Clause, the Court held, in *Plessy v. Ferguson*, that segrega-tion on an intrastate carrier was not a vestige of servitude that Congress could prevent.[44] Only in the waning days of the Warren Court, in 1968, did the jus-tices come to understand the amendment's relevance to civil rights reform. In *Jones v. Alfred H. Mayer*, the Court held that Congress's powers under the En-forcement Clause are so sweeping that it may enact any "necessary and proper" laws rationally related to the incidents or vestiges of servitude.[45]

Congress has rarely tapped into its Thirteenth Amendment power to protect fundamental rights, even though at various times diverse groups—including the labor movement, the NAACP, and the Civil Rights Section of the Justice Department—have realized the amendment's potential for civil reform.[46] The Radical Republicans who pushed for the amendment had envisioned federal activism, based on Revolutionary ideals and abolitionist demands for the pro-tection of natural rights. They had expected it to change the traditional rela-tionship between state and federal governments. That potential for progressive civil rights legislation is still there, ready to be thawed by a civil-rights-minded Congress. The continued narrow reading of the amendment's scope is, in part, the result of the failure to make sense of its Revolutionary and abolitionist foundations.

After the Civil War, national reconstruction radically altered the Constitution of the United States. Between 1865 and 1877 the nation charted a new course. The three constitutional amendments of that era augmented federal power, enabling it to safeguard certain civil and political rights. The addition of the Thirteenth Amendment was the first change in sixty-one years to the nation's organic law.

On January 1, 1863, even before Congress began to debate how best to end slavery, President Abraham Lincoln issued the Emancipation Proclamation. Thereby he dramatically redirected the course of the war, fueling the aspira-tions of reformists who wanted not only to stop the western expansion of slavery but also to destroy the entrenched institution. The proclamation relied on the president's wartime powers as commander in chief of the military. It unfastened the bonds of everyone who was enslaved in states "in rebellion against the United States." That criterion left the South's "peculiar institution" intact in several states, including Delaware, Maryland, Missouri, and Kentucky.

On December 14, 1863, more than a year before General Robert E. Lee sur-rendered to General Ulysses S. Grant at Appomattox Courthouse, an Ohio representative introduced a bill meant to prohibit slavery by constitutional amendment.[47] The Senate orchestrated one and the House of Representatives conducted two debates on the merits of the Thirteenth Amendment before passing it onto the states. Congressman Isaac N. Arnold, of Illinois, considered these three debates to be "the most important in American history. Indeed it would be difficult to find any others so important in the history of the world."[48] On December 18, 1865, Secretary of State William H. Seward announced the ratification of the amendment.[49] The first section of the amendment immediately freed everyone who was still held in slavery or involuntary servitude anywhere in the United States "or any place subject to their jurisdiction." The second section declared that "Congress shall have the power to enforce this article by appropriate legislation," vastly expanding the national government's ability to pass civil rights laws aimed at ending lingering or future forms of forced subordination.

Shortly thereafter, in 1866, Congress relied on the amendment's grant of authority to pass the Civil Rights Act of 1866. That law indicated the new relationship between the federal and state governments. The statute criminalized individual and state discriminations in contract and property-related transactions, judicial proceedings, and estate distributions. Before the addition of the Thirteenth Amendment, all these areas of law had been at the exclusive discretion of state governments, which separately chose whether to prohibit discrimination. Not long after, with the abandonment of Reconstruction and judicial opinions that narrowly construed legislative prerogatives, the Thirteenth Amendment increasingly became a relic of the past.

Even during the 1960s civil rights era, when Congress again began to pass a variety of civil rights laws, lawmakers shied away from resorting to their Thirteenth Amendment power. It was the Supreme Court that revived interest in the amendment through a 1968 opinion that upheld the constitutionality of a statute, which was derived from the 1866 law, prohibiting the use of racial discrimination in real estate transactions.[50] Sidney Buchanan then published a detailed analysis of the history of the amendment and the judicial interpretations of it.[51]

While most current civil rights decisions rely on the Commerce Clause and the Fourteenth Amendment, there are important reasons to revivify the Thirteenth Amendment's mandate of freedom. The Supreme Court has found that the Commerce Clause implicates economic concerns,[52] and it limited the applicability of the Fourteenth Amendment's Due Process Clause to violations of governmental actors.[53] The Thirteenth Amendment, on the other hand, is primarily about individual liberties rather than economic interests, and it enables Congress to prohibit private acts of discrimination.[54]

Many of the Thirteenth Amendment's potential uses remain largely unexplored by the judiciary, Congress, and academe. In a 1951 article, Jacobus tenBroek provided a profound analysis of the amendment. His research indicated that its central purpose is to provide Congress with the discretion to pass statutes against the infringement of natural rights.[55] For the next two decades, with the exception of a dissertation that was republished as a lengthy article, little academic research focused on the Thirteenth Amendment.[56]

Since then, there has been an increased interest in discovering the origins of the amendment and in its relevance to outstanding civil rights issues. Akhil Reed Amar and Douglas Colbert relied on tenBroek's research to parse the amendment's significance for a variety of subjects, including hate speech and jury nullification.[57] Additionally, two books appeared on the ratification of the amendment and on its continued significance.[58] Historians have delved into the Thirteenth Amendment by parsing congressional debates on its passage and on the enactment of the Civil Rights Act of 1866.[59] Other theorists have analyzed a variety of present-day problems, such as the exploitation of labor, racial profiling, and hate crimes, through the lens of the Thirteenth Amendment.[60]

This book is a collection of essays about the history and current relevance of the Thirteenth Amendment. It begins with David Brion Davis's comparative international analysis of obstacles that stood in the way of slave emancipation in America. His chapter also tackles how economic self-interest and racial discrimination strengthened the institution of slavery. Following my introduction is James M. McPherson's narrative of how abolitionists influenced the ratification process. Paul Finkelman addresses the much-debated issue of who liberated the slaves and concentrates his attention on President Abraham Lincoln's commitment to end slavery.

The book next turns to the aftermath of ratification. Michael Vorenberg analyzes the nineteenth-century understanding of freedom, rights, and citizenship. He analyzes the reason the amendment so rarely played a part during the Reconstruction and post-Reconstruction periods: its framers were so concentrated on the immediate need to break from past enslavement that they gave inadequate thought to the future of equal citizenship. Furthermore, the U.S. Supreme Court's narrow interpretation, as William M. Wiecek points out in his chapter, rendered the constitutional guarantee of freedom nearly illusory. Wiecek discusses a series of late-nineteenth- and early-twentieth-century Supreme Court cases reducing the nation's ability to safeguard the equal freedom of its citizens. David M. Oshinsky's chapter describes the use of peonage to further undermine the amendment's prohibition against compulsory service.

Even during its quiescent stage, the principle of equal human liberty continued to influence social protest. The vision of women's freedom at the time of abolition was bound by a narrow notion of freedom denying them the right to full self-mastery. But emancipation from slavery also became a symbol of justice for women seeking to achieve the full status of citizenship.

A quarter century after the ratification of the Thirteenth Amendment, the Supreme Court did much to diminish Congress's ability to use its power to pass civil rights legislation. Several authors criticize the narrow construction of cases such as the *Civil Rights Cases* and *Hodges v. United States.* During the New Deal, as Risa L. Goluboff recounts, U.S. Justice Department attorneys sought to reinvigorate the Thirteenth Amendment in order to facilitate civil rights prosecutions. Goluboff's chapter indicates that in the era before the Court's most important desegregation decision, *Brown v. Board of Education*, Civil Rights Section attorneys construed the Thirteenth Amendment as a repository of affirmative duties requiring that federal attorneys protect individuals' physical security and their labor and economic rights.

The history of the Thirteenth Amendment bespeaks a lost opportunity to end slavery and many public and private discriminatory practices that diminish the fundamental liberties of identifiable groups. Despite Congress's neglect of the Thirteenth Amendment, it remains a source of power to end discrimination. James Gray Pope discusses how the Amendment influenced the twentieth-century labor movement and how labor's vision continues to be relevant. Several unique features of the Thirteenth Amendment are analyzed in the second part of the book. The authors both describe the reach of congressional power to end continuing injustices and predict the amendment's future uses.

The second part begins with George A. Rutherglen's exposition of the meaning of "badges and incidents of slavery" to evaluate the class of discriminatory practices that the Thirteenth Amendment prohibits. The elusive meaning of this proposition determines the current scope of Congress's power to pass anti-discrimination laws pursuant to the amendment's second section. Parsing it is important for deciding what freedoms the American people can reasonably expect their federal government to safeguard against intrusions by state and private actors. Rebecca E. Zietlow optimistically describes Congress's vast but relatively untapped power to enforce the Thirteenth Amendment through the promulgation of civil rights legislation. Aviam Soifer shows how a close analysis of the Civil Rights Act of 1866, which relies on Thirteenth Amendment enforcement authority, sheds light on present-day controversies about subjects such as affirmative action, private education, and rights of the disabled. Andrew Koppelman draws an analogy between involuntary servitude and forced labor, finding the Thirteenth Amendment to be a logical source of abortion rights. His view has echoes of Justice Harry Blackmun's assertion that "restrictive abortion laws deprive" a woman of the "basic control over her life . . . By restricting the right to terminate pregnancies, the State conscripts women's bodies into its service" without compensation.[61]

In the two chapters that follow, Andrew E. Taslitz and William M. Carter, Jr., discuss the Thirteenth Amendment's applicability to criminal law. Taslitz points

out the extent to which the Thirteenth Amendment has already impacted the
American criminal justice system, and he argues that Congress can use its authority to pass additional criminal legislation, such as laws that would punish
violence meant to restrict minorities' access to housing. Carter explains the
amendment's relevance to those criminal cases in which the police rely on evidence obtained through the use of racial profiling. Maria L. Ontiveros elaborates on the exploitation of immigrant laborers, focusing especially on the abuse
of undocumented workers. Darrell A. H. Miller advances an argument about the
present relevance of the Thirteenth Amendment, analyzing it in the context of
felon disenfranchisement, the death penalty, and race-conscious school desegregation plans. The book ends with Robert J. Kaczorowski's epilogue. After putting
the other contributors' chapters into the context of Thirteenth Amendment his-
toriography, Kaczorowski presents an in-depth discussion about the breadth
of congressional power to guarantee citizens' liberties. Based on the historical
record, he finds that the Thirteenth Amendment granted Congress affirmative
plenary power to protect civil rights. Kaczorowski's chapter caps off a collection
of essays demonstrating the enduring possibility of relying on the Thirteenth
Amendment to expand our federal government's role in enforcing the Revolutionary promises of equal liberty.

NOTES

1. ALEXANDER HAMILTON, THE FULL VINDICATION OF THE MEASURES OF
THE CONGRESS 5 (1774); Thomas Paine, *African Slavery in America, in* 1 THE WRIT-
INGS OF THOMAS PAINE 4, 7 (Moncure D. Conway ed., 1894) (1775).

2. MOSES MATHER, AMERICA'S APPEAL TO THE IMPARTIAL WORLD 48 (1775).
See also RICHARD PRICE, OBSERVATIONS ON THE NATURE OF CIVIL LIBERTY, *in*
TWO TRACTS ON CIVIL LIBERTY, THE WAR WITH AMERICA 11 (1778).

3. ALEXANDER HAMILTON, A FULL VINDICATION OF THE MEASURES OF CON-
GRESS 4 (1774); HAMPDEN, THE ALARM (No. III) (Oct. 15, 1773); JOSIAH QUINCY,
JR., *Observations on the Act of Parliament Commonly Called* THE BOSTON
PORT-BILL (1774); JOHN DICKINSON, LETTERS FROM A FARMER IN PENNSYLVA-
NIA, TO THE INHABITANTS OF THE BRITISH COLONIES 53 (1768); THE SPEECHES
OF HIS EXCELLENCY GOVERNOR HUTCHINSON, TO THE GENERAL ASSEMBLY OF
THE MASSACHUSETTS-BAY 34, 44 (1773); PHILIP DAVIDSON, PROPAGANDA AND
THE AMERICAN REVOLUTION 1763–1783, at 341 (1941) (quoting army private).

4. DAVID BRION DAVIS, THE PROBLEM OF SLAVERY IN THE AGE OF REVOLU-
TION 1770–1823, at 274 (1975) (quoting Rush); RICHARD WELLS, A FEW POLITICAL
REFLECTIONS SUBMITTED TO THE CONSIDERATION OF THE BRITISH COLONIES
80 (1774); JOHN ALLEN, THE WATCHMAN'S ALARM TO LORD N____H 27–28 (1774).

5. JAMES OTIS, RIGHTS OF THE BRITISH COLONIES ASSERTED AND PROVED 29 (1764); A LETTER FROM *****, IN LONDON . . . ON THE . . . SLAVE-TRADE 16 (1784); ABRAHAM BOOTH, COMMERCE IN THE HUMAN SPECIES 22 (1792).

6. WINTHROP D. JORDAN, WHITE OVER BLACK: AMERICAN ATTITUDES TOWARD THE NEGRO, 1550–1812, at 298 (1968).

7. Letter from Benjamin Rush to Granville Sharp, Oct. 29, 1773, *in Correspondence of Benjamin Rush & Granville Sharp*, 1 J. AM. STUD. 1, 5 (John A. Woods ed., 1965).

8. JORDAN, *supra*, 291 (1968) (quoting N. H. petitioners); *'Liberty Further Extended': A 1776 Antislavery Manuscript by Lemuel Haynes*, 40 WM & MARY Q. 85, 92 (3d ser., 1983); Thomas J. Davis, *Emancipation Rhetoric, Natural Rights & Revolutionary New England: A Note on Four Black Petitions in Massachusetts, 1773–1777*, 62 NEW ENG. Q. 248, 255 (1989); 1 A DOCUMENTARY HISTORY OF THE NEGRO PEOPLE IN THE UNITED STATES 10 (1951).

9. SAMUEL HOPKINS, A DIALOGUE CONCERNING THE SLAVERY OF THE AFRICANS: SHEWING IT TO BE THE DUTY AND INTEREST OF THE AMERICAN COLONIES TO EMANCIPATE ALL THEIR AFRICAN SLAVES 50 (1776); NATHANIEL APPLETON, CONSIDERATIONS ON SLAVERY 19 (1767); DONALD L. ROBINSON, SLAVERY IN THE STRUCTURE OF AMERICAN POLITICS, 1765–1820, at 74–75 (1971) (quoting Niles); ANTHONY BENEZET, SOME HISTORICAL ACCOUNT OF GUINEA ch. 11 (1771); ANTHONY BENEZET, A SHORT ACCOUNT OF THAT PART OF AFRICA, INHABITED BY THE NEGROES 71–72 (3d ed. 1768).

10. Letter from Patrick Henry to Robert Pleasants, January 18, 1773, reprinted in GEORGE S. BROOKES, FRIEND ANTHONY BENEZET 443–44 (1937).

11. THOMAS JEFFERSON, NOTES ON THE STATE OF VIRGINIA 162–63 (1955) (1787) ("The whole commerce between master and slave is a perpetual exercise of the most boisterous passions, the most unremitting despotism on the one part, and degrading submissions on the other . . . With the morals of the people, their industry also is destroyed . . . I tremble for my country when I reflect that God is just."); Tania Tetlow, *The Founders & Slavery: A Crisis of Conscience*, 3 LOY. J. PUB. INT. L. 1, 11 (2001) (quotes of the Declaration of Independence draft); THOMAS JEFFERSON, A SUMMARY VIEW OF THE RIGHTS OF BRITISH AMERICA 16 (1774) (Jefferson on abolishing slavery); 1 THE PAPERS OF THOMAS JEFFERSON 363 (Julian P. Boyd ed., 1950) (drafts of Virginia Constitution); WILLIAM W. FREEHLING, THE ROAD TO DISUNION: SECESSIONISTS AT BAY 1776–1854, at 8 (1991) (on Jefferson's support for the Ordinance of 1784, which would have banned the spread of slavery after 1800 into southern and northern territories).

12. Letter from Thomas Jefferson to Edward Coles, Aug. 25, 1814, *in* 11 THE WORKS OF THOMAS JEFFERSON 416–19 (Paul L. Ford ed., 1905). Coles eventually freed his slaves after he had confronted James Madison about his participation in slavery. *See* RALPH KETCHAM, JAMES MADISON: A BIOGRAPHY 551–52 (1971).

13. BENJAMIN QUARLES, THE NEGRO IN THE AMERICAN REVOLUTION 40–41 (1961); A DECLARATION OF THE RIGHTS OF THE INHABITANTS OF THE STATE OF VERMONT, available at http://www.yale.edu/lawweb/avalon/states/vt01.htm; N.H. BILL OF RIGHTS art. 2, available at http://www.state.nh.us/constitution/billofrights .html; *Commonwealth v. Jennison* (1783), *quoted in* PHILIP S. FONER , 1 HISTORY OF BLACK AMERICANS 353 (1975); 10 RECORDS OF THE STATE OF RHODE ISLAND AND PROVIDENCE PLANTATIONS IN NEW ENGLAND 132 (1865); Lois E. Horton, *From Class to Race in Early America: Northern Post-Emancipation Racial Reconstruction,* 19 J. EARLY REPUBLIC 629, 639 (1999); J. FRANKLIN JAMESON, THE AMERICAN REVOLUTION CONSIDERED AS A SOCIAL MOVEMENT 25 (1926). By 1830, fewer than 3,000 blacks remained enslaved in northern and middle states compared to those states' 125,000 free black population. GORDON S. WOOD, REVOLUTION & THE POLITICAL INTEGRATION OF THE ENSLAVED & DISENFRANCHISED 13 (1974).

14. *See generally* on slave-protecting clauses of the Constitution Alexander Tsesis, *Furthering American Freedom: Civil Rights & the Thirteenth Amendment,* 45 B.C. L. REV. 307, 319–22 (2004); WILLIAM WIECEK, THE SOURCES OF ANTISLAVERY CON-STITUTIONALISM IN AMERICA, 1760–1848, at 62–83 (1977); Frederick Douglass, *in* VOICES FROM THE GATHERING STORM: THE COMING OF THE AMERICAN CIVIL WAR 40–41 (Glenn M. Linden ed., 2001).

15. WILLIAM L. GARRISON, AN ADDRESS DELIVERED BEFORE THE OLD COL-ONY ANTI-SLAVERY SOCIETY, AT SOUTH SCITUATE, MASS., JULY 4, 1839, at 17 (1839); WILLIAM E. CHANNING, SLAVERY 21 (Edward C. Osborn: repr. 1836); *Principles of the Anti-Slavery Society, in* THE AMERICAN ANTI SLAVERY ALMANAC 30–31 (1837 ed.); Theodore Parker, *The Dangers from Slavery* (July 2, 1854), *in* 4 OLD SOUTH LEAFLETS 1–3 (1897); *Constitution of the New-England Anti-Slavery Society, in* 1 THE ABOLITIONIST: OR RECORD OF THE NEW ENGLAND ANTI-SLAVERY SOCIETY 2 (January 1833).

16. American Anti-Slavery Society, *Declaration of the Anti-Slavery Convention,* Dec. 4, 1833, PROCEEDINGS OF THE ANTI-SLAVERY CONVENTION, ASSEMBLED AT PHILADELPHIA 12, 12 (1833); JOEL TIFFANY, A TREATISE ON THE UNCONSTITU-TIONALITY OF AMERICAN SLAVERY 29 (1849).

17. CHARLES OLCOTT, TWO LECTURES ON SLAVERY AND ABOLITION 88 (1838); GEORGE W. F. MELLEN, AN ARGUMENT ON THE UNCONSTITUTIONALITY OF SLAVERY 55, 63 (1841).

18. CONG. GLOBE, 33rd Cong., 1st Sess., Appendix 268 (Feb. 24, 1854).

19. 2 GEORGE W. WILLIAMS, HISTORY OF THE NEGRO RACE IN AMERICA 45 (1883); ANNA L. DAWES, CHARLES SUMNER 208 (1898).

20. CONG. GLOBE, 39th Cong., 1st Sess. 5 (Dec. 4, 1865).

21. Ashley introduced the proposal on December 14, 1863, during the 38th Con-gress, announcing his intent to submit an amendment "prohibiting slavery, or invol-untary servitude, in all of the States and Territories now owned or which may be

hereafter acquired by the United States." CONG. GLOBE, 38th Cong., 1st Sess. 19 (1863). In the Senate, John Henderson, of Missouri, introduced the proposal on January 13, 1864. *Id.* at 145 (1864).

22. *At the Fair in Baltimore, in Aid of the Sanitary Commission, April 18, 1864, in* ABRAHAM LINCOLN, THE MARTYR'S MONUMENT: BEING PATRIOTISM AND POLITICAL WISDOM OF ABRAHAM LINCOLN 252 (1865).

23. Both congressmen and Lincoln recognized that the Emancipation Proclamation was inadequate for eradicating slavery since its legal justification rested on the president's wartime powers and would have been ineffectual following the end of conflict. The political determination to proceed with a constitutional amendment abolishing slavery was partly predicated in the constitutional uncertainties surrounding the Emancipation Proclamation. *See* HORACE WHITE, THE LIFE OF LYMAN TRUMBULL 222–23 (1913); J. G. RANDALL, CONSTITUTIONAL PROBLEMS UNDER LINCOLN 372–78, 390–91 (rev. ed. 1963); DONALD G. NIEMAN, PROMISES TO KEEP: AFRICAN-AMERICANS & THE CONSTITUTIONAL ORDER, 1776 TO THE PRESENT 55 (1991); Ira Berlin, *Emancipation & Its Meaning, in* UNION & EMANCIPATION: ESSAYS ON POLITICS & RACE IN THE CIVIL WAR ERA 109 (David W. Blight & Brooks D. Simpson eds., 1997).

24. CONG. GLOBE, 38th Cong., 2d Sess. 200 (1865) (Rep. John Farnsworth); CONG. GLOBE, 38th Cong., 2nd Sess. 154 (1865) (Rep. Thomas Davis); Charles L. Black, Jr., *Further Reflections on the Constitutional Justice of Livelihood*, 86 COLUM. L. REV. 1103, 1103 (1986).

25. CONG. GLOBE, 38th Cong., 1st Sess. 2983 (1864).

26. Letter from Alvan Stewart to Dr. [Gamaliel] Bailey, Apr. 1842, *in* WRITINGS & SPEECHES OF ALVAN STEWART, ON SLAVERY 250–51 (Luther R. Marsh ed., 1860); CONG. GLOBE, 38th Cong., 2d Sess. 265 (1865).

27. *Id.* at 142; 38th Cong., 1st Sess. 2955 (June 14, 1864) (Francis W. Kellogg's connection of the proposed Thirteenth Amendment to the Preamble).

28. *Id.* at 2990; CONG. GLOBE, 39th Cong., 1st Sess. 1152 (Mar. 2, 1866).

29. CONG. GLOBE, 38th Cong., 1st Sess. 2989 (1864) (Arnold); James A. Garfield, *Oration Delivered at Ravenna, Ohio July 4, 1865, in* 1 THE WORKS OF JAMES ABRAM GARFIELD 86 (Burke A. Hinsdale ed., 1882); CONG. GLOBE, 39th Cong., 1st Sess. 1152 (Mar. 2, 1866) (Thayer).

30. CONG. GLOBE, 39th Cong., 1st Sess. 41 (1865).

31. *See, e.g., id.* at 74 .

32. CONG. GLOBE, 38th Cong., 1st Sess. 1439–40 (1864); *Jones v. Alfred H. Mayer*, 392 U.S. 409 (1968).

33. CONG. GLOBE, 39th Cong., 1st Sess. 503–4 (1866).

34. CONG. GLOBE, 38th Cong., 1st Sess. 1324 (1864).

35. CONG. GLOBE, 38th Cong., 2d Sess. 216 (1865) (White); *id.* at 291 (1865) (Stiles); *id.* (Kelley); CONG. GLOBE, 38th Cong., 1st Sess. 186 (1864); *id.* at 2941.

36. Ch. 31, § 1, 14 Stat. 27 (1866) (currently codified as amended at 42 U.S.C. §§ 1981–1982 [2000]).

37. The act concerns a variety of contract, property, and procedural rights. Violators were subject to imprisonment for up to one year and a fine of no more than $1,000. Civil Rights Act, 14 Stat. 27 (1866).

38. CONG. GLOBE, 39th Cong., 1st Sess. 42 (Dec. 13, 1865). Senator Howard held a similarly broad construction of the Thirteenth Amendment's guarantee of freedom, "What are the attributes of a freeman according to the universal understanding of the American people? Is a freeman to be deprived of the right of acquiring property, of the right of having a family, a wife, children, home? What definition will you attach to the word 'freeman' that does not include these ideas?" Id. at 504 (Jan. 30, 1866). Any lesser guarantee of freedom, Howard asserted, would be worse than the bondage from which blacks emerged. Id.

39. CONG. GLOBE, 39th Cong., 1st Sess. 1118, 1119 (Mar. 1, 1866).

40. Id. at 1118, 1119 (1866) (Wilson); id. at 41 (1865) (Sherman).

41. Sumner proposed that the Thirteenth Amendment guarantee that "all persons are equal before the law, so that no person can hold another as a slave; and the Congress may make all laws necessary and proper to carry this article into effect everywhere within the United States and the jurisdiction thereof." CONG. GLOBE, 38th Cong., 1st Sess. 1482–83 (Apr. 8, 1864)

42. CONG. GLOBE 39th Cong., 1st Sess. 813 (Feb. 13, 1866); W. R. BROCK, AN AMERICAN CRISIS 276–77 (1963).

43. Civil Rights Cases, 109 U.S. 3, 20, 25 (1883).

44. 163 U.S. 537, 551 (1896).

45. Civil Rights Cases, 109 U.S. 3, 20, 25 (1883); Plessy, 163 U.S. 537, 551 (1896); Jones, 392 U.S. at 439–40.

46. See James G. Pope, ch. 9 this vol.; Risa L. Goluboff, ch. 8 this vol.

47. CONG. GLOBE, 38th Cong., 1st Sess. 19 (1863) (Rep. James M. Ashley).

48. ISAAC N. ARNOLD, THE LIFE OF ABRAHAM LINCOLN 346 (1887).

49. 2 DOCUMENTARY HISTORY OF THE CONSTITUTION OF THE UNITED STATES OF AMERICA, 1786–1870, at 636–37 (1894).

50. Jones v. Alfred H. Mayer Co., 392 U.S. 409 (1968).

51. G. SIDNEY BUCHANAN et al., THE QUEST FOR FREEDOM: A LEGAL HISTORY OF THE THIRTEENTH AMENDMENT (1976).

52. United States v. Morrison, 529 U.S. 598, 611 (2000).

53. Id. at 621; City of Boerne v. Flores, 521 U.S. 507, 533 (1997).

54. See, e.g., Runyon v. McCrary, 427 U.S. 160, 179 (1976).

55. Jacobus tenBroek, Thirteenth Amendment to the Constitution of the United States: Consummation to Abolition and Key to the Fourteenth Amendment, 39 CAL. L. REV. 171 (1951).

56. Howard D. Hamilton, The Legislative & Judicial History of the Thirteenth Amendment, 9 NAT'L B.J. 26 (1951).

57. Akhil R. Amar, *The Case of the Missing Amendment: R.A.V. v. City of St. Paul*, 106 HARV. L. REV. 124, 157 (1992); Akhil R. Amar & Daniel Widawsky, *Child Abuse as Slavery: A Thirteenth Amendment Response to* Deshaney, 105 HARV. L. REV. 1359 (1992); Douglas L. Colbert, *Affirming the Thirteenth Amendment*, 1995 ANN. SURV. AM. L. 403 (1995); *Challenging the Challenge: Thirteenth Amendment as a Prohibition against the Racial Use of Peremptory Challenges*, 76 CORNELL L. REV. 1 (1990).

58. ALEXANDER TSESIS, THE THIRTEENTH AMENDMENT AND AMERICAN FREEDOM: A LEGAL HISTORY (2004); MICHAEL VORENBERG, FINAL FREEDOM: THE CIVIL WAR, THE ABOLITION OF SLAVERY, AND THE THIRTEENTH AMENDMENT (2001).

59. Robert J. Kaczorowski, *Fidelity Through History & to It: An Impossible Dream?*, 65 FORDHAM L. REV. 1663 (1997); Alexander Tsesis, *The Problem of Confederate Symbols: A Thirteenth Amendment Approach*, 75 TEMPLE L. REV. 539 (2002); Douglas L. Colbert, *Liberating the Thirteenth Amendment*, 30 HARV. C.R.-C.L. L. REV. 1 (1995).

60. James Gray Pope, *The Thirteenth Amendment versus the Commerce Clause: Labor and the Shaping of American Constitutional Law, 1921–1957*, 102 COLUM. L. REV. 1 (2002) (labor); Lea S. VanderVelde, *The Labor Vision of the Thirteenth Amendment*, 138 U. PA. L. REV. 437 (1989) (labor); Tobias B. Wolff, *The Thirteenth Amendment & Slavery in the Global Economy*, 102 COLUM. L. REV. 973 (2002) (global labor); William M. Carter, Jr., *A Thirteenth Amendment Framework for Combating Racial Profiling*, 39 HARV. C.R.-C.L. L. REV. 17 (2004) (racial profiling); Alexander Tsesis, *Regulating Intimidating Speech*, 41 HARV. J. LEGIS. 389 (2004) (hate speech).

61. *Planned Parenthood of Southeastern Pennsylvania v. Casey*, 505 U.S. 833, 928 (1992) (Blackmun, J., concurring).

PART 1

Historical Settings

2. In Pursuit of Constitutional Abolitionism

James M. McPherson

The abolitionist movement of the 1830s hoped to end slavery in the United States by converting slaveholders into abolitionists in the same way that evangelical preachers converted sinners into Christian believers. This optimistic crusade soon confronted the reality of self-interest and racism buttressing slavery. The expectation that "moral suasion" would liberate America from the sin of human bondage gave way to a political movement to elect a national government that would curb the expansion of slavery as the first step, in the words of Abraham Lincoln, toward bringing it "in the course of ultimate extinction." When Lincoln was elected president in 1860, leaders of most slave states saw the handwriting on the wall signifying the "ultimate extinction" of their peculiar institution. To forestall that outcome, they seceded from the United States to establish their independent slave republic. The war they provoked by firing on the American flag at Fort Sumter set in train a series of events that did indeed assure the extinction of slavery in an America reunited by that war.

The pursuit of constitutional abolitionism gained momentum on January 1, 1863, when President Abraham Lincoln issued the Emancipation Proclamation. Critics noted that it "emancipated" only those slaves beyond the power of the federal government and exempted those within Union lines. Abolitionists recognized that this was true, but they replied that the proclamation constituted a promise, freedom to all slaves in nonexempt rebel states as soon as the Confederacy was conquered. Edmund Quincy, an abolitionist editor and author, admitted that actual physical emancipation could be accomplished only by the Union army as it advanced southward; but news of the proclamation would "not only spread with immense rapidity over every portion of the South, but [would] . . . exercise everywhere a moral influence mightily efficacious for the freedmen, and against the slaveholder." William Robinson observed dryly: "That old Declaration of July 4, 1776, remained a ridiculous *brutum fulmen* for seven years. No doubt many a mad wag among the Tories of that day had his jeer at it, comparing it to the Pope's bull against the comet."[1]

January 1, 1863, was the climax of the drive for emancipation. But the events of the next two years constituted an important anticlimax. There were still many obstacles to be overcome before the decision to abolish slavery was secured beyond recall. Thomas Wentworth Higginson, colonel of the first regiment of freed slaves enlisted in the Civil War, feared a reaction from the sweeping revolution of emancipation. "Sometimes I feel anxious about the ultimate fate of these poor [Negro] people," he confided to his journal a week after Lincoln had issued the Emancipation Proclamation. "After Hungary, one sees that the right may not triumph, & revolutions may go backward, & the habit of inhumanity in regard to them seems so deeply impressed upon our people, that it is hard to believe in the possibility of anything better. I dare not yet hope that the promise of the President's proclamation will be kept."[2]

Radical Republicans and abolitionists asked one another apprehensively whether Lincoln would bow to conservative pressure and modify his proclamation. The president relieved their anxiety in a public letter of August 26 to James Conkling, of Springfield, Illinois. Relying on antebellum war-power arguments, Lincoln affirmed that he possessed full constitutional power to declare military emancipation. He had done so, and he would not retract his action. He had promised freedom to the slaves, "and the promise being made, must be kept."[3] Abolitionists praised the letter. "We thank the President for that declaration," wrote William Goodell in *Principia*. "We thank God, and take courage."

Republican victories in the 1863 elections gave proponents of emancipation another injection of hope. Lincoln provided abolitionists with further cause for rejoicing in his annual message to Congress on December 8,1863, when he firmly declared that "while I remain in my present position I shall not attempt to retract or modify the emancipation proclamation; nor shall I return to slavery any person who is free by the terms of that proclamation, or by any of the acts of Congress." A member of the New-England Anti-Slavery Society, Henry Wright, wrote fervently, "God bless thee, Abraham Lincoln! With all my heart I bless thee, in the name of God & Humanity." Lincoln's declaration was an important victory for abolition. The president had refused to succumb to the counter-emancipation pressures exerted during 1863 and had placed himself firmly and irrevocably on the side of freedom.[4]

In the spring of 1863 Elizabeth Cady Stanton and Susan B. Anthony organized the Women's Loyal National League to promote loyalty and propagandize for emancipation. Abolitionists had been calling for a congressional emancipation act to reinforce Lincoln's proclamation, and the Women's League decided that its main function would be to circulate petitions urging passage of such an act.[5]

Late in 1863 there was a growing conviction that the confiscation acts and the Emancipation Proclamation, although legitimate wartime measures, might become legally inoperative once peace was concluded. To be permanent, therefore, emancipation must be written into the Constitution. Realizing the force of this argument, abolitionists decided, in December 1863, to press for a constitutional amendment to abolish and prohibit forever the institution of slavery in the United States. The request for a constitutional amendment was included in all petitions circulated by the antislavery societies after December 1863, and in all petitions circulated by the Women's Loyal National League after February 1864.[6]

By early 1864, 2,000 men, women, and children were at work circulating petitions. In February Anthony and Stanton sent the first installment of petitions bearing 100,000 signatures to Senator Charles Sumner. On February 9 two tall black men, symbolizing the struggle for freedom, carried the huge bundles of petitions into the Senate and placed them on Sumner's desk. The senator rose to speak. "This petition is signed by one hundred thousand men and women, who unite in this unparalleled manner to support its prayer," he told the Senate. "They are from all parts of the country and every condition of life . . . Here they are, a mighty army, one hundred thousand strong, without arms or banners, the advanced guard of a yet larger army."[7]

It was clear that the women would come nowhere near their goal of 1 million signatures. Such a goal was unrealistically high for the resources and woman power of the league. By the time Congress adjourned in July 1864, the league had sent in petitions bearing nearly 400,000 signatures. No other petition for a single objective had ever received so many signatures. Senators Sumner and Henry Wilson assured the league that their petition campaign had been of great assistance in the struggle to secure congressional passage of the Thirteenth Amendment.[8]

By 1864 the doom of slavery was not only an abolitionist issue. It had become one of the Republicans' foremost concerns. As military measures, both President Lincoln's Emancipation Proclamation and General Nathaniel Banks's edict declaring slavery "void" in Louisiana would have precarious legal force when the war was over. That was why radicals considered a new constitution abolishing slavery a necessary prerequisite to the election of new state govern-ments in places such as Louisiana. Many congressional Republicans also feared a revival of slavery if conservatives should gain control of a reconstructed Loui-siana. The best solution for this problem was a national constitutional amend-ment abolishing slavery. All Republicans, including Lincoln, united in favor of this in 1864. But the problem persisted. The Senate quickly mustered the neces-sary two-thirds majority for a Thirteenth Amendment abolishing slavery, but Democratic gains in the 1862 congressional elections prevented similar success in the House, where a ninety-three to sixty-five vote for the amendment, on June 15, fell thirteen votes short of success.

In 1864 the controversy over freedmen's policy in Louisiana added its force to the process by which Congress hammered out a Reconstruction bill. As fi-nally passed after seemingly endless debate, the Wade-Davis bill reached Lin-coln's desk on July 4. By limiting suffrage to whites it did not differ from the president's policy. In another important respect—the abolition of slavery—it only appeared to differ. While the bill mandated emancipation and Lincoln's policy did not, the president's offer of amnesty required recipients of pardon to swear their support for all government actions on slavery. The two states thus far "reconstructed," Louisiana and Arkansas, had abolished the institution. Nevertheless a fear persisted among some Republicans that a residue of slavery might survive in any peace settlement negotiated by Lincoln, so they consid-ered abolition by statute vital.

More significant were other differences between presidential and congres-sional policies: the Wade-Davis bill required 50 percent instead of 10 percent of the voters to swear an oath of allegiance, specified that a constitutional con-vention must take place before election of state officers, and restricted the right to vote for convention delegates to men who could take the "ironclad oath" that they had never voluntarily supported the rebellion. No Confederate state (ex-cept perhaps Tennessee) could meet these conditions; the real purpose of the Wade-Davis bill was to postpone Reconstruction until the war was won. Lin-coln, by contrast, wanted to initiate Reconstruction immediately in order to convert lukewarm Confederates into unionists as a means of winning the war.[9]

Lincoln decided to veto the bill. Since Congress had passed it at the end of the session, he needed only to withhold his signature to prevent it from becom-ing law (the so-called pocket veto). This he did, but he also issued a statement explaining why he had done so. Lincoln denied the right of Congress to abolish slavery by statute. To assert such a right would "make the fatal admission" that these states were out of the Union and that secession was therefore legitimate. The pending Thirteenth Amendment, said the president, was the only constitu-tional way to abolish slavery. Lincoln also refused "to be inflexibly committed to any single plan of restoration" as required by the bill, since this would destroy "the free-state constitutions and governments, already adopted and installed in Arkansas and Louisiana."[10]

Lincoln's renomination and reelection were by no means assured. No incumbent president had been renominated since 1840, and none had been reelected since 1832. The Republican convention in Baltimore during the second week of June 1864 exhibited the usual hoopla and love-feast unity of a party renominating an incumbent. The assemblage called itself the National Union convention to attract Civil War Democrats and Southern unionists who might flinch at the name Republican. But it nevertheless adopted a down-the-line Republican platform, including endorsement of unremitting war to force the "unconditional surrender" of Confederate armies and the passage of a constitutional amendment to abolish slavery.

When the latter plank was presented, "the whole body of delegates sprang to their feet . . . in prolonged cheering," according to William Lloyd Garrison, who was present as a reporter for his newspaper the *Liberator*. "Was not a spectacle like that rich compensation for more than thirty years of personal opprobrium?"[11] Even a longtime abolitionist could support Lincoln's renomination on a platform promising to alter the nation's fundamental law.

From that point slavery was as good as doomed. While the South debated the relationship of slavery to its cause, the North acted. Lincoln interpreted his reelection as a mandate for passage of the Thirteenth Amendment to end slavery forever. The voters had retired a large number of Democratic congressmen. But until the Thirty-eighth Congress expired on March 4, 1865, they retained their seats and could block House passage of the amendment by the necessary two-thirds majority. In the next Congress the Republicans would have a three-quarters House majority and could easily pass it. Lincoln intended to call a special session in March if necessary to do the job. But he preferred to accomplish it sooner, by a bipartisan majority, as a gesture of wartime unity in favor of this measure that Lincoln considered essential to Union victory. "In a great national crisis, like ours," he told Congress in his message of December 6, 1864, "unanimity of action among those seeking a common end is very desirable— almost indispensable." This was an expression of an ideal rather than reality, since most war measures, especially those concerning slavery, had been passed by a strictly Republican vote. For the historic achievement of terminating the institution, however, Lincoln appealed to Democrats to recognize the "will of the majority" as expressed by the election.[12]

But most Democrats preferred to stand on principle in defense of the past. Even if the war had killed slavery, they refused to help bury it. The party remained officially opposed to the Thirteenth Amendment as "unwise, impolitic, cruel, and unworthy of the support of civilized people." A few Democratic congressmen believed otherwise, however. The party had suffered disaster in the

1864 election, said one, "because we [would] not venture to cut loose from the dead carcass of negro slavery." Another declared that to persist in opposition to the amendment "will be to simply announce ourselves a set of impracticables no more fit to deal with practical affairs than the old gentleman in Copperfield."[13] Encouraged by such sentiments, the Lincoln administration targeted a dozen or so lame-duck Democratic congressmen and subjected them to a barrage of blandishments. Secretary of State Seward oversaw this lobbying effort. Some congressmen were promised government jobs for themselves or relatives; others received administration favors of one sort or another.[14]

This arm-twisting and the conviction of enough Democrats that public opinion desired emancipation paid off, though until the House voted on January 31,1865, no one could predict which way it would go. As a few Democrats early in the roll call voted aye, Republican faces brightened. Sixteen of the eighty Democrats finally voted for the amendment; fourteen of them were lame ducks. Eight other Democrats had absented themselves. This enabled the amendment to pass with two votes to spare, one hundred nineteen to fifty-six. When the result was announced, Republicans on the floor and spectators in the gallery broke into prolonged and unprecedented cheering, while in the streets of Washington cannons boomed a hundred-gun salute. The scene "beggared description," wrote a Republican congressman in his diary. "Members joined in the shouting and kept it up for some minutes. Some embraced one another, others wept like children. I have felt, ever since the vote, as if I were in a new country." By acclamation the House voted to adjourn for the rest of the day "in honor of this immortal and sublime event."[15]

The Thirteenth Amendment sped quickly through Republican state legislatures that were in session; within a week eight states had ratified it, and during the next two months another eleven did so. Ratification by five additional Northern states was certain as soon as their legislatures met. Of the Union states only those carried by General George B. McClellan in the 1864 presidential election—New Jersey, Kentucky, and Delaware—held out.[16] The "reconstructed" states of Louisiana, Arkansas, and Tennessee ratified readily. Since the Lincoln administration had fought the war on the theory that states could not secede, it considered ratification by three-quarters of all the states, including those in the Confederacy, to be necessary. One of the first tasks of Reconstruction would be to obtain the ratification of at least three more ex-Confederate states to place the amendment in the Constitution.

Among the spectators who cheered and wept for joy when the House passed the Thirteenth Amendment were many black people. Their presence was a visible symbol of the revolutionary changes signified by the amendment, for until 1864 blacks had not been allowed in congressional galleries. Blacks were also admitted to White House social functions for the first time in 1865, and Lincoln went out of his way to welcome Frederick Douglass to the inaugural reception on March 4. Congress and Northern states enacted legislation that began to break down the pattern of second-class citizenship for Northern blacks: admission of black witnesses to federal courts, repeal of an old law barring blacks from carrying mail, prohibition of segregation on streetcars in the District of Columbia, repeal of black laws in several Northern states that had imposed certain kinds of discrimination against blacks or barred their entry into the state, and steps to submit referendums to the voters of several states to grant the ballot to blacks (none of these referendums passed until 1868).

Perhaps the most dramatic symbol of change occurred on February 1, the day after House passage of the Thirteenth Amendment. On that day Senator Charles Sumner presented Boston lawyer John Rock for admission to the Supreme Court Bar. Chief Justice Salmon P. Chase swore him in. There was nothing unusual in this except that Rock was the first black man accredited to the highest court that, eight years earlier, had denied U.S. citizenship to his race. The Court had been virtually reconstructed by Lincoln's appointment of five new justices, including Chase. The transition from the deceased Chief Justice Roger Taney to Chase as leader of the Court was itself the most sweeping judicial metamorphosis in American history.[17]

As for abolitionists they acted with qualified jubilation, much as they had to the Emancipation Proclamation when they realized that it was but a "military necessity." The massive job of aiding the transition of 4 million bondsmen to a new life of freedom, and of persuading white America to accept black Americans as equals, still lay in the future. Abolitionists could not yet retire from the conflict; it was still too early to celebrate the final victory. All abolitionists, even Wendell Phillips, who had initially opposed Lincoln's bid for reelection, hailed the Republican triumph in November as a great victory for freedom. "The people pronounced for the prosecution of the war in the first place, and in the next for the abolition of slavery," said the *Commonwealth*. 'With a logic which never fails them, they linked together there two things and made them one and inseparable." Phillips urged all abolitionists to forget past differences and work together for the common cause. "Now our common duty is to throw all personal matters behind us and rally together to claim of the Republican party the performance of their pledge [the Thirteenth Amendment]," he told Elizabeth Cady Stanton. "On that issue the canvass was conducted, and now we have a right to demand the 'bond,' and they a right to demand that we shall help them attain the capability of granting it." Universal freedom for blacks was assured by Lincoln's reelection; abolitionists must work to persuade the people and their government to take the next step forward—universal equality.[18]

For the rest of their lives, most abolitionists remained active in efforts to fulfill this egalitarian promise of freedom. These efforts took two principal forms.

One was continued activism in reform organizations such as the American Anti-Slavery Society and the Equal Suffrage Association to pressure the government to enact and enforce measures to guarantee equal civil and political rights for freed slaves. These goals were achieved—on paper at least—by the Fourteenth and Fifteenth amendments to the Constitution, the Civil Rights acts of 1866 and 1875, and the Enforcement acts of 1870 and 1871.

The second arena of continued abolitionist activism was black education. Organizations founded by abolitionists, most notably the American Missionary Association, founded hundreds of schools for freed slaves. Several of them evolved into institutions of higher education that are among the leading universities attended by many of their descendants today: Howard University, Fisk University, the Atlanta University Center, including Morehouse and Spelman colleges, and others.

Despite the apparent victory of the struggle for racial equality by the 1870s, the nation soon commenced to backslide on these commitments. By the end of the nineteenth century, the promises of Reconstruction had been all but forgotten and the Fourteenth and Fifteenth amendments eviscerated. Most African Americans found themselves disfranchised, segregated, and suppressed into a second-class citizenship in which economic exploitation reinforced caste discrimination. Abolitionists who survived into the era of Jim Crow watched this process with alarm and anger. Many of their children and grandchildren had inherited their commitment to racial justice. Some of them took the lead in organizing neoabolitionist societies to resist this reactionary course. Three of the founders of the National Association for the Advancement of Colored People (established in 1909) were, for example, sons and grandsons of William Lloyd Garrison: William Lloyd Garrison, Jr., Francis Jackson Garrison, and Oswald Garrison Villard. Stretching from the first William Lloyd Garrison's demand for immediate emancipation in 1831 through Abraham Lincoln's Emancipation Proclamation to Martin Luther King's demand for "Freedom now," the spirit of abolitionism has lived on.

NOTES

1. Quincy, *in* NATIONAL ANTI-SLAVERY STANDARD, Jan. 10, 1863; Robinson, *in* SPRINGFIELD REPUBLICAN, Jan. 8, 1868.

2. Higginson, journal entry of Jan. 8. 1863, Higginson Papers, Houghton Library, Harvard University.

3. THE COLLECTED WORKS OF ABRAHAM LINCOLN 406–10 (Roy C. Basler ed., 1953) (hereafter CWL).

4. PRINCIPIA, Sept. 10, 1863; 7 CWL 51; Henry Wright to Lincoln, Dec. 16, 1863, Lincoln Papers, Library of Congress.

5. NATIONAL ANTI-SLAVERY STANDARD, May 23, 30, June 6, 1863; 2 ELIZABETH CADY STANTON ET AL., HISTORY OF WOMAN SUFFRAGE 50–78 (1881).

6. Samuel May, Jr., to Garrison, Dec. 28, 1863, Garrison Papers, Boston Public Library; LIBERATOR, Jan. 15,1864; S. B. Anthony to Charles Sumner, Mar. 1, 1864, Sumner Papers, Houghton Library, Harvard University.

7. 2 STANTON, HISTORY OF WOMAN SUFFRAGE, *supra*, at 78–87; S. B. Anthony and E. C. Stanton to Sumner, Feb. 4, 1864, Sumner Papers, Houghton Library, Harvard University; CONG. GLOBE., 38th Cong., 1st Sess. 536 (1864).

8. LIBERATOR, Mar. 11, 1864; INDEPENDENT, Apr. 7, 1864; NEW YORK TRIBUNE, May 17, 1864; NATIONAL ANTI-SLAVERY STANDARD, May 28, June 4, 1864; IDA HARPER, THE LIFE AND WORK OF SUSAN B. ANTHONY (3 vols., Indianapolis, 1898–1908), 1:238.

9. CONG. GLOBE, 38th Cong., 1st Sess. 2107–8, 3518 (1864).

10. 7 CWL 433.

11. LIBERATOR, June 24, 1864.

12. 8 CWL 149.

13. CHRISTOPHER DELL, LINCOLN AND THE WAR DEMOCRATS 290 (1975); Anson Herrick, of New York, in CONG. GLOBE, 38th Cong., 2d Sess. 524–28 (1865); Samuel S. Cox, *quoted in* JOEL H. SILBEY, A RESPECTABLE MINORITY: THE DEMOCRATIC PARTY IN THE CIVIL WAR ERA, 1860–1868 183 (1977).

14. JAMES G. RANDALL AND RICHARD N. CURRENT, LINCOLN THE PRESIDENT: LAST FULL MEASURE 307–13 (1955); LaWanda Cox AND JOHN H. COX, POLITICS, PRINCIPLE, AND PREJUDICE 1865–1866: DILEMMA OF RECONSTRUCTION AMERICA 1–30 (1963).

15. *George W. Julian's Journal*, 11 INDIANA MAGAZINE OF HISTORY 327 (1915); CONG. GLOBE, 38th Cong., 2d Sess. 531 (1865).

16. New Jersey ratified the amendment in 1866 after Republicans gained control of the legislature.

17. In June 1864, Lincoln had finally accepted Chase's third offer to resign from the cabinet. In October, Taney died, and two months later the president appointed Chase chief justice in part as a gesture of conciliation to the radical wing of his party.

18. COMMONWEALTH, Nov. 19, 1864; Wendell Phillips to E. C. Stanton, Nov. 20, 1864, Stanton Papers, Library of Congress. *See also* LIBERATOR, Nov. 18, 1864; and a speech by Phillips published in the PHILADELPHIA PRESS, Dec. 19, 1864.

3. The Civil War, Emancipation, and the Thirteenth Amendment

UNDERSTANDING WHO FREED THE SLAVES

Paul Finkelman

In December 1865 all slavery came to an end in the United States with the ratification of the Thirteenth Amendment. That amendment was not the beginning of emancipation, but rather the last piece of a process that began more than four years earlier. To understand the meaning of the Thirteenth Amendment—to even understand why the Constitution has the Thirteenth Amendment—we must first look at the process of emancipation that began during the Civil War. This phase of emancipation—what might be called military, congressional, and presidential emancipation—led to the piecemeal liberation of millions of slaves. The central figure in this process was Abraham Lincoln, but he is not the only important actor. Politicians in the cabinet, members of Congress, military officers, and the slaves themselves all had a part in the process that led to the Thirteenth Amendment.

THE CONSTITUTIONAL PROTECTIONS
OF SLAVERY: 1861

When he took the oath of office Abraham Lincoln faced a crisis unlike any president before him. Seven Deep South states had seceded from the national union and now claimed to be part of a new nation, the Confederate States of America.

Lincoln believed he had a constitutional and moral obligation to resist this destruction of the United States. He implored the South to step away from the precipice of civil war and national disaster. He reminded Southerners that they had taken "no oath in Heaven to destroy the government," while Lincoln had just taken "the most solemn one to 'preserve, protect, and defend'" the nation.[1]

The Confederate states had seceded because they believed Lincoln threatened their most important form of property, human beings held as slaves. Lincoln flatly denied this, declaring, "I have no purpose, directly or indirectly to interfere with the institution of slavery in the States where it exists." Trying to reassure the South, he pointed out that he also had "no lawful right" and no "inclination" to interfere with slavery in the Southern states. He wanted all Americans, Northerners and Southerners alike, to understand that "the property, peace and security of no section [of the nation] are to be in anywise endangered by the now incoming Administration."[2]

Four years after he denied that he had any "lawful right" or any "inclination" to end slavery, Lincoln gave his second inaugural address. During those four years *everything* about American slavery had changed. On January 1, 1863, Lincoln had issued the Emancipation Proclamation, declaring that most slaves owned by rebellious masters were forever free. In December 1864 Lincoln urged Congress to pass the Thirteenth Amendment to end all slavery in the United States. He noted that before the November elections the amendment had passed the Senate but failed to get the requisite two-thirds majority in the House. In the wake of his overwhelming reelection and the election of a stronger Republican majority in Congress, he urged the lame-duck House of Representatives to reconsider the issue. He pointedly noted that "almost certainly" the "next Congress will pass the measure" and it was only a matter of time before the amendment would be sent to the states. Thus he urged the current Congress to pass the amendment, rhetorically asking those members who had voted no earlier in the year, "May we not agree that the sooner better?"[3] A few weeks later the House reconsidered the amendment and passed it, sending it to the states for ratification on January 31, 1865. The next day Lincoln's home state, Illinois, became the first to ratify the Thirteenth Amendment. The text of this amendment was straightforward and simple: "Neither slavery nor involuntary servitude, except as a punishment for crime whereof the party shall have been duly convicted, shall exist within the United States, or any place subject to their jurisdiction."[4] Although Lincoln would not live to see it ratified, by the end of 1865 the Thirteenth Amendment was part of the Constitution and slavery was officially ended in the United States.

In his second inaugural address, looking back over four years of ferocious warfare, Lincoln focused on the cause of this bloodshed. He noted that on the

eve of the war "one eighth of the whole population were colored slaves, not dis-
tributed over the Union, but localized in the Southern part. These slaves constituted a peculiar and powerful interest. All knew that this interest was, somehow,
the cause of the war."[5]

The president also knew that the horror of the Civil War was rooted in the
fundamental immorality of slavery. "If God will that" the war "continue, until
all the wealth piled by the bond-man's two hundred and fifty years of unre-
quited toil shall be sunk and until every drop of blood drawn with the lash, shall
be paid by another drawn with the sword, as was said three thousand years ago,
so still it must be said, 'the judgments of the Lord, are true and righteous
altogether.' "[6]

What had happened in those four years to so change President Lincoln, the
war aims of the United States, and the nature of the American nation? In 1861
Lincoln had called for volunteers to fight to preserve the Union. By 1865 the
U.S. Army had become an avenging angel of liberty, bringing freedom to millions of slaves. In 1861 reunion had been tied to *not* interfering with slavery where
it existed; by 1865 reunion was inextricably tied to emancipation and the ratification of the Thirteenth Amendment. Indeed, as early as 1863 it was impossible
to conceive of reunion without emancipation.

What, indeed, had caused this change? Certainly the reasons for this shift
are complex. Five elements help explain how the war for union became a war
for liberty:

1. Lincoln's deep personal hatred of slavery
2. The clever—indeed brilliant—response to fugitive slaves by some U.S. Army
   generals
3. Actions by Congress in passing laws, resolutions, and sending the Thirteenth
   Amendment to the states
4. The actions of free blacks and slaves in both the Confederacy and the
   United States
5. Military success

An analysis of these elements provides an answer to the question, Who freed
the slaves? and helps us understand both why the Thirteenth Amendment
became part of the Constitution and what that amendment was designed to
accomplish.

It would be foolish to claim that any single one of these factors was, by itself,
decisive in changing the nature of the war and ending slavery. None of these
elements, standing alone, could have led to emancipation and freedom. And
without some or all of them working together slavery might not have come to an
end so quickly and so completely.

To illustrate this point, imagine how the issue of emancipation would have played out if Andrew Johnson, rather than Lincoln, had become president before the war ended. Johnson was a determined unionist and the only senator from a Confederate state who remained loyal to the United States. But Johnson was also a slave owner and a virulent racist. It is not hard to imagine Johnson's bringing the war to a conclusion without ending slavery and without upholding the Emancipation Proclamation that Lincoln had issued. Johnson might not have been able to reenslave those slaves who had become free during the war, but he may very well have negotiated peace by compromising on emancipation and allowing those still in bondage to remain there. We can imagine Johnson's obtaining peace and reunion with the South by renouncing the Emancipation Proclamation and promising federal support for slavery.

Similarly, it is not hard to imagine Lincoln's being pushed *away* from emancipation if that had been the will of his party. If Republicans had opposed emancipation Lincoln would have had much less incentive to issue the Emancipation Proclamation. And, even though Lincoln clearly hated slavery, without political support from his own party, Congress, and the vast majority of Northern whites, moving against slavery would have been difficult or impossible.

Throughout the war slaves ran away from their masters, seeking refuge behind U.S. Army lines. For the most part these slaves were protected by the army and often employed by the War Department, first as noncombatants and later as soldiers. But what would have happened if the army had returned fugitive slaves to their masters? The administration claimed the South had never legally left the Union. The administration could have taken the position that it should vigorously enforce the Fugitive Slave Law of 1850 in order to demonstrate to Southerners that their slave property would be safe if they laid down their arms and returned to the Union. If this had happened the slaves would quickly have learned they could not free themselves and they would have ceased trying to do so.

Alternatively, would emancipation have been possible if the slaves had not furthered their own cause? In hindsight it is hard to imagine the failure of slaves to assert their own freedom during the war, or their refusal to help U.S. soldiers as they marched through the South. But what if the vast majority of the slaves had been too fearful of retaliation by their masters to escape to freedom? What if the possibility of separation from family and friends had prevented most slaves from aiding their own liberation? What if male African Americans had generally refused to take up arms against their former masters and refused to serve in the U.S. Army, either out of fear of warfare or because they mistrusted these strangers in blue uniforms with their unfamiliar accents of Boston, New York, or Cleveland?

Finally, what would have happened to emancipation if the army had failed to win the war? Surely some slaves would have made it to the North and been free. But the majority of slaves were still in the South, behind Confederate lines when the war ended. What if peace had occurred before victory? Would the Emancipation Proclamation have had any value? Would self-liberation have been possible?

To understand how slavery ended—who freed the slaves—we must examine these factors as part of a complex set of issues interacting to create the conditions that led to emancipation during the war and the adoption of the Thirteenth Amendment after the war.

LINCOLN'S HATRED OF SLAVERY

Lincoln's personal views on slavery were clear: he hated slavery and had always believed that "if slavery is not wrong, nothing is wrong."[7] His political career illustrated this.

In 1837 the twenty-eight-year-old Lincoln was one of six members of the General Assembly of Illinois to vote against a proslavery resolution, supported by eighty-three members of that body. The resolution declared that the right to own slaves was "sacred to the slaveholding States." Not only did Lincoln vote against this resolution but he also joined one other representative in framing his own resolution, asserting that slavery was "founded on both injustice and bad policy."[8] A decade later, in his single term in Congress, Lincoln proposed a bill for the gradual abolition of slavery in the District of Columbia. Such an emancipation scheme would have avoided the Fifth Amendment problem of taking property without due process or just compensation, because gradual emancipation did not free any existing slaves but only guaranteed the freedom of as-yet-unborn children of slaves. Lincoln read the proposed emancipation bill on the floor of Congress but in the end did not introduce it. A powerless freshman congressman, he explained, "I was abandoned by my former backers."[9] When running against Stephen Douglas for the Senate in 1858 he constantly reiterated his view that slavery was morally wrong. His campaign began with the argument that the nation should put slavery "where the public mind shall rest in the belief that it is in the course of ultimate extinction."[10]

As president, Lincoln reiterated his hatred for slavery. In the summer of 1862 he had already drafted the Emancipation Proclamation and was patiently waiting for the right moment to issue it. But he could not reveal his plans. Nevertheless, he reminded the nation of his "oft-expressed *personal* wish that all men every where could be free."[11] He later declared in an often quoted letter that slavery was simply "wrong," that he was "naturally antislavery," and could "not remember when" he "did not so think, and feel."[12]

The important point here is that Lincoln was the first president since John Quincy Adams who believed that slavery was morally wrong and must be abolished. He was hemmed in by constitutional limitations, political considerations, and, early in the war, by the military weakness of the United States. He persistently argued that he could not move against slavery until he had the military power to enforce an emancipation proclamation. Thus, he told a group of ministers: "What *good* would a proclamation of emancipation from me do, especially as we are now situated? I do not want to issue a document that the whole world will see must necessarily be inoperative, like the Pope's bull against the comet! Would *my word* free the slaves, when I cannot even enforce the Constitution in the rebel States?"[13] The implications of his statement were clear: when he had the power and the opportunity to end slavery he would do so. In fact, nine days later, in the wake of the U.S. victory at Antietam, Lincoln issued the preliminary Emancipation Proclamation.

CLEVER MILITARY COMMANDERS AND THE CAUSE OF EMANCIPATION

The war had hardly begun when slaves began to stream into the camps and forts of the U.S. Army. The army was not a social welfare agency and was unprepared to feed, clothe, or house masses of propertyless refugees. Initially the army returned slaves to masters who came after them. This situation undermined the morale of U.S. troops, who fully understood that they were returning valuable property to their enemies, and, more important, those enemies would use that property to make war on them. Slaves grew the food that fed the Confederate army, raised and cared for the horses the Confederates rode into battle, and labored in the workshops and factories that produced the metals and weapons necessary to fight the war.[14] As Frederick Douglass noted, "The very stomach of this Rebellion is the negro in the form of a slave."[15] Returning slaves to Confederate masters was hardly different from returning guns or horses to them. However, at the beginning of the war some army officers did just that because the army had no firm policy on runaway slaves. Thus, early on some slaves who tried to free themselves were returned to their masters. A new policy began to emerge at the end of May 1861 and would be more or less complete by the end of the summer. By the following spring Congress had codified this policy.

On May 23 three slaves owned by Confederate colonel Charles K. Mallory escaped to Fortress Monroe, under the command of General Benjamin F. Butler. A day later Butler faced the surrealistic spectacle of Confederate major M. B. Carey, under a flag of truce, demanding the return of the slaves. Major Carey, identifying himself as Colonel Mallory's agent, argued that Butler had an obligation to return the slaves under the Constitution and the Fugitive Slave Law of 1850. Butler, a successful Massachusetts lawyer before the war, had devoted some thought to the issue. He told Carey that the slaves were contrabands of war because they had been used to build fortifications for the Confederacy, and thus Butler would not return them to Mallory.[16] Butler told Carey "that the fugitive slave act did not affect a foreign country, which Virginia claimed to be and she must reckon it one of the infelicities of her position that in so far at least she was taken at her word." Butler then offered to return the slaves if Colonel Mallory would come to Fortress Monroe and "take the oath of allegiance to the Constitution of the United States."[17] Not surprisingly, Colonel Mallory did not accept General Butler's offer.

This ended Colonel Mallory's attempt to recover his slaves, but it was the beginning of a new policy for the United States. Butler, in need of workers, immediately employed the three fugitives, who had previously been used by Mallory to build Confederate defenses. Taking these slaves away from Confederates served the dual purposes of depriving the enemy of labor while providing labor for the United States.

By the middle of the summer significant numbers of slaves were pouring into army forts and camps, where U.S. troops had conflicting orders. Some officers returned slaves to all masters; others returned them only to loyal masters in Maryland, Kentucky, and Missouri; some offered sanctuary to all slaves who crossed their lines.

Clarity of a sort came from Secretary of War Simon Cameron on August 8, when he informed Butler of the president's desire "that all existing rights in all the States be fully respected and maintained" and that the war was "for the Union and for the preservation of all constitutional rights of States and the citizens of the States in the Union." Because of this, "no question can arise as to fugitives from service within the States and Territories in which the authority of the Union is fully acknowledged." This meant that military commanders could not free fugitive slaves in Missouri, Kentucky, Maryland, and Delaware. But the president also understood that "in States wholly or partially under insurrectionary control" the laws could not be enforced and it was "equally obvious that rights dependent on the laws of the States within which military operations are conducted must be necessarily subordinated to the military exigencies created by the insurrection if not wholly forfeited by the treasonable conduct of the parties claiming them." Most important, "rights to services" could "form no exception" to "this general rule."[18]

Thus, through General Butler's ingenious solution to the problem of runaways the military in effect adopted the contraband concept for slaves who escaped from the Confederacy. As these slaves took the first step to free themselves the army protected their new freedom. On the other hand, slaves living in the United States could not yet free themselves by escaping to army camps. Nor could slaves who lived far from army encampments take advantage of the contraband policy.

CONGRESS AND EMANCIPATION

From the beginning of the war Lincoln knew that he had to work with Congress to succeed in preserving the Union. He also knew that if he were ever to attack slavery, he had to have congressional support. At the beginning of the war Congress, like the president, understood that turning the war into a crusade against slavery would have alienated many Northern conservatives and probably forced the loyal slave states into the Confederacy. At the same time, many Republicans in Congress were strongly abolitionist and many more represented communities that truly hated slavery. These individual representatives from antislavery districts had to satisfy their constituents who were clamoring for an end to slavery. Congress also served as a barometer for Lincoln. The more Congress pushed against slavery, the easier it would be for Lincoln to move against bondage. Moreover, if a majority of Congress took actions against slavery, Lincoln could be pretty sure that Northern public opinion had moved in that direction as well. In an age before political polling, Lincoln had to rely on the instincts of those closest to the electorate—the members of Congress—to gauge how fast he could safely move against slavery.

On August 6, 1861, Congress passed the First Confiscation Act, which allowed for the seizure of any slaves used by the Confederacy for military purposes.[19] This law was narrowly crafted to allow for emancipation of only those slaves actually being used by the Confederates for military purposes. It did not jeopardize border state slave owners, even if they were sympathetic to the Confederacy. Freeing slaves under the Confiscation Act might have violated the Fifth Amendment if seen as the taking of private property without due process. This might not have been the case, however, if viewed as a military measure. Surely the army could seize a weapon in the hands of a captured Confederate soldier without a due process hearing, or take a horse from a captured Confederate. Similarly, slaves working on fortifications or being used in other military capacities might be taken. However, in 1861, or even 1865, no one could be certain how the courts would rule on this and subsequent emancipatory acts. The Thirteenth Amendment would make these issues moot.

Ambiguous and cumbersome, the First Confiscation Act did not threaten slavery as an institution. It merely allowed for the seizure of the relatively small number of slaves being used specifically for military purposes. However, the Confiscation Act did indicate a significant political shift toward emancipation.

Neither Congress nor the American people were ready to turn the military conflict into an all-out war against slavery; however, Congress—which presumably reflected its constituents—was ready to allow the government to free some slaves in the struggle to suppress the rebellion.

This law, along with the contraband policy, can be seen as a major step toward eventual public support for emancipation. In the Confiscation Act, Congress embraced the principle that the national government had the power to free slaves as a military necessity. The logical extension of this posture could be the total destruction of slavery. If Congress could free some slaves through the Confiscation Act, or the executive branch could free some slaves through the contraband policy, then the two branches might be able to free all slaves if the military, political, and social conditions warranted such a result.

By early 1862 Congress reflected growing Northern hostility to slavery and the sense in the North that the war had to lead to emancipation. In March 1862 Congress prohibited the military from returning fugitive slaves, whether from enemy masters, loyal masters in the Confederacy, or masters in the border states. Any officers returning fugitive slaves could be court-martialed and, if convicted, dismissed from military service.[20] Here is an example of how Congress, the president, the army, and the slaves themselves worked to end slavery, as least for those slaves who sought to free themselves.

On April 10, 1862, Congress passed a joint resolution declaring the United States would "cooperate with," and provide "pecuniary aid" for, any state willing to adopt a gradual emancipation scheme.[21] For the first time in the history of the nation, Congress was advocating measures that would end slavery. The loyal slave states refused to accept this offer, but the message of the offer was clear to Lincoln: a majority in both houses of Congress was ready to begin to dismantle slavery, and presumably these savvy politicians understood that their constituents would support these moves.

The most important step in this process came later that month, when Congress passed a law abolishing slavery in the District of Columbia and providing compensation for the masters. This law was consistent with Lincoln's longstanding belief that, under the Constitution, the U.S. government had plenary power over the District. The president happily signed this law, which ended slavery in the District more quickly than would have happened under the bill he had wanted to introduce in Congress fifteen years earlier.[22] By providing compensation to the masters, this law was likely to survive a challenge on Fifth Amendment grounds. However, given the Taney Court's decision in *Dred Scott* (1857), it is not inconceivable that the Court might have struck down this law on due process grounds, because it was not a traditional "taking," or because it was not taking private property "for public use," as required by the Fifth Amendment. This law unambiguously answers the question, Who freed the slaves? for those slaves living in the nation's capital. Congress, along with the president, who signed the law, freed the slaves in the District of Columbia.[23] However, the Thirteenth Amendment would still be necessary to absolutely preserve this outcome.

The political message of this law was dramatic. Congress, in an election year, was prepared to begin to dismantle slavery. Members of the House, who were to stand for reelection in the fall, were willing to run on a record that included voting to free some of the slaves. In June Congress abolished slavery in the federal territories, this time without compensation.[24] Once again we have an answer, for the federal territories, to the question of who freed the slaves.

Further evidence of congressional support (and de facto popular support) for emancipation came with the Second Confiscation Act, which Lincoln signed on July 17, 1862.[25] This law was more expansive than the First Confiscation Act. It provided a death penalty as well as lesser penalties—including confiscation of slaves—for treason and also allowed for the prosecution of "any person" participating in the rebellion or who gave "aid and comfort" to it. The law also provided for the seizure and condemnation of the property of "any person within any State or Territory of the United States . . . being engaged in armed rebellion against the government of the United States, or aiding or abetting such rebellion."[26] This would include Confederate sympathizers in the border states as well as in the Confederacy. Two separate provisions dealt, in a comprehensive way, with runaway slaves and contrabands.

Section 9 of the law provided that any slave owned by someone "engaged in rebellion against the government" who escaped to U.S. Army lines or was captured by the army would be "forever free of their servitude, and not again held as slaves." Section 10 prohibited the military from returning any fugitive slaves to any masters, even those in the border states, unless the owner claiming the slave would "first make oath" that he or she had "not borne arms against the United States in the present rebellion, nor in any way given aid and comfort thereto."[27]

The second Confiscation Act was one more step toward creating public opinion that would allow emancipation. It also helped clarify the legal and constitutional issues by once again affirming that, under the war powers, Congress or the president might emancipate slaves. The act did not, however, do much to actually free slaves. The law provided numerous punishments for rebels, but their slaves would become free only after a judicial hearing. Had there been no Emancipation Proclamation or Thirteenth Amendment the act might have eventually been used to litigate freedom, but it would have been a long and tedious process. The only certain freedom created by the act came in sections 9 and 10, which secured liberty to fugitive slaves escaping rebel masters. But this was not really much of a change from existing policy. While not freeing any slaves directly, the act was another clear signal to Lincoln that he could now move against slavery. Five days after he signed the Second Confiscation Act, Lincoln presented his first draft of the Emancipation Proclamation to his cabinet. Congress had now done its part to free the slaves, and Lincoln was soon able to move against slavery.

The final congressional action against slavery would take place in 1864 and early 1865, as Congress drafted, passed, and sent on to the states the Thirteenth Amendment. On April 8, 1864, the Senate overwhelmingly passed the amendment by a vote of thirty-eight to six, eight more votes than were needed to reach the necessary two-thirds majority. On June 15, the majority of the House voted in favor of the amendment, but the votes fell short of the constitutionally mandated two-thirds majority. In the November elections Lincoln won a resounding victory while his party substantially increased its majority in the House. On December 6, Lincoln urged the lame-duck Congress to reconsider the amendment, pointing out that the next Congress would surely pass it. On January 6, 1865, the House began to debate the amendment again. Opposition from Democrats remained strong, but ultimately a significant number accepted the reality of their situation, and on January 31 it passed the house by a vote of one hundred nineteen to fifty-six, with eight abstentions. The next day Illinois ratified the amendment, and by December it was part of the Constitution. At one level, this story is the complete answer to the question of who freed the slaves. It was Congress and the states that ratified the Thirteenth Amendment.

BLACK SELF-LIBERATION

While Congress and the president pondered emancipation, numerous slaves acted on their own to liberate themselves. As we have seen, the army, led by General Benjamin Butler, adopted a policy to deal with these slaves, and Congress and the president joined in. Everyone in the North and the South understood that slavery was the cause of the rebellion. As Alexander Stephens, the vice president of the Confederacy, declared, slavery was the "cornerstone" of the new Southern nation.[28]

From the beginning of the war African Americans in the North also understood this. They realized, far more than most white Northerners did, that the destruction of slavery could come only if the Confederacy itself were defeated; they also understood that Confederate defeat required that its cornerstone— slavery—be torn down. Southern blacks, who were overwhelmingly slaves, did not need to carefully analyze the relationship between slavery and the war. They simply understood that the war provided opportunities for freedom. They also quickly came to understand that the enemies of their masters were their friends.

Thus, in both the North and the South blacks responded to the war with vigor and enthusiasm. Shortly after the war began Frederick Douglass argued that "the very stomach of this Rebellion is the negro in the form of a slave." Douglass wisely observed, "Arrest that hoe in the hands of the Negro, and you smite the rebellion in the very seat of its life."[29]

When the war began Northern blacks immediately tried to enlist in the army. Initially most discovered that their services were not wanted. The war began as a "white man's war." However, racial prejudice was not universal, and a few blacks served early on. Nicholas Biddle, for example, a black from Pottsville, Pennsylvania, marched with Northern troops to protect the nation's capital. A proslavery, pro-Confederate mob in Baltimore attacked these troops with bricks, rocks, and anything else they could throw. Biddle was a special target for this mob because of his race. He arrived in Washington bloody and bruised but still in uniform and still serving his country.[30]

In late 1861 John Boston ran away from his Maryland master. By January 1862 he reported he was "in Safety in the 14th Regiment of Brooklyn." His trip was difficult. "I had a little trouble in getting away," he wrote, "but as the lord led the Children of Israel to the land of Cannan [sic] So he led me to a land where freedom will rain [sic]."[31] The African American William Henry Johnson arrived in Washington, D.C., with the Second Connecticut Volunteers. Johnson later fought at Bull Run and in North Carolina. In North Carolina army camps became havens for runaway slaves. In March 1862 near Roanoke Island, Johnson witnessed rebel masters appealing to General Ambrose Burnside to return their fugitive slaves. Johnson proudly reported his commander's response: "Sir, you misunderstand my mission—I am not here to bag slaves for their owners. No, sir! I am here to teach rebels their duty to their Government, and, with the help of God, I will do it!" With charming irony, Johnson noted that the disgruntled Southern slave owner then *"seceded"* from General Burnside.[32]

By this time General Burnside had the support of Congress on this issue. As already noted, in March 1862 Congress passed legislation forbidding the military from returning escaped slaves to their masters. By February 1863 hundreds of slaves in southeast Missouri were running away to the U.S. Army. Although some were returned to loyal masters, most gained their freedom when they reached the army.[33] By early 1863 more than 10,000 slaves had flocked to Fortress Monroe, in Virginia. Confederates circulated rumors and disinformation to discourage such escapes. One group of slaves asked U.S. officers if it was true that the army planned to "put black men in irons and send them off to Cuba." But these Confederate attempts to confuse slaves and discourage them from running to the U.S. Army failed. More significant was the knowledge of the Emancipation Proclamation, which went into effect on January 1, 1863. Slaves living at Fortress Monroe came from as far away as North Carolina, with some traveling more than 200 miles on foot. Arriving at the fort they told officers that they had heard about the Emancipation Proclamation, and it motivated them to travel hundreds of miles to come under the protection of American troops. Some of the slaves reaching U.S. lines had plans to return home, to bring back family members. One former slave told a U.S. Army captain that he planned to work at the fortress until he had saved some money; then he would return to his master's plantation to rescue his wife from bondage.[34]

The evidence is clear that tens of thousands of slaves ran to the army for protection and to join the fighting. After the Emancipation Proclamation was issued, slaves often left their master's houses when the U.S. Army approached. By the end of the war some 200,000 blacks, most of whom had been slaves in 1861, had served in the U.S. Army and Navy. Many tens of thousands of other slaves left their masters to become civilian employees of the army, working as teamsters, cooks, burial crews, and in other noncombatant jobs. Many others simply followed the army, ran to forts and camps, and in some other way freed themselves from bondage. These slaves answered the question, Who freed the slaves? by voting with their feet. Once regulations, laws, and the Emancipation Proclamation were in place to protect their liberty, these slaves freed themselves. Ultimately, of course, the Thirteenth Amendment would preserve and secure this freedom from legal attack.

While huge numbers of slaves ran to the army and freedom, millions of other black slaves did not leave their homes. They were unable or unwilling to risk running away. Most Southern blacks never left their homes during the war. They did not free themselves. In the end, they would be freed by military success and the Thirteenth Amendment.

MILITARY SUCCESS AND EMANCIPATION

Ultimately, the army freed the slaves by winning the war. Had the United States lost the Civil War, the Emancipation Proclamation would have been a mean-ingless piece of paper, "like the Pope's bull against the comet,"[35] and the Thir-teenth Amendment would have freed only those slaves *inside* what was left of the United States. The tens of thousands of slaves who had freed themselves by running to the lines of the U.S. Army would have been free, but the millions left behind would have remained slaves. The army of course could not have emancipated the slaves without the authority from the president and the Con-gress to do so. The army worked in tandem with Lincoln, carrying his Emanci-pation Proclamation into the South. Similarly, the army worked in tandem with the slaves, who ran to the army to gain their freedom. Initially this process was led by General Butler with his imaginative contraband theory of the law of war.

But the contraband theory, however clever and innovative, would have been useless if Butler and the rest of the army had not carried the war into the South, where emancipation could take place.

From the beginning of the war Lincoln understood that emancipation would not be possible without military success. Many modern scholars argue that Lincoln issued the Emancipation Proclamation in a desperate effort to win the war. In the words of one his harshest critics, Lincoln was "forced into glory" by dwindling military resources and persistent American defeats at the hands of the Confederacy. Critics of Lincoln argue that he eventually moved toward emancipation for military and diplomatic reasons: because he needed black troops to repopulate his army and to prevent Britain and France from giving diplomatic recognition to the Confederacy.[36]

The chronology of emancipation does not support this analysis. Both Lincoln and Congress began to move toward emancipation only after a series of U.S. military successes in early 1862. Lincoln then waited to announce emancipation until after a major battle that stopped Lee's army dead in its tracks—with huge Confederate losses that could never be replaced—at Antietam. Early emancipation would probably have thrown Kentucky and Missouri into the Confederacy, and Lincoln believed this would have doomed the Union cause. While emancipation may properly be seen as one of the elements of victory, it must also be seen as an outcome of the likelihood of ultimate victory. Victory would probably have been possible without emancipation or even black troops. Moreover, wholesale emancipation was not necessary to enlist free blacks in the North and later in the South. Although victory might have been more difficult and perhaps taken longer without emancipation, it would probably have come. The 150,000 or so former slaves who served in the U.S. Army made a difference in how fast the army could occupy the South, but they did not provide a critical margin of victory. Moreover, without emancipation, it is entirely likely that the Confederacy would have accepted defeat earlier than it did, or that individual states might have voluntarily returned to the Union had the slave owners in those states not been faced with the prospect of emancipation. Indeed, it is possible that emancipation prolonged the war.

But, while victory was possible without emancipation, emancipation was clearly impossible without victory. Conditions looked bright after Antietam, when the preliminary proclamation was announced, and Lincoln assumed they would look just as bright in a hundred days, when he planned to sign the proclamation, on January 1, 1863. Thus, rather than being forced into glory when he announced emancipation, Lincoln understood that moral glory—emancipation—was possible only through military glory.

Lincoln also understood that military success was predicated on first securing the loyal slave states. Thus, Lincoln overruled Major General John C. Frémont when the former Republican candidate for president issued an order freeing the slaves in Missouri. On August 30, 1861, Frémont, acting without any authority from the president, declared martial law in Missouri and announced that all slaves owned by Confederate activists in that state were free.[37] Missouri was not part of the Confederacy, and such an order violated the Constitution and, more important, threatened the Union by alienating the four loyal slave states. Lincoln immediately and unambiguously urged Frémont to withdraw his proclamation: "I think there is great danger [that] . . . liberating slaves of traitorous owners, will alarm our Southern Union friends, and turn them against us— perhaps ruin our rather fair prospect for Kentucky." Thus he asked the general to "modify" his proclamation "on his own motion," to conform with the First Confiscation Act, which Lincoln had just signed. Aware of the exaggerated egos of his generals, Lincoln noted, "This letter is written in a spirit of caution and not of censure."[38]

While Lincoln waited for Frémont to act, border-state unionists begged Lincoln to countermand Frémont's order. One Kentucky unionist told Lincoln, "There is not a day to lose in disavowing emancipation or Kentucky is gone over the mill dam."[39] Lincoln understood the issue. He told Senator Orville Browning that "to lose Kentucky is nearly . . . to lose the whole game."[40] Lincoln hoped that Frémont would be politically savvy enough to withdraw the order. Frémont, hoping to set himself up to be the Republican candidate in 1864, refused to comply with Lincoln's request. Instead, Frémont asked Lincoln to formally countermand the proclamation. This would allow Frémont to later blame the president for undermining emancipation. Lincoln "cheerfully" did so, ordering Frémont to modify the proclamation. Still playing politics, Frémont claimed he never received the order but only read about it in the newspapers, and even after Lincoln issued it, Frémont continued to distribute his original order.[41] Frémont's stubbornness, lack of political sense, and military incompetence led to his dismissal by Lincoln on November 2, 1861.[42] He would get another command, fail there, and by the end of the war, Frémont would be marginalized and irrelevant.

Lincoln's response to Frémont has been condemned by many scholars as illustrating his insensitivity to black freedom. Such scholars argue that here was a perfect moment to strike a blow against slavery. Frémont was a national hero and a popular general. By supporting his abolitionist general, critics argue, Lincoln could have turned the war into a crusade against slavery. However, unlike Frémont, Lincoln understood that an unwinnable war would not end slavery. Rather, it would only destroy the Union and permanently secure slavery in the new Confederate nation. His comments to Frémont bear out his realistic assessment that if Kentucky, and perhaps Missouri, joined the Confederacy, the war might be lost. Frémont's proclamation jeopardized the war effort, and that led

Lincoln to overturn it. The fall of 1861 was simply not the time to begin an attack on slavery, especially in the loyal border states.

Lincoln was attacked by some in the abolitionist wing of the Republican Party for his response to the Missouri proclamation. Privately he assured Senator Charles Sumner that the difference between them on emancipation was only a matter of time—a month or six weeks. Sumner accepted this statement and promised to "not say another word to you about it till the longest time you name has passed by."[43] The time would in fact be nearly a year, but there is little reason to doubt that Lincoln was moving toward some sort of abolition plan.

For Lincoln there were three paramount issues to consider: the timing of emancipation, the need to secure the loyal slave states, and the likelihood of military victory. He could attack slavery only if he could win the war; if he attacked slavery and did not win the war, then he accomplished nothing. Critics of Lincoln argue that he eventually moved toward emancipation because he needed black troops to win the war. But the more plausible reading—starting with his correspondence with Frémont—is that he could move against slavery only after he had secured the border states and made certain that victory was possible. Only then could he make emancipation work. Rather than a desperate act to save the war effort, emancipation must be seen as the logical fruit of victory. Frémont's proclamation threatened victory *and* emancipation; consequently, Lincoln countermanded it.

Lincoln clearly underestimated the time needed before he could move against slavery. The preconditions he needed for emancipation—support from Congress and a reasonable expectation of military victory—did not emerge in the time he forecast to Sumner. A call for emancipation had to be tied to a realistic belief that the war could be won; there was no point in telling slaves they were free if the government could not enforce that freedom. The prospect of a military victory was not great in the fall of 1861. The embarrassing defeats at Bull Run and Ball's Bluff did not bode well for the immediate future.[44]

The first half of the next year, however, would be "one of the brightest periods of the war for the North."[45] This bright period actually began before the New Year. In November 1861 Admiral Samuel du Pont seized the South Carolina Sea Islands with the important naval base at Port Royal. Once established, the United States would never be dislodged from this beachhead on the South Carolina coast. At least some of the war would now be fought in the heartland of the rebellion.[46] Although Lincoln could not know it at the time, this was the beginning of the shrinking of the Confederacy. In February, Roanoke Island was captured, and by the end of April the navy and army had captured or sealed off every Confederate port on the Atlantic except Charleston, South Carolina, and Wilmington, North Carolina. Ports such as Savannah, Georgia, remained in Confederate hands, but the rebels no longer had access to the ocean except through blockade runners, which had virtually no affect on the Confederate war effort.

In the west, the United States won a series of crucial victories, securing Kentucky for the Union. Although the Kentucky legislature had voted in September to stay in the Union, support for the Confederacy remained strong in the Bluegrass state. The state's governor, Beriah Magoffin, had resigned to join the Confederacy. In November General George B. McClellan had told General Don Carlos Buell, "It is absolutely necessary that we shall hold all the State of Kentucky" and to make sure that "the majority of its inhabitants shall be warmly in favor of our cause." McClellan believed that the conduct of the "political affairs in Kentucky" was perhaps "more important than that of our military operations." To secure Kentucky he insisted that the U.S. Army respect the "domestic institution"—slavery—in the state.[47]

Underscoring McClellan's concern, later that month some 200 Kentuckians organized a secession convention and declared their state to be in the Confederacy. In December the rebel congress admitted Kentucky into the Confederacy. At times there were more than 25,000 Confederate troops in the Bluegrass state. As the new year opened, Kentucky was hardly secure. That changed in a ten-day period in early February 1862. On February 6, an obscure brigadier general, Ulysses S. Grant, captured Fort Henry on the Tennessee River in northern Tennessee. On the February 16 Grant captured Fort Donelson, on the Cumberland River, along with more than 12,000 Confederate troops. These twin victories established a U.S. presence in the Confederate state of Tennessee. More important, they emphatically secured Kentucky for the Union. By the end of the month the U.S. Army was sitting in Nashville, Tennessee, the first Southern state capital to fall. Instead of Kentucky possibly going into the Confederacy, it was more likely that Tennessee would be returned to the United States.

On the other side of the Mississippi, in early March Confederate forces suffered a devastating loss at Pea Ridge, in Arkansas. The Confederates had planned to march into Missouri and eventually capture St. Louis. But Pea Ridge ended any chance that Missouri would become a Confederate state. Instead, the outcome made it all the more likely that Arkansas would be brought back into the Union. A month later the United States won an important but bloody victory at Shiloh, in southwestern Tennessee. On the same day U.S. troops seized Island No. 10 in the Mississippi River, capturing more than fifty big guns and some 7,000 Confederate soldiers. In April Memphis fell to combined naval and army operations, and on May 1, General Benjamin Butler, who had developed the contraband policy while a commander in Virginia, marched into New Orleans.

This truncated history of the first months of 1862 illustrates how circumstances allowed Lincoln to begin to contemplate emancipation. By June he knew that the border South was unlikely to join the Confederacy. There would still be fighting in that region—especially horrible guerrilla warfare in Missouri—but by June 1862 it was clear that Kentucky, Maryland, Delaware, and Missouri were secure. So too was a good piece of Tennessee as well as the cities of New Orleans, Natchez, and smaller river towns in Mississippi, Louisiana, and Arkansas. Baton Rouge had become the second Confederate state capital to fall to the U.S. Army. There could be no more realistic fears that an emancipation policy would push Kentucky or Missouri into the Confederacy.

Lincoln now had a reasonable chance of implementing an emancipation policy for a substantial number of slaves. Even if the war ended with some part of the Confederacy intact, the president could break the back of slavery in the Mississippi Valley. Once free, these blacks could not be easily reenslaved.

By the spring of 1862 Lincoln had reason to believe that emancipation was possible because the army had secured the upper South. There was now a reasonable chance of military success and emancipation. He was also gaining support in Congress for ending slavery. By midsummer he had drafted the Emancipation Proclamation, and in September he announced it.

CONCLUSION

So, who freed the slaves? In the end, the question is wrongly phrased. The question should be: how did the slaves become free. The answer is by different methods and different agencies. Some freed themselves; some were liberated by the army; some gained freedom through an act of Congress. Many were freed by the Emancipation Proclamation and its implementation. Many, however, remained slaves until the war finally ended.

Some slaves were not freed until the ratification of the Thirteenth Amendment, which was announced to the nation on December 18, 1865. President Lincoln lobbied hard for the amendment in late 1864 and early 1865. In the end, even some Democrats in Congress were persuaded to support it. It was then sent to the states, which ratified it. That amendment resolved all doubts about the legality of the contraband policies, the Confiscation acts, and the Emancipation Proclamation.

Who freed the slaves? It was a group effort: the Congress, the army, the states, and the slaves themselves all had a hand in ending slavery. They were led by a president whose leadership and imagination transformed a struggle to preserve the Union into a constitutional and humanitarian revolution. When we contrast Lincoln with the Lilliputian chief executives who preceded and followed him, it becomes evident that leadership and vision matter in shaping public policy. Fortunately, the president who was intent on preserving the Union and the Constitution was equally intent on redeeming America's soul and providing "that all men everywhere could be free."[48] When the conditions were right, and the opportunity was there, the president led the nation toward "a new birth of freedom."[49]

NOTES

1. Abraham Lincoln, "First Inaugural Address—Final Text," in Roy P. Basler, ed., *Collected Works of Abraham Lincoln* (1955) (hereafter *CW*), 4:262, quoted at 271.

2. Ibid. at 263.

3. Abraham Lincoln, "Annual Message to Congress," *CW*, 8:149.

4. U.S. Constitution, Amendment XIII.

5. Abraham Lincoln, "Second Inaugural Address," *CW*, 8:332.

6. Ibid., 333.

7. Lincoln to Albert G. Hodges, April 4, 1864, *CW*, 7:281.

8. "Protest in the Illinois Legislature on Slavery," *CW*, 1:74–75.

9. Benjamin Quarles, *Lincoln and the Negro* (1962), 30.

10. " 'House Divided,' Speech at Springfield, Illinois," June 22, 1858, *CW*, 2:461.

11. Lincoln to Horace Greeley, August 22, 1862, *CW*, 5:388–89.

12. Lincoln to Albert G. Hodges, April 4, 1864, *CW*, 7:281.

13. "Reply to Emancipation Memorial Presented by Chicago Christians of All Denominations," September 13, 1862, *CW*, 5:419–25, quotations at 420.

14. Charles Dew, *Bond of Iron: Master and Slave at Buffalo Forge* (1994), 264–311.

15. Douglass, quoted in James M. McPherson, *Battle Cry of Freedom: The Civil War Era* (1988), 354.

16. Benjamin F. Butler, *Butler's Book* (1892), 256–57.

17. Maj. Gen. Benjamin F. Butler to Lt. Gen. Winfield Scott, May 24/25, 1861, in *The War of the Rebellion: The Official Records of the Union and Confederate Armies* (1880–1901), ser. 2, 1:752 (hereafter *O.R.*).

18. Simon Cameron to Maj. Gen. Benjamin F. Butler, Aug. 8, 1861, *O.R.*, 1:761–62.

19. "An Act to confiscate Property used for Insurrectionary Purposes," August 6, 1861, *United States Statutes at Large*, 12 (1863), 319.

20. "An Act to make an Additional Article of War," March 13, 1862, ibid., 354. This law modified an important part of the Fugitive Slave Law of 1850, which had authorized the use of the military or the militia to return fugitive slaves.

21. Joint Resolution No. 26, April 10, 1862, ibid., 617.

22. "An Act for the Release of Certain Persons Held to Service or Labor in the District of Columbia" (hereafter D.C. Emancipation Act), April 16, 1862, ibid., 376.

23. In addition to providing payment to masters for the slaves, the D.C. Emancipation Act also provided money for colonization of former slaves in Africa or Haiti.

Critics of Lincoln have often focused on this one provision as proof of Lincoln's racism and his insincerity with regard to both emancipation and black rights. However, a serious analysis of this provision, which such critics rarely offer, undermines the strength of such claims. The law provided up to $100,000 for the colonization of both free blacks already living in the District and the newly emancipated slaves. The operative language, however, is critical. The money was "to aid in the settlement and colonization of such free persons . . . as *may desire to emigrate* to the Republics of Hayti or Liberia, or such other country beyond the limits of the United States as the president may determine." This language, which Lincoln had demanded, did not require or force anyone to leave the United States, and it allowed the president to prevent voluntary emigration if he were to "determine" it was not suitable. The law also limited the amount to be appropriated for each emigrant to $100 (ibid., 378; emphasis added). As a practical matter, this provision was little more than a sop thrown to conservatives and racists, who feared a free black population. In 1860 the census had found over 14,000 blacks in the city, including about 3,200 slaves. The appropriation would have provided money for the colonization of only 1,000 blacks—less than a third of the newly freed slaves and less than 7 percent of the entire free black population of the city in 1860. Moreover, by 1862 the black population in the city was much larger than 14,000, which meant that even a smaller percentage of the population could leave under the appropriation. Furthermore, the $100 was hardly much of an incentive for any free black or former slave to move to a new country. Not surprisingly, no record exists of *any* African American taking advantage of this offer. This law may in fact be unique in American history: the only time that the Congress appropriated a substantial sum of money, to be given out to individuals, and none of the money was spent. Misunderstanding of the colonization bill is common. John Hope Franklin, for example, asserts that the law "provided for the removal and colonization of the freedmen" (*The Emancipation Proclamation* [1963], 17), when in fact it did not provide for "removal" but merely allowed voluntary colonization. This dovetailed with Lincoln's own consistent rejection of "compulsory deportation" and his view that black "emigration must be voluntary and without expense" (Eric Foner, "Lincoln and Colonization," in Eric Foner, ed., *Our Lincoln: New Perspectives on Lincoln and His World* [2008], 146, 157). Foner impressively argues that Lincoln's support for voluntary colonization, which continued as late as 1862, was not a function of his personal racism but rather a realistic assessment that white Americans would never accept black equality or emancipation without some type of colonization and that, for Lincoln and many whites at the time, "colonization represented a middle ground between the radicalism of the abolitionists and the prospect of the United States' existing permanently half slave and half free" (Foner, at 145).

24. "An Act to Secure Freedom to all Persons Within the Territories of the United States," June 19, 1862, *Statutes at Large*, 12:432.

25. "An Act to suppress Insurrection, to punish Treason and Rebellion, to seize and confiscate the Property of Rebels, and for other Purposes," July 17, 1862, ibid., 589.

26. Ibid.

27. Ibid. Like the D.C. Emancipation Act, this law allowed for the colonization of such blacks "as may be willing to emigrate" to other lands. This was a sop to conservatives who feared black freedom, but it would not have required anyone to leave the United States. Significantly, unlike the District of Columbia emancipation bill, the Confiscation Act allowed colonization but did not appropriate any money for it.

28. Charles Lee, *The Confederate Constitutions* (1963), 110.

29. Douglass, quoted in McPherson, *Battle Cry of Freedom*, 354.

30. Edwin S. Redkey, *A Grand Army of Black Men: Letters from African-American Soldiers in the Union Army, 1861–1865* (1992), 9–10.

31. Ira Berlin and Leslie S. Rowland, *Families and Freedom: A Documentary History of African-American Kinship in the Civil War Era* (1997), 23.

32. Redkey, *Grand Army of Black Men*, 18–19.

33. Berlin and Rowland, *Families and Freedom*, 29–30.

34. Ibid., 32.

35. "Reply to Emancipation Memorial Presented by Chicago Christians of All Denominations," *CW*, 5:419–25, quotations at 420.

36. For modern critical assessments of Lincoln and emancipation, see Lerone Bennett, Jr., *Forced into Glory: Abraham Lincoln's White Dream* (2000); LaWanda Cox, "Lincoln and Black Freedom," in Gabor S. Boritt and Norman O. Forness, eds., *The Historian's Lincoln: Pseudohistory, Psychohistory, and History* (1988); Ira Berlin. "Who Freed the Slaves? Emancipation and Its Meaning," in David W. Blight and Brooks D. Simpson, eds., *Union and Emancipation: Essays on Politics and Race in the Civil War Era* (1997); Julius Lester, *Look Out Whitey! Black Power's Gon' Get Your Mama!* (1968); Lerone Bennett, Jr., "Was Lincoln a White Supremacist?" *Ebony* 23 (1968): 35–42.

37. O.R., 3:466–67.

38. Lincoln to John C. Frémont, Sept. 2, 1861, CW, 4:506.

39. Quoted in William E. Gienapp, *Abraham Lincoln and Civil War America: A Biography* (2002), 89.

40. Lincoln to Orville H. Browning, Sept. 22, 1861, CW, 4:531–32.

41. Lincoln to John C. Frémont, Sept. 11, 1861, CW, 4:517–18.

42. General Order No. 28, Nov. 2, 1861, O.R., Additions and Corrections to Series 2, 3:558–59 (1902).

43. Stephen Oates, *With Malice Toward None: The Life of Abraham Lincoln* (1978), 292.

44. McPherson, *Battle Cry of Freedom*, 358–68.

45. Ibid., 368.

46. One of the important results of this was the liberation of thousands of slaves on the Sea Islands, many of whom would later be enlisted when the United States began

to organize black regiments in late 1862. See David Dudley Cornish, *The Sable Arm: Negro Troops in the Union Army, 1861–1865* (1966), and Willie Lee Rose, *Rehearsal for Reconstruction: The Port Royal Experiment* (1976).

47. [General] George B. McClellan to Brig. Gen. D. C. Buell, November 7, 1861, O.R., 1:776–77.

48. Lincoln to Horace Greeley, August 22, 1862, CW, 5:388–89.

49. Abraham Lincoln, "Final Text, Address Delivered at the Dedication of the Cemetery at Gettysburg" (Nov. 19, 1863), in CW, 7:23.

4. Citizenship and the Thirteenth Amendment

UNDERSTANDING THE DEAFENING SILENCE

Michael Vorenberg

Almost from the moment that the Fourteenth Amendment was ratified, in 1868, the Thirteenth Amendment, ratified three years earlier, was regarded as little more than a vestigial appendage to the Fourteenth, a sort of younger, if better-known, sibling. The Thirteenth Amendment has had its moments, to be sure, but they have been short-lived. In 1948, President Harry Truman signed an act declaring February 1 "National Freedom Day," in honor of that day in 1865 when Lincoln signed the Thirteenth Amendment before sending it to the states for ratification. Scholars will tell you that Lincoln did not have to sign the amendment, that he was not even authorized to do so. But no matter. The fact that he signed the measure is counted as little more than presidential trivia, and the holiday that celebrates the signature, not to mention the amendment, has been forgotten.

The amendment resurfaced in 1968, when the U.S. Supreme Court declared that a housing project discriminating against African Americans had violated the Thirteenth Amendment. A rush of legal scholarship on the amendment followed, as law professors vied to gain a new purchase on the mountain of civil rights law. A torrent of legal scholarship spilled onto law review pages, and civil rights activists and scholars looked to the Court. What would it say next on the rediscovered Thirteenth Amendment? Almost nothing, it turned out. But a good number of legal scholars refused to pack it in, insisting that there was more good law to be made from the amendment. Running through all this scholarship has been an effort to make the proper connection between the Thirteenth and Fourteenth amendments. To be more precise, the $64,000 question is this: are the key words and concepts of the Fourteenth Amendment—"citizen," "privileges and immunities," "equal rights," "due process," and, perhaps most important, "no state shall"—embedded in the Thirteenth Amendment, which does not explicitly mention any of those terms?[1]

To answer this question, scholars have pored over archival records, newspapers, and, especially, the debates on the Thirteenth Amendment in the *Congressional Globe*. At the heart of the endeavor has been an assumption that the Fourteenth Amendment might be illuminated by light from the Thirteenth. Indeed, "The Fourteenth Amendment in Light of the Thirteenth" was the title of a chapter of a 1982 constitutional history authored by two of the leading scholars of the era, Harold H. Hyman and William M. Wiecek.[2] The verdict on the Fourteenth Amendment based on new evidence from the Thirteenth has been divided. On one side are those who believe that the broad notions of freedom conveyed by the Thirteenth Amendment, a measure containing a simple but powerful declaration of an end to slavery while remaining unencumbered by a "state action" clause, strengthen the potential of the Fourteenth Amendment to protect a broad range of individual rights against public *or* private abuse. One of the earliest scholars to take this approach was Jacobus tenBroek, whose argument, now more than half a century old, infuses much more recent scholarship on the Reconstruction amendments. On the other side are those who believe that the framers of the Thirteenth Amendment were at least as narrow in their understanding of the nation's obligation to protect individual rights as were those who would frame the later amendment. Charles Fairman offered one of the earliest, most comprehensive statements of this position, and, in recent years, Earl Maltz has done much to reinforce Fairman's argument. For more than thirty years, scholars have interrogated the historical record and yet failed to reach a consensus about the nature of the connection between the Thirteenth and Fourteenth amendments. Is it time to give up and move on?[3]

No—at least not for those among us who believe that the historical context of a measure's creation matters, and that one can always know more about that context. If historical scholarship of recent years is any indication, we have only skimmed the surface of a mountain of records revealing Americans' attitudes toward freedom, rights, and citizenship in the Civil War and Reconstruction era.[4] Among the effects of this newer scholarship will be, I believe, a fuller understanding of the complex relationship among these three core concepts: freedom, rights, and citizenship. Unfortunately, presentist ideas about rights and citizenship in particular still inform much scholarship about the historical meaning of the Reconstruction amendments. There are exceptions to this trend, to be sure. To give but two well-known examples, books by Akhil Reed Amar and Linda K. Kerber have helped to recover early meanings of rights and citizenship. In Amar's scholarship, we see the primacy of federalist structures in older notions of rights; in Kerber's, we see the greater emphasis on obligation over rights in early thinking about citizenship. What does this increased attention to historical context mean for scholarship linking the Thirteenth and Fourteenth amendments? At this point, it is difficult to say, but, at the very least, it necessitates a rewriting of the standard, teleological narrative of the emergence of the Fourteenth Amendment from the Thirteenth.

That narrative runs something like this: A Republican-controlled Congress in 1864 to 1865 passed the resolution sending the Thirteenth Amendment to the states for ratification in order to secure and enhance the Emancipation Proclamation; after the Civil War was over, and even before the amendment was ratified, Southern states began to pass "Black Codes," which infringed on the freedom promised by the amendment; in reaction, a new Republican Congress, in 1865 to 1866, adopted, over President Andrew Johnson's veto, two laws, the Civil Rights Act of 1866 and a new Freedmen's Bureau Act, which empowered federal officials to enforce the Thirteenth Amendment over state interference; and, finally, in order to protect these acts, the same Congress sent to the states a new constitutional amendment—the Fourteenth—which reiterated the Civil Rights Act's promise of "equal" rights as well as that act's declaration that those born in the country had both state and national citizenship. There is nothing wrong with the basic facts of the narrative. But, like all narratives, this one has the potential to create or reinforce assumptions that are flawed, even damaging.[5] The assumption that concerns me most, at least in this essay, is that rights and citizenship are necessarily linked, an assumption that may hold true today but did not hold true through most of the nineteenth century, at least until the Civil War.

The point of this essay is to highlight some of the ways that ideas about rights differed from ideas about citizenship in early nineteenth-century America and then to argue that, although both sets of ideas came powerfully into play during the Civil War, they did not neatly overlap each other. Thus we should not be surprised that a discussion of the meaning of citizenship is not to be found in the congressional debates about the Thirteenth Amendment. Opponents of the amendment occasionally warned that the measure would "elevate" slaves to citizenship and therefore confer voting rights to them.[6] Republicans in the debate did not respond directly to the specter of "negro citizens" armed with voting rights other than to point out that freedom did not necessarily confer suffrage, a fact demonstrated by the many Americans, white women most visibly, who were free but could not vote.[7] Yet that reply evaded the question of whether freed slaves became citizens, and what "citizenship" actually meant. The silence of the Republicans was noticed with frustration by one opponent, who jeered, "You make no provision for making these emancipated slaves citizens of the United States, or giving them any power in the sovereignty of a State."[8] Modern scholars seem equally stymied by the Republicans' silence. Surely, they assume, Republicans must have had some notion of citizenship in mind as they traveled the road toward the Fourteenth Amendment.

The silence on citizenship during the debates on the Thirteenth Amendment is more of a problem for modern legal scholars than it was for most Civil War–era lawmakers and legal theorists. First, those of the period did not know that they were headed toward the Fourteenth Amendment. As Hyman and Wiecek have pointed out, "persons who enacted the Thirteenth [Amendment] in early 1865 and who ratified it later that year did not know that *a* Fourteenth (much less *the* Fourteenth) was to be needed."[9] Second, and more to the point of this essay, even though many of the same people involved in the creation of the earlier amendment took part in the making of the later one, the Fourteenth Amendment was not a logical consequence of the Thirteenth. The road from the Thirteenth to the Fourteenth was more than unpredictable; it was discontinuous. There was a discrete break along the way. The Fourteenth Amendment came to privilege ascriptive, or at least restrictive, notions of citizenship in a way that the Thirteenth Amendment, to the extent it dealt with citizenship at all, did not. Many of the people involved in the Thirteenth Amendment's creation were aware of the measure's potential impact on American citizenship, but most were not yet thinking about citizenship in the ways that those who created the Fourteenth Amendment would. That fact helps to explain the deafening silence one hears when listening for details about American citizenship in the Thirteenth Amendment debates. But, perhaps more important, the disjunct between citizenship as it existed in the Thirteenth Amendment versus the Fourteenth should remind us that the relationship between the two amendments is more in the nature of cousins rather than siblings.

RIGHTS AND CITIZENSHIP IN ANTEBELLUM AMERICA

The relationship between rights and citizenship in antebellum America was not as it has become. Today, the lodestar of rights is citizenship. If an American today wants to claim individual rights, including rights against her own government, she can do no better than to assert her citizenship. In contrast, the lodestar of rights in early nineteenth-century America was not citizenship but freedom. The person harassed by a police officer today objects, "Stop—I am an

American *citizen!*" Two hundred years ago, the same person would have said, "Stop—I am a *free* American."

To be sure, much about rights was contested in the early nineteenth century. Who conferred and regulated rights, the state or national governments? Did all freeborn people have the same rights, regardless of age, gender, or race?

Despite these contests, all for the most part agreed that the source of rights was freedom. The presence of slavery helped create the consensus. People argued among themselves about who had which rights, but all agreed that slaves had none.[10] The destruction of slavery during the Civil War led naturally to efforts by lawmakers to clarify the rights attached to freedom, though only rarely during the Thirteenth Amendment debates themselves did congressmen attempt to spell out these rights.[11] Legal historians tend to treat these rights as falling into identifiable categories: civil rights (rights to contract, to sue, to testify in court); political rights (rights to vote and serve on juries); and social rights (rights to equal accommodations and the right to intermarriage). But such categories, along with their relationship to citizenship, were not as well defined as they would become in the Supreme Court decisions running from *Slaughterhouse* (1873) to *Plessy* (1896).[12] Parallel with the development of clearer categories of rights during Reconstruction was a separate transition, described with detail and elegance by Akhil Reed Amar, from thinking about rights primarily in terms of protections secured by the structures *of* the sovereign people toward thinking about them in terms of protections of the individual *against* the sovereign people.[13] What all these conceptions of rights had in common was that they posed the individual as threatened by something within the body politic, whether an overbearing national government, a tyrannical majority, an aberrant agent of the state, or a harmful fellow person. Whereas slaves were vulnerable to all these threats, free individuals had rights to guard against them.

Yet rights alone did not make these free individuals automatically members of a community, for the emphasis in rights-based thinking tended then as now to be on the rights of an individual, maybe even rights possessed equally by groups, but not on individuals' relationship to one another. Communities, whether acknowledged or imagined, depend, as Benedict Anderson and others have argued, on some connecting thread running through all its members— perhaps language, religion, or ethnicity.[14] Rights might flow from membership in a community, but something besides and beyond rights earned members a place in the community. Communities were not defined by rights—at least in early nineteenth-century America. They were defined by citizenship.

Citizenship prior to the Civil War was primarily about belonging to a common association rather than enjoying particular individual rights. As the historian William J. Novak has argued, the meaning of citizenship in the period was not to be found in the formal law of rights—who enjoyed which sorts of government protections—but rather in what he calls "the common law of status and membership."[15] One's status and membership in the polity (whether local, state, or national) depended primarily on the role that one played in one or more associations sanctioned by the polity. Nineteenth-century Americans, as Alexis de Tocqueville and other foreign observers noted, were prone to join associations, and, as de Tocqueville rightly noted, these associations were as significant for governance as for recreation: "Where in France you would find the government or in England some territorial magnate, in the United States you are sure to find an association."[16] These associations ranged from those we today might immediately think of as political, such as a city or town, to those that we might (mistakenly) categorize as nonpolitical or merely "voluntary," such as universities, corporations, churches, or fire companies. All these associations were involved in some way in governance—if not of formal political entities then of social, economic, or moral conditions. They were not simply symptomatic of civil society but constitutive of it. One's citizenship flowed from membership in one or more of these entities. Membership carried certain rights, usually denoted as "privileges" or "immunities," and these could vary depending on one's status in the association, but they generally involved protection against entities outside the association rather than protection from those within. In other words, the normal ways that one thought of rights in the early nineteenth century—as means to protect free people from excessive uses of power by those in authority— did not describe the privileges and immunities attached to citizenship.[17] Furthermore, just as entities within an association had privileges and immunities, the associations themselves had certain privileges and immunities; that is, as components of a variegated state system, they could claim status within the body politic. This phenomenon, which only in the late nineteenth century would become known as "corporate citizenship," was well established by the time of the Civil War as a staple of federal court jurisprudence.[18]

If one looked hard enough, one could find formal categories of national and state citizenship, and with those categories were associated various privileges and immunities, but these categories competed or were overshadowed by associational citizenship, which, though more informal, carried privileges and immunities as dear to its members as those attached to state and national affiliations. The result was a concept of citizenship that could hardly be more different from today's. Novak explains:

> Whereas a modern conception of national citizenship usually entails a notion of top-down primary memberships and uniformly regulates the general rights and duties of all citizen no matter what their secondary associations, early American rights and duties flowed from the bottom up, hinging on the particular regulations and policies of a panoply of secondary jurisdictions

and institutional affiliations. Constitutional rights of citizenship did not trump or limit the power of these majoritarian organizations. On the contrary, full membership in some of these self-governing associations was the key determinant of the substantive rights of many antebellum Americans.[19]

Any number of examples might capture the situation that Novak describes. Consider the many women in the antebellum period claiming to be citizens who made that claim on the basis not of what formal rights were granted to them but rather on their participation in civic associations, such as schools, churches, and reform groups.[20]

Once one understands the historically specific meanings of rights and citizenship in the early nineteenth century, it becomes increasingly difficult to apply to this context the commonplace terms of civil, political, and social rights. The more historically accurate categories would be, on one side, freedom rights, which corresponded generally to our notion of civil rights but flowed less from the abstract notion of civil society than from the actual presence of slavery; and, on the other side, associational privileges and immunities, which flowed less from explicit categories of citizenship established by state and national law than from membership in any community that could in some way be construed as political. These two categories of freedom rights/associational privileges could blend into each other and were not always easier to identify than were the three categories of civil/political/social rights that modern scholars tend to rely on, but the two-category system more satisfactorily describes the way that people of the time understood the nature of rights and privileges. A constitutional interpreter who puts the text of the Constitution above all else may well prefer the two-category system, as citizenship appears only in the original Constitution, and usually in places describing a community (such as a state), whereas the words "citizen" and "citizenship" do not appear once in the Bill of Rights.

Not only could the two categories of freedom rights and associational privileges become confused with each other, but each category was complicated by exceptions and definitions peculiar to antebellum America. Two distinguishing characteristics were especially noteworthy. The first was the denial of freedom rights to some who were free. In particular, free African Americans in the Midwest and free Chinese Americans in the far West, although tending to receive different treatment before the courts, together suffered from denial of certain rights associated with freedom, such as the right to move from place to place, to hold property, or to bring suit or testify in court. Such disabilities were sometimes, and aptly, termed badges or incidents of slavery, for they signaled that a person or people had not yet made the transition fully from slavery to freedom (although the term was concocted with African Americans in mind—specifically those who had been born as slaves in this country—it had been imposed on others, such as recent Chinese immigrants, who had not been born in the country).[21] The second notable peculiarity in the American legal system was the withering of birthright citizenship. Under the law of most modern nations, including England, from which most American law developed, one's birth in a place assured one's citizenship in the sovereign bodies located there. That formal, political citizenship operated alongside the citizenship that stemmed from membership in associations sanctioned by the state. Contingent circumstances in the United States—most notably the problem of identifying loyalty in the American Revolution, the persistence of racialized slavery, and the evolution of white supremacist thought—combined to steer the nation away from birth and toward volitional allegiance as the basis of citizenship.[22] As a result, associational citizenship became not simply one type of citizenship but increasingly the only type, and allegiance more than birth became the preferred basis of establishing membership in communities and polities.

The people most affected by this peculiarity of the American system were freeborn African Americans. While in other countries, including England, freeborn people, regardless of race, were counted as citizens, in the United States, being born in the country did not assure citizenship to someone of African descent. Through associational life, many freeborn African Americans did come to view themselves as citizens, but they then found themselves running headlong into state and national authorities who refused to acknowledge their citizenship. How could they then become formal, government-acknowledged citizens? Neither the federal nor state governments had laws spelling out how a freeborn person denied citizenship could become a citizen. The only law that seemed relevant was the naturalization law of 1790, but that measure specified only "white" aliens as eligible for citizenship. Some enterprising African Americans attempted to escape the legal limbo by applying for naturalization without mentioning their color and, despite having been born in the United States, claiming to be immigrants from some fictional country, such as "Guinea."[23]

Because of free African Americans' peculiar legal status, they presented the greatest challenge to lawmakers seeking clarity in the meaning of rights and citizenship. The distinction between freedom rights and associational privileges, always a bit unstable, collapsed entirely when free African Americans came before the bench and bar. Witness Justice Roger B. Taney's intellectual gyrations when he decided to resolve once and for all the issue of "negro citizenship" in the *Dred Scott* opinion of 1857. The citizenship question was the least pressing issue of the case—the power of Congress to prohibit slavery in federal territories garnered far more public attention—yet Taney devoted almost half his opinion to it, a reflection of how difficult citizenship was to describe and define. Regardless of what people then or now think of Taney's decision, most agree that the section on citizenship is the most confusing. Most of the confusion came from his determination to treat citizenship and rights as necessarily congruent, when decades of legal development and common experience had led most Americans to think of the two things in different ways.

Taney's very first step took him into the quagmire: "The question is simply this: Can a negro, whose ancestors were imported into this country and sold as slaves, become a member of the political community formed and brought into existence by the Constitution of the United States, and as such become entitled to all the rights, and privileges, and immunities, guarantied by that instrument to the citizen. One of which rights is the privilege of suing in a court of the United States in the cases specified in the Constitution."[24]

The first part of the passage nicely reflects the antebellum notion of citizenship being tied to "community," but he then conflates the privileges associated with membership with at least one right, the right to sue in court, which was not attached to citizenship but rather to the more fundamental condition of freedom. Deeper into the morass he went. Here he found a right listed in an old statute book and uses it to make a claim about citizenship; there he took a restrictive use of the word "citizen" to suggest the necessary denial of rights. The most infamous part of Taney's opinion, that "[Negroes] had no rights which the white man was bound to respect," might have had some legitimacy if it had flowed from Taney's examination of African American rights. But such an examination was not the source of the statement, nor could it have been, for when Taney did that analysis, he found that African Americans in some places had quite a few rights. Rather, he rested his statement on African Americans' citizenship status at the time of the framing of the Constitution. To his credit, he once again, and appropriately, framed citizenship in terms of membership in an association: "[Negroes] had for more than a century before been regarded as . . . altogether unfit to associate with the white race."[25] But to link citizenship to rights in this way—that is, to offer as logical the idea that citizenship was the sole source and indicator of rights—was not only illogical but a gross distortion of the incongruity that in fact existed between rights and citizenship in antebellum America.

Taney has been excoriated for his decision, especially in recent years, but it is not clear that any other justice could have done much better—at least when it came to defining citizenship. Justice John McLean simply equated a citizen with a "freeman"—that is, a free person with rights that included the right to sue.[26] Taney was closer to the mark, in that he understood citizenship and freedom rights as distinct; his conflation of the two things was not as complete as McLean's.

The justice who came closest to understanding the distance between citizenship and freedom rights was Benjamin R. Curtis, whose claim makes sense only in the context of the nineteenth century, not the twentieth: "The truth is, that citizenship, under the Constitution of the United States, is not dependent on the possession of any particular political or even of all civil rights; and any attempt so to define it must lead to error."[27] Citizenship may carry certain privileges and immunities, Curtis argued, but those were always determined by the more intimate community rather than the general one. Thus in the particular federal system of the United States, states took a greater role than the nation in determining and regulating privileges. Abraham Lincoln echoed Curtis in his debates with Senator Stephen Douglas a year later: "The different States have the power to make a negro a citizen under the Constitution of the United States if they choose. The *Dred Scott* decision decides that they have not that power [to which Lincoln, like Curtis, objected]. If the State of Illinois had that power I should be opposed to the exercise of it."[28] Lincoln, like Curtis, focused only the controversial issue of state versus national citizenship, but he might have added that further regulations of the privileges attached to citizenship took place in even smaller communities than states, such as municipalities, some of which still had property-holding requirements for voting well into and beyond the Civil War.[29]

If one accepts the categories of freedom rights on one side and citizenship privileges on the other, then puzzlement is likely to follow a reading of Curtis's statement that "what civil rights shall be enjoyed by [United States] citizens, and whether all shall enjoy the same, or how they may be gained or lost, are to be determined in the same way" that states regulate the privileges of citizenship.[30] What does Curtis mean by "civil rights" here, and doesn't this statement suggest that he sees freedom rights and citizenship privileges as congruous? The choice of the word "rights" does indeed create confusion, for that would be precisely the word used to describe the protections all free people enjoy. But the confusion begins to fade once one sees that Curtis was talking only about rights among "citizens," not all free people. He was using "rights" to mean a citizen's status within a community, not the rights enjoyed by a free person regardless of his or her various affiliations with associations. This was a discussion about the law of status and membership, not about the law of freedom. Yet Curtis's statement serves as another reminder of how unstable the categories of freedom rights and citizenship privileges could be, and thus how likely it was that a jurist or any American could use imprecise language in describing these categories.

Despite this imprecision, it is possible to make one further generalization about the distinction between freedom and citizenship, one especially relevant to the meanings of the Thirteenth and other Reconstruction amendments: whereas freedom rights were generally regarded as expansive, citizenship privileges tended to be ascriptive. Whether rights were the product of natural law, positive law, or some combination of the two, theorists and ordinary Americans from the seventeenth century onward tended to see rights as legal protections belonging to free people, and, once granted, irrevocable. With time, and the discovery of new sorts of rights that a free people should have, freedom rights expanded, with some notable exceptions, such as occasional but short-lived retractions of rights for free African Americans in the nineteenth century. The expansive trajectory of rights was assumed by James Madison when he warned of the danger of enumerating rights during the Constitutional Convention: if the law treated rights as static, Madison believed, then it might preclude the granting of rights needed but not yet known. Hence the Ninth Amendment— Madison's clever means of ensuring that unenumerated rights, including rights not yet imagined, were "retained by the people" and not to be denied through interpretation of enumerated rights.

Citizenship, by contrast, was never assumed to be an expanding category. Rather, according to Rogers M. Smith, it was by its nature ascriptive; that is, citizenship was as much about who was *not* a citizen as about who was one. In the same way, states composed of citizens tended to be established on exclusionary principles. As Anthony Marx has argued, excluding people was not merely an incident but a defining feature of the modern state. The expansive trajectory of freedom rights and the exclusionary tendency of citizenship privileges signaled, yet again, that rights and citizenship, while related, operated at cross planes with each other.[31]

RECONSTRUCTING RIGHTS AND CITIZENSHIP IN THE CIVIL WAR ERA

Wartime circumstances forced Americans to clarify the meaning of rights and citizenship as well as the relationship between the two categories. But, with a few important exceptions, they did remain as two distinct, if related, categories. They may even have remained as such well into the postwar Reconstruction years had not lawmakers, in creating legislation to enforce the Thirteenth Amendment, made the innovative yet, in hindsight, illiberal move of tangling the categories hopelessly together so that freedom rights, once regarded as expansive, would thenceforth be tainted with the ascriptive qualities of citizenship.

Even before the firing on Fort Sumter in 1861, but certainly after it, the sectional crisis created circumstances in which various groups asserted rights, often with the successful effect of having those rights given the imprimatur of positive, written law. The best known of these groups was the 4 million African Americans still enslaved at the time of the outbreak of the war. Slavery was well on the way to oblivion before Congress took up the Thirteenth Amendment in late 1863. Although the precise rights obtained by slaves freed in the areas of the

Southern states described by the Emancipation Proclamation of January 1, 1863, would not be delineated until well after that date, the rights of those freed in 1862 in areas under exclusive congressional jurisdiction—federal territories and the District of Columbia—were more explicit and included the right of habeas corpus to prevent former masters from holding them in servitude in the face of abolition law. Later, slaves who served in the military secured not only their own freedom but the freedom of their families. Emancipation raised rights consciousness and activated or accelerated rights movements for other groups besides slaves. Free African Americans, women of all races, labor groups, Mexican Americans, and Native Americans were just some of the groups that invoked wartime slave emancipation as a basis for their claims to rights.[32]

Meanwhile, as is always the case in war, especially in civil war, people were forced to declare their citizenship or, alternatively, others delimited it for them. Delegates to the convention to create a Confederate constitution argued about who would be citizens of the new nation. After a number of criteria were proposed and rejected, the convention agreed finally to make citizenship in the nation depend entirely on whether one was a citizen of a state within that nation. A number of states took the cue and passed laws defining citizenship. Georgia, for example, declared resident aliens there citizens unless they declared citizenship elsewhere within three months after secession.[33] But ambiguity remained. What happened if a person moved from one state of the Confederacy to another? And what about U.S. citizens who moved south, swore an oath to the Confederacy, and took up arms against their former country: did they immediately become citizens not only of the Confederate States of America but also of the state where they resided? This could have been a real problem in Florida, for example, which banned from state citizenship all people who had been U.S. citizens as of 1862. And what about onetime citizens of a Confederate state who had taken up residence in a Union state: had they forfeited their citizenship status? The quest for definitive answers to such questions led only to frustration. A clerk in a Confederate federal district court in Tennessee wrote to a counterpart in Virginia to ask how the Virginia court had been handling the thorny question of whether "a citizen of the State [may] elect, or choose, between the two governments at war." "Is he absolutely bound by the sovereign act of the state, and made a citizen thereof?"[34] When it came to establishing rules of citizenship, officials seemed to be making it up as they went along.

Meanwhile, ordinary Americans with overlapping associational identities found it increasingly difficult not to privilege political citizenship—especially national citizenship—over all sorts of citizenship. If nationalism was on the rise, so was the scramble to establish one's citizenship. Among other benefits of putting one's citizenship on record was the protection of property. By late 1861, both the Union and the Confederacy had instituted confiscation policies against those allied with their enemies. The best way to immunize oneself from confiscation was to establish one's citizenship before a court, a military official, or some other agent of the nation.[35]

Questions of who was a citizen or how a person became one now coursed through public discussion. The Confederacy and the Union passed new laws of naturalization, they established or clarified the citizenship status of military enlistees and conscripts, and, most important, they administered oaths of an implicit if not explicit ascriptive nature. Oath takers swore allegiance to one and only one entity, and oath taking was denied to those deemed not eligible for citizenship. Refusal to take the oath, or outright renunciation of citizenship, led to alienation, perhaps even imprisonment. Consider the fictional Philip Nolan, the tragic central figure of Edward Everett Hale's 1863 story "The Man Without a Country," set fifty years prior to the war but, as Hale himself conceded, informed by discussions of loyalty, disloyalty, and citizenship during the Civil War. Having denounced the United States, Nolan is banished from the country and ordered to live adrift on ships never to dock. In one episode, he encounters a group of slaves and finally seems part of a community. Where once the pariah was the slave, now it was the noncitizen.[36]

A turning point in the Union's efforts to define citizenship came in late 1862, when Salmon P. Chase, the secretary of the treasury, asked Edward Bates, the attorney general, to issue an opinion on the citizenship of freeborn African Americans. Like many Republicans, Chase had been looking for an opportunity to have a national pronouncement that would reverse the *Dred Scott* opinion's declaration against "negro citizenship," and the perfect situation presented itself when his treasury agents captured a ship piloted by a freeborn African American who had stolen the ship from the South and piloted it to Union waters. Bates's opinion began by venting the frustration that so many others had felt when trying to offer a single, simple statement of the meaning of citizenship: "Eighty years of practical enjoyment of citizenship, under the Constitution, have not sufficed to teach us either the exact meaning of the word, or the constituent elements of the thing we prize so highly."[37] Bates concluded that the man was indeed a U.S. citizen, for he had been born free in the country and, to the extent he might feel allegiance to any political entity, it would be to the United States. Republicans approved of the opinion. A Maine man was grateful that Bates had reasserted "the essential facts of birth and allegiance" as the basis of citizenship, rather than relying on more recent standards of "the fact of color and of the more or less curl of the hair."[38] Chase had the opinion he wanted, and he eventually sent copies of it to his agents in Louisiana to provide justification for the plan he was attempting to put into effect there, under which African Americans would take part in unionist conventions, rewrite the state constitution, and apply for readmission to the Union.[39]

Historians have tended to treat Bates's opinion as one more piece of evidence that African Americans were rapidly acquiring rights during and because of the Civil War. But, once again, we should be careful not to treat rights and citizenship as somehow equivalent. Even though it was an important departure from *Dred Scott*, Bates's opinion failed to provide a clear definition of citizenship to substitute for the one Taney had offered. Nor did the opinion discuss what specific rights were attached or not attached to citizenship. And when partisan opponents claimed that Bates's opinion was yet another sign that Republicans meant to give suffrage rights to blacks, Republicans such as the editor of the *Cincinnati Gazette* denied the charge in predictable fashion: "The right to vote has nothing to do with citizenship," the editor claimed, as evidenced by the fact that many women and children were citizens but could not vote.[40] Bates's opinion also followed the pattern of antebellum assertions of citizenship, in that it was ascriptive rather than expansive. That is, unlike the acts freeing slaves in federal territories and the District of Columbia, which asserted certain rights under freedom and said nothing about rights denied, thus allowing for the possibility of further rights not yet stated, Bates's opinion was as engaged with the question of who was not a citizen as it was with the citizenship status of this particular person. Indeed, one of the first steps he took in the opinion was to state that blacks born slaves but now free were not covered by his opinion, and that certainly those still enslaved were not citizens.

When Congress took up the Thirteenth Amendment beginning in late 1863, the debates focused on rights, not citizenship. Supporters of the measure said nothing about Bates's 1862 opinion, even though opponents baited them to say something about citizenship. Even when Republicans invoked blacks' military service to the Union as justification for the amendment, they did not frame that argument in terms of citizenship. Instead of asserting that black soldiers were necessarily citizens, a claim made by many black and white abolitionists, not to mention black soldiers themselves, they treated black military service more in the nature of an exchange: for blacks' onetime service to their country, they would get freedom and the rights attached to freedom.

Outside Congress, many Americans talked of "negro rights" and "negro citizenship" in the same breath. They always had, and they were inclined to do so now more than ever, as both phenomena had gained greater visibility during the war, and both involved some sort of legal protection or legal status.

But those trained in law or well read in legal and political theory were much less likely during the Thirteenth Amendment debate to conflate citizenship privileges and freedom rights. The most telling episode about the meaning of citizenship under the Thirteenth Amendment took place not in the congressional debate but in a private correspondence between two renowned legal theorists:

Horace Binney and Francis Lieber.[41] Inspired by the initiative to create an anti-slavery amendment, Lieber drafted, in 1864, a slate of constitutional amendments, which not only abolished slavery but also set out specific rights due to the free people and specific punishments due to those who interfered with their freedom. Like his fellow Republicans in Congress, Lieber thought of freedom in terms of rights more than of citizenship. And he was at least a year ahead of them in imagining what sort of legislation would be needed to secure those rights. When Binney read Lieber's draft amendments, he responded by saying that the whole matter of specific rights and punishments should be put aside—Congress could later decide what rights and punishments to dole out—and instead there should be a different sort of amendment, one that defined citizenship. "The word *citizen* or *citizens* is found ten times at least in the Constitution of the United States," Binney complained, "and no definition of it is given anywhere." Binney drafted a citizenship amendment that looked much like the Fourteenth Amendment, to be passed by Congress a year later. Binney's measure said nothing about "rights" such as due process and equal protection but instead spoke only of "privileges . . . in courts of judicature as elsewhere." Perhaps Binney would have seen the "due process" and "equal protection" clause of the Fourteenth Amendment as synonymous with the "privileges" clause he had drafted, but it is nonetheless significant that he chose to use the language of privileges rather than rights; indeed, he had purposefully announced to Lieber that rights need not be mentioned at all. Binney was upholding the antebellum tradition of treating freedom rights and citizenship privileges as distinct though related instruments.

Lieber's pamphlet, published in 1865, confounded Binney's request and conflated freedom rights and citizen privileges by adding Binney's amendment to Lieber's slate of amendments but keeping in that slate Lieber's measures specifying rights and punishments. Congress would make a similar move when it framed the Fourteenth Amendment a year later.

Had Binney had his way, the abolition of slavery would have triggered two separate, distinct initiatives: legislation (or, if necessary, though Binney did not think it necessary, a constitutional amendment) establishing the rights attached to freedom, and a constitutional amendment defining citizenship. History almost played out in the way that Binney would have wanted, a way that would have been consistent with the distinction between freedom rights and citizen privileges that inhabited the thoughts of legal-minded Americans in the antebellum period. Instead, the nation ended up with the Fourteenth Amendment, which drew citizenship and rights together in its first clause, leading to more than a century of unresolved debate about the meaning of rights versus privileges and immunities and, more tragically, to an ascriptive reading of rights that would have puzzled if not offended Binney and others of his cohort.

How did this happen? How did the ascriptive tendency of citizenship worm its way into freedom rights, which were generally thought of in expansive terms? It was not an inevitable development but rather an incidental one. When Congress set out, in the winter of 1865 to 1866, to enumerate the rights under the Thirteenth Amendment, an initiative that Binney had predicted would happen, and that would culminate in the passage of the Civil Rights Act of 1866, it began with a Senate version declaring that there would be "no discrimination in civil rights or immunities among the inhabitants . . . ," and it then listed what those rights were. Criticism arose inside and outside Congress that the measure would grant rights to people who might not deserve them, such as Chinese-born Americans. The problem was not that the rights were too expansive—again, it was natural for people to assume that rights would be expansive—but rather who would receive them. To placate the critics, wording was needed to signal that the people granted rights would be delimited in some way. What better way to signal delimitation than by the term "citizen," which had always been regarded as ascriptive? In the House of Representatives, James Wilson, of Iowa, altered the first sentence of the bill so that "inhabitants" now read as "citizens." That did the trick: the bill was passed, ultimately over President Andrew Johnson's veto. The veto, in combination with the fear that the act might not withstand judicial review or the approval of some later Congress, led Congress to import the language of the act into the first clause of a proposed constitutional amendment. The word "citizen" necessitated further definition, which ultimately appeared in the assertion of birthplace as the basis of citizenship. The first clause of the Fourteenth Amendment was now set. Thus it was that a piece of legislation initially meant to secure expansive rights under freedom ultimately became tinged with the ascriptive language of citizenship. A constitutional amendment defining citizenship was needed, to be sure, but such an amendment was not the logical next step from the Thirteenth Amendment. The logical next step was a civil rights act, or even a civil rights amendment, that made no mention of citizenship.[42]

Had this logical next step been taken, would the history of civil rights under the Thirteenth Amendment have turned out any differently? Maybe, maybe not. But at least freedom under the amendment would have retained more of the expansive quality it had in the antebellum era, and less of the ascriptive quality that it would come to have in the century after the adoption of the Fourteenth Amendment. It is long past time to separate the Fourteenth Amendment from the Thirteenth at the family table: the Thirteenth has freedom to share; the Fourteenth has only citizenship to deny.

NOTES

1. See Michael Vorenberg, *Final Freedom: The Civil War, the Abolition of Slavery, and the Thirteenth Amendment* (New York: Cambridge University Press, 2001), chap. 8.

2. Harold M. Hyman and William M. Wiecek, *Equal Justice Under Law: Constitutional Development, 1835–1875* (New York: Harper & Row, 1982), 386–438.

3. Jacobus tenBroek, *Equal Under Law* (originally published as *The Antislavery Origins of the Fourteenth Amendment*) (1951; repr., New York: Collier Books, 1965); Charles Fairman, *Reconstruction and Reunion, 1864–1888: Part One*, vol. 6, *History of the Supreme Court of the United States* (New York: Macmillan, 1971), esp. chaps. 19 and 21; Earl M. Maltz, *Civil Rights, the Constitution, and Congress, 1863–1869* (Lawrence: University Press of Kansas, 1990). For a fuller review of the literature on the subject as it existed in 1987, see Robert J. Kaczorowski, "To Begin the Nation Anew: Congress, Citizenship, and Civil Rights after the Civil War," *American Historical Review* 92 (February 1987): 45–47. For an example of recent legal scholarship making the case for the Thirteenth Amendment over the Fourteenth Amendment as the basis of modern civil rights law, see Alexander Tsesis, "Furthering American Freedom: Civil Rights and the Thirteenth Amendment," *Boston College Law Review* 45 (March 2004): 307.

4. For a review of some of this scholarship, see Michael Vorenberg, "Reconstruction as a Constitutional Crisis," in Thomas J. Brown, ed., *Reconstructions: New Perspectives on the Postbellum United States* (New York: Oxford University Press, 2006), 141–71.

5. Hayden White, "The Value of Narrativity in the Representation of Reality," in Joyce Appleby et al., eds., *Knowledge and Postmodernism in Historical Perspective*, 395–409 (New York: Routledge, 1996); Peter Brooks and Paul Gewirtz, eds., *Law's Stories: Narrative and Rhetoric in the Law* (New Haven, Conn.: Yale University Press, 1996).

6. See, for example, *Congressional Globe* (hereafter CG), 38th Cong., 1st sess., 2982 (Robert Mallory); *CG*, 38th Cong., 1st sess., 2987 (Joseph K. Edgerton).

7. See, for example, *CG*, 38th Cong., 2d sess., 202 (John R. McBride).

8. *CG*, 38th Cong., 2d sess., 154 (Andrew J. Rogers).

9. Hyman and Wiecek, *Equal Justice Under Law*, 389.

10. The literature on the relationship between slavery and freedom, including the impact of that relationship on ideas about rights, is vast. For an analysis and synthesis of the relevant works, see Eric Foner, *The Story of American Freedom* (New York: Norton, 1998), esp. chaps 1–5. Despite the fact free people thought of slaves as beings without rights, slaves themselves were capable of thinking of themselves as having rights. For example, on American slaves' assumption of their own property rights, see Dylan C. Penningroth, *The Claims of Kinfolk: African American Property and Com-*

munity in the Nineteenth-Century South (Chapel Hill: University of North Carolina Press, 2003).

11. Vorenberg, *Final Freedom*, 103–5, 132–33, 189–91.

12. Hyman and Wiecek, *Equal Justice Under Law*, 395–97 (see esp. diagram at 396). For an overview of the process by which rights gained definition by the Supreme Court in the period, see William E. Nelson, *The Fourteenth Amendment: From Political Principle to Judicial Doctrine* (Cambridge, Mass.: Harvard University Press, 1988), 148–96.

13. Akhil Reed Amar, *The Bill of Rights: Creation and Reconstruction* (New Haven, Conn.: Yale University Press, 1998).

14. Benedict Anderson, *Imagined Communities: Reflections on the Origin and Spread of Nationalism*, rev. ed. (1983; repr., London: Verso, 2006). For a review of the most pertinent literature on "imagined communities" that engages Anderson's formulation of the concept, as well as attempts to apply such theories to American nationalism and citizenship, see Ed White, "Early American Nations as Imagined Communities," *American Quarterly* 56 (March 2004): 49–81.

15. William J. Novak, "The Legal Transformation of Citizenship in Nineteenth-Century America," in Meg Jacobs, William J. Novak, and Julian E. Zelizer, eds., *The Democratic Experiment: New Directions in American Political History*, 85–119 (Princeton, N.J.: Princeton University Press, 2003).

16. Alexis de Tocqueville, *Democracy in America*, ed. J. P. Mayer (1966; repr., Garden City, N.Y.: Anchor Books, 1969), 513.

17. Much recent work besides Novak's stresses the connection between government-sanctioned associations and citizenship in the United States, especially in the Early Republic period. For an example of this work and a review of the literature, see Johann N. Neem, "The Elusive Common Good," *Journal of the Early Republic* 24 (fall 2004): 381–417.

18. Austin Allen, *Origins of the Dred Scott Case: Jacksonian Jurisprudence and the Supreme Court, 1837–1857* (Athens: University of Georgia Press, 2006).

19. Novak, "Legal Transformation of Citizenship in Nineteenth-Century America," 101–2.

20. Nancy Isenberg, *Sex and Citizenship in Antebellum America* (Chapel Hill: University of North Carolina Press, 1998), chap. 4.

21. See, in this vol., George Rutherglen, "The Badges and Incidents of Slavery and the Power of Congress to Enforce the Thirteenth Amendment."

22. James H. Kettner, *The Development of American Citizenship, 1608–1870* (Chapel Hill: University of North Carolina Press, 1978), chaps. 7–10.

23. Kunal M. Parker, "State, Citizenship, and Territory: The Legal Construction of Immigrants in Antebellum Massachusetts," *Law and History Review* 19 (fall 2001): 583–643. ("Guinea" would not become an official political entity until 1890, and it would not become an independent nation until the mid-twentieth century.)

24. *Dred Scott v. John F. A. Sandford*, 19 Howard 403 (1857).

25. Ibid., 407.

26. Ibid., 532.

27. Ibid., 583.

28. Roy P. Basler, ed., Marion Dolores Pratt and Lloyd A. Dunlap, asst. eds., *The Collected Works of Abraham Lincoln* (New Brunswick, N.J.: Rutgers University Press, 1953), 3:179.

29. See, for example, Sven Beckert, "Democracy in the Age of Capital: Contesting Suffrage Rights in Gilded Age New York," in Jacobs, Novak, and Zelizer, *Democratic Experiment*, 146–74. The restriction of suffrage rights among locales is one of many subjects detailed in Alexander Keyssar, *The Right to Vote: The Contested History of Democracy in the United States* (New York: Basic Books, 2000).

30. Ibid., 583.

31. Rogers M. Smith, *Civic Ideals: Conflicting Visions of Citizenship in U.S. History* (New Haven, Conn.: Yale University Press, 1997); Judith Shklar, *American Citizenship: The Quest for Inclusion* (Cambridge, Mass.: Harvard University Press, 1991); Anthony W. Marx, *Faith in Nation: Exclusionary Origins of Nationalism* (New York: Oxford University Press, 2003). For a different argument, one emphasizing the liberalizing trajectory of citizenship, see Michael Schudson, *The Good Citizen: A History of American Civic Life* (New York: Free Press, 1998).

32. Eric Foner, "The Meaning of Freedom in the Age of Emancipation," *Journal of American History* 81 (September 1994): 435–60.

33. Kettner, *Development of American Citizenship*, 337 (including n. 9).

34. Matthew T. Haynes to Archimedes Davis, Knoxville, June 13, 1863, "CSA v. William H. Smith," Record Group 21, Confederate District Court for the Western District of Virginia, National Archives Mid-Atlantic Region, Philadelphia.

35. Daniel W. Hamilton, *The Limits of Sovereignty: Property Confiscation in the Union and the Confederacy during the Civil War* (Chicago: University of Chicago Press, 2007).

36. Edward Everett Hale, *The Man Without a Country* (1863; repr., Boston: Roberts, 1891), 17–18. On the Civil War's effect on formal and informal citizenship identification during the Civil War, see Vorenberg, "Reconstruction as a Constitutional Crisis," 168–71.

37. Edward Bates, "Citizenship," *Opinions of the Attorney General* 10 (November 29, 1862): 382–83.

38. John Appleton to William P. Fessenden, December 11, 1862, William Pitt Fessenden Papers, Western Reserve Historical Society, Cleveland, Ohio.

39. For Chase's use of the Bates opinion, see Chase to Robert Dale Owen, September 6, 1863, Salmon P. Chase Papers, Historical Society of Pennsylvania, Philadelphia.

40. *Cincinnati Gazette*, December 30, 1862, 2.

41. Vorenberg, *Final Freedom*, 66–69.

42. On the creation of the Civil Rights Act of 1866, and the relation of that act to the Fourteenth Amendment, see Kaczorowski, "To Begin the Nation Anew," and Maltz, *Civil Rights, the Constitution, and Congress*, chaps. 5–6. Because of space limitations, this essay does not delve into the details of the process by which Congressman Wilson's language, which used "citizen," became the accepted language of the Civil Rights Act, and thus the Fourteenth Amendment. The process is well detailed in a number of books on the creation of the Fourteenth Amendment, perhaps the most succinct and readable of which is Nelson, *Fourteenth Amendment*.

5. Emancipation and Civic Status

THE AMERICAN EXPERIENCE, 1865–1915

William M. Wiecek

What is the legal effect of abolition through the Thirteenth Amendment on the civic status of a formerly enslaved person?[1] When an individual or an entire people become free, what place do they occupy in the society that had formerly enslaved them? What rights and immunities may they claim? What disabilities and inequalities may be imposed on them? A spectrum of answers to these questions is theoretically available. At one extreme the former slave might be treated as an outlaw, subject to being killed or reenslaved with impunity, unable to claim any rights or status in society. At the other conceptual extreme, the liberated individual might enjoy complete equality with those who had formerly enslaved her, with no difference whatever in her status, rights, or opportunities from those of her former masters. The historical experience of the world's slave societies furnishes examples of all possibilities along this spectrum, but the question of interest to us is: what became the civic status of African Americans in the United States after 1865?

This last question can be answered only at two levels, the formal and the realistic. By 1900, Americans of African descent enjoyed a formal, nominal equality, supposedly fully rights endowed as compared with their fellow Americans of European descent. But that was of course illusory, as everyone understood at the time and acknowledges now. The reality was that black Americans occupied a subordinated, quasi-servile status similar to that found under South African apartheid before 1994. It is a question of some moment how and why this two-tiered system of status came about, and that is the issue addressed here.

The abolition of slavery, first by statute and desuetude in the states, then by the Thirteenth Amendment nationwide, necessarily had to result in a new legal status for the freedpeople, which, for lack of a more exact term, we may call freedom. But the meaning and content of that freedom were not obvious or preordained. It was a new legal regime that would be defined only by experience. What did freedom mean as a legal and constitutional status, and how did African Americans experience it?[2] To answer those questions we must turn to antebellum experience. Freedom after 1865 with the ratification of the amendment can be understood only in reference to the differing legal regimes of the free and the slave states before 1860. This chapter explores those differing understandings, follows their respective ascendancies, and sketches the compromised resolution of their incompatibilities that was achieved by 1900.

In compressed outline, the explanation for America's two-tiered law of race in 1900—formal equality as a veneer covering universal inequality—begins with the 1772 Kings Bench decision of *Somerset v. Stewart*. Flowing into the common law of all American states after independence, the principles of *Somerset* structured the law of personal status of the separate American states, as well the relationships among the states themselves in the matter of individuals' status. After the Missouri crises of 1819 to 1821, the law of the slave states began to diverge from that of the free states in its treatment of individual emancipation. Each section, North and South, unthinkingly assumed that *its* law of status would control the rights and opportunities of people formerly enslaved. Under the slave states' neo-*Somerset* understanding of status, a former slave had only one right, locomotion, the ability to go where he or she wanted. (And even that right was constricted by statutory law and social controls such as the slave patrols.) All other elements of personal status were determined by positive law. In the free states, by contrast, a person formerly enslaved assumed many of the usual rights of other free people. This understanding left ample room for racial discrimination and did not necessarily confer access to political power, but it did prescribe at least a quasi-egalitarian legal status for individuals in the private-law domains of contract, property, family status, and legal capacity.

Nationwide abolition by 1865 forced an abrupt resolution of this potential conflict between the laws of the former slave and free states. At first, the slave states' understandings dictated the status of the freedpeople, since this was purely a matter of state law at that time, and nearly all the freedpeople lived in the ex–slave states. This outcome was totally unacceptable to the victorious North, which immediately nullified the expression of slave-state understanding, the Black Codes, and substituted the free-state vision of personal status as law throughout the nation—and in so doing federalized what had previously been a matter exclusively for the states. But this free-state solution was in turn unacceptable to most whites in the former slave states, and they began a campaign through both legitimate and extralegal means to replace it with the two-tier system of formal, nominal equality imposing apartheid and rightslessness on African Americans. To paraphrase Frederic W. Maitland, by 1900 the slave law of the South may have been dead, but it ruled us from its grave.

THE ANTEBELLUM ERA, 1772–1860: SECTIONAL DIVERGENCES

The law of personal status in the American states was the evolutionary product of multiple influences. But a major determinant of that law, as far as slaves were concerned, was the judgment of William Murray, 1st Earl of Mansfield, in the 1772 decision of *Somerset v. Stewart*.[3] Awarding a writ of habeas corpus to James Somerset, who had been brought from Virginia and Massachusetts to London as a slave and who escaped in London only to be recaptured and consigned for shipment and sale back into slavery in Jamaica, Mansfield held that: [1] "The state of slavery is of such a nature, that it is incapable of being introduced on any reasons, moral or political; but only [by] positive law . . . It's so odious, that nothing can be suffered to support it but positive law" and [2] "So high an act of dominion must be recognized by the law of the country where it is used."[4] It would logically follow from the first point that if a human being's natural state was freedom, and slavery an unnatural condition imposed by positive law, then when the unnatural condition was removed, the person became not only free but capable of claiming rights like those enjoyed by freeborn people.

Because it was decided before American independence, *Somerset* passed into the common law of all American jurisdictions. Its principles were at first absorbed into the law of status in the slave states. In several prominent early decisions by the supreme courts of Mississippi, Louisiana, and Kentucky, Southern jurists upheld the free status of slaves who had been taken from slave jurisdictions into free states and then returned to slave states, adopting the principle sometimes avowed by earlier English courts of deciding such questions *in favorem libertatis* (in favor of freedom) and, in the Louisiana case, endorsing the extension of this idea embodied in the principle "free for a moment, free forever."[5] Each of these courts explicitly contrasted the "municipal law" (i.e., positive law) that imposed slavery with the constitutionally guaranteed "natural right" to freedom and decided "in favour of liberty."[6]

We cannot know whether this momentum might have developed in the direction of leading slave-state courts to hold that an emancipated slave assumed the status and rights of freeborn people. Any potential in that direction was annihilated by the Missouri crises of 1819 to 1821 and subsequent events of the 1820s that traumatized slave-state political leaders and convinced them that the internal security of all slave societies was mortally imperiled.[7] This mind-set produced ever more draconian statutory and common law that degraded the status and rights of free blacks in order to secure the absolute subjugation of the enslaved population. This reaction led Southern jurists to repudiate *Somerset*, its aspersions on slavery, and its liberating possibilities.

The racial justification for American slavery came to override any doubts about its compatibility with natural law. The Georgia judicial fire-eater Joseph Henry Lumpkin expressed this idea vehemently in *Cleland v. Waters* (1855): "I utterly repudiate the whole current of decisions . . . from Somerset's case down . . . which hold that the bare removal to a free country . . . will give freedom . . . This fungus has been engrafted upon [free-state] Codes by the foul and fell spirit of modern fanaticism."[8] In the leading authority on the subject of the effects of manumission, *Bryan v. Walton* (Ga. 1853), Chief Judge Lumpkin defined the civil status of free blacks:

> Manumission confers no other right but that of freedom from the dominion of the master, and the limited liberty of locomotion; . . . it does not and cannot confer any of the powers, civil or political, incident to citizenship.
>
> The status of the African in Georgia, whether bond or free, is such that he has no civil, social or political rights or capacity, whatever, except such as are bestowed on him by Statute.[9]

Emancipation conveyed no right or power except locomotion. Echoing *State v. Mann* (N.C. 1829)[10] and anticipating the *Dred Scott* case (1857), Lumpkin based his absolute, fatalistic reasoning on race, insisting that blacks could never enjoy civil capacity equal to that of whites.[11] For good measure, he urged the legislature to prohibit manumission. Georgia confirmed Lumpkin's view of status in its 1861 Civil Code: "The free person of color is entitled to no right of citizenship, except such as are [*sic*] specially given by law. His status differs from that of the slave in this: No master having dominion over him he is entitled to the free use of his liberty, labor and property, except so far as he is restrained by law. All laws enacted in reference to slaves, and in their nature applicable to free persons of color, shall be construed to include them, unless specially excepted."[12]

The Mississippi Supreme Court endorsed Lumpkin's position in *Mitchell v. Wells* (1859): "'The law . . . confers on [the slave] no rights or privileges except such as are necessary to protect [his] existence. All other rights must be granted specially'" by the legislature. Manumission "requires the act of the state to clothe him with civil and political rights."[13]

Chief Justice Roger B. Taney, in some *Dred Scott* dicta, affirmed the rightslessness principle when he described African Americans "as a subordinate and inferior class of beings, who . . . , whether emancipated or not, . . . had no rights or privileges but such as those who held the power and the Government might choose to grant them."[14] In this view, for which the chief justice of the United States spoke authoritatively, emancipation produced a legally naked individual, stripped of any status or protection of law, almost totally devoid of legally enforceable rights, subject to the absolute and arbitrary control of positive law.

Meanwhile, legal development and public policy in the free states went in a radically different direction. The Northern states too received *Somerset's* principles into their common law, but at first found little occasion to apply them as they adopted gradual or immediate abolition. They did not have to deal with slavery as a domestic legal institution. With few slaves in their jurisdictions, free-state jurists encountered issues relating to emancipation less frequently than their Southern brethren. This differing social environment incubated an antislavery impulse that took activist form in the early republic as agitation against the international slave trade and against kidnapping in the free states. This activism in turn encouraged a proto-egalitarianism recognizing the humanity of blacks and leading to a concern for their rights.[15]

The issue of blacks' rights began to come to the fore as Northern states commenced adopting personal liberty laws in the 1820s that guaranteed some minimal rights of procedural due process to individuals seized by slave catchers claiming them to be slaves.[16] Pennsylvania adopted the bellwether personal liberty act in 1826, leading to the momentous decision in *Prigg v. Pennsylvania* (1842) invalidating the act but opening up *Somerset* conflicts-of-laws issues by dicta stating that the Northern states did not have to provide facilities or personnel to assist in slave hunting.[17] It was but a short step from insisting on rights of allegedly enslaved Southern blacks to providing protection for the rights of free blacks. "Providing protection for rights" is misleading, though; it was more a matter of *not denying* rights, because of the prevailing Northern assumption that all free individuals, irrespective of race, possessed a given minima of rights qua human beings.

At the same time, and somewhat inconsistently with this trend, some of the free states adopted various forms of discriminatory legislation denying blacks equality within their jurisdictions, such as prohibiting their service in militias, denying them the vote, prohibiting interracial marriage, and even going so far as to forbid their entry into the state. Civil rights in the North for blacks were always subject to discriminatory diminution, Indiana and New Jersey being the worst offenders in this respect. Full legal equality existed nowhere in the North.

Such statutes have misled some scholars[18] into overstating the scope and extent of Northern discrimination. But as Paul Finkelman has shown,[19] Northern resentment at the heavy-handed intrusion of the Fugitive Slave acts and slave catching, combined with an underdeveloped sense of racial justice, produced a social climate in which people of the free states could at least partially dissociate racial preconceptions from their thinking about fundamental liberties, citizenship, and civil rights. Further, the enactments imposing racial discrimination confirmed *Somerset's* point that positive law was necessary to degrade an individual below general social norms.

In such a climate, a person formerly enslaved, and increasingly even self-liberated fugitives, could claim an undefined but significant range of rights as a human being, far beyond the mere locomotion conceded by slave-state jurists. These would include, for example, the right to habeas corpus or other personal-liberty writs (such as the antique writ of *de homine replegiando*), the right to jury trial, and the right to be tried by the same procedures as used in the trials of whites. These fell short of full equality, to be sure, but all Northern legal regimes, even the most discriminatory, were more benign than the slave states' and accorded African Americans varying degrees of civic status. Northern societies may be best described as regimes of "differential equality."

Thus a rudimentary sense of justice created a different legal status for blacks in the free states, as compared with the slave states. When fired in the crucible of war and social revolution, this impulse eventually produced the postbellum Northern attitude that when the positive law of slavery fell away, the former slave was left with a broad panoply of basic civil rights. In the Northern view, emancipation came to mean that a legal disability, and an unnatural one at that, had been removed, leaving the individual as he would have been had the disability never existed—that is, a free person comparable in status to native whites. This default civil status had been defined by Justice Bushrod Washington in *Corfield v. Coryell* (1823); it consisted of "those privileges and immunities which are, in their nature, fundamental; which belong, of right, to the citizens of all free governments; [including] protection by the government; the enjoyment of life and liberty, with the right to acquire and possess property of every kind, and to pursue and obtain happiness and safety; subject nevertheless to such restraints as the government may justly prescribe for the general good of the whole."

Washington then enumerated by way of illustration what such rights might include: the right to go into any state and to reside there; the right to the writ of habeas corpus; the ability to litigate, to own real and personal property; equality of taxation; and, finally, the right to vote.[20] A half century later, the Supreme Court declared Washington's description of the privileges and immunities of national citizenship to be canonical to state citizenship.[21]

THE BLACK CODES, 1865–1866: SLAVERY REVIVED

After states ratified the Thirteenth Amendment in December 1865, slavery was abolished throughout the United States. Each section expected that its understanding of postemancipation status would prevail, scarcely aware that the other section entertained a radically different expectation. The ensuing generation of constitutional development displayed the following pattern: At first (1865–1866), the Southern view prevailed, imposing a legal regime little removed from the assumptions of *Bryan v. Walton*. An outraged Congress overthrew this legal order and imposed a radically different one based on premises of equality. This prevailed only partially, and only until around 1880, when white Southerners established the two-tiered regime of brutal inequality rationalized by a gauzy pretense of nominal equality.

In the immediate aftermath of the Civil War, Southern whites embodied their assumptions about emancipation's limited effects in the Black Codes that were enacted in ten of the former slave states.[22] These reimposed both of the traditional incidents of slavery, labor coercion and race control, on the people who were now nominally freed by the Thirteenth Amendment. As a Louisiana Republican noted at the time, the point of the Black Codes was "getting things back as near to slavery as possible."[23] The earliest measures adopted were apprenticeship laws, modeled on antebellum laws controlling the children of free blacks, which took young people from the custody of their parents and forced them to work for some employer. In the optimistic first flush of early Reconstruction, Chief Justice Salmon P. Chase, sitting as a circuit judge, held such a Black Code provision unconstitutional as a de facto reimposition of slavery.[24] But this had little impact on lower-court practices of binding out black children to white employers.

The labor laws most obnoxious to Northerners were the vagrancy statutes. The most draconian was Mississippi's 1865 act, which defined vagrants as "persons who neglect their calling or employment, misspend what they earn" plus "all other idle and disorderly persons."[25] It also included whites and blacks who intermingled "on terms of equality." Alabama defined vagrants as "a stubborn or refractory servant; a laborer who loiters away his time" and as "any runaway, stubborn servant or child; . . . and any person, who, depending on his labor, habitually neglects his employment."[26] The offense of vagrancy was punishable by a $100 fine in Mississippi, and someone unable to pay it (i.e., all blacks) could be hired out at auction to anyone who would pay the fine. The penalty of hiring out was not limited to vagrancy; it attached to most petty offenses. The other eight jurisdictions did not go so far as Mississippi and Alabama, but most enacted some sort of vagrancy/hiring-out law.

In addition to using vagrancy and apprenticeship laws, states controlled black labor by requiring blacks to provide written evidence of employment, by authorizing an involuntary return to a job that the black employee had left ("deserted" was the statutory term; the employees were "runaways") where there was a labor contract, by prohibiting other employers from "enticing" a black worker from his current employment, by banning the sale of farm produce by blacks, by banning blacks from leasing rural land, and by prohibiting them from working at skilled trades. The labor contract, potentially an empowering opportunity, instead enmeshed African American workers in a snare that limited their freedom to seek and do work. Finally, though not as part of the Black Codes themselves, the states began creating crop-lien farming systems.[27]

The Black Codes' labor-coercion elements stunted labor and entrepreneurial freedom, while the race-control provisions prescribed demeaning and irksome restraints on everyday behavior.[28] Most of them were reenacted from antebellum statutory controls on free blacks, though some came from the slave codes as well. The states banned interracial marriage and punished rape of a white woman by black man with death. African Americans were prohibited from owning firearms and lesser weapons such as bowie knives and dirks. The criminal law specified capital punishment for crimes such as arson and insurrection and criminalized behavior for blacks not prohibited to whites, such as malicious mischief or insolent gestures. A racial etiquette of deference began to appear in provisions controlling the way that blacks addressed whites ("insulting gestures, language or acts"). Blacks were subject to curfews or required passes to move about and could not congregate. Sale of alcoholic beverages to blacks was prohibited. Special criminal punishments were prescribed for blacks, including whipping (that universal symbol of slavery), the pillory, the treadmill, the chain gang, and hiring out. Blacks were excluded from juries, office holding, and voting. Some states prohibited immigration by blacks.

Three states enacted early Jim Crow statutes requiring separate accommodations for blacks in transportation. Municipal ordinances restricted blacks from owning or renting real property. Blacks were forbidden to reside in specified locations and were required to provide proof of residence on demand. Finally, lest something be overlooked, Mississippi provided that all extant laws concerning slaves and free blacks "are hereby reenacted, and declared to be in full force and effect," thereby salvaging much of the old slave code as a special law for the freedpeople.[29]

The Black Codes had their positive features as well. In conformity with antebellum Southern juristic assumptions, the Southern state legislatures conferred and defined civil status by positive law. Thus, with variations from state to state, the former slave states conferred on blacks the right to buy, sell, own, use, and bequeath property; to enter into binding contracts to establish legally recognized family relationships, including marriage and parentage; and juridical capacity, which included the right to sue in state courts and to appear as a witness, though this latter was usually limited to testifying against or about other blacks. In this way, positive law conferred on the freedpeople the rudiments of citizenship and civil status as members of the polity. But the very act of granting these capacities affirmed that the freedpeople could have only the status and rights that were given by statute. They could claim no inherent natural civil status as a member of society as of right, by virtue of their birth or presence in the society. In this sense, *Dred Scott* remained good law.

RECONSTRUCTION, 1867–1876: EQUALITY UNDER LAW

The *Chicago Tribune* bespoke Northern reaction to the Black Codes when it editorialized: "We tell the white men of Mississippi that the white men of the North will convert the State of Mississippi into a frogpond before they will allow such laws to disgrace one foot of soil in which the bones of our soldiers sleep and over which the flag of freedom waves."[30] Implementing this sentiment, the free states, acting through Congress, immediately overrode the Black Codes by the Civil Rights Act of 1866,[31] which implemented the Northern assumptions about the consequences of emancipation. Congress relied on its Thirteenth Amendment enforcement power to achieve the substantive aims of abolition. Its first section laid out in lawyerlike detail the free-state understanding of freedom. It comprised the following elements: "all persons born in the United States" were declared to be "citizens of the United States."[32] That citizenship in turn conferred on them "the same right . . . as is enjoyed by white citizens" in three areas: (1) contracts: "to make and enforce contracts"; (2) access to courts as party and witness: "to sue, be parties, and give evidence"; and (3) property: "to inherit, purchase, lease, sell, hold and convey real and personal property."

These three fundamental rights of civil capacity were capped by a fourth general and comprehensive guarantee of equality before the law: entitlement "to the full and equal benefit of all laws and proceedings for the security of person and property, . . . and shall be subject to like punishment, pains and penalties, and to none other." This last provision embodied the abolitionist ideal of equality before the law: the freedpeople were to come under the protection of laws, and were to come under its discipline as well—but now by laws that were administered equally.

The 1866 Civil Rights Act, enacted under Congress's Thirteenth Amendment authority to end the incidents of slavery and involuntary servitude, is the key to understanding the meaning of freedom, equality, and civil status after abolition. Together with its predecessor, the Freedmen's Bureau Act,[33] this statute confirmed the understanding of most Republicans that the Thirteenth

Amendment, in Congressman James A. Garfield's words, did more than confer "the bare privilege of not being chained."[34] It began to flesh out the specific meaning of freedom and its necessarily concomitant right, equality.[35] The acts were based on federal authority derived from section 2 of the Thirteenth Amendment (the Fourteenth not yet having been proposed or ratified). As such, they represent the fullest understanding of that amendment,[36] since ratification of the due process and equal protection clauses in 1868 shifted the terms of debate and the assumptions underlying them.

Whether seen as conservative[37] or as revolutionary,[38] the Civil Rights Act established the Northern, free-state understanding of the meaning of emancipation as the law of the land, to be enforced everywhere but most particularly in the former slave states. This was, to understate the matter, unacceptable to most Southern whites in 1866, and they responded in two ways, first by counterrevolutionary violence, then subversion by subterfuge. The outcome, by the end of the century, was a legal status for African Americans in the Southern states that regressed to the Black Codes of 1865 to 1866, imposing many of the disabilities and inequalities of the slavery era in less extreme form, under the cover of a nominal equality.

Northern Republicans reacted to this Southern counterrevolution with exemplary rationality. They first investigated conditions in the former Confederate states, relying heavily on General (later Senator) Carl Schurz's firsthand written observations gleaned from an extensive tour he took of the region in the late summer of 1865.[39] Schurz's picture of violence and oppression informed the 1866 Report of the Joint Committee on Reconstruction, which confirmed his impressions by extensive testimony from Freedmen's Bureau agents and Southern loyalists attesting to violence directed against blacks, Northerners, and unionists. This evidence of Southern terror enabled all factions of the Republican Party to come together on a program of systematically reconstituting the Southern state governments and reordering political society there.

President Andrew Johnson's vetoes first of the Freedmen's Bureau Bill and then of the Civil Rights bill in 1866 convinced congressional Republicans of all ideological shades that they could not hope to work cooperatively with him in reconstituting Southern legal relationships, so they took matters into their own hands. In 1866 to 1867, in the Joint Committee on Reconstruction, they hammered out the components of a comprehensive plan of Reconstruction, both of the states and of legal relationships within those states. It consisted of the following elements, in the order in which they were enacted:

1. The Civil Rights Act of 1866 (discussed above), enacted over Johnson's veto
2. The Freedmen's Bureau Act of 1866, also enacted over Johnson's veto, which mandated an active role for the federal government in protecting

the freedpeople in the exercise of their newly acquired rights, whatever those might eventually be

3. The Fourteenth Amendment, adopted by Congress and sent out to the states for ratification in 1866, and ratified in 1868

4. The Military Reconstruction Acts, 1867–1868,[40] which created the actual processes for implementing Reconstruction

5. The Enforcement Act of 1870[41] and its successors, which suppressed counterrevolutionary terror throughout the South

By 1867, congressional Republicans had been forced to abandon the prevalent free-state assumption that the end of slavery would automatically elevate the freedpeople to full civil status. In place of that expectation, now dispelled by reality, Northern Republicans adopted a positive-law program spelling out in considerable detail exactly what rights accompanied emancipation. The centerpiece of that effort was the Fourteenth Amendment.[42]

Section 1 of the amendment conferred four distinct but related attributes on the emancipated people. First and foundationally, they were declared to be citizens of the United States and of the state where they reside. Everything else followed from their embodiment in the body politic. Second was a refashioned privileges-and-immunities vision.[43] States could no longer discriminate by law among their citizens in the matter of privileges and immunities. Now all "citizens of the United States" were protected against any state laws that might "abridge" those rights. Third came the due process guarantee, and fourth, of course, was the guarantee of equal protection of the states' laws. The latter two attributes extended to all "persons," not just citizens.

Two other provisions of the Fourteenth Amendment added to the legal construction of a free person. Section 2 embodied the Republicans' assumption that the new black citizens (that is, the adult males among them) ought to be able to vote, though the authors of the amendment stopped short of guaranteeing that as a right. In fact, the provision can be read only as assuring the states the power to deny black voters the ballot if they were willing to incur the penalty of reduced representation in the House. Section 5 of the amendment empowered Congress to enforce all the foregoing, emphasizing, as had section 2 of the Thirteenth Amendment, the primacy of federal power in the matter of enforcing rights. Recognizing the inadequacy of section 2 of the Fourteenth Amendment, Congress returned to the task in 1870, approving the Fifteenth Amendment, which prohibited denial of the ballot on the basis of race. Finally, these rights-enabling provisions were backed up by two series of statutory enforcement measures already noted, the Military Reconstruction acts and the Enforcement acts.

REDEMPTION, 1876–1915: SERVITUDE

Southern whites were now faced with a seeming Northern determination to impose a free-state version of civil status on the freedpeople. By 1874, this forced those opposing a regime of equality to abandon large-scale resistance, though not individual acts of terror. In its stead, they put in place a comprehensive program of legal subterfuge to reinstate the Southern view. In this they were consistently abetted by the U.S. Supreme Court, which rejected the more expansive abolitionist/Republican vision of a rights regime secured by federal power and unwittingly created legal opportunities for malevolent Southern legal ingenuity.

To understand the politics of redemption, it is useful to invert Carl von Clausewitz's best-known dictum: in Reconstruction and its aftermath, politics was the continuation of war by other means. Beginning with the Black Codes, which were themselves a continuation of slavery by other means, Southern Democrats, abetted by their Northern party allies and then enabled by Republican weltschmerz, implemented political programs that drove Republicans from power in most Southern states within a decade.[44] In this political vacuum, Democratic Redeemer regimes ensconced themselves in power so effectively that they were not dislodged for a century—and then only by mass conversion of conservative white southern Democrats into Sunbelt Republicans.

The implementation of a postwar regime of subordinated status for African Americans derived from slave law premises and reflected the values of that system. This took place concurrently in four arenas: the political, social, economic, and extralegal (illegal but condoned violence).[45]

Once in power, the Redeemers inexorably drove blacks from the political arena.[46] At first, they resorted to traditional electoral fraud: ballot-box stuffing and intimidation. But these nonsystematic techniques eventually gave way to the "Mississippi Plan," a package of constitutional amendments and their statutory implementation after the Mississippi constitutional convention of 1890. The Mississippi Plan erected a comprehensive cascade of pretextual voter qualifications (literacy tests, registration requirements, poll tax, good character, residency, grandfather clauses, and so on) to eliminate black voters. It was adopted by South Carolina in 1895, Louisiana in 1898, North Carolina in 1900, Alabama in 1901, Virginia in 1902, Georgia in 1908, Oklahoma in 1910, and piecemeal in the remaining former Confederate states.[47] The failure of the Lodge Federal Elections bill in 1890 confirmed black disfranchisement because there would now be no national impediments to "home rule."[48] By World War I, this produced the virtual elimination of black political power and, with it, the status of blacks as participating citizens and members of the body politic. Senator Walter George, of Georgia, later boasted of how disfranchisement functioned behind the facade of nominal equality: "Why apologize or evade?" he asked. "We have been very careful to obey the letter of the Federal Constitution—but we have been very diligent in violating the spirit of such amendments and such statutes as would have a Negro to believe himself the equal of a white man."[49]

In the social realm, parallel developments ended up, by the turn of the century, in universal and formal status degradation for all black people. After the Civil War, a pattern emerged: exclusion gave way to de facto (and occasional de jure) segregation in the Black Code years (1865–1866), followed by brief and temporary desegregation during Reconstruction, which was then overturned by de jure segregation imposed by law.[50] Prejudice was elevated to legally binding social custom, and then into legislation, reaching into the most insignificant minutiae of social interaction. Whites accomplished this by legislating a comprehensive regime of Jim Crow, based on segregation, disparate treatment, and denial of fundamental civil rights, such as mobility and freedom of contract.

By 1890, the Southern states began to adopt Jim Crow laws and ordinances mandating segregation and subordination in interstate, intrastate, and local transportation (trains, streetcars, interurbans, steamboats, buses, and the waiting rooms serving them), theaters, hotels, restaurants, inns, lunch counters, libraries, hospitals, prisons, cemeteries, restrooms, beaches, swimming pools, and generally all places serving the public, including, most important, schools.[51] These segregation laws were supplemented by statutes prohibiting miscegenation and interracial marriage.

Separate was never equal; "colored" facilities were invariably crowded, inferior, primitive, noisome, unsanitary, or nonexistent. Anyone who lived or traveled in the pre-1960 South carries indelible memories of these ubiquitous marks of status degradation. Their message was unmistakable and was understood by everyone, black and white. "Every one knows that the statute," wrote Justice John M. Harlan in his *Plessy* dissent (referring to Louisiana's recently enacted railroad segregation statute), was meant to declare that "colored citizens are so inferior and degraded that they cannot be allowed to sit in public coaches occupied by white citizens[.] That, as all will admit, is the real meaning of such legislation."[52] But the point is that all did *not* admit it, least of all Harlan's eight colleagues.

The political and social structures of quasi-servile civic status were buttressed by an intricate network of legal-economic barriers to freedom in a market economy, which had the effect of virtually nullifying the Thirteenth Amendment.[53] As the postbellum South slid into widespread sharecropping, tenancy, and crop-lien arrangements,[54] the Southern states revived Black Code provisions designed to compel blacks' labor and to restrict their economic opportunities. The net result of these laws was a condition best described as "servitude," a kind of crypto-slavery, for most African Americans in the South. Men were limited to unskilled agricultural field labor, women to field labor or domestic service. These forms of unfree labor constituted a transitional stage of economic development between the formally unfree system of slavery and the nominally free system of a market economy.[55]

Convict lease systems and prison labor were the most oppressive forms of labor coercion, providing the states with a bounty of unpaid and unfree workers on public works (roads and bridges mostly). They also provided private employers such as railroads, coal mines, lumber companies, and the turpentine plantations along the Florida-Georgia border with cheap labor, whom they all too often literally worked to death. Begun in Georgia in 1868, convict lease and prison labor lasted well into the twentieth century, especially as they mutated into the notorious chain gang.[56] As David Oshinsky explains in his contribution to this collection, the exploitation of convict labor perpetuated slavery through the ruse of criminal sentencing.

Shorter-term unfree black labor was funneled into the Southern economy through the combined operation of vagrancy and criminal-surety statutes. Vagrancy acts had first appeared in the Black Codes and then, when those were overridden politically, in late-Reconstruction legislation enacted after 1890. A 1903 Alabama statute permitted courts to hire out "any person wandering or strolling about in idleness, who is able to work, and has no property to support him; or any person leading an idle, immoral, profligate life, having no property to support him."[57] A 1907 Florida statute defined vagrants as "rogues and vagabonds, idle or dissolute persons," "common night-walkers," "persons who neglect their calling," and the catchall "all able-bodied male persons over eighteen years of age who are without means of support."[58]

In two states by statute,[59] and elsewhere by customary practice, the criminal-surety system permitted a third party (would-be employers) either to bail out or to pay the fines and costs of persons who had been convicted of various misdemeanors, such as chicken stealing and other forms of petty larceny, breach of the peace, disorderly conduct, and, of course, vagrancy. The liberated jail prisoner would then be obligated to work for his benefactor to pay off the "debt." The U.S. Supreme Court held the Alabama statute void under the federal Anti-Peonage Act (1867),[60] but that did not put an end either to the vagrancy laws or to their enforcement as a way of rounding up involuntary black labor.

Contract-enforcement laws converted the dream of civic status through contractual capacity into the nightmare of forced labor. Florida legislation enforced these labor contracts criminally by making "willful disobedience of orders" or "wanton impudence" a misdemeanor. In 1897, South Carolina criminalized refusal to work after receiving an advance on the crop or wages. A federal district court judge held the statute violated the Anti-Peonage Act. He explained that though "the white people of the state . . . [are] better acquainted with the negro, his capacities and limitations" are the best judges of sound social policy, "the one sufficient answer to [that] argument is that the question of human liberty is not one of merely local concern. It rests upon the Constitution of the United States."[61] Coming from a man who was himself a Confederate veteran, such an acknowledgment was remarkable.

Two other programs round out this assemblage of policies designed to deny blacks economic opportunity. Enticement laws prohibited employers from luring workers away from their current job to come to work for the enticer. The emigrant-agent laws penalized labor brokers who tried to hire black workers for employment out of state. Unlike the peonage-inflected cases noted earlier, the constitutionality of emigrant-agent laws was upheld by the U.S. Supreme Court against a commerce-clause challenge.[62]

Throughout all these political, economic, and social developments, the U.S. Supreme Court abetted the Southern program. The process began in the *Slaughterhouse Cases* (1873), where Justice Samuel F. Miller imposed a conservative answer to the question of how far the Reconstruction amendments had revolutionized the antebellum constitutional system. Not much, he concluded. He feared that a broad reading of the amendments would transfer to Congress "the entire domain of civil rights heretofore belonging exclusively to the States," which in turn would "fetter and degrade the State governments by subjecting them to control of Congress" and "radically change" the American constitutional system. "We do not see in these amendments any purpose to destroy the main features of the general system," he concluded.[63] *Slaughterhouse* drained away nearly all the egalitarian potential of the Republican response to the Black Codes.

After 1873, the Court fatally weakened the effectiveness of the 1870 Enforcement Act by imposing a requirement of racial motivation, which was impossible to prove, especially in the climate of the times (*United States v. Reese*, 1873),[64] or of racial animus in prosecutions under the Enforcement acts (*United States v. Cruikshank*, 1875).[65] The justices sustained Jim Crow innovations in railway transportation, striking down state antisegregation statutes on the grounds that they would interfere with interstate commerce in railway traffic, yet upholding a segregation statute despite the obvious impediment to interstate travel.[66] In a trio of companion jury cases decided in 1880,[67] the Court suggested, in dicta, that the states could "make discriminations" on the basis of sex, property ownership, age, and education (but not race) in the selection of jurors. The jury cases perniciously suggested ways for Southern state courts to pretextually exclude blacks, drawing the line only at explicit exclusion on the grounds of race.[68]

In the *Civil Rights Cases* (1883),[69] the Court invented the state-action doctrine to strike down the Civil Rights Act of 1875,[70] limiting federal power under section 5 of the Fourteenth Amendment to acts done under "State authority in the shape of laws, customs, or judicial or executive proceedings." The decision also denied that public segregation was an incident of slavery or involuntary servitude that had abrogated the right to equal liberty under the Thirteenth Amendment. Justice Joseph Bradley expressed impatience with congressional efforts to protect African Americans' rights, insisting that "there must be some stage in the progress of his elevation when he takes the rank of a mere citizen, and ceases to be the special favorite of the laws."

Recognizing that the justices were throwing the door wide open to evasion, and reading implicit assurances from both the political and judicial sectors that the North would not interfere with discriminatory practices after the political bargain known as the Wormley Compromise of 1877, Southern whites went forward unobstructed with their program of racial degradation. Having been stymied in their frontal assault on equality of civic status, they learned to achieve their goals indirectly and gradually.

Once a regime of servility was in place, the Court ratified most of it. In *Plessy v. Ferguson* (1896),[71] the Court gave its blessing to the pretextuality that was at the heart of blacks' new rights-deprived status: segregation laws "do not necessarily imply the inferiority of either race to the other." Only Justice Harlan, writing in dissent, argued that those laws imposed civil limitations on blacks that were analogous to the status of slavery. It resoundingly affirmed the constitutionality of Jim Crow, grounding it in custom and the states' police powers to maintain civil peace: "the established usages, customs, and traditions of the people, and with a view to the promotion of their comfort, and the preservation of the public peace and good order." Race, racism, and the social arrangements produced by them were innate: "In the nature of things, it could not have been intended to abolish distinctions based upon color, or to enforce social, as distinguished from political, equality." Any attempt to meliorate such racism was futile: "Legislation is powerless to eradicate racial instincts, or to abolish distinctions based upon physical differences."

The Court then sustained the political deracination of African Americans that had been achieved by the Mississippi Plan.[72] In *Williams v. Mississippi* (1898),[73] a case challenging the constitutionality of the poll tax (a major element of the Mississippi Plan), Justice Joseph McKenna, for a unanimous Court, openly acknowledged what was going on, quoting the candid admission of the Mississippi Supreme Court that "within the field of permissible action under the limitations imposed by the federal constitution, the [constitutional] convention swept the circle of expedients to obstruct the exercise of the franchise by the negro race . . . Restrained by the federal constitution from discriminating against the negro race [openly], the convention discriminated against its characteristics and the offenses to which its weaker members were prone."[74] McKenna shrugged this off: "But nothing tangible can be deduced from this. If weakness were to be taken advantage of, it was to be done 'within the field of permissible action under the limitations imposed by the federal constitution,' and the means of it were the alleged characteristics of the negro race, not the administration of the law by officers of the state." Then he salvaged the whole process by pretextuality: "Besides, the operation of the constitution and laws is not limited by their language or effects to one race. They reach weak and vicious white men as well as weak and vicious black men."

By 1900, the Court had thrown up formidable barriers to the possibility that blacks might regain the franchise. *Cruikshank* had denied relief for private violence; *Reese* shut off federal remedies for racial exclusion from state elections; *Williams* upheld the Mississippi Plan and pretextuality. In 1903, when black voters sought a federal injunction to compel their registration before the Alabama version of the Mississippi Plan took effect, Justice Oliver Wendell Holmes disappointed them in *Giles v. Harris*,[75] arguing that it would be illogical to compel their registration under a statutory scheme that they alleged was illegal. But more to the point, he held that federal courts had no power, either constitutional or practical, to remedy a statewide wrong, even if perpetrated by the state or its agents. With an air of indifferent resignation, Holmes remitted the black petitioners to Congress and the president, two certain dead ends. *Plessy, Williams*, and *Giles* confirmed the new racial order. Jim Crow and white supremacy reigned.

During the half century following the Civil War, the Thirteenth Amendment was effectively abrogated by white southerners' implacable determination to restore the status quo ante bellum of racial subordination as closely as possible. Nominally, all people in the United States were free; peonage (debt bondage) had been made a federal felony; and "involuntary servitude, except as a punishment for crime whereof the party shall have been duly convicted," had been abolished.[76] But if the form of slavery was defunct, the reality of crypto-slavery endured, bringing misery into the lives of the people who, after 1865, had so joyously embraced freedom as their new birthright. If we understand "freedom" to mean equal participation in the civil and economic lives of the polity, a window had opened to the freedpeople by emancipation, only to be inexorably closed within about fifteen years in most Southern jurisdictions. As insurrectionary violence and Jim Crow stripped most blacks of civic status and economic opportunity, the Thirteenth Amendment seemed to subside into a status of constitutional irrelevance similar to that of the Letters of Marque and Reprisal Clause[77] or the Third Amendment.

At the turn of the twentieth century, Joseph Henry Lumpkin enjoyed a posthumous triumph. A half century after he penned these lines in *Bryan v. Walton* (1853), his words still described the actual civic status of black Americans: "Freedom does not and cannot confer any of the powers, civil or political, incident to citizenship. The status of the African . . . is such that he has no civil, social or political rights or capacity, whatever, except such as are bestowed on him by Statute."[78] The slave-state understanding of the effects of emancipation prevailed. Blacks might now be citizens of state and nation, and might enjoy nominal rights under the Fourteenth Amendment, the most hollow of which was equal protection of the laws. But the reality on the ground for all black people was a netherworld of rightslessness. The regime of status rejected in 1866 was now de facto law in the Southern states, and its malignant influence seeped into the Northern states as well. The abolitionist vision of freedom was an empty formality. Lacking political power by 1910, confined to low-paid menial labor, hemmed about in a thousand ways, petty and major, by the code of segregation and Jim Crow, subject to random violence both legal and extralegal, most black Americans in the years before the Great War were little better off than their grandparents under slavery or their parents under the Black Codes. They were, as Taney had described them in *Dred Scott*, "a subordinate . . . class of beings" who enjoyed only those "rights and privileges [that] those who held the power and the Government might choose to grant them."[78] It would take another fifty years of suffering and struggle to weaken the grip of the antebellum law of status of the slave states.

NOTES

1. I presented an oral version of this chapter at a conference on the *Dred Scott* case at the Law School of Washington University, St. Louis, March 2, 2007.

2. I explore the closely related question of the meaning of equality after emancipation in an article that is a companion to this chapter: Wiecek, "The Emergence of Equality as a Constitutional Value: The First Century," 82 *Chi.-Kent L. Rev.* 233 (2007).

3. Somerset's case has become the focus of growing scholarly interest, as evidenced by an international conference, "Too Pure an Air: Law and the Quest for Freedom, Justice, and Equality," held at the University of Gloucestershire, June 2006. See George Van Cleve, "Somerset's Case and Its Antecedents in Imperial Perspective," 24 *Law & Hist. Rev.* 601 (2006) (reviewing recent literature).

4. *Somerset v. Stewart*, Lofft 1 at 19, 98 Eng. Rpt. 499 at 510 (K.B. 1772).

5. *Harry v. Decker & Hopkins*, 1 Miss. (Walker) 36 (1818); *Lunsford v. Coquillon*, 14 Mart. 465 (La. 1824); *Rankin v. Lydia*, 9 Ky. (2 A.K. Marshall) 467 at 470 (1820).

6. *Harry v. Decker & Hopkins*, 1 Miss. at 43.

7. William M. Wiecek, *The Sources of Antislavery Constitutionalism in America, 1760–1848* (1977), 106–49.

8. 19 Ga. 35, 41–42 (1855).

9. 14 Ga. 185, 198–200 (1853) (italics omitted and order of quotations reversed) (holding that a free black had no capacity to convey property, in this case, slaves).

10. 13 N.C. 168 (1829).

11. *Contra* Thomas R. R. Cobb, *An Inquiry into the Law of Negro Slavery* (1858), who claimed that a manumitted ex-slave has all the rights of a free person under natural law but remains under any disabilities imposed by positive law. He insisted that the degraded status of the former slave in Georgia is the product of legislatively imposed disabilities, not anything innate in the status of slavery.

12. 1861 Georgia Code, §§ 1612–1613.

13. 37 Miss. 235 (1859) at 260 (approvingly quoting Cobb, *Law of Negro Slavery*, § 89).

14. *Dred Scott v. Sandford*, 19 How. (60 U.S.) 393, 404–5 (1857).

15. Matthew Mason, *Slavery and Politics in the Early American Republic* (2006), 130–57.

16. See generally Thomas D. Morris, *Free Men All: The Personal Liberty Laws of the North, 1780–1861* (1974), and Paul Finkelman, *An Imperfect Union: Slavery, Federalism, and Comity* (1980).

17. 16 Pet. (41 U.S.) 608 (1842). See Paul Finkelman, "Story Telling on the Supreme Court: Prigg v. Pennsylvania and Justice Joseph Story's Judicial Nationalism," 1994 *Sup. Ct. Rev.* 83; Finkelman, "Sorting out Prigg v. Pennsylvania," 24 *Rutgers L. J.* 605 (1993); Finkelman, "Prigg v. Pennsylvania and Northern State Courts: Antislavery Use of a Pro-Slavery Decision," *Civil War Hist.* 25 (1979): 5.

18. Leon Litwack, *North of Slavery: The Negro in the Free States, 1790–1860* (1961); Raoul Berger, *Government by Judiciary: The Transformation of the Fourteenth Amendment* (1977).

19. Paul Finkelman, "The Protection of Black Rights in Seward's New York," *Civil War Hist.* 34 (1988): 211; ibid., "Prelude to the Fourteenth Amendment: Black Legal Rights in the Antebellum North," 17 *Rutgers L. J.* 415 (1986). See also Robert J. Cottrol, "The Thirteenth Amendment and the North's Overlooked Egalitarian Heritage," 11 *Nat'l Black L. J.* 198 (1989).

20. *Corfield v. Coryell*, 6 F. Cas. 546, 551–52 (C.C.Pa. 1823) (No. 3230).

21. *Slaughterhouse Cases*, 16 Wall. (83 U.S.) 36, 75–76 (1873).

22. Mississippi, Alabama, Louisiana, and South Carolina in 1865; Florida, Tennessee, Virginia, Georgia, Texas, and North Carolina in 1866. Theodore B. Wilson, *The Black Codes of the South* (1965), 61–80, 96–115. Arkansas, Missouri, Maryland, Delaware, and Kentucky did not adopt comprehensive codes, though some of them enacted fragmentary bits of legislation that were common in the Black Codes of the Deep South. "Codes" is something of a misnomer; the provisions appeared in constitutions, statutes, and ordinances; none were codified in a technical sense.

23. Quoted in Eric Foner, *Reconstruction: America's Unfinished Revolution, 1863–1877* (1988), 199.

24. In re Turner, 24 Fed. Cas. 337 (C.C.N.D.Md. 1867), on which see Harold M. Hyman, *The Reconstruction Justice of Salmon P. Chase: In Re Turner and Texas v. White* (1997).

25. 1865 Mississippi Laws, ch. 73.

26. 1865–66 Alabama Acts, chs. 108, 112.

27. See, e.g., "An Act for the Encouragement of Agriculture," 1867 Mississippi Laws, ch. 465.

28. Leon Litwack has movingly described the actual experiences of the freedpeople under the immediate postwar regime in *Been in the Storm So Long: The Aftermath of Slavery* (1979).

29. 1865 Mississippi Laws, ch. 23.

30. Quoted in Eric McKitrick, *Andrew Johnson and Reconstruction* (1960), 178.

31. Act of 9 April 1866, ch. 31, 14 Stat. 27.

32. No mention was made of state citizenship, an omission soon rectified by section 1 of the Fourteenth Amendment.

33. Act of 16 July 1866, ch. 200, 14 Stat. 173.

34. "Oration Delivered at Ravenna, Ohio, July 4, 1865," in Burke A. Hinsdale, ed., *The Works of James Abram Garfield* (1882), 1:86.

35. On the meaning and egalitarian potential of the Thirteenth Amendment, see Alexander Tsesis, *The Thirteenth Amendment and American Freedom* (2004), esp. 34–58 and *passim*.

36. Michael Vorenberg, *Final Freedom: The Civil War, the Abolition of Slavery, and the Thirteenth Amendment* (2001), esp. 234–39.

37. Michael Les Benedict, *Preserving the Constitution: Essays on Politics and the Constitution in the Reconstruction Era* (2006), 3–22, 214–28.

38. Robert J. Kaczorowski, "Revolutionary Constitutionalism in the Era of the Civil War and Reconstruction," 61 *N.Y.U.L.Rev.* 863 (1986), and Kaczorowski, "To Begin the Nation Anew: Congress, Citizenship, and Civil Rights after the Civil War," *Am. Hist. Rev.* 92 (1987): 45.

39. Carl Schurz, *Report on the Condition of the South* (1867, repr. 1969).

40. Act of 2 March 1867, ch. 152, 14 Stat. 428; Act of 23 March 1867, ch. 6, 15 Stat. 2; Act of 19 July 1867, ch. 30, 15 Stat. 14; Act of 11 March 1868, ch. 25, 15 Stat. 41.

41. Act of 31 May 1870, ch. 114, 16 Stat. 140.

42. On the evolution of rights guarantees in the drafting of the amendment, see Garrett Epps, *Democracy Reborn: The Fourteenth Amendment and the Fight for Equal Rights in Post–Civil War America* (2006).

43. The original being the *interstate* privileges-and-immunities provision of Article IV.

44. The best background study of redemption remains C. Vann Woodward's classic, *The Origins of the New South* (1951).

45. On the experiences of African Americans during redemption, see Leon F. Litwack, *Trouble in Mind: Black Southerners in the Age of Jim Crow* (1999); see, on segregation laws after 1890, 215–79; Edward L. Ayers, *The Promise of the New South: Life after Reconstruction* (1992), 132–59.

46. J. Morgan Kousser, *The Shaping of Southern Politics: Suffrage Restriction and the Establishment of the One-Party South, 1880–1910* (1974).

47. Woodward, *Origins of the New South*, 321.

48. Charles W. Calhoun, *Conceiving a New Republic: The Republican Party and the Southern Question, 1869–1900* (2006), 226–63.

49. Quoted in George B. Tindall, *The Emergence of the New South, 1913–1945* (1967), 160–61.

50. Howard N. Rabinowitz, *Race Relations in the Urban South, 1865–1890* (1978), 165–72.

51. Pauli Murray provides a survey of the statutory foundations of racial segregation in the mid-twentieth century in *States' Laws on Race and Color* (1951, repr. 1997), as does Charles S. Johnson in *Patterns of Negro Segregation* (1943); see 156–72 of the latter on their historical evolution.

52. *Plessy v. Ferguson*, 163 U.S. 537, 560 (1896). In this dissent, Harlan was relying on the Thirteenth and Fourteenth amendments.

53. See generally Daniel A. Novak, *The Wheel of Servitude: Black Forced Labor after Slavery* (1978); William Cohen, "Negro Involuntary Servitude in the South, 1865–1940: A Preliminary Analysis," *Journal of Southern History* 42 (1976): 31; William Cohen, *At Freedom's Edge: Black Mobility and the Southern Quest for Racial Control, 1861–1915* (1991).

54. Carefully analyzed by Harold D. Woodman, "Postwar Southern Agriculture and the Law," *Agricultural History* 53 (1979): 319.

55. Barbara J. Fields, *Slavery and Freedom on the Middle Ground: Maryland during the Nineteenth Century* (1985), 157–66, 194–206.

56. See generally David M. Oshinsky, *"Worse Than Slavery": Parchman Farm and the Ordeal of Jim Crow Justice* (1996) ; Alex Lichtenstein, *Twice the Work of Free Labor: The Political Economy of Free Labor in the New South* (1996); Matthew J. Mancini, "Race, Economics, and the Abandonment of Convict Leasing," *Journal of Negro History* 63 (1978): 339.

57. 1903 Alabama Laws, ch. 229.

58. 1907 Florida Acts, ch. 5720.

59. 1874 Georgia Acts, no. 25; 1907 Alabama Code, §§ 6846 and 6847.

60. Act of 2 March 1867, ch. 187, 14 Stat. 546. *United States v. Reynolds*, 235 U.S. 133 (1914). The Peonage Act was adopted under Congress's Thirteenth Amendment authority. On the Court's surprising role in peonage suppression, see Alexander M. Bickel and Benno C. Schmidt, Jr., *The Judiciary and Responsible Government, 1910–*

1921 (1984) (vol. 9 of *The Oliver Wendell Holmes Devise History of the Supreme Court of the United States*), 820–906.

61. Ex parte Drayton, 153 F. 986, 996 (D.S.C. 1907).

62. *Williams v. Fears*, 179 U.S. 270 (1900).

63. 83 U.S. at 77–78, 82 (1873).

64. *United States v. Reese*, 92 U.S. 214, 217 (1875) ("The Fifteenth Amendment does not confer the right of suffrage upon any one.").

65. *United States v. Cruikshank*, 92 U.S. 542 (1875).

66. Respectively: *Hall v. DeCuir*, 95 U.S. 485 (1877); *Louisville, New Orleans, and Texas Railway v. Mississippi*, 133 U.S. 587 (1890).

67. *Strauder v. West Virginia*, 100 U.S. 303, 307 (1880) (quote); Ex parte Virginia, 100 U.S. 339 (1880); *Virginia v. Rives*, 100 U.S. 313 (1880).

68. For realizations of this possibility, see *Smith v. Mississippi*, 162 U.S. 592 (1896); *Murray v. Louisiana*, 163 U.S. 101 (1896).

69. 109 U.S. 3, 17, 25 (1883). See also *United States v. Harris*, 106 U.S. 629 (1883).

70. Act of 1 March 1875, ch. 114, 18 Stat. 235.

71. 163 U.S. 537, 544, 550–51 (1896).

72. Kousser, *Shaping of Southern Politics*.

73. 170 U.S. 213, 222 (1898).

74. *Ratliff v. Beale*, 74 Miss. 247, 20 So. 865 at 868 (1896).

75. 189 U.S. 475, 489 (1903).

76. The sinister potential of that regrettable exception has been realized by the widespread practice of felon disfranchisement, permitted because of the phrase in section 2 of the Fourteenth Amendment prohibiting disfranchisement "except for participation in rebellion, *or other crime*" (italics added). See *Richardson v. Ramirez*, 418 U.S. 24, 54 (1974), where Justice Rehnquist read the exceptions as "an affirmative sanction" for a practice that has diminished the civic status of countless African Americans.

77. U.S. Const. art. I, § 8, cl. 11.

78. 14 Ga. at 198.

79. *Dred Scott v. Sandford*, 19 How at 405–6 (1857).

6. Convict Labor in the Post–Civil War South

INVOLUNTARY SERVITUDE AFTER THE THIRTEENTH AMENDMENT

David M. Oshinsky

In the fall of 1865, the year the Thirteenth Amendment was ratified, Governor Benjamin Humphreys, of Mississippi, addressed the "Negro problem" before a special session of the state legislature. A planter by profession and a general during the war, Humphreys had just been pardoned by President Andrew Johnson, allowing him—and hundreds of other Confederate leaders—to reenter the political arena. His speech about the Negro was a major event, the first of its kind by a Southern governor in the new era known as Reconstruction. "Under the pressure of federal bayonets," Humphreys began, slavery had been abolished. That decision was final. "The Negro is free, whether we like it or not; we must realize that fact, now and forever."

But freedom had its limits, Humphreys warned. It protected the Negro's person and property, but it did not guarantee him political or social equality with whites. Indeed, the "purity and progress" of both races required a strict caste system, with the Negro dutifully accepting his place at the bottom of the pile. His new life after slavery would remain largely unchanged; he would labor at the same tasks, on the same land, with the same whites directing his efforts. Such was the rule of the plantation, said Humphreys, and the "will of God."[1]

In the following weeks, the Mississippi legislature passed a series of laws known as the Black Codes to undermine Radical Reconstruction. The Black

Codes' aim was twofold: to ensure the survival of white supremacy and to maintain a cheap supply of plantation labor despite the Thirteenth Amendment's ban on slavery. While noting that "some of [these codes] may seem rigid and stringent to sickly modern humanitarians," the legislators insisted that they were only protecting the freedman from his many "vices." Others agreed. The Mississippi Black Codes would be copied, sometimes word for word, by legislators in South Carolina, Georgia, Florida, Alabama, Louisiana, and Texas.[2]

Unfortunately, the Thirteenth Amendment had created a gaping hole for white Southerners to exploit. By banning slavery and involuntary servitude, "except as a punishment for crime whereof the party shall have been duly convicted," the amendment left open the door to criminal peonage, a legal device begun by the Black Codes, of 1865, that would ensnare Southern blacks for decades, sending thousands of them to prison and leaving many more in a state of economic dependence eerily similar to the slave conditions they had faced in the years before the Civil War.

The Black Codes listed crimes for the "free Negro" alone: "mischief," "insulting gestures," and the "vending of spirituous or intoxicating liquors." Free blacks were also prohibited from keeping firearms and from cohabiting with whites. (The penalty for intermarriage, the ultimate taboo, was "confinement in the state penitentiary for life.") Equally important were the vagrancy and enticement laws, designed to keep the newly freed slaves from leaving their former masters. The Vagrancy Act (1865) provided that "all free negroes and mulattoes over the age of eighteen" must carry written proof of employment; those who did not "*shall be deemed vagrants*, and on conviction . . . fined a sum not exceeding fifty dollars." The Enticement Act (1865) made it a crime to lure a worker away from his employer by offering inducements of any kind. Its purpose, quite simply, was to restrict the flow (and price) of labor by keeping plantation owners from "stealing each other's Negroes."[3]

These codes were vigorously enforced. If a "vagrant" did not have fifty dollars to pay his fine—a safe bet—he could be hired out to any white man willing to pay it. Of course, a preference was given to the vagrant's former master, who could then "deduct and retain the amount so paid from the wages of such freedman." In one sense, these restrictions sought to return the post–Civil War South to the racial certitudes of antebellum life as if the Thirteenth Amendment had not been ratified. But they also reflected how much had changed. Following emancipation, black crime and punishment moved well beyond the plantation. Thousands of former slaves were now being arrested, tried, and convicted for acts that had once been dealt with by the master alone. Black crime was no longer a private matter but rather an offense against the state. Law enforcement meant keeping the Negro in line.

Stealing was the most common offense. From across the South came reports of ex-slaves looting "pigs, turkeys, chickens, melons, and roasting ears" from white families who seemed perilously close to poverty themselves. "The negroes are so destitute they will keep stealing," wrote a Mississippi woman in 1866. "They think, to the last of them, that they have a right to what belongs to their former owners." White reaction was intense. Some state legislatures considered proposals to employ the gallows for serious property crimes and the whipping post for lesser ones. In Alabama, vigilantes punished hundreds of "thieving niggers" on their own. Some were flogged; others were lynched. In Mississippi, land owners were urged to gun down suspected black felons and "let the buzzards hold an inquest over [their] remains."[4]

It didn't take long for the new outlines of crime and punishment to emerge. The fear of white lawlessness—a matter of serious concern in antebellum times— was pushed to the side. "Wherever larceny, burglary, arson, and similar crimes are committed in the South," said a Charleston attorney, "no one is suspected [anymore] save Negroes." And almost no one save Negroes went to trial. When a local newspaper described a typical day at the Richmond police court in the late 1860s, it could have been writing about the one in Vicksburg or Atlanta, in Galveston or New Orleans. "Africa was on the rampage," it reported in the distinctive prose of that time and place. "The dock was thronged with forlorn, degraded, and sulky eboshins," including "a negro city buck," "a kinky-headed culprit," "a flat-nosed, bullet-headed, asp-eyed little darkey," "a decrepit old negress," and a "lady of color" charged with "stealing three pounds of butter from John (not Jim) Crow."[5]

As convictions mounted, Southern prisons turned black. "In slavery times," a freedman recalled, "jails was all built for the white folks. There warn't never nobody of my color put in none of them. No time . . . to stay in jail; they had to work; when they done wrong they was whipped and let go." Now this pattern was reversed. By 1866, as Congress debated the Civil Rights Act and the proposed Fourteenth Amendment, the Natchez city jail held sixty-seven black prisoners and just eleven whites. In Grenada, to the north, there were seventeen blacks and one white. In Columbus, to the east, there were fifty-three blacks and no whites. Almost overnight, the Southern jailhouse had become a "Negro preserve."[6]

Across the Reconstruction South, emancipation placed strains upon a modest prison system already gutted by war. Most of the facilities lay in ruins. There was no money to rebuild them or to house the flood of black defendants now pouring through the courts. In Mississippi—a state with the highest percentage of ex-slaves—these problems were especially severe. The penitentiary in Jackson had been torched by General Sherman's Union troops, and the county jails were crumbling from neglect. "Emancipation will require a system of prisons," a state official observed. "The one in Jackson was nearly full *when the courts had little to do with the negroes.* How will it be now?"[7]

The question was answered by a Mississippi businessman named Edmund Richardson, who had parlayed a small inheritance into an antebellum empire of cotton plantations and general stores. When the Civil War began, his assets totaled $1 million; when it ended, most everything was gone. In 1868, Richardson struck a bargain with federal authorities in his state. He needed cheap labor to clear some land he had bought in the Mississippi Delta; the authorities controlled a decrepit prison system overflowing with ex-slaves. The result was a contract placing hundreds of convicts under Richardson's supervision. He promised to guard them, feed them, clothe them, and treat them well. The authorities agreed to pay him $18,000 a year for their maintenance, plus the cost of transportation to and from his primitive Delta camps. Richardson got to keep all the profits he derived from the labor of these men. The era of convict leasing had begun.[8]

What started as a stopgap measure to control an exploding postwar prison population would grow into one of the South's most distinctive and deplorable institutions, pitting rich against poor, white against black, and ex-master against former slave. For many, the freedom achieved through the Thirteenth Amendment became a mere illusion. Until recently, the subject of convict leasing has received little scholarly attention. Much has been written about Southern honor and violence, about what went on in Southern courtrooms, and what went into the making of Southern law. Far less is known about the incarceration of Southern convicts—who they were, what they endured, and how their lives and labor connect to broader issues of economic development, punishment for profit, and racial control.

Thankfully, this is no longer the case. Historians have begun to examine the ways in which convict leasing provided economic elites with the tools to modernize the Southern economy while also keeping the "criminal" black element in line. It's a complicated picture. The latest studies show convict leasing to have been less a coherent regional system than a grab bag of individual practices, distinctly Southern yet tailored to the needs of specific industries in the different states. Indeed, what began for similar reasons—a shortage of prisons, a fear of exploding "black crime," a need for pliable bodies to do the dirtiest work with the least resistance, a belief that African Americans could not be made to labor without coercion—would remained a scattered system, effective and profitable in some places, less so in others.[9]

In theory, at least, the benefits of convict labor to a private employer were readily apparent. Despised, powerless, and expendable, a prisoner could be made to do any job, at any pace, in any location. Why? "Because he is a *convict*," a Southern railroad official explained, "and if he dies it is a small loss, and we can make him work there, while we cannot get free men to do the same kind of labor for, say, six times as much as the convict costs."[10]

Convicts' lives were always in peril. A year or two on the Western North Carolina Railroad was akin to a death sentence: convicts were regularly blown apart in tunnel explosions, buried in mountain landslides, and swept away in springtime floods. At a prison camp of the Greenville and Augusta Railroad, convicts were devoured faster than the South Carolina authorities could supply them. Between 1877 and 1879, the railroad "lost" 128 of their 285 prisoners to gunshots, accidents, and disease (a death rate of 45 percent) and another 39 to escapes. It was even worse in Arkansas, where the graveyards surrounding the convict labor camps were packed with wooden crosses. One Southern employer put it this way: "Before the war we owned the Negroes. If a man had a good nigger, he could afford to take care of him; if he was sick, get a doctor. He might even put gold plugs in his teeth. But these convicts: we don't own 'em. One dies, get another."[11]

Convict labor was widely viewed as cheaper and more reliable than free labor. A study of the convict lease in Texas concludes that the state's sugar industry would have been hard-pressed to survive without it. By the early 1900s, more than half the state's 4,000 prisoners were being leased to outside farms at a monthly rate of twenty-one dollars for a "first-class" field hand. Three-fifths of these convicts were black, though African Americans made up less than one-fifth of the Texas population. The average prisoner was a young, illiterate male Negro serving a first-time offense for burglary. Typically, his trial took place without an attorney, in a matter of minutes, before an all-white jury prone to discard "nigger testimony" as worthless.[12]

In Alabama, the chief engineer of the Tennessee Coal and Iron Company told industrialist Henry Clay Frick that convicts, who constituted about a quarter of his workforce, "mined the cheapest coal ever produced by the company." He wasn't merely boasting. "It is an indisputable fact," said a mining superintendent in Birmingham, that "coal cannot be produced by free labor within 20 cents per ton of what it can be produced by convicts." By 1900, more than one-quarter of all miners in the booming Birmingham district were prisoners, and more than half of all coal miners in the state had learned their trade while in chains.[13]

The size of the convict workforce in Alabama was directly related to the labor needs of the coal operators and the revenue needs of the counties and the state. When demand was high, authorities would comb the streets for thieves and vagrants, arresting hundreds of black men, sentencing them to ninety days in prison (plus court costs), and then delivering them to a "hard labor agent," who would march them to the train. A visitor to Alabama in the 1880s vividly recalled the scene: "In filthy rags, with vile odors and the clanking of shackles . . . , nine penitentiary convicts chained to one chain, and ten more chained to one another, dragged laboriously into the compartment . . . The keeper of the convicts told me he should take them . . . two hundred miles that night . . . They were going to the mines."[14]

Many never returned. When Alabama's infamous Banner Mine blew up in 1911, 128 convicts died in the blast. Next to their names, the local newspapers listed the crimes that had led them to their awful fate: gambling, bootlegging, and vagrancy topped the list. "Several Negroes from this section . . . were caught in the Banner Mine explosion," a rural newspaper reported. "That is a pretty tight penalty to pay for selling booze."[15]

In Florida, private employers were hard-pressed to find workers willing to do "turpentine labor"—a dangerous, physically exhausting job. So convicts filled the void, working long shifts in deep mud and thick underbrush. "We go from can't to can't," said one. "Can't see in the morning to can't see at night." Since Florida had no state prison in this era, its convicts were leased to a single bidder—a Jacksonville businessman named C. H. Barnes—who never actually employed these men. Barnes simply "subleased" them, at twice his cost, to the labor-starved turpentine operators of the north Florida woods. A local journalist described the all-too-common "recruitment process" in his county. Together, he wrote, the sheriff and the big employers "made up a list of some 80 Negroes known to both as good, husky fellows, capable of a fair day's work." Promised five dollars for each one he landed, the sheriff arrested them "on various petty charges—gambling, disorderly conduct, assault, and the like." Most were cornered "at Saturday-night shindies, and hailed to the local justice, who was in [on] the game."[16]

Convict labor had other benefits as well. In Alabama and Tennessee, free miners worked in constant fear of being replaced. They understood the perils of joining a union or going out on strike; they knew that if they walked off their jobs to protest low pay or poor working conditions, they might lose their jobs for good. Convict labor served to intimidate free labor, undermine worker solidarity, and act as a serious drag on wages. In Alabama, it reached the point where authorities felt secure enough to lease convicts to coal companies at rates roughly comparable to the pay scale for free miners.

Throughout the South, convict leasing added millions of dollars in desperately needed revenue. It lowered the tax rate for average citizens and generated money for bridges, schools, and roads. Furthermore, the system served a cultural need by bolstering the walls of white supremacy as the South moved from an era of racial bondage to one of racial caste. In a region where dark skin and forced labor went hand in hand, convict leasing became a functional replacement for slavery, a human bridge between the Old South and the New.

Alabama was the last state to outlaw it, in 1928. But this raises the obvious question: why did a system this profitable not last longer than it did? Previous wisdom has pointed to the growing moral outrage on the part of reformers, church groups, and humanitarians, whose relentless publicity regarding the evils of convict leasing eventually shamed the public into action. But recent scholarship has moved in other directions, noting that convict leasing always presented serious problems for employers and state authorities alike. In Tennessee, for example, free miners rose up in armed revolt against it, triggering one of the bloodiest working-class insurrections in American labor history. Before long, the cost of keeping National Guard troops on duty in the Tennessee coalfields far exceeded the $100,000 per year that mine owners were paying to lease the state's 1,600 prisoners. Stripped of its profit-making magic, the system quickly died out.

Over time, it appears, employers across the South came to see convict labor as less productive than they had originally believed—that the prisoners they leased, mostly first-time offenders, were unskilled, undisciplined, and thoroughly uninterested in their tasks. To compound the problem, state governments increasingly required employers to sign fixed contracts, meaning that the convicts could no longer be returned to the state when economic times were slow. While fully aware of the secondary part played by reformist rhetoric and political squabbling, the latest scholarship sees convict leasing as a system of declining profitability to employers and, eventually, to the states themselves.

Parchman Farm, the state penitentiary of Mississippi, is a sprawling 20,000-acre plantation in the cotton-rich land of the Yazoo-Mississippi Delta. Its legend has come down from different sources: the work chants and field hollers of the convicts who toiled there; the Delta blues of inmates like Eddie "Son" House and Washington "Bukka" White; the memoirs of William Alexander Percy and Hodding Carter; the novels of William Faulkner, Eudora Welty, and, most recently, John Grisham, who seem mesmerized by the mystique of this huge Delta farm. One of Faulkner's characters in *The Mansion*, a young attorney, tells his luckless client: "It's Parchman . . . destination doom . . . You can't escape it." And "Bukka" White sings these words in his "Parchman Farm Blues":

> Oh listen you men,
> I don't mean no harm,
> If you wanna' do good,
> . . . stay off old Parchman Farm.[17]

Parchman Farm is perhaps the closest thing to slavery to have survived the ratification of the Thirteenth Amendment. Its story is one of race, punishment, forced labor, and plantation culture in the darkest corner of the American

South—a story bolstered by the musty prison records and plantation ledgers that map the daily lives of these convicts, as well as the voluminous pardon files that describe every prisoner who applied for early release. In Mississippi, a convict requesting a pardon had to put a petition in his local newspaper, alerting the community of his intentions. Since most convicts were illiterate, their families or supporters would hire a white attorney to compose the petition and get it published. Thus alerted, the community members would respond by writing letters of support or opposition to the governor, who made the final decision. Correspondence would pour in from plantation owners, merchants, ministers, police chiefs, district attorneys, and, of course, the victim (or victims) of the crime. Each pardon file amounted to a social history of the convict, telling of his background, his work habits, his family ties, and his standing in the community.

These pardon files spoke volumes about the forms of racial etiquette and oppression that defined and regulated all aspects of daily life. "Carson Alexander has lived on my place nearly all his life," a planter assured the governor in 1911. "This darkey's reputation is far above average in fact he is a white man's negro." Or, "I have known Lewis ever since he was born . . . He was a faithful slave and since the surrender has been a good and dependable citizen." Or, a collective plea from the "best" white people of a small Delta town for "old-time uncle" Charlie Berry, who "stood so nobly by our own people during the gloom of war, when 'old master' was away on distant battlefields fighting 'neath the grandest battle flag that ever hovered over our land."[18]

Some letters had a practical bent. One planter asked for the return of Ben Jeter, "as I need him to pick cotton." A second requested a "temporary pardon" for John Cook, "an exceptionally good negro," so he could come home to "complete his crop." Other letters reversed the equation by describing the convict as too sick or weak to do the work required of him—what lawyers cynically called "the broken-down Negro approach." Either way, however, the attorney would take care to portray the convict's criminal past in biological terms, as the destiny of a savage, impulsive race. Time and again, a pardon would be requested—and granted—with the explanation that "it was just a normal case where one nigger killed another." In 1911, for example, a lawyer requested a pardon for his client, Prince Berry, on the grounds that Berry posed no danger to the white community since all his previous offenses had been committed against blacks. In the lawyer's chilling words, "Wouldn't it be the wisest course to grant Berry's pardon, turn him out, and take chances on his killing another negro?"[19]

Blacks rarely wrote the governor about their views on a particular clemency case. The gesture was not only futile, it also could be dangerous by pitting the writer against powerful white forces in his town. But cases did arise in which the races differed, and their resolution is instructive. One involved a convict named Charles Collins, who had been sentenced to hang for killing a "colored fiddler" at a "negro frolic" in the Delta. Collins was such a valued field hand that his employer had taken the unusual step of hiring a state senator to write the pardon letter. In it, the senator freely admitted that the black community wanted Collins to hang, viewing him as "wild" and "reckless" and fully deserving of his fate. He added, however: "This is an industrious boy, polite and popular with whites . . . We are asking that you take his good character into consideration and that whites think well of him, that your Excellency will let him have the benefit of merciful clemency." Collins got his pardon.[20]

These are but a few of the artifacts of Mississippi's unique and appalling penal history. No other part of the post–Civil War South would remain more resistant to economic change, more frozen in time. Indeed, with the exception of the short, violent era of Reconstruction, Mississippi would be dominated by the same planter elite that had ruled in the antebellum era, led the charge toward secession, and run the Confederate state government during the Civil War. These, too, were the men who would write the Black Codes of 1865, undermine the fragile Reconstruction efforts in Mississippi, criminalize the newly emancipated black majority, and bring convict leasing to the South.

In 1876, following the fall of the biracial Reconstruction government in Mississippi, the state legislature passed two bills to control "Negro crime." The first was the so-called Pig Law, which redefined "grand larceny" to include the theft of a farm animal or any property valued at ten dollars or more. As expected, arrests shot up dramatically. The number of state convicts rose from 272, in 1874, to 1,072 by 1877. All would be leased to private businesses and plantations, and all would be former slaves or their descendants.[21]

The Pig Law was followed, a few weeks later, by "AN ACT to provide for leasing the . . . convict labor of the state"—a law intended to codify the informal arrangement made with businessman Edmund Richardson several years before. All prisoners, it declared, may "work outside the penitentiary in . . . any private labor or employment." With the gates now officially open, the state leased more than a thousand of its convicts in one fell swoop. They included the likes of Rause Echols, a "colored of Lauderdale County," who was handed a three-year sentence for stealing an "old suit of clothes." And Lewis Luckett, of Canton, Mississippi, "a pure and simple Negro," who received a two-year sentence for the theft of a hog. And Robert Hamber, a "colored of Chickasaw County, who got five years for stealing a horse." And Will Evans, a "flat-nosed Negro" from Washington County, whose "vital facts" were these:

Height: 4 feet, 5 inches
Occupation: Errand Boy
Term: 2 years
Weight: 70 pounds

Crime: Grand Larceny
Habits of Life: Good
Use of Tobacco: Yes
Education: Very Little
Build: Child
Style of Whiskers Worn When Received: None

Will Evans was convicted of stealing some change from the counter of a dry goods store. He was eight years old.[22]

The Leasing Act was designed exclusively for blacks. It cleverly made this distinction by setting aside the old penitentiary in Jackson to house convicts serving a sentence of ten years or more. The intent, said lawmakers, was to keep the most dangerous prisoners behind bars. In truth, however, the real issue was race. Though far fewer in numbers, white convicts in post–Civil War Mississippi received longer sentences than blacks because the courts did not normally punish whites for anything except the most heinous of crimes. The Pig Law rarely applied to them.

Convict leasing amounted to state-run slavery, with Mississippi delivering its human cargo to willing employers for the sum of nine dollars per body per month. In letters to state officials, these employers preferred convicts over Asians ("too fragile"), Irish ("too belligerent"), and local blacks ("too slow"). Indeed, some employers—especially the planters—seemed to forget that consti-tutional abolition had occurred. "The crop [here] is being considerably dam-aged by want of sufficient labor," said one. "I hope you will send additional convicts without a moment's delay." "When you get a moment," said another, "won't you send a slave out to fix my cemetery fence?"[23]

The Mississippi leasing records tell a story of astonishing brutality and ne-glect. On Delta plantations, the convicts ate and slept on bare ground. They were punished for "slow hoeing" (ten lashes), "sorry planting" (five lashes), and "being light with cotton" (five lashes). Many dropped from exhaustion, malaria, pneu-monia, sunstroke, dysentery, gunshot wounds, and "shackle poisoning" (the constant rubbing of chains and leg irons against bare flesh). A doctor sent by the state on a rare plantation visit wrote that the word "unsanitary" didn't begin to express the filthy conditions of the "convict cage": bloodstained dirt floors, over-flowing waste buckets, and vermin-covered walls. In 1882, for example, 126 of 735 black state convicts perished, as opposed to 2 of 83 whites. It is little wonder that George Washington Cable, the noted social reformer, described leasing in Mis-sissippi as "the system at its worst."[24]

Some observers went further, portraying the convict lease as "worse than slavery." The reason, quite simply, was that antebellum slaves represented a large capital investment for the planter. Economic reality, and varying degrees of paternalism, ensured that the slave would be fed, clothed, and cared for, even in old age. Convict leasing was different: the state shifted its responsibility for prisoner care to the lessees, who had no economic incentive to behave humanely. "It is to be supposed that [the lessee] takes convicts for the purpose of making money out of them," wrote a prison doctor, "so naturally the less food and clothing used and the more labor derived from their bodies, the more money in the pocket of the lessee." If a convict died or escaped, the lessee lost nothing. He simply hired a replacement—at nine dollars a month.[25]

In Mississippi and other Southern states, individual counties could lease their convicts as well. This was a major enterprise, involving thousands of freedmen and hundreds of freedwomen convicted of violating a local ordinance and sentenced to a term of one year or less. Historians of debt peonage in the South have focused mainly on the share-cropping system, which is understandable. That is where the most widespread and well-publicized abuses occurred. But the leasing of county convicts in Mississippi provides a sobering example of debt peonage in its rawest early form. In 1884, the system ensnared the likes of Walter Blake, "a crap-shooting little colored boy," who received a $50 fine for gambling. Though sentenced to no jail time, Blake spent a full year on the county chain gang working off his debt. "He is being charged 60 cents per day for board," a local attorney noted, "and at present the fine and accumulated board amounts to approximately $89.20, and it will never be possible for him to serve out his time."[26]

In the Delta, labor agents literally camped at the courthouse door. A look at the record book of contractor David Hearn shows how the system worked. Among the many entries is a freedman named Henry Gale, sentenced to ninety days, a $5 fine, and $9.95 in court costs for being "a tramp." Hearn paid the $14.95 in fines and costs, took control of Henry Gale, and leased him to a local planter for $8 a month. Hearn made close to a $9 profit, the planter got himself a field hand, and Gale served his three-month sentence on a plantation, without ever spending a moment in jail.[27]

Convict leasing ended in Mississippi in 1890, when a new state constitution was written, spurred by a desire to fully disfranchise black voters, who were falsely held responsible for instituting the fraud and violence that had marred previous elections. A newspaper headline put it well: "White Supremacy—The One Idea of the Convention." For many delegates, however, the issue was not simply white supremacy but rather which whites should be supreme. The once-solid Democratic Party in Mississippi, dominated for years by the planter class, was now in crisis. Smaller farmers, feeling squeezed and cheated, were demanding a host of reforms, from debt relief to railroad regulation to the abolition of convict leasing. To their thinking, the forced labor of black prisoners had provided an unfair advantage to the state's planter elite—the people who deserved and needed it least. The reformers won some battles and lost others at this convention. But convict leasing was abolished, with state funds set aside to establish a new penitentiary in the coming years.[28]

The end result—Parchman Farm—was seen as a major penal reform at this time, and in some ways it was. The brainchild of Mississippi governor James K. Vardaman, it certainly improved upon the unspeakable conditions of the convict lease. Known as the "White Chief," Vardaman stood out among the racist demagogues of that era—or *any* era—for his inflammatory rhetoric, his open support of lynching, and his promises to protect white women from the "brutish biological failings" of the "colored race." Freedom had been a disaster for the Negro, Vardaman believed. It had failed to make him more responsible or to teach him self-restraint. "He is a barbarian still," the White Chief thundered, with a "thin veneering of civilization" and an "increased capacity for crime."[29]

Vardaman saw Parchman Farm as a way to resocialize the state's African American population. He was particularly concerned about young black men, who had never experienced the "civilizing influences" of slavery. For Vardaman and his supporters, Parchman would re-create the slave experience, providing discipline to the convicts and profits to the state. Its 20,000 acres, deep in the cotton-rich Delta, were divided into fifteen field camps, positioned at least half a mile apart. There were no walls or fences. The illusion of escape was everywhere, but the reality was something else again—marksmen on horseback, packs of well-trained bloodhounds, mile upon mile of open vista, access to posses filled with earnest volunteers.

The Parchman superintendent, akin to the plantation master, lived in a Victorian mansion on the grounds, attended by a small army of convict servants. State law required him to be "an experienced farmer," not a professional penologist, capable of bringing in a good cotton crop. "His annual report to the legislature is not of salvaged lives," a newspaper remarked. "It is of profit and loss statements, with the accent on profit."[30]

The field camps were segregated by race and sex (although black males constituted more than 90 percent of the prison population). Each was directed by a sergeant, or overseer, who set the work schedule, meted out the discipline, and inspected the crops. The sergeant's job was a lifetime occupation, passed down from father to son. One study described the typical sergeant "short on formal education and grasp of penological principles, but long on [knowledge] of the rural Southern subculture."[31]

Below each sergeant were two assistant sergeants, or "drivers," known as "Cap'n" to the men. One driver worked the convicts in the fields, the other ran the barracks where they lived. The field driver, riding a mule, set the pace for the day. "He is the one who says how fast you can go and how much work you can do and cannot," a Parchman official explained. "The man on the mule is the man who . . . does the driving."[32]

Under the drivers were convicts known as "trusty shooters," who watched over the regular inmates in the fields. On horseback, armed with high-powered rifles, they formed a floating barrier that kept order and prevented escapes. A long line of a hundred inmates picking or hoeing cotton required about six trusty shooters. Chosen for their ability to intimidate—most were serving sentences for murder—they received the sort of incentives that encouraged blind loyalty, and more. By tradition, a trusty shooter who shot or captured a fleeing convict was given a pardon, no questions asked. This was the stuff of legend, but it happened all the time. A look at the prison's "discharge books" shows case after case of one convict winning his freedom at the expense of another convict's life. Thus, trusty shooter Robert Garrison was released "for meritorious service as guard, killing Silas Todd." George Pat was pardoned "for shooting and killing George Thomas trying to escape, both balls entering his head." As the Parchman superintendent wrote Governor Theo Bilbo in 1929:

> A [Negro] in the plow gang #8 broke and ran for freedom today and was shot from a considerable distance by [trusty shooter] Andrew Coleman, #1104. This shot Negro made the statement before being put to sleep on the operating table, that he was running to escape and that he intended to get away . . .
>
> I feel that it is necessary to release this guard immediately to keep up the wonderful morale that now exists all over the institution among our guards.

Andrew Coleman got his pardon.[33]

The convict's day began at 4:30 A.M. Following a breakfast of biscuits, syrup, and coffee, he was marched to the fields. Each man belonged to a work gang with a quota to fill. In the fall, that meant picking 200 pounds of cotton daily as part of the "long line." The pace was set by a caller, chosen from the ranks, with the men working to his chanting tempo. The callers all had nicknames: "Red Worm" (he killed a man over fish bait), "Burndown" (an arsonist), and "Twenty-two" (serving twenty-two years). They sang about day-to-day life at Parchman and the world they left behind. Some verses drew knowing laughter:

> Oh wasn't I lucky when I got my time,
> Babe, I didn't get a hundred, got a ninety-nine.

And shouts of approval:

> Take this hammer
> Take it to the sergeant
> Tell him I'm gone.

And pleas to make the sun move faster:

> Been a great long time since Hannah went down
> Oh, Hannah, go down
> Been a great long time since Hannah went down
> Oh, Hannah go down![34]

The fabled symbol of authority and discipline at Parchman was the thick leather strap known as "Black Annie," which hung from the driver's belt. Whipping had a long history in the South, with racial overtones going back to slavery. By 1900, corporal punishment for convicts had been outlawed in all Northern states except Delaware. But in Mississippi, as in other parts of the South, the whipping of convicts enjoyed strong public support. "The whip makes no appeal to hidden virtue," said the Jackson *Clarion-Ledger*, "but it is a sure and effective means of planting fear . . . in the hearts of criminals. It is retribution, and retribution hurts."[35]

For Parchman officials, whipping needed no fancy defense. It was, they believed, the ideal punishment for the wayward children of former slaves. A well-supervised whipping sent a message to the convict without interfering with his ability to do his job. "You spank a fellow right," claimed one superintendent, "and he'll be able to work on." The average was ten powerful strokes to the naked lower back. Often a caller chanted the cadence:

> One . . . he's a gitten de leather,
> Two . . . he don't know no better,
> Three . . . cry niggah, stick yo' finger in yo' eye
> Four . . . niggah thought he had a knife,
> Five . . . got hit off'n his visitin' wife,
> Six . . . now he'll git time for life
> Seven . . . lay in trusty man!
> Eight . . . wham! Wham! He gotta wu'k tomorra,
> Nine . . . he got chop cotton in de sun
> Ten . . . dat's all, trusty man, you's done.[36]

Parchman perfectly reflected the static culture of Mississippi. Well into the twentieth century, it remained what it had always been, what Governor Vardaman had intended it to be—a vast penal plantation with convicts taking the role of slaves. Blacks streamed through the front gate as illiterate field hands and left the same way. That was their lot in life. As a general rule, Parchman's population rose and fell with the fortunes of the cotton economy. In flush times, when the big plantations needed laborers, Parchman was rarely full. But in hard times, it was jammed to capacity (around 2,500 inmates), partly because the large planters showed less interest in shielding surplus workers from the law. "It is obvious to me," Mississippi governor Mike Connors said in 1936, "that when labor is plentiful in the Delta, the accused is permitted to go to the penitentiary."

What Parchman did do, consistently, was to generate huge profits for the nation's poorest state—putting millions of dollars into the revenue stream while remaining perfectly self-sufficient. Most whites saw it as a model prison, and the newspapers carried endless stories of its successful ways: "Parchman Is a Self-Supporting Institution," "Penitentiary Crops in Excellent Shape," "Prison System Puts Money in State Coffers and Makes Inmates Healthy." Until the 1960s, Parchman remained a stable and successful business enterprise, linked to the fortunes of King Cotton but better able than neighboring plantations to deal with dramatic economic swings. As a labor-intensive operation, Parchman depended far less on the tractors and cotton-picking machines that revolutionized southern agriculture—and spurred the black migration north. Parchman's crop was prized for being hand-picked, which made for a cleaner product. Equally important, a prison official noted, "a cotton-picking inmate is less likely to promote mischief than one who stands around watching a machine do his job."[37]

What changed Parchman, in the end, was the civil rights struggle that engulfed Mississippi in the 1960s. Originally, segregationist leaders like U.S. senator James O. Eastland and Governor Ross Barnett had expected to use the Delta prison as a weapon against the "Northern agitators" who first arrived during the Freedom Rides and vowed to return in larger numbers for Freedom Summer, 1964. One Jackson (Miss.) newspaper even boasted sarcastically of Parchman's Southern charm:

ATTENTION RESTLESS RACE-MIXERS
Whose Hobby is Causing Trouble
FULFILL THE DREAM OF A LIFETIME
HAVE A "VACATION" ON A REAL PLANTATION
Here's All You Do
Buy yourself a Southbound ticket . . . Check in and Sign the guest register, Then spend the next 4 months at our 21,0000-acre Parchman Plantation . . . Meals furnished. Enjoy the wonders of chopping cotton, warm sunshine, plowing mules and tractors, feeding the chickens, slopping the pigs, scrubbing floors, cooking and washing dishes, laundering clothes. Sun lotion, bunion plasters, as well as medical service free. Experience the "abundant" life under Socialism. Parchman prison fully air-cooled by Mother Nature.
    (We cash U.S. Government Welfare Checks.)[38]

In fact, the reverse occurred. The civil rights workers sent to Parchman in the 1960s were hailed as heroes, survivors of the "toughest" prison in the nation's most repressive state. For the first time, moreover, the press beyond Mississippi got a good glimpse of a legendary penal farm that had been carefully hidden from public view. Parchman now became a national issue, part of the larger black struggle for civil rights. Shortly thereafter, several Parchman inmates, aided by northern civil rights attorneys, filed a federal lawsuit (*Gates v. Collier*) alleging that "deplorable conditions and practices" at the Delta penal farm had deprived them of their rights guaranteed under the First, Eighth, Thirteenth, and Fourteenth amendments to the U.S. Constitution.

The federal judge who heard the case, a white Mississippian, went to Parchman to have a look for himself. What he saw—kitchens overrun with rodents, open ditches filled with feces and medical waste, polluted water supplies, evidence of trusties brutalizing inmates who, in turn, brutalized one another—led him to qualify the lawsuit as a class action under federal guidelines, covering all inmates at the prison. The judge issued a series of injunctions, ordering an end to dawn-to-dusk field work, the abolition of corporal punishment, the dismantling of the trusty-shooter system, the appointment of a professional penologist to run the facility, and the hiring of professional guards. "Defendants shall exert every effort to obtain competent civilian personnel," he declared, "making special appeals to the black community for qualified persons."[39]

Parchman remains a distant, isolated place today, a mixture of the present and the past. The convict population is about 70 percent black—twice the percentage of black residents in Mississippi—and the rate of recidivism, a depressing 49 percent, has remained stable for many years. Parchman doesn't grow much cotton anymore, and few inmates work in the fields. The majority of guards and administrators are African American. They come from all over the Yazoo Delta, and few would ever think of living on the prison grounds. Parchman is a job to them, not a way of life.

There's a modern hospital at the prison, a handsome Spiritual Life Center, a fully equipped gymnasium, and a sizable law library, perhaps the most popular spot of all. The prisoners spend much of the day killing time; gang violence is a serious problem, as it is in prisons everywhere. "These are not submissive inmates," a Parchman official observed. "Those days are long gone. A lot of the people we get have no roots. They have no discipline. They are very angry. They resent us more than they fear us, and they need more help than a prison can provide."

About a decade ago, a group of longtime Parchman inmates spoke about the changes they had seen. They were veterans of handpicked cotton and hard labor in the fields. They could recall the beatings and shootings by the trusties, the sound of Black Annie hitting raw flesh, and the raw sewage that ran through their camps. One of them was a plaintiff in *Gates v. Collier*, and all are grateful for the good that it did. Yet these men also insisted that the new Parchman could learn something from the old. What is missing today, said a Parchman veteran of fifty years, is "the feeling that work counted for something," that the farm had a rhythm—"awful bad as it was in most camps, that kept us tired and kept us together and made me feel better inside."

"I'm not looking to go backwards," he said. "I know the troubles at old Parchman better than any man alive. I'm seventy-three years old. But I look around today and see a place that makes me sad."[40]

NOTES

1. William C. Harris, *Presidential Reconstruction in Mississippi* (1967), 104–20; *Mississippi House Journal* (1865), appendix, 44–46.

2. Daniel A. Novak, *The Wheel of Servitude* (1978), 1–8; Vernon L. Wharton, *The Negro in Mississippi* (1947), 80–96; Harris, *Presidential Reconstruction*, 121–53.

3. Wharton, *Negro in Mississippi*, 91–105; Harris, *Presidential Reconstruction*, 141; Eric Foner, *Reconstruction* (1988), 276–80.

4. Michael Wayne, *The Reshaping of Plantation Society* (1983), 144–45; William C. Harris, *The Day of the Carpetbagger* (1979), 27–28; William Sallis, "The Color Line in Mississippi Politics, 1865–1915," (Ph.D. diss., University of Kentucky, 1967), 6; Dwyn Monger, "Lynching in Mississippi" (master's thesis, Mississippi State University, 1961), 50–75; Wharton, *Negro in Mississippi*, 237; Edward Ayers, *Vengeance and Justice* (1984), 176.

5. Alrutheus Taylor, *The Negro in the Reconstruction of Virginia* (1926), 46.

6. "Autobiography of Squire Irvin," in George Rawick, ed., *The American Slave: A Composite Autobiography*, suppl. series 1, vol. 8, *Mississippi Narratives* (1977), part 3:1082; Wharton, *Negro in Mississippi*, 234–36.

7. Lyda Shivers, "A History of the Mississippi Penitentiary" (master's thesis, University of Mississippi, 1930), 26–45; Ayers, *Vengeance and Justice*, 187.

8. David M. Oshinsky, *"Worse Than Slavery"* (1996), 35–37.

9. See, especially, Matthew Mancini, *One Dies, Get Another: Convict Leasing in the American South, 1866–1928* (1996); Alex Lichtenstein, *Twice the Work of Free Labor: The Political Economy of Convict Labor in the New South* (1996); Oshinsky, *"Worse Than Slavery"*; Karin Shapiro, *A New South Rebellion: The Battle Against Convict Labor in the Tennessee Coal Fields* (1998); Douglas Blackmon, *Slavery by Another Name* (2008).

10. Frenise Logan, *The Negro in North Carolina* (1964), 192.

11. Hilda Zimmermann, "Penal Systems and Penal Reforms in the South Since the Civil War" (Ph.D. diss., University of North Carolina, 1947), 129; Alfred Oliphant,

Evolution of the Penal System of South Carolina (1916), 5–9; George Tindall, *South Carolina Negroes* (1952), 267–71; Hilda Zimmermann, "The Convict Lease System in Arkansas," *Arkansas Historical Quarterly*, autumn 1949, 171–88.

12. Donald Walker, *Penology for Profit: A History of the Texas Prison System* (1988).

13. Carl Harris, *Political Power in Birmingham* (1977), 203.

14. George Washington Cable, *The Silent South* (1885), 27–28.

15. Wayne Flint, *Poor but Proud: Alabama's Poor Whites* (1989), 137; Robert Ward and William Rogers, *Convicts, Coal, and the Banner Mine Tragedy* (1987), 55–56.

16. Jerrell Shofner, "Forced Labor in the Florida Forests," *Journal of Forest History* January 1981, 17; Robert Lauriault, "From Can't to Can't: The North Florida Turpentine Camp," *Florida Cosmopolitan Magazine*, March 1907, 488.

17. Oshinsky, *"Worse Than Slavery,"* 1–2.

18. See pardon files of Carson Alexander, Alf Hudson, and Lewis Luckett, RG 27, Governor's Papers, Mississippi Department of Archives and History, Jackson, Miss. (hereafter MDAH).

19. Pardon files of Ben Jeter, John Cook, and Prince Berry, ibid.

20. Pardon file of Charles Collins, ibid.

21. J. H. Jones, "Penitentiary Reform in Mississippi," *Publications of the Mississippi State Historical Society* (1902): 116; Neil R. McMillen, *Dark Journey* (1989), 221; *Mississippi Laws*, 1876, c. 110, sec. 1, 3, pp. 194–95.

22. Pardon files of Rause Echols, Lewis Luckett, Robert Hamber, and Will Evans, RG 27, Governor's Papers, MDAH.

23. "Report of House Investigating Committee," *House Journal*, Mississippi (1888), appendix, 3–4; *Raymond Gazette* (Miss.), May 8, 1884; Shivers, "History of the Mississippi Penitentiary," 48; Charles Scott to Warden M. L. Jenkins, May 4, 1896; J. H. O'Donnell to Jenkins, both in RG 49, no. 3, file 1896, MDAH.

24. R. D. Farish to Board of Control, May 23, 1896, RG 27, 110. 228; E. J. Turner to Sec. of State Bd. of Health, October 12, 1896, RG 49, no. 3, file 1896; Cable, *Silent South*, 168–71.

25. Dr. D. A. M'Callum, "Mississippi and Her Convicts," *Proceedings of the Annual Congress of the American Prison Association* (1910): 120–24.

26. Pardon file of Walter Blake, RG 27, no. 214, MDAH.

27. Account Book, Hearn & Jones, 1884, David Hearn Family Papers, box 1, MDAH.

28. Oshinsky, *"Worse Than Slavery,"* 51–53.

29. Governor James K. Vardaman, "To the Officers of the Counties, Cities, Towns, and Villages of Mississippi" (n.d.), MDAH.

30. *New York Post*, January 9, 1957.

31. William McWhorter, "Inmate Society: A Study of Inmate Guards at the Mississippi State Penitentiary" (1981), 11–26 (copy in author's possession).

32. Ibid.

33. Board of [Prison] Trustees Minute Book, 1906–1916, 305, 312, RG 49, vol. 31, MDAH; J. F. Thames, "Remarks on Prison Conditions in Mississippi," *Proceedings of the Annual Congress of the American Prison Association* (1925), 81–86; J. W. Williamson to Governor Theo Bilbo, July 26, 1929, Andrew Coleman Pardon File, RG 27, no. 579, MDAH.

34. Oshinsky, *"Worse Than Slavery,"* 145–47

35. Jackson *Clarion-Ledger,* July 20, 1935.

36. Oshinsky, *"Worse Than Slavery,"* front matter.

37. Ibid., 223–29.

38. Ibid., 233–34.

39. *Nazareth Gates et al. v. John Collier et al.,* no. GC-71-6-K, 349 F. Supp. 881, 1972, 881–905.

40. Interviews with Parchman inmates Horace Carter, Delbert Driscoll, James Lewis, Robert Phillips, and Matthew Winter.

7. The Thirteenth Amendment and a New Deal for Civil Rights

Risa L. Goluboff

Like much of the United States Constitution, the Thirteenth Amendment is what its interpreters make of it. Scholars, lawyers, and the occasional judge have found in the Thirteenth Amendment prohibitions against not only the chattel slavery the amendment most directly targeted but also a whole host of other wrongs: child abuse, forced reproduction, hate crimes, segregation and discrimination of all kinds, and various constraints on the freedom of workers. Unsurprisingly, dominant currents of political thought have influenced interpretations of the amendment at any given moment.[1]

This chapter explores the ways in which political developments affected the understanding of the Thirteenth Amendment during the fifteen years of constitutional and civil rights uncertainty that lasted from the New Deal revolution until the Supreme Court's decision in *Brown v. Board of Education*. During that time, lawyers in the newly created Civil Rights Section (CRS) of the Department of Justice (DOJ) refashioned a *Lochner*-era, contract-based Thirteenth Amendment for the post–New Deal world.

When CRS lawyers began aggressively prosecuting Thirteenth Amendment cases in the late 1930s and 1940s, they inherited a way of thinking about the amendment closely tied to the *Lochner* era. During the early twentieth century, the Department of Justice had prosecuted southern officials and individual employers under the Anti-Peonage Act (1867). A statutory enforcement of the Thirteenth Amendment, that act prohibited peonage, a form of involuntary servitude in which a worker was forced to work out a debt to an employer. In the 1905 case of *Clyatt v. United States* and the 1914 case of *United States v. Reynolds*, the Court upheld the Anti-Peonage Act and indictments under it. Moreover, in the 1911 state criminal case of *Bailey v. Alabama*, the Court invalidated a state contract labor law common in the South. The law presumed a criminal intent to defraud when an employee accepted an advance from an employer but broke his labor contract without repaying his debt to his employer.[2]

The Court's opinions in these cases predictably reflected a *Lochner*-era focus on contractual freedom. The problem in *Bailey*, as the Court saw it, was that the Alabama law functionally required specific performance for the breaking of a labor contract. Although decided under the Anti-Peonage Act and the Thirteenth Amendment, the language and logic of contract law and contract rights pervaded the opinion. "The full intent of the constitutional provision could be defeated with obvious facility if, through the guise of contracts under which advances had been made, debtors could be held to compulsory service . . . The contract exposes the debtor to liability for the loss due to the breach, but not to enforced labor." In these peonage cases, as in many *Lochner*-era cases, the Supreme Court saw itself as intervening sporadically into private relationships to ensure the contractual freedom of the parties.[3]

Even after the *Lochner* framework began to lose its hold on constitutional understandings of individual rights in the late 1930s, the debt element of peonage kept enforcement of the Thirteenth Amendment closely tied to its contract-based interpretation. Although many instances of forced labor during the first half of the century did not involve contracted debt—as where employers maintained immobility through violence or threats of violence—every successful federal involuntary servitude prosecution before 1937 involved contractual indebtedness. All three involuntary servitude cases that reached the Supreme Court during World War II—*Taylor v. Georgia, United States v. Gaskin*, and *Pollock v. Williams*—also conformed to the conventional definition of peonage. All three involved contracted debt. All three arose under the 1867 Anti-Peonage Act.[4]

During World War II, however, lawyers in the CRS began to unshackle the Thirteenth Amendment from the contract-based framework of the *Lochner* era. They began to draw on the New Deal rather than *Lochner* as they conceptualized both the government's role in enforcing the Thirteenth Amendment and the substance of the amendment's prohibitions. As to the first, the lawyers shifted their understanding of the government's role from one in which the government occasionally intervened into private contracts that had gone wrong to one in which the government had an ongoing obligation to protect individuals from rights violations. As to the second, the CRS lawyers drew on two types of New Deal protections to inform the content of the Thirteenth Amendment: its commitment to free labor and its guarantee of a minimum standard of living and working.

The New Deal influenced the CRS lawyers' understanding of the Thirteenth Amendment in the first instance by providing the lawyers with a new model of the role of government in protecting rights. During the *Lochner* era, lawyers and judges had thought about peonage in terms of debt and the policing of contracts. Once the New Deal offered wide-ranging statutory protections to many Americans, the government lawyers began to see an ongoing relationship between individuals and the federal government, with the government offering affirmative protection of rights. They increasingly understood peonage as a "federally-secured right to be free from bondage."[5]

This conceptual transformation was rooted in the New Deal's overall guarantees of security. "Security" in the economic sense was the watchword of the federal government's attack on the Depression of the 1930s. New Deal legislation attempted to provide such economic security (mostly for white men) through unemployment insurance, public works projects, Social Security, relief, the protection of unions, and other economic and social welfare programs. The New Deal thus demonstrated that the exercise of government power, rather than its restraint, might serve to safeguard the vulnerable. Attorney General Francis Biddle made this very point in a lecture he delivered at the end of 1942. He acknowledged that the Founders had been most concerned with a limited government. He argued, however, that after the Industrial Revolution, Americans came to realize that "the powers of unregulated business had to be checked by transferring much of their control from private to public hands."[6]

The Truman administration reinforced this new emphasis on the government's provision of affirmative protections. When President Harry S. Truman created his groundbreaking Committee on Civil Rights in 1946, he declared the end of complacency "with a civil liberties program which emphasizes only the need of protection against the possibility of tyranny by the Government." Modern conditions required the creation of "new concepts of civil rights to safeguard our heritage." The "extension of civil rights today," Truman announced, "means not protection of the people *against* the Government, but protection of the people *by* the Government."[7]

In its final report, Truman's committee argued that increased national authority for protecting civil rights extended the "positive governmental programs designed to solve the nation's changing problems." The report described how the Supreme Court had found in the Constitution a "basis for governmental action at the national level . . . for such policies as the control of prices; regulation of agricultural production; requirement of collective bargaining; social security benefits for millions of people; prohibitions of industrial monopolies," and more. The committee built on those interpretations, concluding that "freedom in a civilized society is always founded on law enforced by government."[8]

Truman and his committee also rejected the notion that the new governmental duty to provide security began and ended with economic security. Invoking FDR's identification of "freedom from fear" as one of the Four Freedoms, the committee's report made clear that fear did not stem from economic hardship and uncertainty alone. It grew as well out of the personal insecurity of living as a racial minority in a society that publicly and privately, systematically and informally, oppressed such minorities. As a result, freedom from fear now required not only the economic safety net the New Deal had provided mostly white workers but also freedom from involuntary servitude, lynching, and police brutality for African Americans.[9]

By the late 1940s and early 1950s, then, the New Deal's catchphrase of "economic security" had mutated in some contexts into the "security of the person" or "the safety and security of the person." The phrase drew on a venerable but long-submerged understanding of civil rights, with common law roots traceable to Blackstone's 1765 *Commentaries* and statutory roots in the 1866 Civil Rights Act and the Freedmen's Bureau Bill of the same year. Eighty years later, the security of the person formed a central component of the report, in 1947, of the President's Committee on Civil Rights. And it was the phrase used to describe the category of harms that included involuntary servitude and peonage, lynching, and police brutality in the first casebook on civil rights, published in 1952.[10]

Drawing on this conception of "the security of the person," and this New Deal approach to civil rights more generally, the CRS lawyers rejected the essence of *Lochner*-era peonage cases as the occasional interference of courts into private contracts. Instead, they focused on a direct, ongoing relationship between the executive branch of the federal government and its citizens. In fact, they saw the Thirteenth Amendment as a particularly apt site for this new conception because, as CRS lawyer Sidney Brodie noted, the victims of peonage were often "defenseless or without capacity to pursue [their] personal remedies," and the government needed to "act on its own initiative."[11]

Once the CRS lawyers based their understanding of the government's role in Thirteenth Amendment cases on a positive conception of rights, their use of the amendment and related statutes changed. They began to use the Thirteenth Amendment beyond the specific, timeworn cases of peonage proper and beyond prosecutions under the Anti-Peonage Act itself. In Circular no. 3591, Attorney General Biddle requested that U.S. attorneys "defer prosecutions under the peonage statute in favor of building the cases around the issues of involuntary servitude and slavery . . . disregarding entirely the element of debt." To accomplish this shift from contract-based peonage to the "federally-secured right to be free from bondage," the CRS lawyers revitalized other statutory weapons from the recent and distant past. The CRS put to use a slave-kidnapping statute from 1866, which prohibited the holding of a person as a slave, as well as the 1932 Lindbergh law, a federal kidnapping law passed after the abduction of Charles Lindbergh's infant son. Most significant, for the first time since the ratification of the Thirteenth Amendment, the Department of Justice used general civil rights laws to prosecute involuntary servitude cases not based on an underlying debt. Once the CRS lawyers read the Thirteenth Amendment as establishing a federal right, a pair of Reconstruction criminal civil rights statutes could provide far broader authority for prosecution than the Anti-Peonage Act alone. Section 51 of the criminal code criminalized all conspiracies to violate rights guaranteed against private interference, and section 52 criminalized all governmental violations of constitutional rights. Because the Thirteenth Amendment lacked a state action requirement, it protected the right to be free from bondage against virtually all comers.[12]

Even before Biddle made it a policy to use these general civil rights statutes, the CRS had begun experimenting with a variety of statutory cocktails suggesting the New Deal demotion of debt and contract. The celebrated prosecution of the notorious William T. Cunningham, in Oglethorpe County, Georgia, offers a prime example. As antipeonage crusader William Henry Huff and others publicized, Cunningham had provided his workers with so little food they frequently went hungry. He threatened to beat them with a pistol if they could not keep his pace. And he hunted his terrified, escaping workers all the way from Georgia to Chicago, where he convinced the police to arrest them. Cunningham's indictment included counts of conspiracy to deprive the farmworkers of the right to be free from slavery and involuntary servitude under section 51 and counts of holding them as slaves under the slave-kidnapping statute, as well as the traditional counts of peonage under the 1867 act.[13]

CRS investigations into the servitude of young black men working in the Florida cane fields illustrate the change even more dramatically. After Biddle's circular, case titles altered from "Peonage" to "Involuntary Servitude," and so did the emphasis of the FBI's questions and the lawyers' analyses of their trial evidence. Before Biddle's circular, questions and memos had focused on the amount and details of the debts the youngsters owed the sugar company. Afterward, the lawyers wrote memos organizing their investigative reports by references to threats, shootings, and beatings, among other things.[14]

Safeguarding the security of Americans against both public and private rights violations was institutionally, doctrinally, and culturally different from enforcing the narrow terms of the Anti-Peonage Act. The New Deal had begun this trend with its promise of economic security. The CRS lawyers broadened it to include African Americans' rights to the "safety and security of the person," prime among which was the right to be free from bondage. This conceptual shift suggested that African Americans as well as whites deserved "security," that that security went beyond economics, and that affirmative federal power could and should be used to protect individuals. When the CRS expanded the "economic security" of the New Deal into the "safety and security" of African Americans, they transformed the Thirteenth Amendment from a bulwark against constitutionally problematic contracts into a positive guarantee of freedom from servitude.

The CRS lawyers drew on the New Deal not only in thinking about the role of government in enforcing the Thirteenth Amendment but also to fill in the very substance of the amendment's protections. Since the debates that accompanied its proposal, advocates of an expansive vision of the Thirteenth Amendment had generally agreed that it was meant not only to end slavery and involuntary servitude but that it should, in the words of Attorney General Biddle, also guarantee "a system of completely free and voluntary labor . . . throughout the United States." What made labor free for the CRS lawyers during and after World War II differed substantially from what had made it free in the free-labor ideology of Reconstruction and in the freedom-of-contract jurisprudence of the *Lochner* era, however. During the Reconstruction era, the term carried connotations of the right to pursue a calling, the dignity of labor, and the autonomy of the individual. It also embraced the opportunity to find jobs, to advance economically, and to receive a just compensation for labor. This ideal provided part of the basis for *Lochner*-era liberty of contract, and it persisted with some force even after the *Lochner* era ended.[15]

The "free and voluntary labor" to which Biddle tied the Thirteenth Amendment drew more directly on the New Deal, however. The essence of free labor became rights to organize, bargain, and strike. "The tendency of modern economic life toward integration and centralized control," an early version of the National Labor Relations Act (NLRA) stated, "has long since destroyed the balance of bargaining power between the individual employer and the individual employee, and has rendered the individual, unorganized worker helpless to exercise actual liberty of contract, to secure a just reward for his services, and to preserve a decent standard of living." In order for the free-labor ideology of the Reconstruction and *Lochner* eras to become a reality in the twentieth-century United States, workers had to have the right to act collectively.[16]

Even as the New Deal took steps to protect these labor rights, it largely forsook black workers' rights by accommodating the racial hierarchies and economic coercion of the southern labor market. The NLRA, the Fair Labor

Standards Act (FLSA), and the Social Security Act (SSA) all exempted from coverage the agricultural and domestic work that most African Americans in the South performed. The National Recovery Administration failed to eliminate regional wage differentials, and its local administrators maintained racial differentials through discriminatory implementation. Locally administered federal relief agencies similarly catered to the southern system by customarily cutting from the rolls workers needed for agricultural work during planting and harvesting seasons. And the Agricultural Adjustment Act even strengthened the economic power of white planters at the expense of white and black tenants and sharecroppers. New Deal legislation thus simultaneously embraced a new, robust definition of free labor and excluded from it a significant portion of American workers. Without addressing these New Deal biases and attacking the southern labor market as a whole, the CRS lawyers realized, free labor would remain an elusive goal.[17]

Drawing on this New Deal conception of free labor, the CRS used the Thirteenth Amendment to broaden the application of New Deal principles beyond the federal protections themselves. CRS lawyers' Thirteenth Amendment practice targeted for constitutional protection precisely those workers the New Deal left unprotected and unions left organized. As the lawyers saw the problem, workers who could not move physically or occupationally to exert market pressure were poor candidates for labor organization. The immobility created by pervasive southern laws—vagrancy, hitchhiking, contract labor, antienticement, and emigrant agent licensing laws—posed a barrier to organization and bargaining. It therefore posed a barrier to the full and effective implementation of New Deal free-labor principles. The ability to protect oneself from coercion by exercising the right to strike and the right to work for minimum wages under minimally acceptable conditions had become the means by which American workers would resist labor exploitation. They were the means by which workers could protect themselves against the kind of involuntary servitude the Thirteenth Amendment prohibited. Contemporary commentator Howard Devon Hamilton recognized this when he included "resistance to organization and movement of agricultural labor" among the obstacles workers faced in violation of "the Thirteenth Amendment's objective of a system of completely free and voluntary labor throughout the United States."[18]

Over the course of World War II, top Justice Department officials increasingly tied the Thirteenth Amendment to such unfettered regional and national mobility. By the time Justice (and former attorney general) Robert Jackson penned the opinion in the 1944 peonage case of *Pollock v. Williams*, Attorney General Biddle had set himself squarely behind using the Thirteenth Amendment to create a unified labor market unimpeded by southern attempts to control the region's black laborers. In *Pollock*, the Court invalidated a contract labor statute similar to the laws the Court had struck down more than thirty years earlier in *Bailey v. Alabama* and less than two years before in *Taylor v. Georgia*. Despite the doctrinal similarities, the Court's language indicated a newly expansive view of unconstitutional involuntary servitude deeply inflected with New Deal conceptions of free labor.[19]

Where the *Bailey* opinion had emphasized the constitutionality of various mechanisms of enforcing contracts, *Pollock* emphasized the relationship between this particular law and the labor market as a whole. Justice Jackson could not fathom the purpose behind a law meant to bind employees to particular employers. Rather, he saw "the right to change employers" as the worker's prime "defense against oppressive hours, pay, working conditions, or treatment." He maintained that when "the master can compel and the laborer cannot escape the obligation to go on, there is no power below to redress and no incentive above to relieve a harsh overlordship or unwholesome conditions of work." Jackson warned that the "resulting depression of working conditions and living standards affects not only the laborer under the system, but every other with whom his labor comes in competition." Laws such as Florida's contract labor statute, Jackson cautioned, not only imposed immobility on particular individuals but they also depressed the labor market as a whole and infringed on the rights of all workers.[20]

Justice Department lawyers took Justice Jackson's observations and ran with them. They saw that many state and local laws were designed to keep the southern labor market impermeable. So long as such laws continued to restrict some laborers in their bargaining power, laborers of all kinds and in all regions of the nation would not be truly free. Echoing Jackson, CRS lawyer Brodie discussed in 1951 the "depressing effect of slave labor upon our society and economic system." He described "the detriment suffered by the public as well as by the individual victim who is forced to work for another against his will [as] serious and substantial." A U.S. attorney from Alabama was even more specific about the relationship between peonage and the labor market. The purpose of using contract labor laws, he explained, was to get individuals "to work for less money than labor could be obtained ordinarily in the open market."[21]

Biddle and the lawyers in the Justice Department thus read *Pollock* and the other wartime cases as "substantially strengthen[ing] the federal guaranty of freedom from involuntary servitude." According to Biddle, *Pollock* placed "the right to freedom from involuntary servitude on so broad a base that the way has been opened to an attack on the 'enticing labor' and 'emigrant agent' statutes, and some of the vagrancy statutes and 'work or fight' orders." The department had learned from experience that such laws had "proved to be in reality indirect means of enforcing involuntary servitude, especially against Negro farm hands and laborers." These laws were the very ones that minimized African American mobility, that made employment recruitment impracticable in the South, and that closed off the channels of information necessary to facilitate widespread migration for work.[22]

As a result, CRS lawyers and U.S. attorneys during and after the war made wholesale, rather than retail, efforts to eliminate peonage by ensuring that justices of the peace, county sheriffs, and local prosecutors knew when they were violating the Thirteenth Amendment. U.S. attorneys lobbied legislatures to repeal contract labor statutes like those the Supreme Court had struck down. They tried to educate law enforcement officials by speaking at events such as annual meetings of the Georgia Peace Officers Association. And they repeatedly wrote local officials about laws the Supreme Court had held unconstitutional. They told the officials to "read [the *Pollock* opinion] in full, so that you will understand the ruling of the Supreme Court."[23]

In its second use of the New Deal to inform the Thirteenth Amendment, then, the CRS not only targeted laws that created a particular employment relationship from which exit was difficult but also the larger legal framework that made it difficult for workers to leave all employment relationships. Drawing on unrealized New Deal aspirations for a free national labor market, Biddle concluded that vindicating the Thirteenth Amendment meant far more than stopping a particular employer from directly coercing a particular employee. It meant protecting truly free labor, even in the South and even, "especially," for southern African Americans. Biddle and his staff thus took the old, abolitionist, free-labor ideology, transformed it from the *Lochner* era for service in the post–New Deal era, and tried to make it constitutionally foundational.

The third influence of the New Deal on the CRS's understanding of the Thirteenth Amendment similarly reflected unfulfilled New Deal aspirations. As the nation put the war behind it, and predictions of a postwar recession largely fell flat, the CRS began to suggest that black agricultural and domestic workers, who had not shared significantly in either the wartime economic boom or the nation's postwar prosperity, might nonetheless find some measure of economic security in the Thirteenth Amendment. More than a decade after the New Deal promised better working conditions and an economic safety net for most Americans, these African American men and women were still denied rights to the most basic economic security. The New Deal's guarantees of economic security in the FLSA, the SSA, and other laws were as racially exclusionary as the NLRA's protections of labor rights. As the CRS turned its attention to the conditions in which these workers lived and worked, its cases suggested that no worker in the United States, not even those excluded by political compromise, could constitutionally endure such extreme economic privation. The lawyers suggested that the Thirteenth Amendment might protect workers unable to take advantage of New Deal economic rights, just as it might protect those un-able to take advantage of New Deal labor rights.

As the CRS lawyers increasingly defined the Thirteenth Amendment in terms of economic coercion in the late 1940s, they drew on changing academic, political, and popular meanings of peonage and involuntary servitude. These meanings stemmed from the social and economic "realities" of involuntary ser-vitude, which the earlier attention to contract had overshadowed. Political sci-entist Howard Devon Hamilton, for example, defined peonage "in every day parlance" as "used loosely to cover almost any variety of forced labor, or simply exploited labor." Moreover, Hamilton extended his discussion of the Thirteenth Amendment from peonage proper to "peonage-like conditions," condemning the latter as those in which "men get sick or die from overwork or bad conditions." He discussed how contract workers were "farm[ed] out" to other employers dur-ing slack periods and how Mexican workers endured "hideous living conditions and . . . low wages." Hamilton was not alone in thinking that peonage encom-passed all these coercions and indignities. Although some lawyers continued to emphasize the importance of forced immobility in making out legal claims, the conditions of the work, the hardship it entailed, and the inadequate pay often suf-ficed to demonstrate "practical peonage" among nonlawyers.[24]

Complaints to the Department of Justice and to organizations like the NAACP reflected these changes in the meaning of involuntary servitude. Male agricultural laborers began to protest their lack of amenities, rather than the vio-lent or contractual means by which they were forced to work. They "wore rags" and slept in "chicken house[s]" or on "old rusty cot[s]."[25] Moreover, a new group of workers began to complain about involuntary servitude in similar terms. Fe-male domestic workers such as Elizabeth Coker, Polly Johnson, and Dora Jones complained about the poor conditions of their working lives, their isolation from American freedom, and their exclusion from its plenty. They emphasized lack of pay, degrading conditions, and work too onerous for their sex. They rarely mentioned forced immobility. In fact, Polly Johnson testified not that she was kept by force but that "she was not allowed to leave [her employer's] prem-ises except when her employer sent her to the store and then she had to return within a given period." Because Johnson could leave her workplace and home unaccompanied, the essence of her servitude was not in the force by which she was held but rather the conditions that ensured that she would indeed "return within a given period." At the heart of such complaints was the sense that these women, as Elizabeth Coker put it, had "never enjoyed any of the privileges of a free person."[26]

Dora Jones's similar complaints led to a watershed case in 1947. Judge Jacob Weinberger decided that the conviction of Elizabeth Ingalls for holding Jones as a slave was novel and important enough to warrant the publication of his opinion denying Ingalls's motion for a new trial. Because the case was prose-cuted under the Slave Kidnapping Act, the trial court emphasized the condi-tions of Jones's life in a way never before discussed in a published opinion. The essence of slavery for the court was the subjection of the will of one individual to that of another. For more than twenty-five years, Jones had been "required to arise at an early hour in the morning and perform practically all of the household labor in connection with the maintenance of the Ingalls household. She was forbidden to leave the household except for the commission of errands and performed drudgery of the most menial and laborious type." All this, he noted, was performed "without compensation, . . . days off[,] . . . or vacation[s]." Jones's "quarters were among the poorest in the several homes occupied by the defendant during this period of years." Her board "was of a substantially lower standard than that common to servants generally."[27]

After detailing additional poor treatment, the court concluded that "the servant, Dora L. Jones, was a person wholly subject to the will of defendant; that she was one who had no freedom of action and whose person and services were wholly under the control of defendant and who was in a state of enforced com-pulsory service to the defendant." The facts of Jones's life spoke for themselves: an individual exercising her free will would simply not have countenanced such treatment. That Jones had opportunities to leave and did not suggested all the more that she was indeed "wholly subject to the will of the defendant" with no "freedom of action" of her own. She was, as the *Los Angeles Times* put it, "a 20th century slave."[28]

The chain of reasoning that led to a conviction in *Ingalls* differed greatly from that which had led to peonage convictions less than a decade earlier. In the intervening period, promising complaints began to include not only physi-cal restraint and imprisonment but also the quality of the victims' lives and the conditions of their work. By 1952, *Ingalls* represented an acute example of the modern slavery and involuntary servitude the Thirteenth Amendment prohib-ited. In discussing the question whether "slavery" and "involuntary servitude" should be considered the same thing, CRS lawyer Sydney Brodie concluded that because *Ingalls* had been such an extreme case, it had not "disposed of the prob-lem." "The sordid facts of the case actually established more than mere unwill-ing labor, service rendered another because of duress, fear, threats or intimida-tion," Brodie wrote. Even someone with "privileges such as going home after work, receiving some remuneration, maintaining a form of private life," privileges that Jones most certainly did not enjoy, might still "clearly be in a condition of involuntary servitude" even if not slavery itself.[29]

Elizabeth Ingalls's sentence also represented this new gloss on the Thir-teenth Amendment. Prior to *Ingalls*, criminal prosecutions of involuntary ser-vitude, like criminal prosecutions generally, primarily aimed to vindicate the government itself. The perpetrator's fine and prison term served as restitution owed for violating the laws of the nation. In a departure from the past, Judge Weinberger required Ingalls to provide restitution to Jones in the amount of $6,000. This was above and beyond Ingalls's suspended prison sentence and a $2,500 fine she had to pay the government. The harm, then, was not only against the government but also against Dora Jones personally. The case had made much of the Ingallses' failure to pay Jones, and the sentence provided her with remuneration for her work.

As *Ingalls* drew headlines, waves of similar complaints hit the DOJ. Whereas in 1946, CRS attorney Leo Meltzer had described Polly Johnson's case as "not the ordinary type of peonage or involuntary servitude situation," by 1948 such cases were legion. The complainants described, almost uniformly, how the victims worked long, hard hours with little or no pay other than paltry room and board and some clothing to wear. The lack of schooling these victims received, and the lack of modern amenities they could access, indicated that such workers lacked freedom in the modern, postwar sense of the word.[30]

The CRS saw some success in other cases like *Ingalls*. Yet the CRS lawyers still sought better enforcement mechanisms for such cases. Though the conditions in which some people lived seemed "shocking," U.S. attorneys and the lawyers in Washington lamented that they were "only a violation of the laws of civilized society and not the laws of the Federal Government." In 1951, both the Senate and the House considered legislation to bolster the legal tools for eliminating involuntary servitude. As part of the House consideration of the bill, CRS chief George Triedman testified before a subcommittee about the need for further changes to the involuntary servitude statutes. Complaints of forced labor conditions kept "coming up and hitting us constantly," Triedman reported. He and his attorneys found themselves "powerless to go forward" with prosecutions under the laws as they then stood. They were "frustrated with a situation where a condition exists like this." Although the CRS had few attorneys and no need "to borrow any more work," it nonetheless pursued wider jurisdiction in involuntary servitude cases. "There are actual cases of happenings that have come across my table as well as members['] of my section and there are no other laws to meet them," Triedman explained. "That is what prompted us, even at this late date, even after 75 years, to come in and see if we can modernize them a bit."[31]

The cases Triedman brought to Congress's attention illustrated how much the CRS's view of the Thirteenth Amendment and involuntary servitude was now informed by the New Deal's economic protections. The classic case of peonage—of the poor black man in the rural South held for debt in either agricultural or rural nonagricultural work (like timber or sugar refining) by violence, threats of violence, and arrest—had given way to a New Deal–based understanding about who was forced to work and how. Of the four prototypical cases

Triedman described to the committee, only two conformed to the traditional image of involuntary servitude: one employer held his worker through violence and another through threats of arrest. The other two both involved female victims, one of whom was a domestic worker. Triedman spent a considerable part of his testimony describing the women's plight and the federal law's inability to help them.[32]

The CRS thus used its Thirteenth Amendment practice to complement the gaps in the New Deal's economic protections. The CRS aimed to protect not just industrial and agricultural workers but all workers. The CRS included domestic workers normally thought to occupy a private sphere immune from governmental intervention. Although Triedman tried to assure his congressional audience that his bill "would effect no radical change in existing law and would not extend the jurisdiction of the Department to any new situation or type of case," his domestic worker example belied those reassurances. Such examples were revolutionary, as they indicated a willingness to use federal law to intrude into relationships of household labor, relationships that Congress had deemed local, private, and off-limits to the federal government.[33]

The content of the Thirteenth Amendment in the CRS's cases thus came once again from the New Deal. The economic coercion that ensured immobility in such cases—evidenced not by violence or force of law but by the individual's apparent inability to save herself from objectionable conditions—had never before received systematic federal attention. But the New Deal's partial promise to provide economic security to the American people had wrought a revolution in expectations about work, working conditions, and free will. Against the backdrop of promised federal protection for minimum wages, maximum hours, collective bargaining, and free movement within the labor market, a person choosing his or her employment would obviously not choose to work very long days under squalid and dehumanizing conditions. The baseline was a low one. As the judge had suggested in *Ingalls*, Dora Jones was properly compared to other domestic workers who were not enslaved, not to some middle-class or even working-class ideal. It was not, however, necessary for the conditions to deteriorate so far that the victims became slaves without any free will at all before the federal government could intervene. Rather, as CRS lawyer Sydney Brodie made clear in 1951, the Thirteenth Amendment could protect even those who (unlike Jones) enjoyed "privileges such as going home after work, receiving some remuneration, [and] maintaining a form of private life."[34]

By the early 1950s, then, much had changed from the *Lochner* era. In slightly different ways, each of the CRS's three expansive interpretations of the Thirteenth Amendment showed how African Americans could benefit from new, New Deal–based conceptions of positive rights. The first interpretation understood New

Deal promises of "security" to encompass the "safety and security of the person," including peonage and involuntary servitude. The second expanded the New Deal's free-labor protections to the South and to the African American agricultural and domestic workers purposefully restricted by state laws and purposefully unprotected by federal ones. And the last expanded New Deal rights to economic security to the same two groups legislatively excluded from such protections.

Each of these expansions of the Thirteenth Amendment's protections built on a different application of the New Deal's concern for workers to African American workers specifically. Where the New Deal had emphasized labor and economic rights and assisted African Americans only partially and incidentally, these novel involuntary servitude prosecutions aimed to bring African Americans within the New Deal rights framework. Following changing trends within the involuntary servitude complaints of African Americans themselves, the CRS lawyers went about expanding the meaning of involuntary servitude— and the accompanying protection of the Thirteenth Amendment—in order to make the Constitution serviceable for African Americans in the post–New Deal era.

The close correspondence between the CRS's Thirteenth Amendment practice and New Deal conceptions of governmental protections of rights becomes even clearer when viewed in contrast not only to the *Lochner*-era, contract-based Thirteenth Amendment paradigm that preceded it but also to the conception of the Thirteenth Amendment in the succeeding era. When the Supreme Court discussed the Thirteenth Amendment at length for the first time in twenty-five years in the 1969 case of *Jones v. Alfred Mayer and Co.*, the amendment was hardly recognizable. In *Jones*, the Court addressed the question of whether a civil rights statute passed pursuant to the Thirteenth Amendment could proscribe private discrimination in housing. According to the Court, the amendment empowered Congress to protect the freedom of African Americans "at the very least . . . to buy whatever a white man can buy, the right to live wherever a white man can live." In concurrence, Justice William O. Douglas offered a long list of the "badges of slavery" he thought Congress could prohibit under the Thirteenth Amendment. These included discrimination in voting and jury service; segregation of courtrooms, schools, transportation, public accommodations, and housing; and bans on interracial marriage. In this description, the prohibitions of the Thirteenth Amendment were essentially the same as those of the Fourteenth Amendment, with one major difference: unlike the Fourteenth Amendment, the Thirteenth had no state-action requirement. Because the Thirteenth Amendment prohibited slavery and involuntary servitude wholesale, the Court reasoned, legislation passed on the basis of the Thirteenth Amendment, like that at issue in *Jones*, could proscribe private as well as public discrimination.[35]

From the perspective of the pre-*Brown* era, the most striking thing about the *Jones* Court's description of the Thirteenth Amendment was not what it included but what it omitted: any mention of labor or economic rights. Although labor questions pervaded the Reconstruction-era history the Court cited to support its view of the amendment, that labor pedigree was detached from the Court's description of how the Thirteenth Amendment operated in 1969. Justice Douglas's long list of racial wrongs did not even mention labor or employment.

Just as the early twentieth-century understanding of the Thirteenth Amendment derived from *Lochner*-based free contract and the midcentury paradigm took its cues from the New Deal, the Court's framing of the Thirteenth Amendment in this way was a product of the times. In the aftermath of *Brown v. Board of Education* in 1954, lawyers, courts, and commentators had generally converged on a civil rights framework characterized by a focus on formal equality and a negative understanding of rights as constraining rather than enabling government action. By 1969, equal protection analysis under the Fourteenth Amendment had become the dominant way of thinking about civil rights: it prevented government actors from segregating or discriminating on the basis of race in a variety of circumstances. As a result, by the time the Court decided *Jones*, it was difficult to envision the Thirteenth Amendment as anything but an equal protection guarantee without a state-action requirement.

The disappearance of the pre-*Brown* understanding of the Thirteenth Amendment in the 1960s highlights a critical difference between the CRS lawyers' relationship to the *Lochner*ian past they had inherited and the Supreme Court's relationship to the New Deal past it had inherited. The lawyers in the 1940s CRS had been deeply attentive to the contours of the Thirteenth Amendment during the *Lochner* era. Though they rejected the limitations of those contours, they understood them, and they used them as a base from which to expand. The justices writing in *Jones*, by contrast, were wholly unaware that the Thirteenth Amendment had had a life as a complement to the New Deal. The disappearance of that earlier understanding of the Thirteenth Amendment was both the result of the ascendance of an equal-protection-based framework for civil rights and the reason the Court felt free to remake the amendment in the image of that new framework.

The very different relationships the CRS lawyers and the *Jones* justices maintained with the constitutional frameworks that had preceded them suggests that such relationships can have a substantial effect on the meaning of the Constitution at any given moment. Lawyers, scholars, and judges take their cues not only from contemporary political thought; they take them as well from their understandings of the past. This is true both for what they remember of the past and for what they do not even know has already been forgotten.

NOTES

1. See William M. Carter, Jr., "Race, Rights, and the Thirteenth Amendment: Defining the Badges and Incidents of Slavery," *U.C. Davis Law Review* 40 (2007): 1311–79 (collecting articles on uses of the Thirteenth Amendment); see also James Gray Pope, "The Thirteenth Amendment versus the Commerce Clause: Labor and the Shaping of American Constitutional Law, 1921–1957," *Columbia Law Review* 102 (2002): 1–122.

2. 197 U.S. 207; 235 U.S. 133; 219 U.S. 219, 241.

3. 219 U.S. at 242. Similarly, the Court treated the criminal surety law it struck down in *United States v. Reynolds* as punishing the violation of the contract between the criminal and the surety for whom he agreed to work in lieu of time served on the state chain gang (235 U.S. 133, 147 [1914]). See generally Aziz Z. Huq, "Peonage and Contractual Liberty," *Columbia Law Review* 101 (2001): 351–91.

4. 315 U.S. 25, 26–30 (1942); 320 U.S. 527, 527–28 (1944); 322 U.S. 4, 5–13.

5. Sydney Brodie, "The Federally-Secured Right to Be Free from Bondage," *Georgetown Law Journal* 40 (1952): 367–98.

6. Francis Biddle, *Democratic Thinking and the War: The William H. White Lectures at the University of Virginia, 1942–1943* (New York, 1944), 19.

7. Harry S. Truman, "Statement on Executive Order 9808 Establishing the President's Committee on Civil Rights," December 5, 1946, quoted in President's Committee on Civil Rights, *To Secure These Rights: The Report of the President's Committee on Civil Rights* (Washington, D.C., 1947), vii; Harry S. Truman, "Address before the National Association for the Advancement of Colored People" (Lincoln Memorial, Washington, D.C., June 29, 1947), in *Public Papers of the Presidents of the United States: Harry S. Truman, 1947* (Washington, D.C., 1963), 311–13, 311.

8. *To Secure These Rights*, 106, 103.

9. Truman, "Statement on Executive Order 9808," vii; see also Frank Coleman, "Freedom from Fear on the Home Front," *Iowa Law Review* 29 (1944): 415–29.

10. William Blackstone, *Commentaries on the Laws of England* (Oxford, 1765), 1:125; Civil Rights Act of 1866, ch. 31, § 1, 14 Stat. 27. Freedmen's Bureau Bill, ch. 200, § 14, 14 Stat. 173, 176 (1866). See also *To Secure These Rights*, 20; Thomas I. Emerson and David Haber, *Political and Civil Rights in the United States: A Collection of Legal and Related Materials* (Buffalo, 1952), 1. Language about the "security of the person" also occasionally resurfaced in some of the signal civil rights dissents of the late-nineteenth century, such as the *Slaughterhouse Cases* and *Plessy v. Ferguson* (83 U.S. 36, 115–19 [1873] [Bradley, J., dissenting]; 163 U.S. 537, 555–56, 560 [1896] [Harlan, J., dissenting]).

11. Brodie, "Federally-Secured Right to Be Free from Bondage," 367, 376.

12. Department of Justice Circular no. 3591, December 12, 1941, 1–3, in *Justice Department Civil Rights Policies prior to 1960: Crucial Documents from the Files of*

Arthur Brann Caldwell (New York, 1991), 61–63, 61. See also O. John Rogge to all United States attorneys, memorandum, "Federal Criminal Jurisdiction over Violations of Civil Liberties," May 21, 1940, Department of Justice Circular no. 3356, supp. no. 1, 1–31, repr., ibid., 12–51, 21–51; John T. Elliff, "Aspects of Federal Civil Rights Enforcement: The Justice Department and the FBI, 1939–1964," in Donald Fleming and Bernard Bailyn, eds., *Law in American History* (Boston, 1971), 608–9; Brodie, "Federally-Secured Right to Be Free from Bondage," 367. For the statutes, see An Act to Prevent and Punish Kidnapping, ch. 86, 14 Stat. 50 (1866), subsequently codified at ch. 321, § 268, 35 Stat. 1141–42 (1909), and 18 U.S.C. § 443 (1940) (current version at 18 U.S.C. § 1583 [2000]); Lindbergh Kidnaping Act, ch. 271, 47 Stat. 326 (1932) (current version at 18 U.S.C. §§ 1201–1202 [2000]), codified during the 1940s at 18 U.S.C. § 408(a), (c) (1940); *United States v. Gantt*, No. 10,031n (N.D. Ala. Nov. 5, 1949), cited in Brodie, "Federally-Secured Right to Be Free from Bondage," 374n34.

13. "Federal Prosecution of a Georgia Planter for Peonage," *Daily Worker*, November 20, 1939, 1; Pete Daniel, *The Shadow of Slavery: Peonage in the South, 1901–1969* (New York, 1973), 175; Memorandum, May 1941, Record Group 60, National Archives (hereafter DOJ Files), 50-708.

14. DOJ files, 50-18-15.

15. Francis Biddle, "Civil Rights and the Federal Law," in *Safeguarding Civil Liberty Today: The Edward L. Bernays Lectures of 1944 Given at Cornell University* (Ithaca, N.Y., 1945), 109–44, 115. For the classic treatment of antebellum free labor ideology, see Eric Foner, *Free Soil, Free Labor, Free Men: The Ideology of the Republican Party before the Civil War* (New York, 1970), 11–51. For an excellent discussion of laborers' changing conceptions of free labor in the postbellum period, see William E. Forbath, "The Ambiguities of Free Labor: Labor and the Law in the Gilded Age," *Wisconsin Law Review* (1985): 767–817, 782–87, 801–14. See also James Gray Pope, "Labor and the Constitution: From Abolition to Deindustrialization," *Texas Law Review* 65 (1987): 1071–1136, 1096–1104; James Gray Pope, "Labor's Constitution of Freedom," *Yale Law Journal* 106 (1997): 941–1031, 962–66; Lea S. VanderVelde, "The Labor Vision of the Thirteenth Amendment," *University of Pennsylvania Law Review* 138 (1989): 437–504, 437–39; Risa L. Goluboff, "The Work of Civil Rights in the 1940s: The Department of Justice, the NAACP, and African American Agricultural Labor" (Ph.D. diss., Princeton University, 2003), 17–63.

16. Labor Disputes Act, S. 2926, 73rd Cong. § 2 (1934), *Congressional Record* 78, part 4:3444. See generally Pope, "Thirteenth Amendment versus the Commerce Clause," 46–122.

17. National Labor Relations Act, ch. 372, § 2(3), 49 Stat. 449, 450 (1935) (current version at 29 U.S.C. §§ 151–169 [2000]); Fair Labor Standards Act, ch. 676, § 13(a) (6), 52 Stat. 1060, 1067 (1938) (current version at 29 U.S.C. §§ 201–219 [2000 & Supp. II 2002]); Social Security Act, ch. 531, §§ 210(b) (1), (2), 811(b) (1), (2), 907(c) (1), (2), 49 Stat. 620, 625, 639, 643 (1935) (current version at 42 U.S.C. §§ 301–1397jj [2000 & Supp. II

2002]). See also Harvard Sitkoff, *A New Deal for Blacks: The Depression Decade* (New York, 1978), 1:34–57; Nancy J. Weiss, *Farewell to the Party of Lincoln: Black Politics in the Age of FDR* (Princeton, 1983), 163–68; William E. Forbath, "Caste, Class, and Equal Citizenship," *Michigan Law Review* 98 (1999): 1–91, 76; Ira Katznelson, *When Affirmative Action Was White* (New York, 2005). For discussions of the existence of a separate southern labor market until World War II, see Gavin Wright, *Old South, New South: Revolutions in the Southern Economy since the Civil War* (New York, 1986); Bruce J. Schulman, *From Cotton Belt to Sunbelt: Federal Policy, Economic Development, and the Transformation of the South, 1938–1980* (New York, 1991), 1–85

18. Howard Devon Hamilton, "The Legislative and Judicial History of the Thirteenth Amendment," *National Bar Journal* 10 (1952), part 2:7–85, 72.

19. 322 U.S. 4.

20. 219 U.S. at 241; 315 U.S. at 26–30; 322 U.S. at 16, 18.

21. Brodie, "Federally-Secured Right to Be Free from Bondage," 398 (footnote omitted); Percy C. Fountain to attorney general, July 15, 1948, DOJ Files, 50-1-24.

22. Biddle, "Civil Rights," 137–38, 138.

23. J. Sewell Elliott to William M. Sneed, Justice of the Peace, and Sheriff J. R. Nix, n.d., DOJ Files, No. 50-19M-48. See also, e.g., John P. Cowart to attorney general, December 28, 1949, DOJ Files, 50-19-37; Alexander M. Campbell to director, FBI, October 26, 1948, DOJ Files, 50-19-31; Herbert S. Phillips to Hon. Warren Olney, III, April 16, 1953, DOJ Files, 50-18-63; John P. Cowart to attorney general, April 13, 1950, DOJ Files, 50-19-37.

24. Hamilton, "Legislative and Judicial History of the Thirteenth Amendment," part 2:15, 57, 57–58; ibid., *National Bar Journal* 9 (1951), part 1:26–134, 69. See also, e.g., "Peonage," selections from *A Monthly Summary of Events and Trends in Race Relations*, August–October 1946, in August Meier, ed., *Papers of the NAACP* (Frederick, Md., 1982), part 13C, rl. 12:650–51 (hereafter *NAACP Papers*); Allan Keller, "22 Brooklyn Boys Flee Slave Farm," N.Y. *World-Telegram and Sun*, August 6, 1953, 1–2, 1; NAACP, "FBI Asked to Probe New York State Farm," news release, August 6, 1953, in *NAACP Papers*, part 13A, rl. 19:213. See also Marian Wynn Perry to Edward Knott, Jr., December 1, 1947, ibid., part 13C, rl. 12:690.

25. See, e.g., Clay A. William to Thurgood Marshall, February 18, 1946, in *NAACP Papers*, part 13C, rl. 12:847–48.

26. Affidavit of Polly Johnson, 1946, 1, ibid., 764–66, 764; Affidavit of Elizabeth Coker, January 30, 1947, ibid., 390–91, 391. See also Miss Mattie Lomax to NAACP, March 10, 1946, ibid., 752; Walter Pate, FBI Report, February 24, 1945, DOJ Files, 50-67-9.

27. *United States v. Ingalls*, 73 F. Supp. 76, 77 (S.D. Cal. 1947).

28. Ibid. at 78; "Daughter Tells More 'Slave' Case Details," *Los Angeles Times*, February 27, 1947, part 2:1, DOJ Files, 50-12-3.

29. Brodie, "Federally-Secured Right to Be Free from Bondage," 388.

30. Leo Meltzer to file, memorandum, October 22, 1946, DOJ Files, 50-79-2; FBI Report, Maurice D. duBois, October 20, 1950, DOJ Files, 50-35-6. See also, e.g., Henry A. Donahoo, FBI Report, January 5, 1948, DOJ Files, 50-1-23; Joseph A. Canale, FBI Report, March 13, 1952, DOJ Files, 50-40-22; Special Agent George A. Gunter, FBI Report, July 1, 1948, DOJ Files, 50-350; T. Vincent Quinn to James M. Carter, January 26, 1948, DOJ Files, 50-12-6; John B. Honeycutt, FBI Report, April 3, 1948, DOJ Files, 50-41-51; Andrew M. Smith, FBI Report, November 16, 1951, DOJ Files, 50-1-30.

31. Chester L. Sumners to attorney general, June 23, 1950, DOJ Files, 50-40-18; T. Vincent Quinn to director, FBI, memorandum, December 30, 1947, DOJ Files, 50-80-2; Hamilton, "Legislative and Judicial History of the Thirteenth Amendment," part 2:57; Henry Putzel, "Federal Civil Rights Enforcement: A Current Appraisal," *University of Pennsylvania Law Review* 99 (1951): 439–54, 445. U.S. House Committee on the Judiciary, Subcommittee No. 4, "H. R. 2118: Peonage and Slavery[; Hearing]," 82nd Cong., 1st sess., 1951, 13–14, 18 (statement of George Triedman), 29, in *Unpublished U.S. House of Representatives Committee Hearings, 1947–1954* (Bethesda, Md., 1992), microfiche, 82 HJ-T.15, B4–B5, B9, C6. See also H.R. 2118, 82nd Cong. (1951); A Bill to Strengthen the Laws Relating to Convict Labor, Peonage, Slavery, and Involuntary Servitude, S. 1739, 82nd Cong. (1951).

32. "H. R. 2118 Hearing," 14–15, 21–25, in *Unpublished House Hearings, 1947–1954*, 82 HJ-T.15C5.

33. Ibid., 28. Cf. Suzanne Mettler, *Dividing Citizens: Gender and Federalism in New Deal Public Policy* (Ithaca, N.Y., 1998), xi–xii.

34. Brodie, "Federally-Secured Right to Be Free from Bondage," 388.

35. 392 U.S. 443, 445–46 (Douglas, J., concurring).

8. The Workers' Freedom of Association Under the Thirteenth Amendment

James Gray Pope

Long before the Thirteenth Amendment, white American workers claimed the freedoms to organize and strike under principles of both natural law and republican citizenship.[1] Enslaved black workers did not issue public claims of right, but they did join together to engage in job actions and "forms of collective labour bargaining customarily associated with industrial wage labourers." At the risk of flogging and other harsh punishments, they limited the pace of work, secured the dismissal of abusive overseers, and established norms limiting the master's power.[2] Following emancipation, black workers promptly formed unions and staged strikes to improve conditions and defend their jobs against the attempts of white workers to drive them from desirable trades. The rights to organize and strike received little attention, however, as white elites unleashed a wave of terror directed at eliminating the rights of black people to engage in *any* form of political or economic association.[3] Meanwhile, white workers continued to claim the rights to organize and strike, but not under the recently ratified Thirteenth Amendment. Having experienced the amendment as a black emancipation measure, they neglected to consider whether its text—which prohibited "involuntary servitude" as well as slavery—might apply to their situation. Around the turn of the twentieth century, however, a new generation of workers looked at the text afresh. Confronted by the recently invented labor injunction, the yellow dog contract, and proposals for the compulsory arbitration of labor disputes, workers of all colors turned to the Thirteenth Amendment as a source of collective labor rights.

This chapter recounts the fate of labor's Thirteenth Amendment claims in the twentieth century and assesses their viability in the twenty-first.

From the early 1900s to the 1950s, the U.S. labor movement claimed the rights to organize and strike under the U.S. Constitution. When employers or the government interfered with the rights to organize and strike, labor leaders and activists invoked the Thirteenth Amendment. They declared yellow dog contracts, labor injunctions, and antistrike laws unconstitutional.[4] They campaigned for legislation to enforce the amendment. If the American Federation of Labor had prevailed, the Norris-LaGuardia Anti-Injunction Act (1932) would have commenced with this declaration: "Every human being has under the Thirteenth Amendment to the Constitution of the United States an inalienable right to the disposal of his labor free from interference, restraint or coercion by or in behalf of employers of labor, including the right to associate with other human beings for the protection and advancement of their common interests as workers, and in such association to negotiate through representatives of their own choosing concerning the terms of employment and conditions of labor, and to take concerted action for their own protection in labor disputes."[5]

Critics maintained that any worker who enjoyed the individual right to quit could not possibly be in a condition of "involuntary servitude"; if she could quit, then surely her servitude must be *voluntary*.[6] From the perspective of many workers, however, the right to quit fell woefully short of negating involuntary servitude. In their experience, the employer occupied a structural position of dominance over unorganized workers notwithstanding the individual right to quit. "The average employer can discharge one man without noticing it," explained coal miner and union activist John Hunter Walker, but "it costs the man and his wife and children everything that they have."[7] Accordingly, the notion that a lone worker could avoid employer control by quitting was, as AFL president Samuel Gompers put it, a "subterfuge": "Just imagine what a wonderful influence such an individual would have, say for instance [on] the U.S. Steel Corporation."[8] A worker might exchange one relation of servitude for another, but she would remain in servitude either way, and not by choice. CIO general counsel Lee Pressman explained: "The simple fact is that the right of individual workers to quit their jobs has meaning only when they may quit in concert, so that in their quitting or in their threat to quit they have a real bargaining strength."[9]

The AFL did not wait for official approval to put this constitutional theory into practice. Beginning in 1909, the federation held that a worker confronted with an unconstitutional injunction had an "imperative duty" to "refuse obedience and to take whatever consequences may ensue."[10] Thousands of workers defied court orders, undermining the legitimacy of the labor injunction and spurring Congress to pass the Norris-LaGuardia Act.[11] In what was perhaps the single most dramatic campaign of resistance, the AFL declared the Kansas Industrial Court Act (1920) unconstitutional under the Thirteenth Amendment, and Alexander Howat led the Kansas district of the United Mine Workers in a four-month winter strike "against the political powers of the state of Kansas, monopoly, [and] the industrial court law."[12]

The Thirteenth Amendment tended to enhance the possibilities for principled unity among workers of all colors. After its ratification, white workers could no longer "derive satisfaction from defining themselves as 'not slaves,'" and the struggle of black workers for freedom from slavery became a model for many.[13] In order to accept that the Thirteenth Amendment was relevant to their situation, white workers had to abandon the comforting thought that their racial status immunized them from such a lowly condition as involuntary servitude. At the same time, black workers drew on the Thirteenth Amendment to insist that full emancipation required not just nondiscrimination (as some black entrepreneurs and professionals maintained) but also effective labor freedom. "Let us call your attention to the Thirteenth Amendment," wrote one black unionist in an article opposing labor injunctions. "It grew out of the suffering of our race." Testifying before a congressional committee on the suppression of a West Virginia coal strike, black coal miner and union activist George Echols commented that he "was raised a slave . . . and I know the time when I was a slave, and I feel just like we feel now."[14] Members of the mostly black Brotherhood of Sleeping Car Porters combined the amendment's thrusts toward labor freedom and race equality, holding that the amendment would remain a "dead letter" until white employers dealt on an equal basis with black workers through their chosen union. Only by organizing could they win full citizenship and avoid the "lash of the master."[15]

Slowly, labor's Thirteenth Amendment claims gained ground. Members of Congress echoed them during debates over workers' rights legislation. Senator George Norris charged that antiunion injunctions brought about "involuntary servitude on the part of those who must toil in order that they and their families may live." Senator Robert Wagner contended that without legal protection for the right to bargain collectively, there would be "slavery by contract."[16] The Norris-LaGuardia Anti-Injunction Act and the Wagner (National Labor Relations [1935]) Act did not specifically mention the Thirteenth Amendment, but they did endorse the core idea that without organization the individual worker was "helpless to exercise actual liberty of contract and to protect his freedom of labor." By midcentury, some lower courts had cited the amendment to justify invalidating antistrike laws and injunctions, and leading legal scholar Archibald

Cox had conceded the logic of the Thirteenth Amendment right to strike.[17] When Supreme Court justices Wiley Rutledge and Frank Murphy declared that the question of the Thirteenth Amendment right to strike was "momentous," it appeared that labor's constitutionalists might be on the verge of winning official sanction for their claimed rights.[18]

LABOR'S CASE FOR THE THIRTEENTH AMENDMENT RIGHTS TO ORGANIZE AND STRIKE

To labor's constitutionalists, the rights to organize and strike flowed from the same reasoning that the Supreme Court had applied to justify the Thirteenth Amendment right to quit. In *Bailey v. Alabama*, decided in 1911, the Court invalidated Alabama's debt peonage law despite the fact that the plaintiff laborer had voluntarily agreed to satisfy his debt with labor. The Court explained that the Thirteenth Amendment was intended not only to abolish slavery but also "to render impossible any state of bondage; to make labor free, by prohibiting that control by which the personal service of one man is disposed of or coerced for another's benefit which is the essence of involuntary servitude."[19] The evil, then, was to be found in the relation of control and not in the presence or absence of consent to be controlled. The Court stressed this point thirty-three years later in *Pollock v. Williams*, another peonage case: "In general the defense against oppressive hours, pay, working conditions, or treatment is the right to change employers. When the master can compel and the laborer cannot escape the obligation to go on, there is no power below to redress and no incentive above to relieve a harsh overlordship or unwholesome conditions of work."[20]

Under *Bailey* and *Pollock*, the case for the rights to organize and strike was simple and straightforward. In an economy dominated by large corporations, the individual right to quit was not enough; only by organizing and collectively withholding their labor could workers gain sufficient "power below" to give employers the "incentive above" to avoid a "harsh overlordship." By 1935, both the Supreme Court and Congress had endorsed this conclusion in other legal contexts. In an opinion by Chief Justice William Howard Taft, the Court declared that a single employee without organization "was helpless in dealing with an employer." Echoing John Hunter Walker and other labor intellectuals, Taft explained that the worker "was dependent ordinarily on his daily wage for the maintenance of himself and family," so that if "the employer refused to pay him the wages that he thought fair, he was nevertheless unable to leave the employ and to resist arbitrary and unfair treatment." Accordingly, "union was essential to give laborers opportunity to deal on equality with their employer."[21] Congress repeated the point in the Norris-LaGuardia Act and the NLRA, stressing the "inequality of bargaining power between employees who do not possess full freedom of association or actual liberty of contract, and employers who are organized in the corporate or other forms of ownership association."[22] All that remained was to plug these conclusions into the language of *Bailey* and *Pollock*.

LABOR'S THIRTEENTH AMENDMENT CLAIMS IN CONGRESS, 1908–1935

Labor's constitutionalists sought help first from Congress, and not from courts. It was the judicial branch that had developed the labor injunction and, in their view, trampled labor's rights to organize and strike. Accordingly, they petitioned Congress to enforce the Constitution against the courts. For the first several decades of the twentieth century, anti-injunction legislation headed the list of labor's political demands.

Andrew Furuseth, president of the Seamen's Union from 1908 to 1938, provided intellectual leadership for the campaign. Lacking formal education, Furuseth had trained himself in constitutional advocacy while campaigning for the individual right of sailors to quit their jobs. The old maritime law made it a crime for a sailor to "desert" his job while under contract. In 1897, the Supreme Court upheld this rule against a Thirteenth Amendment challenge organized by the Seamen's Union.[23] Undaunted, Furuseth campaigned relentlessly for legislation permitting sailors to quit, taking his constitutional argument to legislators and audiences across the country. When Congress rewarded his efforts by passing the LaFollette Seamen's Act (1915), Senator LaFollette proclaimed that the Thirteenth Amendment had become "a covenant of refuge for the seamen of the world."[24] But to Furuseth, mere individual liberty would not suffice; only the rights to organize and strike could ensure labor freedom.

Many labor leaders claimed victory when Congress passed sections 6 and 20 of the Clayton Antitrust Act (1914), which appeared to exempt most peaceful concerted activities from federal court injunctions. During the legislative debates, a number of senators and representatives had justified the labor exemptions as necessary to prevent slavery and involuntary servitude, and section 6 declared that "the labor of a human being is not a commodity or article of commerce."[25] Not unreasonably, some lawyers concluded that the exemptions had been passed "in support of the Thirteenth Amendment rather than under the Interstate Commerce provisions of the United States Constitution."[26]

While labor's constitutional claims were gaining ground among legislators, however, they remained anathema to another highly influential group: legal professionals. Until the 1920s, prolabor congressmen generally deferred to the

AFL in shaping legislative proposals protecting labor rights. During that decade, however, a cadre of elite, progressive lawyers and scholars challenged unionists for leadership in the field of labor reform. Harvard law professors Felix Frankfurter and Francis B. Sayre, Columbia law professor Herman Oliphant, Chief Librarian Edwin Witte, of the Wisconsin Legislative Library, and Donald Richberg, a railroad labor attorney and legal scholar, disparaged the legal ideas of labor leaders and pressed them to accept lawyerly leadership. Writing anonymously, Frankfurter urged labor to accept progressive intellectuals as a "general staff" for labor. "Mr. Gompers will learn," he vowed, "that 'intellectuals' may have as deep a social sympathy and understanding as men who work at crafts." Richberg penned a thinly disguised autobiographical novel in which the protagonist, a young lawyer, goes to court and provides a brilliant defense for oppressed workers who would have been "voiceless" without a skilled advocate like himself. Sayre advised unionists to abandon their campaign for legislation to enforce the Thirteenth Amendment and proposed instead that they hire "the best legal talent available" to conduct studies and draft state legislation.[27]

In 1921, the Supreme Court effectively nullified the labor provisions of the Clayton Act, making it clear to unionists that new legislation would be required.[28] For the next decade, the progressive lawyers disputed labor's constitutionalists over the content of reform. The struggle swayed back and forth, with each side proposing its own bills and disparaging those of the other side.[29] In late 1931, the issue came down to a choice between two bills. The first, drafted by a "committee of experts" consisting of Frankfurter, Sayre, Witte, Oliphant, and Richberg, endorsed labor's claim that "the individual unorganized worker is commonly helpless to exercise actual liberty of contract and to protect his freedom of labor," but without mentioning the Thirteenth Amendment.[30] The second, endorsed by the AFL, was expressly grounded on the amendment. It incorporated most of the experts' bill but with some substantial modifications, including a ringing declaration, quoted at the beginning of this chapter, that the Thirteenth Amendment guaranteed the rights to organize and engage in concerted activity.[31]

The reaction of the progressive lawyers was curiously bifurcated. In public, they ignored the paragraph on the Thirteenth Amendment, instead criticizing the AFL bill on other grounds. But in private, the amendment took center stage. Felix Frankfurter confided to Roger Baldwin of the ACLU that he felt "particularly strongly" about the AFL bill's embrace of the Thirteenth Amendment theory. "The talk about the Thirteenth Amendment," he scoffed, "is too silly for any practical lawyer's use." Baldwin conveyed Frankfurter's opinion to Senator Norris with the admonition that it must, "of course," remain confidential since Frankfurter "would not want to put himself in a position publicly of attacking the A.F. of L. bill." Frankfurter also moved to head off the possibility that

Senator Henrik Shipstead, of Minnesota, a supporter of labor's constitutional claims, might introduce a bill incorporating the Thirteenth Amendment theory. "The notion that the Thirteenth Amendment can serve as an obstruction to the evils against which we are contending," he warned the senator, "seems to me of a simplicity that borders on the fantastic."[32] The professor did not deign to explain why unionists' ideas were so "silly" or "fantastic." After a series of discussions involving Richberg, Frankfurter, and Norris, AFL president William Green agreed—over the vigorous dissent of labor constitutionalist Victor Olander—to go along with the senator's strategy of minimizing opposition by reintroducing the old bill without the AFL's amendments. Not long afterward, the bill passed the Senate and House by margins of seventy-five to five and three hundred sixty-three to thirteen.[33]

A similar but less-focused clash over constitutional foundations played out during the buildup to the Wagner Act, which outlawed employer interference with the rights to organize and engage in concerted activities. Once again, the bill echoed labor's claim that "the individual, unorganized worker" was "helpless to exercise actual liberty of contract" but without mentioning the Thirteenth Amendment. Labor freedom was constitutionally significant not in itself but because it led to strikes and inadequate mass purchasing power with "consequent detriment to the general welfare and the free flow of commerce."[34] In the spring of 1935, Furuseth wrote Senator Wagner a twelve-page letter urging that the bill be grounded on the Thirteenth Amendment instead of the Commerce Power.[35] This time, however, Furuseth wrote without the AFL's backing. The failed effort to ground the Norris-LaGuardia Act on the Thirteenth Amendment was still fresh on the minds of labor leaders, and some labor constitutionalists were suspicious of the NLRA because of its reliance on injunctions against employers, which they (presciently, as it turns out) feared would soon be turned against unions as well.[36]

Despite the AFL's retreat, Furuseth had reason to hope that Wagner would heed his argument. If any of the bill's three goals—realizing worker freedom, increasing worker purchasing power, and fostering industrial peace—was primary to Wagner, it was that of worker freedom. "I would not buy peace," he said, "at the price of slavery." He invoked all of the essential elements of labor's Thirteenth Amendment theory in defense of the bill, including the claim that if workers did not enjoy the right to bargain collectively, there would be "slavery by contract."[37] Other leading legislators also spoke in terms of slavery, freedom, and inherent rights. "As Lincoln freed the blacks in the South," summarized Representative Truax, "so the Wagner-Connery bill frees the industrial slaves of this country from the further tyranny and oppression of their overlords of wealth."[38]

But Wagner adhered to his Commerce Clause strategy. Even after the Supreme Court's famous *Schechter Poultry* decision, which convinced many supporters of the Wagner bill that it could not be sustained under the Commerce Power, Wagner breezily insisted to Furuseth that he had "no doubt that the bill . . . will be sustained by the courts."[39] Eventually it was, but its Commerce Clause foundation had little to do with the result. The act was upheld because of a "tide of forces for change which the Court could no longer resist," a tide that included President Roosevelt's court-packing plan and a wave of sit-down strikes idling millions of workers and stoking fears of revolution.[40] Under this kind of pressure, it is unlikely that the Court would have rejected a congressional finding that rights of self-organization and collective action were essential to negate a condition of involuntary servitude. Just as the interconnectedness of the modern economy had become a commonplace, so had the idea that labor freedom necessarily included the rights to organize and strike.[41]

LABOR'S THIRTEENTH AMENDMENT CLAIMS IN LAW OFFICES AND COURTS, 1894–1950

While pressing Congress for legislation, the labor movement also fought a defensive battle in the courts. Here, workers and unions raised the Thirteenth Amendment as a shield against labor injunctions and antistrike laws. The first judge to apply the Thirteenth Amendment to a strike injunction was Justice John Marshall Harlan (riding circuit) in the 1894 case of *Arthur v. Oakes*. The court held that strikers could not be enjoined to return to work, reasoning in part that "one who is placed under such constraint is in a condition of involuntary servitude." Harlan's opinion merely applied to strikers the general ban on specific performance of labor contracts, leaving the government free to award damages or impose criminal penalties.[42] Since Harlan's day, however, a scattering of courts have invoked the Thirteenth Amendment more broadly as a justification for overturning antistrike injunctions and statutory strike prohibitions.[43]

By the 1950s, however, a growing majority of lower courts had come to the conclusion that the amendment does not reach the right to strike, either because strikers cease work collectively instead of individually,[44] or because they quit work temporarily instead of permanently.[45] None of the lower court opinions—pro or con—contained any reasoning to explain why the right to strike either was or was not necessary to negate a condition of involuntary servitude. The potentially relevant Supreme Court precedents, including *Bailey* and *Pollock*, were ignored or peremptorily distinguished.[46]

What about the Supreme Court? The short answer is that, although the Court has effectively accepted the lower court consensus, it has never squarely addressed the issue. At first glance, this might seem incredible. How could a constitutional claim promoted so passionately over such a long period of time evade a reasoned resolution by the Supreme Court? The answer is to be found in the same clash of allies that frustrated labor's Thirteenth Amendment claims in Congress. In each of two major waves of cases, progressive legalists blocked a resolution.

The first wave arose from constitutional challenges to the Kansas Industrial Court Act, one of a number of antistrike laws enacted after World War I. The act banned strikes and temporary shutdowns in key industries and established an industrial court to arbitrate labor disputes. Workers and unions declared the act unconstitutional under the Thirteenth Amendment and conducted a campaign of constitutional resistance culminating in a four-month political strike against the law. In the 1923 case of *Charles Wolff Packing Company v. Court of Industrial Relations,* the Supreme Court invalidated the law, reasoning in part that the strike ban deprived the individual worker of "that means of putting himself on an equality with his employer which action in concert with his fellows gives him."[47] Even Felix Frankfurter, a relentless opponent of labor's constitutional claims, acknowledged that "the right to strike, generally, is in the Wolff Packing Company case recognized as a constitutional right."[48] But the Court relied on the Fourteenth Amendment liberty of contract instead of the Thirteenth Amendment freedom of labor. At first glance, this appears odd, for the Court's reasoning appeared far more compatible with Thirteenth than Fourteenth Amendment jurisprudence. To Chief Justice Taft, who authored the majority opinion, the worker's right to strike was "a most important element of his freedom of labor" because it gave him a "means of putting himself on an equality with his employer."[49] This positive valuation of actual equality, consistent with the *Bailey* Court's focus on preventing the "coercion" of employees to the benefit of employers, found no analogue in the Fourteenth Amendment labor decisions, where inequality between workers and employers was not only "natural" but "legitimate."[50]

When we look at the briefs, however, we discover that labor's Thirteenth Amendment theory never reached the Court. This omission was not especially surprising in *Wolff Packing,* since the constitutional challenge was brought by an employer, but workers and unions did bring other challenges to the act, one of which reached the Court in 1926.[51] While the strikers passionately defended their Thirteenth Amendment right to strike, the lawyers who "represented" them relied on the liberty of contract allegedly protected by the Fourteenth. Unabashedly drawing on the commodity theory of labor, they argued that an individual laborer enjoyed the constitutional right to "sell his labor for what he thinks best . . . just as his employer may sell his iron or coal." They regarded themselves as clever strategists, turning antilabor decisions to labor's advantage. None had any clue that the Kansas strike might be part of a long-term struggle to change the law, or that the precedents they were relying upon would soon be repudiated by the Supreme Court.[52] In short, then, labor's Thirteenth Amendment claim was defeated in the law offices of labor's attorneys—an arena from which there was no avenue of appeal.

The second wave of cases arose in response to antistrike legislation and injunctions during and after World War II. This time, labor's lawyers did bring the movement's claims to the Court but failed to secure a reasoned response. In *United States v. United Mine Workers*, the Court upheld a strike injunction against the union's Thirteenth Amendment challenge but without mentioning the amendment. The only indication that the claim might have been considered came in the following sentence: "We have examined the other contentions advanced by the defendants but have found them to be without merit."[53] Two years later, in *UAW Local 232 v. Wisconsin Employment Relations Board* (WERC), the Court held that the Thirteenth Amendment did not prohibit a state from outlawing intermittent, unannounced strikes. The Court explained that because the state had not made "it a crime to abandon work individually . . . or collectively," there had been no "purpose or effect of imposing any form of involuntary servitude."[54] This reasoning implied that workers might enjoy the right to abandon work collectively, but—despite various opportunities to do so—the Court never addressed the merits of that issue.[55]

Why did the justices so assiduously avoid the question? Part of the answer lies in the Court's composition. Within a year of announcing that the question of the Thirteenth Amendment right to strike was "momentous," both Frank Murphy and Wiley Rutledge were dead. This development was especially unfortunate for labor because it left Felix Frankfurter unchallenged as the Court's expert on industrial relations. During the debates over the constitutional foundation of the Norris-LaGuardia Act, then professor Frankfurter had maneuvered behind the scenes to prevent prolabor senators from introducing legislation grounded on the Thirteenth Amendment.[56] Now, in the Supreme Court, he would maintain his public silence on the merits of the claim while leading the Court in its de facto rejection.

The problem facing Frankfurter was how to repudiate labor's Thirteenth Amendment claims while respecting the emerging, post–New Deal regime of constitutional jurisprudence. His silence on the issue may have reflected his failure to develop a principled solution. As outlined in the famous *Carolene Products* footnote 4, legislatures were henceforth generally entitled to judicial deference, but not in cases involving "a specific prohibition of the Constitution, such as those of the first ten amendments." Under this schema, the involuntary servitude clause would seem to resemble more closely the first ten amendments than "the general prohibitions of the Fourteenth Amendment."[57] Unlike the clauses guaranteeing "equal protection" or "liberty," it had never been used by courts as a roving mandate to overturn legislation. To date, it had generated only two rights: the individual rights of workers to quit their jobs and to change employers.[58] The labor movement's claims were closely tied to these rights. The right to strike could be framed as the right to quit temporarily and in association with others, while the right to organize flowed closely from the reasoning behind the right to quit.[59]

It would appear, then, that the justices could not provide a principled answer to labor's claims without addressing the question whether the rights to organize and strike were, like the right to quit, necessary to prevent "that control by which the personal service of one man is disposed of or coerced for another's benefit which is the essence of involuntary servitude."[60] And if the justices were to answer that question, they would have to confront the numerous statements by the Court and Congress, the most compelling of which had been coauthored by Frankfurter himself, endorsing labor's claim that "the individual unorganized worker is commonly helpless to exercise actual liberty of contract and to protect his freedom of labor."[61] In light of these difficulties, it is not surprising either that the Supreme Court avoided any public treatment of the issue or that the lower courts—which could not entirely dodge the question—provided no reasoning in support of their conclusions.

TAFT-HARTLEY, THE COLD WAR, AND THE DEMISE OF THIRTEENTH AMENDMENT LABOR RIGHTS

By the early 1950s, then, Frankfurter and his allies had deflected labor's Thirteenth Amendment claims both in Congress and in the Supreme Court. But defeat in official forums could not, by itself, do away with the Thirteenth Amendment freedom of association. Workers and unions had asserted and acted upon their claimed rights for decades without official approval. Even conservative business unionists had declared statutes and injunctions to be unconstitutional (or, in the case of the NLRA, constitutional) despite court rulings to the contrary. In the late 1940s, however, the Taft-Hartley "Slave Labor" Act and the onset of the cold war severely tested the movement's constitutional commitments.

The Taft-Hartley Act (1947) imposed a variety of restrictions on strikes and union political activity, including a total ban on secondary labor boycotts and a requirement that all union officials sign anticommunist affidavits as a condition of remaining in office. Unionists charged that the antistrike provisions violated the Thirteenth Amendment, while the political restraints contravened the First. The AFL and the CIO denounced the act as a "slave labor law" and threatened a massive campaign of constitutional resistance. Alabama coal miners launched a protest strike that quickly spread to more than 200,000 miners in ten states. John L. Lewis called for a boycott of the NLRB, citing the AFL's long-standing policy of defying unconstitutional laws.[62] But most labor leaders soon lost enthusiasm for the struggle. With the cold war in full swing and the labor movement singled out as a seedbed of communism, constitutional defiance seemed un-American. AFL secretary George Meany, who had initially invoked the Thirteenth Amendment and warned that the inevitable worker resistance would "torpedo" America's international crusade against communism, now urged compliance. For the next half century the movement dutifully lobbied and electioneered for labor law reform. Labor's Thirteenth Amendment theory lay dormant as the Supreme Court dodged the issue and labor leaders gradually forgot about it as they grew increasingly dependent on government protection.[63]

THE THIRTEENTH AMENDMENT AND THE DECLINE OF UNIONISM IN THE UNITED STATES

The peak of the Thirteenth Amendment freedom of association was also the peak of the American labor movement. Private-sector union membership has fallen from nearly 40 percent of the private workforce in 1955 to about 7.6 percent today.[64] Many scholars attribute this drop to the law, especially weak remedies for employer unfair labor practices.[65] At the same time, the strike appears to be withering away due to legal restrictions and the permanent replacement rule, according to which employers may give economic strikers' jobs to strikebreakers.[66] Economic inequality has skyrocketed. In 2005, the top 1 percent of households received more than 20 percent of all pretax income, the most since 1928.[67] The richest 1 percent of households now holds about 34 percent of the nation's private wealth, more than the bottom 90 percent combined.[68]

These developments can be traced, in part, to Senator Wagner's choice to ground the NLRA on the Commerce Power instead of the Thirteenth Amendment. No sooner had the act been signed into law than employers began to challenge its constitutionality. Had the law been grounded on the Thirteenth Amendment, the issue of constitutionality would have focused on whether the rights to organize and engage in concerted activity were necessary for labor freedom. Under the Commerce Clause, however, government attorneys were drawn to defend the act as an exercise of Congress's power to "control" and "punish" strikes, thereby preventing disruptions to interstate commerce.[69] During the early, formative period of NLRA jurisprudence, each exercise of the NLRB's authority was constitutionally defended not in terms of labor freedom but as an effort to facilitate commerce. In its anxiousness to prevail on this issue, the board stressed the disruptive potential of strikes and virtually ignored other NLRA policies that more strongly supported workers' rights—policies such as "restoring equality of bargaining power between employers and employees" and "encouraging the practice and procedure of collective bargaining."[70] Workers' rights were to be protected not because they were important in themselves but because protecting them would help to eliminate strikes.

Having been introduced to the NLRA as an antistrike measure, judges soon began to interpret its ambiguous provisions in line with their thinking on what would most effectively prevent strikes. Within a few years of its passage, the Supreme Court had announced that the workers' section 7 right to strike did not prevent employers from giving strikers' jobs permanently to strikebreakers. And, since worker rights had no value in themselves, employers that violated them were guilty of no great offense. Despite statutory language empowering the board to "to take such affirmative action . . . as will effectuate the policies of this Act," the Court held that it could not penalize employers so as to prevent them from committing future violations. When courts were called upon to balance workers' rights against employer property rights, as in cases involving union organizer access to company property, the constitutionally grounded employer rights tended to prevail.[71] Although Wagner's Commerce Clause gambit succeeded in the short run, then, it eventually provided a vivid illustration of the danger that even victorious constitutional claims can impair the long-term prospects for social change because of "the ideological implications of the way in which the legal claims were made."[72]

THE THIRTEENTH AMENDMENT FREEDOM OF ASSOCIATION TODAY

Could the Thirteenth Amendment once again serve as a basis for constitutional labor rights? On the merits, the case for the workers' freedom of association appears stronger now than in its heyday.[73] In the 1940s, when the Supreme Court dodged labor's Thirteenth Amendment claims, there was no constitutional concept of a freedom to associate.[74] Since then, however, the Court has developed a vibrant doctrine with two basic elements. First, claimants must prove that they are doing something that they have a constitutional right to do; then they must show that if they are prohibited from doing it in combination, their exercise of the right will be rendered ineffective.[75] Labor's case for the Thirteenth Amendment right to strike prefigured these elements. Workers and unions maintained that (1) employees enjoy the Thirteenth Amendment right to quit individually and (2) if they are prohibited from exercising that right in combination, then the whole point of the right to quit—preventing a "harsh overlordship" or "unwholesome conditions of work"—would be defeated.[76] The first element is not disputed, and the second finds support in strong statements by both Congress and the Supreme Court, for example that "the individual unorganized worker is commonly helpless to exercise actual liberty of contract and to protect his freedom of labor."[77] Since the development of the doctrine, the Court has not heard a Thirteenth Amendment argument for the right to strike. The last time the Court addressed any claim of a constitutional right to strike, it assumed that the right existed but held that the statute at issue (which denied food stamps to the families of striking workers) did not violate the right.[78]

The core of labor's Thirteenth Amendment idea—that labor freedom necessarily includes the rights to organize and strike—is now embodied in international labor standards. The International Covenant on Civil and Political Rights, ratified by the United States in 1992, requires an "effective remedy" for violations of "the right to form and join trade unions."[79] As a member of the International Labor Organization (ILO), the United States is also obligated to respect ILO conventions.[80] The ILO's Committee on Freedom of Association has determined that various features of U.S. law—including the permanent replacement rule, the flat ban on secondary boycotts, and the failure to protect the right to organize with effective remedies—run afoul of those conventions.[81] Although the relevance of non-U.S. law to American jurisprudence is disputed, the continued vitality of these rights internationally demonstrates, at a minimum, that the conclusions reached by Congress and the Court in the twentieth century reflect more than a temporary political victory for organized labor or a time-bound response to employment conditions generated by mass production industry.[82] Now that the labor movement has abandoned its traditional hostility to new immigrants, the Thirteenth Amendment could also provide a constitutional foundation for workplace rights for immigrant workers.[83]

In 2007, the Supreme Court of Canada repudiated its own precedents and held for the first time that the right of collective bargaining is protected under the Canadian Charter of Rights.[84] Although the charter lacks an equivalent of the Thirteenth Amendment, the Court's reasoning (grounded on the charter's freedom of association provision) incorporated the essentials of the argument raised by American labor constitutionalists. The Court noted that one of the "fundamental achievements of collective bargaining is to palliate the historical inequality between employers and employees" and went on to quote the U.S. Supreme Court's observation that unions "were organized out of the necessities of the situation; that a single employee was helpless in dealing with an employer."[85] The opinion also rejected two arguments that have long been deployed against labor's constitutional claims in the United States. First, the notion that the "rights to strike and to bargain collectively are 'modern rights' created by legislation, not 'fundamental freedoms,'" was found unpersuasive because "the fundamental importance of collective bargaining to labour relations was the very reason for its incorporation into statute."[86] The policy statements and legislative histories of the principal U.S. labor statutes, which resound with references to "labor freedom" and "actual liberty of contract," suggest that the same is true here.[87] Second, the contention that labor law "involves policy decisions best left to" the elected branches did not provide sufficient reason to deny the right. "It may well be appropriate for judges to defer to legislatures on policy matters expressed in particular laws," the Canadian Court conceded. "But to declare a judicial 'no go' zone for an entire right on the ground that it may involve the courts in policy matters is to push deference too far."[88]

Given its present personnel, nobody would expect the U.S. Supreme Court to follow suit. In the context of a struggle dating back centuries, however, the Court's composition at any particular moment seems relatively ephemeral. More important, the vitality of a constitutional freedom does not necessarily depend on acceptance by judges. Famous examples include the First Amendment freedom of speech and the Second Amendment right to bear arms, both of which fueled social movements and influenced government policy long before the Supreme Court lifted a finger to enforce them.[89] As we have seen, the Thirteenth Amendment freedom of association served similar functions for the labor movement during the period leading up to the enactment of federal workers' rights statutes in the 1930s. Now that those statutes have declined in effectiveness, the Thirteenth Amendment once again beckons.

NOTES

1. WILLIAM H. SYLVIS, THE LIFE, SPEECHES, LABORS & ESSAYS OF WILLIAM H. SYLVIS 101, 117 (James C. Sylvis ed., 1872) (1968); EDWARD A. WIECK, THE AMERICAN MINERS' ASSOCIATION 204–5, 217–18 (1940); SEAN WILENTZ, CHANTS DEMOCRATIC: NEW YORK CITY & THE RISE OF THE AMERICAN WORKING CLASS 1788–1850 290–94 (1984).

2. Mary Turner, *Introduction, in* MARY TURNER ED., FROM CHATTEL SLAVES TO WAGE SLAVES: THE DYNAMICS OF LABOR BARGAINING IN THE AMERICAS 1, 7–9 (1995); Lorena S. Walsh, *Work and Resistance in the New Republic: The Case of the Chesapeake 1770–1820, in* FROM CHATTEL SLAVES TO WAGE SLAVES, *supra* this note, at 97, 111–12.

3. ERIC ARNESEN, WATERFRONT WORKERS OF NEW ORLEANS: RACE, CLASS, AND POLITICS, 1863–1923 ix (1991); MICHAEL W. FITZGERALD, THE UNION LEAGUE MOVEMENT IN THE DEEP SOUTH 6 (1989); ERIC FONER, NOTHING BUT FREEDOM: EMANCIPATION AND ITS LEGACY 91–106 (1983); SUSAN EVA O'DONOVAN, BECOMING FREE IN THE COTTON SOUTH 230, 232 (2007); JULIE SAVILLE, THE WORK OF RECONSTRUCTION: FROM SLAVE TO WAGE LABORER IN SOUTH CAROLINA, 1860–1870 113–14, 140–41, 147, 149, 177–79 (1994); PAUL ORTIZ, EMANCIPATION BETRAYED:

THE HIDDEN HISTORY OF BLACK ORGANIZING AND WHITE VIOLENCE IN FLOR-
IDA FROM RECONSTRUCTION TO THE BLOODY ELECTION OF 1920 46–53 (2005);
Rebecca J. Scott, *Fault Lines, Color Lines, and Party Lines: Race, Labor, and Collective
Action in Louisiana and Cuba, 1862–1912, in* FREDERICK COOPER, THOMAS C. HOLT
& REBECCA J. SCOTT eds., BEYOND SLAVERY: EXPLORATIONS OF RACE, LABOR,
CITIZENSHIP IN POSTEMANCIPATION SOCIETIES 61 (2000); William C. Hine, *Black
Organized Labor in Reconstruction Charleston,* 25 LAB. HIST. 504 (1984).

4. WILLIAM E. FORBATH, LAW AND THE SHAPING OF THE AMERICAN LABOR
MOVEMENT 135–41 (1991); James Gray Pope, *Labor's Constitution of Freedom,* 106
YALE L. J. 941–1031 (1997); James Gray Pope, *The Thirteenth Amendment versus the
Commerce Clause: Labor and the Shaping of American Constitutional Law, 1921–1957,*
102 COLUM. L. REV. 1–122 (2002). "Yellow dog" contracts prohibited workers from
joining a union without the employer's approval. Workers could plausibly claim that
such contracts violated the Thirteenth Amendment because it, unlike other constitutional rights guarantees, applies to private as well as governmental action. Civil Rights
Cases, 109 U.S. 3, 20 (1883).

5. AFL Executive Council, *Text of the Anti-Injunction Bill Approved by the Executive Council of the American Federation of Labor* 1 (pamphlet, 1931). The Norris-
LaGuardia Act eliminated federal court jurisdiction to enforce yellow dog contracts
or to enjoin peaceful strikes and picketing.

6. *See, e.g.,* Ernest C. Carman, *The Outlook from the Present Legal Status of Employers and Employees in Industrial Disputes,* 6 MINN. L. REV. 533, 557–58 (1922);
Sidney Post Simpson, *Constitutional Limitations on Compulsory Industrial Arbitration,* 38 HARV. L. REV. 753, 784–85 (1925).

7. J. Walker, *Only Worker Suffers,* WORKERS CHRON., Apr. 29, 1921, at 3. For an
analysis of this argument and its implications, *see* WILLIAM M. REDDY, MONEY AND
LIBERTY IN MODERN EUROPE: A CRITIQUE OF HISTORICAL UNDERSTANDING
64–73 (1987).

8. DEBATE BETWEEN SAMUEL GOMPERS AND HENRY J. ALLEN AT CARNEGIE
HALL, NEW YORK, MAY 28, 1920 15 (1920).

9. Lee Pressman, *Memorandum on Ball-Taft-Smith Bill (S.55), in* HEARINGS BE-
FORE THE COMMITTEE ON LABOR AND PUBLIC WELFARE, U.S. SENATE, ON S.
55 & S.J. RES. 22, 80th Cong., 1st Sess. 1150 (1947).

10. AFL, REPORT OF THE PROCEEDINGS OF THE TWENTY-NINTH ANNUAL
CONVENTION 313–14 (1909) (hereafter AFL PROCEEDINGS); AFL PROCEEDINGS
1919, at 361–62.

11. FORBATH, SHAPING, *supra,* at 158–63.

12. *Miners Vote to Stop Work,* PITTSBURG DAILY HEADLIGHT, Oct. 3, 1921, at 1
(quoting strikers' resolution); Pope, *Labor's Constitution, supra.*

13. DAVID ROEDIGER, THE WAGES OF WHITENESS: RACE AND THE MAKING
OF THE AMERICAN WORKING CLASS 170, 173–76 (1991).

14. Forbath, Shaping, *supra*, at 138–39; Joe William Trotter, Jr., Coal, Class, and Color: Blacks in Southern West Virginia 1915-32 114 (1990). For additional quotations from black workers, *see id.*; Pope, *Labor's Constitution, supra*, at 981-82.

15. Beth Tompkins Bates, Pullman Porters and the Rise of Protest Politics in Black America, 1925–1945 89–90, 92–93 (2001).

16. Limiting Scope of Injunctions in Labor Disputes: Hearings before the Subcommittee of the Senate Committee on the Judiciary, 70th Cong., 1st Sess. at 672 (1928); 75 Cong. Rec. 4502 (1932); 78 Cong. Rec. 3679 (1934).

17. Archibald Cox, *Strikes, Picketing and the Constitution*, 4 Vand. L. Rev. 574, 576–77 (1951); Pope, *Thirteenth Amendment, supra*, at 100–101.

18. Norris-LaGuardia Anti-Injunction Act § 2, 29 U.S.C. 102 (1994); National Labor Relations Act § 1, 29 U.S.C. § 151 (1994); *AFL v. American Sash Co.*, 335 U.S. 538, 559 (1949) (Rutledge, J., joined by Murphy, J., concurring).

19. 219 U.S. 219, 241 (1911).

20. 322 U.S. 4, 17 (1944).

21. *American Steel Foundries v. Tri-City Central Trades Council*, 257 U.S. 184, 209 (1921) (Taft, C.J.); *see also Charles Wolff Packing Company v. Court of Industrial Relations*, 262 U.S. 522, 540 (1923) (discussed *infra*, text accompanying notes 47–50).

22. National Labor Relations Act § 1, 29 U.S.C. § 151 (1994); Norris-LaGuardia Anti-Injunction Act § 2, 29 U.S.C. 102 (1994).

23. *Robertson v. Baldwin*, 165 U.S. 275, 282–83, 287–88 (1897); Hyman Weintraub, Andrew Furuseth: Emancipator of the Seamen 2, 28–30 (1959).

24. *Id.* at 132 (quoting LaFollette).

25. Clayton Act, ch. 323, 6, 38 Stat. 731 (1914); Forbath, Shaping, *supra*, at 155–57; Pope, *Thirteenth Amendment, supra*, at 24–25.

26. Harold Henderson to John L. Lewis (Apr. 11, 1922), District 14 Correspondence, UMWA Records, Pennsylvania State University Labor Archives; Henry J. Allen, The Party of the Third Part: The Story of the Kansas Industrial Relations Court 78 (1921) (quoting Frank P. Walsh).

27. Philip Kurland ed., Felix Frankfurter on the Supreme Court 68, 76 (1970); Donald Richberg, A Man of Purpose 295–304 (1922); Thomas Vadney, The Wayward Liberal: A Political Biography of Donald Richberg 50 (1970); Sayre to Edelman (Nov. 16, 1927), Frankfurter Papers, Library of Congress, Manuscript Division, reel 94, frame 839 (1983).

28. *Duplex Printing Press Co. v. Deering*, 254 U.S. 443, 468–71 (1921); Edwin E. Witte, The Government In Labor Disputes 273 (1932).

29. *See* Ruth O'Brien, Workers' Paradox: The Republican Origins of New Deal Labor Policy, 1886–1935 151–69 (1998); Pope, *Thirteenth Amendment, supra*, at 30–38.

30. Felix Frankfurter & Nathan Greene, The Labor Injunction 280–81 (1930) (reprinting text of substitute bill).

31. *See supra* note 5 & accompanying text.

32. Frankfurter to Baldwin (Dec. 9, 1931), Norris Papers, Library of Congress, Manuscript Division, box 285; Baldwin to Norris (Dec. 10, 1931), *id.*; Frankfurter to Shipstead (Mar. 23, 1931), *id.*; *see also* Witte to Baldwin (Dec. 24, 1931), *id.*

33. AFL Executive Council Minutes, Feb. 2–12, 1932, at 28; Olander to Woll (Dec. 11, 1931), Victor A. Olander Papers, Chicago Historical Society, Chicago, Ill., box 47; Olander to Green (Dec. 11, 1931), *id.*; O'Brien, *supra*, at 168–69.

34. Hearings on S. 2926, 73d Cong. tit. 1 2 (1934), *reprinted in* 1 NLRB, Legislative History of the National Labor Relations Act 1 (1949).

35. Furuseth to Wagner (Apr. 16, 1935), Robert F. Wagner Papers, Georgetown University Special Collections, Labor Series, box 4, folder 39.

36. Frey to Olander (Oct. 27, 1939), in John P. Frey Papers, Manuscript Division, Library of Congress, box 13; Olander to Frey (Oct. 25, 1939), *id.*

37. 1 NLRB, Legislative History, *supra*, at 1224, 1241; Pope, *Thirteenth Amendment*, *supra*, at 47–50; Rebecca Zietlow, Enforcing Equality: Congress, the Constitution, and the Protection of Individual Rights 75 (2006).

38. 2 NLRB, Legislative History, *supra*, at 3093, 3185; Zietlow, *supra*, at 76–77; Pope, *Thirteenth Amendment*, *supra*, at 48–49.

39. Wagner to Furuseth (June 7, 1935), Wagner Papers, *supra*, box 4; Irving Bernstein, The New Deal Collective Bargaining Policy 120 (1950); Drew D. Hansen, *The Sit-Down Strikes and the Switch in Time*, 46 Wayne L. Rev. 49, 63–64 (2000).

40. Peter H. Irons, The New Deal Lawyers 289, 272 (1982); Pope, *Thirteenth Amendment*, *supra*, at 89–97; *but see* Barry Cushman, Rethinking the New Deal Court: The Structure of a Constitutional Revolution 42–43 (1998).

41. *See* Bernstein, New Deal, *supra*, at 18–22; *see also supra* notes 21–22 & accompanying text.

42. 63 F. 310, 318 (7th Cir. 1894).

43. *See United States v. Petrillo*, 68 F. Supp. 845, 849 (N.D. Ill. 1946), *rev'd on other grounds*, 332 U.S. 1 (1947) (overturning criminal prosecution for calling a radio strike in violation of the Federal Communications Act); *Kemp v. Division No. 241, Amalgamated Ass'n of Street & Elec. Ry. Employees*, 255 Ill. 213, 219–20, 99 N.E. 389, 392 (1912) (overturning an injunction that prohibited a union from calling a strike); *Henderson v. Coleman*, 7 So. 2d 117, 121 (Fla. 1942) (invalidating injunction compelling union workers to unload nonunion goods, where injunction did not prohibit employees from quitting their employment altogether); *State ex rel. Dairyland Power Coop. v. Wis. Employment Relations Bd.*, 21 L.R.R.M. (BNA) 2508, 2510 (Wis. Ct. App. 1948) (overturning statute prohibiting strikes by employees of public utilities); *County*

Sanitation Dist. v. Los Angeles County Employees Ass'n, 38 Cal. 3d 564, 593–609 (1985) (Bird, C.J., concurring) (maintaining that California's statutory ban on public employee strikes violated the Thirteenth Amendment).

44. *See, e.g., Dayton Co. v. Carpet, Linoleum & Resilient Floor Decorators Union, Local 39* N.W.2d 183, 197 (Minn. 1949), *app. dismissed*, 339 U.S. 906 (1950); *New Orleans S.S. Ass'n v. General Longshore Workers, ILA Local Union No. 1418*, 626 F.2d 455, 463 (5th Cir. 1980), *aff'd sub nom. Jacksonville Bulk Terminals, Inc. v. International Longshoreman's Ass'n*, 457 U.S. 702 (1982).

45. *See, e.g., NLRB v. National Maritime Union*, 175 F.2d 686, 692 (2d Cir. 1949); *United States v. Martinez*, 686 F.2d 334, 345–46 (5th Cir. 1982).

46. In *NLRB v. National Maritime Union*, for example, the Second Circuit Court of Appeals upheld an administrative order barring union officials from calling a strike. The court distinguished *Pollock* on the ground that the administrative order did not "expressly forbid employees to leave their jobs, individually or in concert." The court failed, however, to explain why that factual distinction should make a legal difference in light of the claim that the order deprived workers of the power below and employers of the incentive above to avoid servitude. *NLRB v. National Maritime Union*, 175 F.2d 686, 692 (2d Cir. 1949).

47. 262 U.S. 522, 540 (1923). The challenge was brought by an employer, but the Court opined that the law's requirement of continuous production imposed a "more drastic exercise of control" on the worker than on the owner and declared that such a requirement could not be forced on either in the absence of "a conventional relation to the public somewhat equivalent to the appointment of officers and the enlistment of soldiers and sailors in military service." *Id*. at 541.

48. KURLAND ed., *supra*, at 141 (reprinting Frankfurter's unsigned editorial from the *New Republic*, June 27, 1923).

49. 262 U.S. 522, 540, 542 (1923).

50. *See, e.g., Coppage v. Kansas*, 236 U.S. 1, 17 (1915) (invalidating state legislative ban on yellow dog contracts, reasoning that "since it is self-evident that, unless all things are held in common, some persons must have more property than others, it is from the nature of things impossible to uphold freedom of contract and the right of private property without at the same time recognizing as legitimate those inequalities of fortune that are the necessary result of the exercise of those rights").

51. *Dorchy v. Kansas*, 272 U.S. 306 (1926). In *Dorchy*, the Court framed the issue narrowly as whether a state could prohibit a strike called to collect a former employee's two-year-old wage claim and concluded that "to collect a stale claim due to a fellow member of the union who was formerly employed in the business is not a permissible purpose" for a strike. *Id*. at 309, 311.

52. Brief of Plaintiff in Error at 8–13, *Dorchy v. Kansas*, 272 U.S. 306 (1926) (No. 119). Pope, *Labor's Constitution, supra*, at 1019–22.

53. 330 U.S. 258, 307 (1947) (Vinson, C.J., plurality opinion); Brief for United Mine Workers and John L. Lewis, *United States v. United Mine Workers*, 330 U.S. 258 (1947), at 50–54; Brief for the Congress of Industrial Organizations as *Amicus Curiae*, at 27–28.

54. 336 U.S. 245, 250–51 (1949).

55. Seth Kupferberg, *Political Strikes, Labor Law, and Democratic Rights*, 71 Va. L. Rev. 685, 734 (1985); *see, e.g.,* cases cited *supra* notes 47, 51, 53–54.

56. *See supra* text accompanying notes 31–33.

57. *United States v. Carolene Prods. Co.*, 304 U.S. 114, 152 n.4 (1938).

58. *Bailey v. Alabama*, 219 U.S. 219, 241 (1911); *Pollock v. Williams*, 322 U.S. 4, 17 (1944); *Shaw v. Fisher*, 113 S.Car. 287, 292 (1920); *Thompson v. Box*, 147 Miss. 1, 12–14 (1927).

59. *See supra* text accompanying notes 7–9, 20–22.

60. 219 U.S. 219, 241 (1911).

61. Norris-LaGuardia Anti-Injunction Act § 2, 29 U.S.C. 102 (1994); *see also supra* text accompanying notes 20–22.

62. *Executive Council Launches All-Out War on Slave Bills*, Am. Federationist, May 1947, at 3, 4; *Murray Warns Labor Will Use Every Moral Means to Kill T-H*, CIO News, Sept. 22, 1947, at 5; AFL Proceedings 1947 at 487, 490, 492 (1947).

63. George Meany, *The Mandate of Big Business*, Am. Federationist, May 1947, at 5; AFL Proceedings 1947 at 495; Pope, *Thirteenth Amendment, supra*, at 105–11.

64. Paul C. Weiler, Governing the Workplace: The Future of Labor and Employment Law 8–9 (1990); Bureau of Labor Statistics, U.S. Dept. of Labor, *Union Members in 2008*, USDL 09-0095 (January 28, 2009) (http://www.bls.gov/news.release/union2.nr0.htm).

65. *See, e.g.,* Weiler, *supra*, at 105–18, 225–41; Charles J. Morris, *A Tale of Two Statutes: Discrimination for Union Activity Under the NLRA and the RLA*, 2 Emp. Rts. & Emp. Pol'y J. 317 (1998).

66. Josiah Bartlett Lambert, "If the Workers Took a Notion": The Right to Strike and American Political Development 1–5, 151–54 (2005).

67. Thomas Piketty & Emmanuel Saez, *Income Inequality in the United States, 1913–2005, in* A.B. Atkinson and T. Piketty eds., Top Incomes Over the Twentieth Century: A Contrast Between European and English-Speaking Countries § 21.8 (2007).

68. Lawrence Mishel, Jared Bernstein & Sylvia Allegretto, The State of Working America, 2006/2007 (Economic Policy Institute, 2006), table 5.1 and figure 5F (34.3).

69. *See* Arguments in the cases arising under The Railway Labor Act and The National Labor Relations Act before the Supreme Court of the United States, February 3–11, 1937, U.S. Cong., Senate Document No. 52

(75th Cong., 1st Sess.) at 124, 171; Petitioner's Brief, *NLRB v. Jones & Laughlin Steel Corp.*, 301 U.S. 1 (1937), at 21–24.

70. *See* Jones & Laughlin, 301 U.S. at 30–31; *Consol. Edison Co. v. NLRB*, 83 L. Ed. 126, 132 (1938) (Lawyers' Edition summary of NLRB General Counsel's argument); NLRA § 1, 29 U.S.C. § 151 (2000).

71. *NLRB v. Mackay Radio & Telegraph Co.*, 304 U.S. 333 (1938); *Consolidated Edison Co. v. NLRB*, 305 U.S. 197, 235–36 (1938); *NLRB v. Babcock and Wilcox Co.*, 351 U.S. 105, 112 (1956); *Eastex, Inc. v. NLRB*, 437 U.S. 556, 580 (1978) (Rehnquist, J., dissenting); James Gray Pope, *How American Workers Lost the Right to Strike, and Other Tales*, 103 MICH. L. REV. 518–53 (2004).

72. MARK TUSHNET, TAKING THE CONSTITUTION AWAY FROM THE COURTS 142 (1999).

73. For a detailed discussion of the present-day case for the Thirteenth Amendment freedom of association, *see* James Gray Pope, *Contract, Race, and Freedom of Labor in the Constitutional Law of "Involuntary Servitude,"* 119 YALE L.J. (forthcoming 2009–10), part V.

74. The first mentions of a constitutional freedom of association came in the 1950s, in cases involving investigations of communism. *See, e.g., Wieman v. Updegraff*, 344 U.S. 183, 195 (1952) (Frankfurter, J., concurring); 354 U.S. 234, 245, 250 (1957).

75. *See NAACP v. Alabama ex rel. Patterson*, 357 U.S. 449, 460–61 (1958); SHELDON LEADER, FREEDOM OF ASSOCIATION: A STUDY IN LABOR LAW AND POLITICAL THEORY 22–23 (1992).

76. *See supra* text accompanying notes 7–9, 20–22.

77. Norris-LaGuardia Anti-Injunction Act § 2, 29 U.S.C. § 102 (1994); *see also* sources cited, *supra* notes 21–22.

78. *Lyng v. International Union*, 485 U.S. 360, 368 (1988) (reasoning that "the strikers' right of association does not require the Government to furnish funds to maximize the exercise of that right").

79. International Covenant on Civil and Political Rights, Articles 2 & 22.

80. The United States has not ratified the relevant conventions, but membership in the organization carries with it the obligation to respect them. Janice Bellace, *The ILO Declaration of Fundamental Principles and Rights at Work*, 17 INT'L J. COMP. LAB. LAW AND IND'L REL. 269–87 (2001).

81. HUMAN RIGHTS WATCH, UNFAIR ADVANTAGE: WORKERS' FREEDOM OF ASSOCIATION IN THE UNITED STATES UNDER INTERNATIONAL HUMAN RIGHTS STANDARDS 18, 31, 171–90, 209–13 (2000).

82. *Cf. County Sanitation Dist. v. L.A. County Employees Ass'n*, 699 P.2d 835, 838 n.8 (Cal. 1985) (overturning California's common law ban on public employee strikes partly to avoid constitutional questions, and observing that the "United States is virtually alone . . . in upholding a . . . prohibition of public employee strikes").

83. Maria L. Ontiveros, *Immigrant Workers' Rights in a Post-Hoffman World: Organizing Around the Thirteenth Amendment*, 18 GEO. IMMIGRATION L.J. 651, 676–78 (2004); Ruben J. Garcia, *Labor as Property: Guestworkers, International Trade, and the Democracy Deficit*, 10 J. GENDER RACE & JUST. 27, 53–54 (2006).

84. *Health Services and Support—Facilities Subsector Bargaining Assn. v. British Columbia*, 2 S.C.R. 391 (2007), 2007 SCC 27, ¶ 20.

85. *Id.*, ¶ 84.

86. *Id.*, ¶ 25.

87. *See supra* note 22 & accompanying text.

88. *Id.*, 26.

89. MICHAEL KENT CURTIS, FREE SPEECH, "THE PEOPLE'S DARLING PRIVILEGE" (2000); David Kairys, *Freedom of Speech, in* THE POLITICS OF LAW: A PROGRESSIVE CRITIQUE 140, 151–58 (David Kairys ed. 1982); Sanford Levinson, *The Embarrassing Second Amendment*, 99 YALE L.J. 637, 641–42 (1989). The Supreme Court did not begin enforcing the First Amendment until the 1930s, or the Second until 2008.

PART 2

Current Legal Landscapes

9. *The Badges and Incidents of Slavery and the Power of Congress to Enforce the Thirteenth Amendment*

George A. Rutherglen

The Supreme Court has rarely considered the scope of the Thirteenth Amendment, perhaps because of nearly unanimous agreement on two basic propositions: first, that the amendment reaches private action because, unlike the Fourteenth Amendment, it has no "state action" restriction on its coverage; and, second, that Congress has the power under section 2 of the amendment to eliminate the badges and incidents of slavery. It follows from the first proposition that the only limit on congressional power to enforce the amendment depends upon the elusive meaning of the second proposition and, in particular, the phrase "badges and incidents of slavery." This phrase does not appear in the amendment itself, which simply gives Congress the "power to enforce this article by appropriate legislation," and it has received diametrically opposed interpretations in the leading decisions on the Thirteenth Amendment.

The *Civil Rights Cases*,[1] decided in the aftermath of Reconstruction, declared the Civil Rights Act of 1875 unconstitutional, holding that its prohibitions against private discrimination in public accommodations exceeded the powers of Congress under both the Thirteenth and the Fourteenth Amendments. Under the Thirteenth Amendment specifically, the Supreme Court reasoned that private discrimination in inns, theaters, and public transport had historically been practiced against free blacks in the antebellum era and that it could not, for that reason, be classified as a badge or incident of slavery. Eighty-five years later, the Court reached nearly the opposite conclusion in *Jones v. Alfred H. Mayer Co.*,[2] where it interpreted the Civil Rights Act of 1866 to prohibit private racial discrimination in housing and it upheld the act as so interpreted. The Court reasoned that Congress could rationally classify this form of discrimination as among the persistent badges and incidents of slavery that it had the power to prohibit under the Thirteenth Amendment.

These decisions agreed in their common use of "badges and incidents of slavery" as the test for congressional power under the Thirteenth Amendment but on little else about the meaning or application of this phrase. The *Civil Rights Cases* drastically limited congressional power to prohibit private discrimination under the Thirteenth Amendment, while *Jones v. Mayer* greatly expanded it. How could one phrase bear such different meanings and be invoked to justify such inconsistent conclusions? This essay offers an answer to this question by analyzing the literal and figurative senses that were given to the "badges and incidents of slavery" in political and legal discourse. The inherent ambiguity in this phrase is the key to understanding its role, initially in political thought and then in constitutional interpretation.

ORIGINS AND ANTEBELLUM MEANING

Of the two attributes of slavery identified as badges and incidents, the "incidents" of slavery had a far more definite and accepted legal sense than the "badges." The "incidents of slavery" could be taken literally as accepted legal usage, just like the incidents of ownership of property or the incidents of office, while the "badges of slavery" took on a sense that was at least partially figurative.

As the *Oxford English Dictionary* defines the term, "incident" means "attaching itself, as a privilege, burden, or custom, *to* an office, position, etc."[3] It also cites English legal sources from the fifteenth through the nineteenth centuries that used the term to refer to the legal consequences of a status or position. In 1828, Noah Webster defined the term in much the same sense in his *American Dictionary of the English Language*: "appertaining to or following the chief or principal. A court baron is *incident* to a manor."[4]

Within a few decades, "incidents of slavery" acquired its own specialized meaning. George M. Stroud used the phrase as the title of a chapter in his abolitionist treatise, recounting the various disabilities imposed upon slaves in different Southern states.[5] Theophilus Parson, a professor of law at Harvard, also offered a survey of the institution of slavery in his treatise on contracts, beginning with the observation that attempts to "ascertain the nature and incidents of slavery, as it exists in this country, by reference to feudal or civil law had proved to be largely unsuccessful."[6] This usage of the word "incident," as indicated by the definition given earlier, just invoked the literal meaning of the term.

By contrast, the phrase "badges of slavery" could be given no such straightforward literal sense. Taken literally, it means a "distinctive device, emblem, or mark . . . worn as a sign of office, such as a sheriff's badge." Figuratively, it is a "distinguishing 'sign,' emblem, token, or symbol of any kind,"[7] as in *The Red Badge of Courage*, the famous novel about the Civil War, in which the blood of soldiers is the emblem of their bravery. Only slightly less figurative is the "badge of shame" represented in *The Scarlet Letter*, published in 1850, where the heroine must wear the letter embroidered on her clothing as a tangible sign of adultery.[8]

As applied to the Thirteenth Amendment, only the figurative sense of "badges" gives any meaning to the power of Congress to eliminate the badges of slavery. American slaves did not wear actual badges, with the single exception of slaves who were free to move about Charleston, South Carolina.[9] They were, instead, identified by the color of their skin and other physical characteristics. Ironically, it was free blacks who had to carry something close to actual badges, in the form of papers establishing that they were free.[10] Congress could abolish such requirements, but it could not abolish the physical characteristics of race. The analogy between actual badges and skin color cannot yield a literal sense of the "badges of slavery" that Congress has the power to prohibit under the Thirteenth Amendment. What Congress can act upon, of course, are the social consequences of race, but these are badges only in a figurative sense.

How far to take this figurative sense has been the central question under section 2 of the Thirteenth Amendment: which consequences of slavery can Congress prohibit? In the *Civil Rights Cases*, the Supreme Court took a narrow view of these consequences, essentially limiting them to the "necessary incidents" of slavery, defined by comparing the status of slaves with the status of free blacks before emancipation.[11] Although the Court assumed that Congress also had the power to eliminate the "badges of slavery,"[12] the Court failed to give any independent significance to this term. Either it meant the same as "incidents of slavery" or it added only metaphorical connotations that had no operative legal effect. The reference to badges amounted, at most, only to a more colorful way of referring to the legal consequences of slavery.

"Badges of slavery" certainly could be used in this narrow sense, as it was by William Lloyd Garrison when he referred to the prohibition against the marriage of interracial couples as "a disgraceful badge of servitude."[13] The denial of the capacity to marry was among the disabilities imposed upon slaves.[14] Garrison's remark was controversial, not in drawing attention to this incident of slavery but in drawing the analogy between denial of the capacity to marry and denial of the capacity to marry someone of a different race. The first was an inference *from* slave status in a literal sense, while the second was an inference *to* slave status in a figurative sense. Laws against miscegenation, insofar as they applied to whites and free blacks, did not draw out a consequence of actual slavery but were an indication of symbolic slavery.

This figurative sense derived from the literal meaning of "badge" as a sign deliberately worn to indicate position or status. From certain external features, an individual's social position could be inferred. Thus, in an argument before the Supreme Court in 1843, a lawyer for a slave seeking freedom through a conditional manumission offered the following observation about American slavery: "Colour in a slaveholding state is a badge of slavery. It is not so where slavery does not exist."[15] Being black was evidence of being a slave.

This sense of "badge" rarely appeared in the law of slavery, which relied far more frequently on "incident" to denote the consequences of being a slave.[16] "Badge," when it was used in legal discourse, appeared in an entirely different field, as "badges of fraud": evidence that a transaction was designed to put a debtor's assets beyond the reach of existing creditors. This terminology was well established in the law of bankruptcy and creditors' rights by the middle of the nineteenth century. As one treatise defined the term and its synonyms, they all "simply denote an act which has a fraudulent aspect,"[17] confirming the sense of "badge" as evidence permitting an inference from external appearances to legal status. A transaction with the badges of fraud, such as a secret transfer of the debtors' assets, supports the inference that it is a fraudulent conveyance.

This shift in focus from the consequences of legal status to evidence for that status underlies the most common sense in which "badges of slavery" was used before the Civil War: as evidence of political subjugation. In *The Wealth of Nations*, Adam Smith used the phrase in a famous passage denouncing British mistreatment of the American colonies. Restrictions on trade and manufacture in the colonies, he wrote, "are only the impertinent badges of slavery imposed upon them without any sufficient reason, by the groundless jealousy of the merchants and manufacturers of the Mother Country."[18] This passage was well known in the nineteenth century, as evidenced by its appearance in Bancroft's *History of the United States*,[19] and Smith's writings generally were familiar to leading Americans.[20] Wholly apart from Smith's use of the term, it appears in the writings of leading political figures such as George Washington, John Adams, and Edmund Burke.[21] The use of the phrase can be traced in English political discourse at least as far back as the English Civil War[22] and much further back through the analogous Latin term *imaginem servitii*, which appears in Tacitus.[23] According to one nineteenth-century history of English law, the phrase refers to "those badges of slavery which are imposed upon a conquered people."[24]

Unlike its legal use, the political use of this phrase was common in the antebellum era. As Bernard Bailyn famously pointed out: "'Slavery' was a central concept in eighteenth-century political discourse. As the absolute political evil, it appears in every statement of political principle, in every discussion of constitutionalism or legal rights, in every exhortation to resistance."[25] The Revolution resulted in political independence, even if it left chattel slavery in place, in order to free the colonies from the badges of slavery that Adam Smith had previously identified. The inconsistency inherent in this position became only more apparent after independence, causing abolitionists to insist that chattel slavery could not be reconciled with the principle that "all men are created equal." The decades leading to the Civil War further intensified the rhetorical connection between slavery and political power, ironically one invoked as frequently in the South as in the North. Southerners saw the rise of the Republican Party and the election of Lincoln as the prelude to their political enslavement. Northerners saw the spread of slavery to new states and territories in the same terms.[26] Political slavery was inextricably intertwined with chattel slavery in political discourse connecting both the figurative and the literal in debates over slavery. It was against this background that "badges of slavery" entered into legal debates over the meaning of the Thirteenth Amendment.

"BADGES AND INCIDENTS OF SLAVERY" IN CONGRESS

It was not until after the Thirteenth Amendment was ratified that "badges and incidents of slavery" became the touchstone for determining the scope of congressional power under section 2. In Congress, the "badges of slavery" and the "incidents of slavery" were mentioned only once in the debates over the Thirteenth Amendment. Section 2 was itself rarely discussed, and mainly by opponents of the amendment who saw a threat of federal encroachment on the power of the states. What the opponents lacked in precision they made up for in the extremism of their rhetoric, arguing that the amendment itself was unconstitutional and predicting the demise of state government if the amendment were adopted. Supporters, on the other hand, remained largely silent on the scope of congressional power conferred by the amendment, hoping to win over the votes needed for the two-thirds majority in each house in Congress and subsequent ratification by three-quarters of the states. Neither side addressed this question in terms of the "badges and incidents of slavery," or indeed acknowledged any specific test for the scope of congressional power to enforce the amendment. This phrase entered into debates over congressional power only when Congress considered the Civil Rights Act of 1866, but even this appearance of the phrase was not without irony, since it was doubts about the constitutionality of the act that led to adoption of the Fourteenth Amendment.

As noted in the previous section, "incidents of slavery" has a far more definite meaning than "badges of slavery." This conclusion is evident in the only speech that comes close to using both phrases to describe the practice of slavery. Senator James Harlan, of Iowa, gave a long list of the "incidents of slavery," like the antebellum treatises cited earlier. The enumerated incidents of slavery were offered as defining features of the institution, as the senator said with respect to the inability of slaves to marry: "If you continue slavery you must continue this necessary incident of its existence."[27] He made no reference to the power of Congress but implied that this, and other, incidents of slavery would be abolished by the amendment itself. Earlier in his speech, he used the phrase "badge of degradation" in describing the practice of slavery in the ancient world: "Color at Rome was not even a badge of degradation. It had no application to the question of slavery." This broad and figurative sense of "badge" follows the political usage of the term, but it was not echoed in the remarks of any other legislator.

Other supporters of the amendment were anxious to limit its effect, denying, for instance, that it affected the right to vote. Even the prominent Radical Republican, Representative Thaddeus Stevens, took this position, saying that he did not believe in "equality in all things—simply before the laws, nothing else."[28] Senator Charles Sumner offered a specific criticism of section 2 of the amendment, but only in formal terms, arguing that it should have been consolidated with the provisions of section 1, by analogy to the Full Faith and Credit Clause in Article IV.[29] In fact, section 2 derived from a proposal by Representative Wilson, of Iowa, to cure problems with prior legislation that had freed the slaves in occupied Confederate territory but had made no provisions for enforcement.[30]

The scope of congressional power, and questions of federalism generally, figured far more prominently in the arguments advanced against the Thirteenth Amendment. Opponents of the amendment argued that, if ratified, it would fundamentally alter the balance of power between the states and the federal government, so much so that the amendment itself was unconstitutional. This argument might strike the modern reader as an obstinate refusal to acknowledge the necessary consequence of the amending process, but it did identify a defining feature of the Thirteenth Amendment: unlike any previous amendment, it expanded federal power at the expense of the states, injecting the federal government into the regulation of "domestic relationships" like that between master and slave.[31] This argument carried over directly to section 2 of the amendment, since that expanded federal power even further by authorizing federal legislation without any of the checks imposed on amendments to the Constitution.[32] Legislators who doubted that Congress had the power to propose the Thirteenth Amendment by a two-thirds vote would have had even stronger objections to giving it the power to enforce the amendment by ordinary legislation.

Supporters of the amendment met these concerns by addressing the weakest of the opponents' arguments, based on the unconstitutionality of the amendment itself. This argument failed almost on its terms. Article V does contain limitations on the amending power, but these only confirm how broad the amending power otherwise is. The limited exception with respect to slavery—preventing repeal of the limitation on congressional power to prohibit importation of slaves before 1808—had long since lapsed. On the more immediate issue of the expansion of congressional power, the supporters of the amendment responded with studied ambiguity. Like Thaddeus Stevens, they conceded only that the amendment conferred something less than full equality on the newly freed slaves, without ever specifying quite what that was. They argued that it conferred "equality before the law," or "civil rights," or "natural rights," but not "political rights," or "social equality," or "full citizenship." By implication, the enforcement power conferred by section 2 must have been subject to the same limits, but the supporters of the amendment did not say what those limits were.

Some of the supporters' strongest disclaimers simply forced a reconciliation between the amendment's abolitionist aims and its limited effect. As Representative Thomas T. Davis, a Republican from New York, framed the issue, the only way to secure equality before the law was "by removing every vestige of African slavery from the American Republic."[33] Others conceded the limited effect of the amendment. Senator John B. Henderson, a Republican from Missouri, who participated in the process of drafting the amendment, offered a candid but ambivalent account of its consequences. In denying that the amendment conferred citizenship on the freedmen, he said: "So in passing this amendment we do not confer upon the negro the right to vote. We give him no right except his freedom, and leave the rest to the States." He then went on to deny that the amendment would result in miscegenation: "I will not be deterred from doing an act of simple justice from fear of the consequences. It is impossible that great evil should spring from such acts of justice. We may not be able now to solve the many problems that universal emancipation may present."[34] Senator Henderson was content to leave these problems to the future and to be addressed, at least in the first instance, by the states. A more extreme version of this position was taken by some reluctant Democratic supporters of the amendment, whose votes were nevertheless necessary for it to pass the House. One of them, Representative George Yeaman, from Kentucky, thought that the amendment would preempt the need for further abolitionist legislation: "In passing this amendment we do make sure the final extinction of slavery, but so far from indorsing the radical abolition party, we rob them of their power."[35]

The arguments in Congress were echoed in the ratification debates in the state legislatures, but with a sharper focus on section 2. In some Northern states, such as Indiana and Illinois, intense debates over the expansion of federal power preceded the eventual vote to ratify the amendment.[36] The border state of Kentucky, however, refused to ratify for this reason, and among Southern states, Mississippi took the same course. South Carolina tried to find a middle course, reluctantly voting to ratify with a resolution approving section 1 of the amendment but not section 2.[37] Secretary of State Seward nevertheless counted South Carolina as ratifying the entire amendment and declared the amendment ratified when Georgia supplied the final resolution in its support. If the marginal states most reluctant to ratify had determined the meaning of the amendment, then it would have granted Congress hardly any enforcement powers at all.

The rhetoric of "badges and incidents of slavery," despite its absence from the debates over the amendment, captured the ambivalence of its supporters, who espoused the revolutionary aim of freedom for all but remained reluctant to expand federal power to the full extent necessary to achieve that goal. The amendment set an oppressed race free from the badges of their subservience, but it immediately abolished only the necessary incidents of slavery. "Badges and incidents" was a phrase adequate to encompass the deep-seated conflicts over the meaning of the amendment but not to resolve all the contradictory impulses behind its adoption. These emerged as soon as Congress sought to exercise its newly conferred powers under section 2.

Senator Trumbull first invoked the phrase in support of the Freedmen's Bureau Bill and the Civil Rights Act of 1866. After several Southern states had enacted "black codes" restricting the rights of the newly freed slaves, Trumbull denounced such laws for reinstating the badges and incidents of slavery: "With the destruction of slavery necessarily follows the destruction of the incidents to slavery." And, "With the abolition of slavery should go all the badges of servitude which have been enacted for its maintenance and support."[38] In his opinion, these extended to any statute that denied civil rights to some citizens but not others, thereby imposing "a badge of servitude which, by the Constitution, is prohibited."[39] When the power of Congress to enact legislation to invalidate the Black Codes was questioned, Trumbull interpreted the amendment to grant Congress nearly sole discretion to decide what measures were "appropriate legislation" under section 2.[40] He admitted, however, that he had not expressed this opinion in the debates over the Thirteenth Amendment, offering the explanation that it was so obvious as to be unnecessary.[41] In fact, continuing in the same vein, he explained that some members of Congress did not think that section 2 was needed at all, because the Constitution already authorized all legislation "necessary and proper to put its provisions into effect."[42] In his view, section 2 simply clarified what the existing powers of Congress already were.

Other legislators took a different view, among them Senator John Sherman, of Ohio, who argued that section 2 was added to the amendment to avoid problems that had arisen in enforcing the Privileges and Immunities Clause of Article IV. This clause had no corresponding enforcement provision, leading to doubts about the power of Congress to assure equal privileges and immunities of citizens in states different from their own.[43] These concerns echoed those that led Representative Wilson to introduce the provision that eventually became section 2. His interpretation of "appropriate legislation" rested squarely on the famous passage in *McCulloch v. Maryland* broadly interpreting the power of Congress under the Necessary and Proper Clause: "Let the end be legitimate, let it be within the scope of the Constitution, and all means which are appropriate, which are plainly adapted to that end, which are not prohibited, but consist with the letter and spirit of the Constitution, are constitutional."[44]

This appeal to precedent, however, did little to reduce the controversy over congressional power under section 2. When President Johnson vetoed the Civil Rights Act of 1866, he invoked the same language of "necessary and proper" but limited it to the end of abolishing slavery, which he thought had already been accomplished.[45] Although his veto of the Civil Rights Act of 1866 was overridden, his veto of the Freedmen's Bureau Bill on similar grounds was not, and a more moderate Freedmen's Bureau Act was proposed again, and again vetoed, but eventually enacted into law.[46] Doubts about the constitutionality of the Civil Rights Act of 1866 also persisted beyond its enactment, leading directly to congressional consideration of the Fourteenth Amendment as one way to put those doubts to rest. And, indeed, after ratification of that amendment, Congress moved quickly to reenact the Civil Rights Act of 1866.[47]

If it were not for doubts about its own constitutionality under the Thirteenth Amendment, the Civil Rights Act of 1866 would give us the best evidence of what Congress thought the "badges and incidents of slavery" were at the time. The act lists a variety of rights guaranteed to the newly freed slaves, from specific rights that were denied to slaves, such as the "right to make and enforce contracts" to the general right to the "full and equal benefit of all laws and proceedings for the security of person and property." As it progressed from specific to general, the act gave less and less determinate content to what constituted the badges and incidents of slavery. The act also purported to confer citizenship on the newly freed slaves, a provision eventually incorporated in the Fourteenth Amendment. Likewise, the "full and equal benefits" clause in the statute was the model for the Equal Protection Clause in the amendment. The presence of these two provisions in the Civil Rights Act of 1866 reproduced the full range of ambiguity about the nature and degree of freedom created by the Thirteenth Amendment. Questions about the meaning of the amendment were not answered—or perhaps even fully appreciated—before it was ratified, and they were put to rest afterward only by the simple expedient of making them questions about the Fourteenth Amendment.

One great difference between the amendments persists, however. The Fourteenth Amendment applies only to state action. The Thirteenth Amendment reaches private action. This question dominated interpretation of the Civil Rights Act of 1866 toward the end of the twentieth century, but it has indirectly figured in interpretation of the Thirteenth Amendment from the beginning. If state action does not operate as a restriction on this amendment, then what does? All that remains is the inherently ambiguous phrase "badges and incidents of slavery," which soon became canonical in interpreting the amendment. The decisions that reached this conclusion are the subject of the next part of this essay.

"BADGES AND INCIDENTS OF SLAVERY" IN THE SUPREME COURT

From its origins in the scattered statements of a single senator, "badges and incidents of slavery" quickly became the Supreme Court's standard gloss upon the powers of Congress under the Thirteenth Amendment. The trajectory of its rise to prominence was from Senator Trumbull to Justice Bradley, who first referred to "a badge of slavery" in his dissent in *Blyew v. United States*[48] and then to "badges and incidents of slavery" in his majority opinion in the *Civil Rights Cases*.[49] From there, it found its way into almost every subsequent decision of the Supreme Court on the Thirteenth Amendment. At the moment this phrase became authoritative, it also lost its expansive implications, when the Supreme Court struck down the provisions on public accommodations in the Civil Rights Act of 1875. According to Justice Bradley, to hold that such discrimination was a badge or incident of slavery "would be running the slavery argument into the ground."[50] This argument by reductio ad absurdum, however, would not prove to be the last word on section 2, but only the beginning of a long and inconsistent line of opinions.

The significance of this entire line of opinions depends upon another distinction introduced by the *Civil Rights Cases*: between the regulation of private action under the Thirteenth Amendment and the regulation of state action under the Fourteenth Amendment, which applies *only* to state action. In addition to holding the Civil Rights Act of 1875 unconstitutional under the Thirteenth Amendment, the Court also held it unconstitutional under the Fourteenth. Congress lacked the power to regulate public accommodations under the Fourteenth Amendment because the private operators of those facilities did not engage in sufficient state action to be subject to the amendment.[51] According to Justice Bradley, the Fourteenth Amendment authorized no "primary and direct" legislation that operated on individuals and private firms, while the Thirteenth Amendment did.[52]

The Court's dictum on the Thirteenth Amendment's coverage of private action came closer to a holding in *Clyatt v. United States*,[53] a case involving a prosecution of private individuals under the Anti-Peonage Act (1867). The Court found the indictment sufficient, despite the absence of any allegation that the defendants engaged in state action (although they had commenced state proceedings against the individuals taken into peonage).[54] The indictment also failed to allege any element of racial discrimination, following the principle of the *Civil Rights Cases* that "the Thirteenth Amendment has respect, not to distinctions of race, or class, or color, but to slavery."[55] The crucial issue in a prosecution for peonage is reducing an individual to the condition of "involuntary servitude," not discrimination on the basis of race. Peonage, according to the Court, "may be defined as a status or condition of compulsory service, based upon indebtedness of the peon to the master."[56] The race of the peon did not matter, a conclusion foreshadowed by the *Slaughterhouse Cases*.[57] Although the Court there emphasized protection of African Americans as the animating purpose of the Reconstruction amendments, it also acknowledged that the literal terms of the Thirteenth Amendment prohibited all forms of servitude, regardless of race.[58]

The scope of this prohibition was the crucial issue in the *Civil Rights Cases*, and in all subsequent cases under the Thirteenth Amendment. Only the limited subject matter of the amendment prevented it from authorizing federal regulation of all kinds of private activity previously reserved to the states. Denial of public accommodations did not fall within the scope of the amendment. "Mere discriminations on account of race or color were not regarded as badges of slavery."[59] Only the rights that free blacks had before the Civil War, and that the slaves did not, constituted the necessary incidents of slavery that could be remedied under the Thirteenth Amendment. Since free blacks were subject to pervasive discrimination before emancipation, the same would also be true of the newly freed slaves.

This narrow construction of the "badges and incidents of slavery" survived well into the twentieth century, providing one of the pillars in the legal foundation for the segregationist regime of Jim Crow. Along with the state-action doctrine and "separate but equal"—what Charles Black called "the Medusan caryatids of racial injustice"[60]—a narrow construction of the Thirteenth Amendment provided crucial support for the preservation of segregation. Indeed, this construction figured in a subsidiary holding in *Plessy v. Ferguson*, which found a state law requiring "separate but equal" facilities in public accommodations to be constitutional under both the Thirteenth and Fourteenth Amendments. Segregation, the Court said, "has no tendency to destroy the legal equality of the races, or reestablish a state of involuntary servitude."[61]

The Court imposed a similarly narrow interpretation of the powers of Congress in several decisions in the early twentieth century that further limited the scope and significance of the Thirteenth Amendment. Thus in *Hodges v. United States*,[62] the Supreme Court held that the amendment did not cover the right to keep a job free from private violence. In that case, a federal indictment alleged that black laborers were forcibly expelled from their jobs at a sawmill by the white defendants, in violation of their right to engage in free labor under the Thirteenth Amendment. The Court found, however, no badge or incident of slavery in the denial of the right to work, even if it was based on race. Wrongful action on the basis of race was not enough because "it was not the intent of the Amendment to denounce every act done to an individual which was wrong if done to a free man and yet justified in a condition of slavery." The denial of the right to work was not unique to slavery because, the Court reasoned, the same right could be denied to immigrants. The badges and incidents of slavery were narrowed to the essential distinguishing features of slavery as an institution, with a corresponding limit on the power of Congress to enforce the amendment.

This entire restrictive approach persisted for more than a century after ratification of the Thirteenth Amendment, only to be suddenly overthrown by the Warren Court. In *Jones v. Alfred H. Mayer Co.*, the Court held that the Civil Rights Act of 1866, the first legislation enacted under the amendment, prohibited private discrimination in addition to discrimination by government. Having interpreted the act to reach private discrimination, the Court had to decide whether Congress could enact a statute with such broad coverage. The Court held that Congress could because it need only find a rational basis for determining what constitutes a badge or incident of slavery. "Surely Congress has the power under the Thirteenth Amendment rationally to determine what are the badges and the incidents of slavery, and the authority to translate that determination into effective legislation."[63] Among the badges and incidents of slavery, according to the Court, were private racial discrimination in housing because, in the language of the act, it denied blacks "the same right . . . to inherit, purchase, lease, sell and convey property, as is enjoyed by white citizens."[64]

Jones v. Mayer took a broad view of "badges and incidents of slavery" where the *Civil Rights Cases* had taken a narrow view, greatly expanding the ends for which Congress could legislate under the Thirteenth Amendment. Under the framework of *McCulloch v. Maryland*, the legitimate ends under the amendment expanded from abolition of slavery to eliminating the consequences of slavery, with a concomitant increase in the appropriate means that Congress could choose to reach those ends. This reasoning closely follows the modern decisions under the Commerce Clause expanding the scope of congressional regulation to any activities that "substantially affect interstate commerce."[65] These decisions conferred doctrinal legitimacy on *Jones v. Mayer* at the same time as they minimized its immediate consequences, which were only to augment the coverage and remedies available to victims of housing discrimination under the Civil Rights Act of 1968.[66]

That act, like other modern civil rights legislation, had been enacted under the Commerce Clause, avoiding the limitations on congressional power imposed by the *Civil Rights Cases*. The vast expansion of federal power on this ground had been solidified in the New Deal and transformed the background against which *Jones v. Mayer* was decided. As a practical matter, the decision added little to existing civil rights law, and, as a theoretical matter, it invoked an understanding of congressional power under a combination of the Commerce Clause and the Necessary and Proper Clause. A broad interpretation of the latter clause carried over directly to the Thirteenth Amendment by way of the phrase "appropriate legislation" in section 2. As we have seen, that phrase was viewed by the framers of the amendment as an implicit reference to *McCulloch v. Maryland*. An expansion of what was necessary and proper to the regulation of commerce led, with seeming ease and inexorability, to a corresponding expansion of the power to enforce the Thirteenth Amendment.

Subsequent decisions have not given Congress nearly so much discretion to enforce the Reconstruction amendments. In particular, legislation to enforce the Fourteenth Amendment must exhibit "congruence and proportionality between the injury to be prevented or remedied and the means adopted to that end."[67] The phrase "appropriate legislation" again provides the connecting link between interpretation of the Fourteenth Amendment and interpretation of the Thirteenth, since all the Reconstruction amendments use this phrase in their enforcement provisions. The standard of "congruence and proportionality" would be markedly more stringent than that applied to legislation under the Commerce Clause. At least with respect to purely economic activity, Congress need not establish any degree of proportionality between the means it has chosen and the resulting effect on commerce. Regulation of noneconomic activity raises other questions under the Commerce Clause, but under existing law, there remains a gap between what is "necessary and proper" to enforce the Commerce Clause and what is "appropriate" to enforce the Fourteenth Amendment.

Jones v. Mayer falls nearer to the Commerce Clause side of this gap, even though the terminology of "badges and incidents of slavery" has few associations with commerce. What it does have is the same capacity to embrace the consequences of an activity undeniably subject to congressional regulation. On a broad construction, it would give Congress the power to eliminate the residual effects of slavery, just as Congress can regulate activity with substantial effects on commerce. *Jones v. Mayer* exploited the potential breadth of the "badges and incidents of slavery" to expand the ends that could be achieved under the Thirteenth Amendment, moving from abolition of the narrowly defined incidents of slavery to prohibiting the badges of continued racial discrimination.

Moreover, the Court accomplished this result without departing from the terms used in the *Civil Rights Cases*, although it gave them a very different sense and spirit. The Court grudgingly recognized that the *Civil Rights Cases* could not really be reconciled with the validity of modern civil rights legislation under the Commerce Clause,[68] but because Congress enacted the Civil Rights Act of 1866 only under the Thirteenth Amendment, the Court had to give the "badges and incidents of slavery" a much broader interpretation than they had received in the *Civil Rights Cases*. In general, Congress had the power "to eradicate the last vestiges and incidents of a society half slave and half free," and, in particular, it could act to prohibit private discrimination with respect to any of the rights enumerated in the 1866 act.

This holding has since coexisted uneasily with the *Civil Rights Cases*. Both decisions serve as defining instances of appropriate legislation under the Reconstruction amendments, but both have been doubted and limited as precedents. The statutory holding in *Jones v. Mayer* soon came under attack as an unjustified judicial extension of the Civil Rights Act of 1866 to private discrimination, and the decision was then limited in some respects, although not on constitutional grounds.[69] Ultimately, however, the full force of the decision was reinstated by Congress in the Civil Rights Act of 1991, a recent instance of federal civil rights legislation that fittingly sought to revive and confirm a broad understanding of the very first civil rights act. In the 1991 act, Congress codified the broad scope of the 1866 act in two respects: first, it made clear that the act applied to all forms of discrimination, whether public or private; and second, that the act applied to all forms of discrimination in contracting, including how a contract was performed in addition to how it was made.[70] The Civil Rights Act of 1991 provides no independent support for the constitutional holding in *Jones v. Mayer*, since Congress simply took advantage of the legislative power conferred by the decision. Yet the concurrence of Congress in the decision inevitably contributed political support to its interpretation of the Thirteenth Amendment.

A similar process of indirect ratification resulted from the Supreme Court's reliance on the *Civil Rights Cases* in decisions invalidating legislation attempting to enforce the Fourteenth Amendment. These decisions did not mention the Thirteenth Amendment holding in the *Civil Rights Cases* that had been called into question by *Jones v. Mayer*. Yet the endorsement of the *Civil Rights Cases* in one respect might well carry over to its force as a precedent in another, since, as noted earlier, Congress can enforce both amendments only by "appropriate legislation." The crucial difference between the two amendments—with the Thirteenth Amendment extending to private action and the Fourteenth Amendment limited to state action—might mitigate any such effect by altering the permissible ends Congress could seek to achieve. "Appropriate legislation" might have the same meaning under each amendment but with very different implications as applied to legislation aimed at private activity. Such uncertainties contribute to the continued coexistence of *Jones v. Mayer* with the surviving holding of the *Civil Rights Cases*, minimizing the likelihood of any direct conflict between the decisions and any need to resolve the obvious tensions between them. The ambiguity inherent in the Thirteenth Amendment may be more durable than any attempt to resolve it.

CONCLUSION

Some may find the "badges and incidents of slavery" to be a constitutional standard of dubious provenance, uncertain meaning, and unprincipled application.[71] Others may see it as the constitutional foundation of racial equality and federal civil rights legislation.[72] The historical record contains enough ambiguity to support both views, and many in between. To the extent that a single phrase can capture all the contradictory aspirations and limitations of the Thirteenth Amendment, "badges and incidents of slavery" does so: "badges" because of its breadth and resonance with ideals of political independence and "incidents" because of its narrow reference to the immediate legal implications of slavery. This essay on the origins of this phrase and its introduction into constitutional discourse cannot reconcile all the disparate and conflicting arguments that have surrounded the Thirteenth Amendment since it was proposed. All this exegesis of this standard can do is to indicate how these different strands of interpretation could credibly be brought together under a single heading, how a single fragment of constitutional doctrine could do justice both to the moral imperatives of emancipation and to the political limitations on its realization. These issues, like the consequences of slavery itself, remain as alive for us as they were for the framers of the Thirteenth Amendment.

NOTES

1. 109 U.S. 3 (1883).

2. 392 U.S. 409 (1968).

3. VII Oxford English Dictionary 793 (2d ed. 1989).

4. Noah Webster's First Edition of an American Dictionary of the English Language (1828; repr. 1967).

5. George M. Stroud, A Sketch of the Laws Relating to Slavery in the Several States of the United States of America (2d ed. 1856).

6. I Theophilus Parson, The Law of Contracts 399 (5th ed. 1864).

7. I Oxford English Dictionary at 876.

8. Nathaniel Hawthorne, The Scarlet Letter 212, 257 (Library of America 1983).

9. This practice was required by law in some other Southern cities, but there is evidence for it only in Charleston. Harlan Greene, Harry S. Hutchins, Jr. & Brian E. Hutchins, Slave Badges and the Slave-Hire System in Charleston, South Carolina, 1783–1865, at 6–8 (2004). I am grateful to Michael Vorenberg for calling this point to my attention.

10. For an account of this practice, *see* Hodges v. United States, 203 U.S. 1, 19 (1906).

11. *Id.* at 20–25.

12. *Id.* at 20 ("It is assumed, that the power vested in Congress to enforce the article by appropriate legislation, clothes Congress with power to pass all laws necessary and proper for abolishing all badges and incidents of slavery in the United States.").

13. The Liberator (June 11, 1831), *quoted in* Louis Ruchames, *Race, Marriage and Abolition*, 40 J. Negro Hist. 250, 253 (1955). I am grateful to Alex Tsesis for this reference.

14. Stroud, *supra*, at 99.

15. *Williams v. Ash*, 42 U.S. 1, 8 (1843) (argument for defendant in error).

16. For some additional examples, *see* Thomas D. Morris, Southern Slavery and the Law, 1619–1860 35 (1996); *Neal v. Farmer*, 9 Ga. 555, 567 (1851) ("The condition of a villein, had many of the incidents of slavery. His service was uncertain, and he was bound to do whatever his lord commanded."); *Jacob v. State*, 22 Tenn. 493, 505 (1842) (argument of counsel that "it is certainly true that many of the disabilities incident to slavery are inconsistent with the common law").

17. Orlando Bump, A Treatise upon Conveyances Made by Debtors to Defraud Creditors 29 (3d ed., James Gray ed., 1896). For antebellum cases using the term, *see, e.g., Warner v. Norton*, 61 U.S. 448, 459 (1857); *200 Chests of Tea*, 22 U.S. 430, 443 (1824); *Sexton v. Wheaton*, 21 U.S. 229, 250 (1823). The standard provision on this subject today, although not one using the term, is the Uniform Fraudulent Transfer Act § 4(b).

18. Adam Smith, An Inquiry in the Nature and Causes of the Wealth of Nations 582 (R. H. Campbell, A. S. Skinner, W. B. Todd eds., 1981) Bk. IV, ch. 7 (1776). He also notes, but dissents from, the opinion "that poll-taxes of all kinds have often been represented as badges of slavery." *Id.* at 857.

19. 8 George Bancroft, History of the United States from the Discovery of the American Continent 174 (1868).

20. Samuel Flieshacker, *Adam Smith's Reception Among the American Founders, 1776–1790*, 59 Wm. & Mary Q. 897 (2002).

21. 6 The Writings of George Washington 486 (Jared Sparks ed., 1834) (remarking during the Revolution that Britain's ability to raise troops was frustrated by the Irish, "who feel the importance of a critical moment to shake off those badges of slavery, which they have worn so long"); 4 The Works of John Adams 206

(Charles Francis Adams ed., 1851) (arguing that the legislature should choose a governor and "*divest him of most of those badges of slavery called prerogatives*") (emphasis in original); 5 THE WORKS AND CORRESPONDENCE OF EDMUND BURKE 393 (1852) (the principle of voluntary contributions during the French Revolution led the populace "to throw off the regular methodical payments to the state as so many badges of slavery").

22. JOHN BRISTOL, A DISCOURSE SHEWING THE GREAT HAPPINESSE, THAT HATH, AND MAY STILL ACCRUE TO HIS MAJESTIES KINGDOMES OF ENGLAND AND SCOTLAND, BY RE-UNITING THEM INTO ONE GREAT BRITAIN 197 (1641) ("We will weare the Badge of slavery on our sleeve, to brag to the world, that we are not ashamed to be conquered.")

23. TACITUS, ANNALS Bk. 15 [31]. He recounts an incident in which a Roman general was asked to treat a conquered Parthian king so that he "might not have to endure any badge of slavery."

24. OWEN FLINTOFF, THE RISE AND PROGRESS OF THE LAWS OF ENGLAND AND WALES 139 (1840).

25. BERNARD BAILYN, THE IDEOLOGICAL ORIGINS OF THE AMERICAN REVOLUTION 232 (1967).

26. MICHAEL F. HOLT, THE POLITICAL CRISIS OF THE 1850S 188–91, 242–43, 258–59 (1978).

27. CONG. GLOBE, 38th Cong., 1st Sess. 1439 (1864). For a discussion of this passage, *see* ALEXANDER TSESIS, THE THIRTEENTH AMENDMENT AND AMERICAN FREEDOM: A LEGAL HISTORY 121 (2004); Senator Wilson made a similar point in enumerating the "privileges and immunities" denied to slaves. *Id.* at 1202.

28. CONG. GLOBE, 38th Cong., 2d Sess. 125 (1865). For a discussion of these passages, *see* MICHAEL VORENBERG, FINAL FREEDOM: THE CIVIL WAR, THE ABOLITION OF SLAVERY, AND THE THIRTEENTH AMENDMENT 190–91 (2001).

29. CONG. GLOBE, 38th Cong., 1st Sess. 1488 (1864).

30. Vorenberg, *supra*, at 50.

31. *See id.* at 107–10, 194–97.

32. *See id.* at 132–33, 190–91.

33. CONG. GLOBE, 38th Cong., 1st Sess. 155 (1864).

34. *Id.* at 1465.

35. CONG. GLOBE, 38th Cong., 2d Sess. 171 (1865)

36. VORENBERG, *supra*, at 219–21.

37. *See id.* at 216–18, 228–33.

38. CONG. GLOBE, 39th Cong., 1st Sess. 322, 323 (1866). Representative Thayer used the language of "incidents" in a similar sense. *Id.* at 1151.

39. *Id.* at 474.

40. *Id.* at 43, 475.

41. *Id.* at 43.

42. *Id.* at 43.

43. *Id.* at 41.

44. *Id.* at 1118. *See also id.* app. at 157. Senator Trumbull eventually took a similar position, arguing that section 2 "authorizes us to do whatever is necessary to protect the freedman in his liberty." *See also id.* at 1124 (Rep. Cook).

45. *Id.* at 1681.

46. Act of July 16, 1866, 14 Stat. 173.

47. Act of May 31, 1870, 16 Stat. 140.

48. 80 U.S. 581, 599 (1872) (Bradley, J., dissenting).

49. 109 U.S. 3, 20, 21 (1883).

50. *Id.* at 24.

51. *Id.* at 18–19.

52. 109 U.S. at 19, 20.

53. 197 U.S. 207 (1905).

54. *Id.* at 215–18. The Court also held, however, that the evidence was insufficient to prove a "return . . . to a condition of peonage" as alleged in the indictment. *Id.* at 219–20. Other decisions of the period also pointed out that the Thirteenth Amendment covered private activity. *Robertson v. Baldwin,* 165 U.S. 275, 282 (1897); *Bailey v. Alabama,* 219 U.S. 219, 241 (1911).

55. 109 U.S. at 24.

56. *Clyatt,* 197 U.S. at 215. Accord, *Bailey v. Alabama,* 219 U.S. 219, 241–43 (1911); *Hodges v. United States,* 203 U.S. 1, 16–17 (1906).

57. 83 U.S. 36 (1873).

58. *Id.* at 72.

59. 109 U.S. at 24, 25.

60. Charles L. Black, Jr., *Foreword: "State Action," Equal Protection, and California's Proposition 14,* 81 HARV. L. REV. 69, 70 (1967).

61. 163 U.S. 537, 543 (1896).

62. 203 U.S. 1, 17–19 (1906).

63. *Jones v. Mayer,* 392 U.S. at 440.

64. Civil Rights Act of 1866 § 1, 42 U.S.C. § 1982, *quoted in Civil Rights Cases,* 109 U.S. at 22.

65. *Gonzales v. Raich,* 545 U.S. 1, 15–17 (2005); *Wickard v. Filburn,* 317 U.S. 11, 121–25 (1942); *United States v. Darby,* 312 U.S. 100, 121 (1941).

66. *Jones v. Mayer,* 392 U.S. at 441 n. 78.

67. *City of Boerne v. Flores,* 521 U.S. 507, 520 (1997); *see United States v. Morrison,* 529 U.S. 598, 619–27 (2000).

68. *Jones v. Mayer,* 392 U.S. at 441 n. 78. Only *Hodges v. United States* had to be overruled. *See id.*

69. *See Patterson v. McLean Credit Union,* 491 U.S. 164 (1989).

70. 42 U.S.C. § 1981(b), (c) (2000).

71. For David Currie, it represents "a triumph of the Trojan Horse theory of constitutional adjudication." DAVID P. CURRIE, THE CONSTITUTION IN THE SUPREME COURT: THE FIRST HUNDRED YEARS 1789–1888 401 (1985).

72. MARK DEWOLFE HOWE, *Federalism and Civil Rights, in* CIVIL RIGHTS, THE CONSTITUTION, AND THE COURTS 30, 48–51 (1967).

10. *The Promise of Congressional Enforcement*

Rebecca E. Zietlow

In recent years, the Supreme Court has placed restrictions upon congressional power to enact civil rights laws. For example, in *City of Boerne v. Flores*, the Court articulated a stringent "congruence and proportionality" test for evaluating Congress's power to enforce the Fourteenth Amendment, and in subsequent rulings, the Court applied that test to strike down several federal statutes making civil rights enforceable against both state governments and private actors.[1] In *U.S. v. Lopez*, the Court tightened its scrutiny of the Commerce Power, and in *U.S. v. Morrison*, the Court applied that test (as well as the congruence and proportionality test) to strike down the civil rights remedy in the Violence Against Women Act.[2] These cases present a challenge for members of Congress wishing to expand rights of belonging, those rights that promote an inclusive vision of who belongs to the national community of the United States and that facilitate equal membership in that community.[3] However, the oft-overlooked section 2 of the Thirteenth Amendment has considerable potential to resolve this dilemma.[4]

Section 2 of the Thirteenth Amendment empowers Congress to enact "appropriate" measures to enforce the abolition of slavery accomplished by section 1 of that amendment. The Reconstruction Congress intended the enforcement power granted by section 2 to be broad, and the Court generally has been deferential to that power. Moreover, while the Court has interpreted the Fourteenth

Amendment enforcement power to apply only to state action, the language of the Thirteenth Amendment makes it clear that it empowers Congress to remedy violations of civil rights by private individuals as well as by state actors.[5] Thus, section 2 of the Thirteenth Amendment holds great promise for a Congress seeking to define and protect our rights of belonging.

The framers of the Thirteenth Amendment intended their enforcement power to be quite broad. To them, the amendment did more than just abolish slavery, it also served as a font of rights of belonging. As Senator Lyman Trumbull explained, "It is idle to say that a man is free who cannot go and come at pleasure, who cannot buy and sell, who cannot enforce his rights. These are rights which the first clause of the constitutional amendment meant to secure to all."[6] Senator William Sherman agreed, noting that the Thirteenth Amendment was "not only a guarantee of liberty to every inhabitant of the United States, but an express grant of power to Congress to secure this liberty by appropriate legislation."[7] This would be a daunting task. As Senator Jacob Howard pointed out during the debate over the 1866 Civil Rights Act,

> We are told that the amendment simply relieves the slave from obligation to render service to his master. What is a slave in contemplation of American law, in contemplation of the laws of all of the slave states? We know full well . . . he had no rights nor nothing which he could call his own. He had not the right to become a husband or a father in the eye of the law, he had no child, he was not at liberty to indulge the natural affections of the human heart for children, for wife, or even for friend. He owned no property, because the law prohibited him. He could not take real or personal estate either by sale, by grant, or descent or inheritance. He did not own the bread he carried and ate. He stood upon the face of the earth completely isolated from the society in which he happened to be.[8]

What possible remedy could there be for this injustice? After the Thirteenth Amendment was ratified, the framers' first solution was the 1866 Civil Rights Act, which they intended to eliminate race discrimination and bestow basic fundamental rights such as the right to contract and to own property. As Howard explained, with "respect to all civil rights there is to be hereafter no distinction between the white race and the black race."[9] Senator Henry Lane agreed that the goal of the act was to ensure "that these freedmen shall be secured in the possession of all the rights, privileges and immunities of freemen; in other words, that we shall give effect to the proclamation of emancipation and to the constitutional amendment."[10]

The Civil Rights Act of 1866 illustrates the breadth of the enforcement power understood by the majority of the framers of the Thirteenth Amendment. The act provided that all persons would enjoy the same right "to make and enforce contracts, to sue, be parties, and give evidence, to inherit, purchase and lease, sell, hold and convey real and personal property and to full and equal benefit of the laws and proceedings for the security of person and property as is enjoyed by white citizens."[11] Opponents of the act argued that Congress lacked the power to enact it because section 2 enabled Congress only to end slavery, not to address the conditions related to that institution.[12] The Republican majority considered such criticism to be contrary to the purposes of the amendment.[13]

The more influential criticism came from Representative John Bingham, a Republican member of Congress who had long held abolitionist views. Although Bingham supported the principles behind the act, he opposed it because he did not believe that it fell within the Thirteenth Amendment enforcement power. He later proposed the Fourteenth Amendment in order to clearly empower Congress to enact a wider range of civil rights legislation.[14] Representative Bingham was well respected, and his fellow Republicans acted quickly to ratify "his" amendment. However, few of them joined him in opposing the 1866 act, which was approved by an overwhelming majority over the veto of President Johnson.[15]

The framers also had a broad view of their own power to enforce the Thirteenth Amendment. Perhaps the most dramatic provision of the 1866 act was its first section, in which Congress declared that all persons born within the jurisdiction of the United States were U.S. citizens. This provision directly conflicted with the Court's ruling in *Dred Scott v. Sandford* that people of African descent could not be American citizens.[16] Opponents of the bill argued that Congress lacked the power to overrule the Supreme Court with this legislation.[17] However, supporters of the bill asserted their authority to themselves determine the scope of their section 2 power notwithstanding Court rulings to the contrary. Senator Trumbull explained, "What that 'appropriate legislation' is, is for Congress to determine, and nobody else."[18] They repeatedly invoked the broad test for congressional power in the Supreme Court case of *McCulloch* to illustrate the meaning of the word "appropriate" in section 2.[19] As Representative John Kasson explained, "I do assert that Congress, as the power originally creating the clause, has the right to construe it, and that there is not a loyal tribunal in this country that will dare to treat with disrespect the construction given by this body to this clause of the Constitution."[20] Hence, members of the Reconstruction Congress believed that they had the authority to interpret the constitution.[21]

Because the slavery and involuntary servitude prohibited by the Thirteenth Amendment were an exploitative employment relationship based on an ideology of racial supremacy, Congress has used its enforcement power to address both conditions of employment and race-based discrimination. Regulating employment, in 1867, Congress prohibited the slavery-like practice of peonage and made it a crime to hold or place a person in condition of peonage.[22] Congress revised and updated the antipeonage statute several times, most recently expanding its protections with the Victims of Trafficking and Violence Protection Act of 2000 (TVPA) Violence Protection Act (2000).[23]

Congress has relied on its section 2 power to enact civil rights legislation. Two sections of the 1866 Civil Rights Act—now codified as 42 U.S.C. § 1981, which includes its prohibition on race discrimination in the making and enforcing of contracts, and 42 U.S.C. § 1982, which prohibits race discrimination in real estate transactions—provide significant remedies for victims of private race discrimination. In 1968, Congress enacted two more provisions based on section 2, the antiblockbusting provision of the Fair Housing Act (1968), which prohibits realtors from using race-based rumors to scare people into selling their homes at a reduced rate, and the 1968 Hate Crimes Act, which makes it a crime for a person to interfere in certain "federally protected activities" on the basis of race.[24]

However, the farthest-reaching civil rights statute based on the Thirteenth Amendment is the 1871 Enforcement Act, or Ku Klux Klan Act, which created civil and criminal penalties for conspiracies to deprive a person from exercising "any right or privilege of a citizen of the United States."[25] By 1871, rampant violence in southern states had convinced members of Congress that the federal authorities could not maintain order without stronger enforcement provisions.[26] They intended the Enforcement Act to give the federal government more power to enforce the new rights that it had created, including the 1866 Civil Rights Act. Its criminal provision, now codified as 18 U.S.C. § 242, is still used often by the federal government to prosecute civil rights violations. The civil remedy, now codified as 42 U.S.C. § 1985, remains a potent weapon for victims of racially motivated violence.[27]

Initially, the Court was skeptical about the scope of the section 2 power. The first case interpreting Congress's power to enforce the Thirteenth Amendment, the *Civil Rights Cases*, contains dicta broadly delineating Congress's power to enforce the Thirteenth Amendment. Specifically, the Court noted that the enforcement power could extend to private activity, "for the amendment is not a mere prohibition of state laws establishing or upholding slavery, but an absolute declaration that slavery or involuntary servitude shall not exist in any part of the United States."[28] In that case, then, the Court held that Congress could use section 2 to address private and public "badges and incidents of slavery." However, the Court applied the test in a nondeferential manner, finding that the 1875 Civil Rights Act did not fall within the section 2 power because the Court did not believe that race discrimination in places of public accommodation amounted to a badge or incident of slavery.[29]

In the 1906 case of *Hodges v. U.S.*, the Court again applied a narrow definition of "badges and incidents" when it struck down the indictment of white men who used force to scare African American workers away from the lumberyard in which they were employed.[30] The government argued that the defendants had violated the statute now codified as 18 U.S.C. § 242 by conspiring to deprive the workers of their Thirteenth Amendment right to work for compensation. The indictment alleged that the right to work for compensation was one of the rights or privileges protected by the Thirteenth Amendment. The Court rejected the government's argument, holding that the Thirteenth Amendment was limited to addressing slavery or involuntary servitude.[31]

As a result of *Hodges*, the Thirteenth Amendment lay dormant for many years. It was not until the late 1930s, when President Franklin Roosevelt created the Civil Rights Section (CRS) of the Department of Justice, that the federal government again embarked on a program revitalizing the Thirteenth Amendment by expanding the meaning and scope of the Thirteenth Amendment–based statutes. To do so, the lawyers in the CRS aggressively enforced antipeonage statutes and brought civil rights actions against abusive police officers.[32] This litigation strategy coincided with the rise and growth of the modern civil rights movement. In 1948, Congress expanded the Anti-Peonage Act and, as the civil rights movement gained momentum, adopted the 1964 Civil Rights Act and the 1965 Voting Rights Act.[33] The Warren Court responded by taking a deferential approach to review legislation enacted pursuant to congressional power to protect rights of belonging.[34] The Court's deference extended not only to the recently enacted statutes but also to the Reconstruction-era statutes, including those enacted to enforce the Thirteenth Amendment.[35]

In *Jones v. Mayer*, an African American couple sued a private actor, a real estate developer, alleging that he had refused to sell them a home because of their race, in violation of 42 U.S.C. § 1982. The Court held that the statute was not limited to addressing state action because the members of the Reconstruction Congress "plainly meant to secure that right [to purchase real estate] against interference from any source whatever, whether government or private."[36] Citing the *Civil Rights Cases*, the Court specifically held that Congress's section 2 power extends to eliminating the badges and incidents of slavery. Adopting language reminiscent of the congressional debates over the Thirteenth Amendment enforcement power, the Court held that "Congress has the power under the Thirteenth Amendment rationally to determine what are the badges and incidents of slavery, and the authority to transform that determination into effective legislation."[37] Congress could rationally determine that racial discrimination in real estate transactions was a badge and incident of slavery because "the exclusion of Negroes from white communities became a substitute for the Black Codes" that members of the Reconstruction Congress intended the statute to abolish.[38] In subsequent decisions, the Court continued to defer to Congress in this manner. For example, the Court cited *Jones* in holding that students denied admission to private schools on the basis of race could bring a cause of action under 42 U.S.C. § 1981 because schools and students had a contractual relationship.[39]

The Warren Court reached the zenith of its deference to Congress's section 2 power in the case of *Griffin v. Breckenridge.* In that case, a unanimous Court upheld a cause of action under 42 U.S.C. § 1985(3) brought by a group of African American men against private citizens who had beaten them up based on the mistaken belief that the victims were civil rights workers.[40] The indictment alleged that the defendants conspired to deprive the victims of their rights to freedom of speech, movement, association, and assembly and their right to petition the government for redress of their grievances.[41] The Court held that § 1985(3) was a valid exercise of the section 2 power because "the varieties of private conduct that [Congress] may make criminally punishable or civilly remediable extend far beyond the actual imposition of slavery or involuntary servitude. By the Thirteenth Amendment, we committed ourselves as a nation to the proposition that the former slaves and their descendants should be forever free."[42] Accordingly, in *Griffin*, the Court held that the Thirteenth Amendment authorized Congress to protect virtually all civil rights from violation by private actors, as long as those actors were motivated by "some racial, or perhaps otherwise class-based, invidiously discriminatory animus."[43]

Hence, in *Jones* and *Griffin* the Court issued an open invitation to Congress to use section 2 of the Thirteenth Amendment as a source of legislation protecting rights of belonging. However, the modern Congress has not accepted that invitation and indeed has shied away from using section 2. Other than its revisions to the antipeonage statute, the only statutes enacted by Congress in the twentieth century in which Congress expressly relied on section 2 were two enacted the same year as *Jones* was decided: the antiblockbusting provision of the Fair Housing Act and the 1968 Hate Crimes Act.[44]

There is reason to believe that Congress's reluctance to use section 2 may be ending. Congress began the twenty-first century by enacting the section 2–based TVPA, and, in 2009, Congress enacted the Local Law Enforcement Hate Crimes Prevention Act, based in part on its section 2 authority.[45] Those members of Congress who wish to use section 2 to protect rights of belonging confront two issues. First, what are the protected categories under the Thirteenth Amendment? In other words, is the amendment limited to prohibiting race discrimination? Second, how far can Congress go in defining the badges and incidents of slavery? This is a particular concern, because, while the Warren Court and the early Burger Court were extremely deferential to Congress, there is ample reason to believe that the Roberts Court may not be so deferential.

The Court's rulings in *Boerne* and *Morrison* indicate that the extent of Congress's section 2 power likely will depend on the degree to which Congress's decisions are consistent with the Court's interpretation of the Thirteenth Amendment.

The first issue is the extent to which Congress's section 2 power is limited to remedying discrimination based on race. While it is clear that the principal concern of the Reconstruction-era Congress was to protect the rights of the newly freed slaves and their Northern sympathizers, those members of Congress did not intend the protections of the Thirteenth Amendment to be limited to newly freed slaves. They intended to protect all races from invidious discrimination. This is evidenced in the language of the Civil Rights Act of 1866, which granted "any person" the same rights as a white citizen, and the Enforcement Act, which protected "any person or class of persons" from conspiracies to deprive them of their civil rights, and the 1867 Anti-Peonage Act, which abolished the system of peonage throughout the United States.[46] Thus, it is apparent that the framers of the Thirteenth Amendment viewed it as a broad font of liberty-based rights not just for slaves but also for every person within its jurisdiction.

In *Griffin v. Breckenridge*, the Court interpreted § 1985 to apply only to conspiracies based on "racial, or perhaps otherwise class-based, invidiously discriminatory animus."[47] However, the Court has interpreted the meaning of race broadly, to cover any group of people considered to be a different race from the Caucasian race by the framers of the Thirteenth Amendment. In *Hodges*, the Court held that the Thirteenth Amendment "reaches every race and individual, and if in any respect it commits one race to the nation, it commits every race and every individual thereof. Slavery or involuntary servitude of the Chinese, of the Italian, of the Anglo-Saxon, are as much within its compass as slavery or involuntary servitude of the African."[48] In a 1987 case, *Saint Francis College v. Al-Khazraji*, the Court pointed out that at the time of Reconstruction, the racial classifications commonly used in the twentieth century were divided into a number of subsidiary classifications, and the legislative history of the Thirteenth Amendment is filled with references to a variety of races, including Scandinavian, Chinese, Latin, Spanish, Anglo-Saxon, Jewish, Mexican, Mongolian, Gypsy, and German. Thus, "plainly all those who might be deemed Caucasian today were not thought to be of the same race at the time § 1981 became law," and a person of Arabic descent could bring a discrimination claim under § 1981.[49]

The Court has also held that Jewish plaintiffs could raise claims under §§ 1981, 1982 and 1985(3) when their synagogue had been sprayed with anti-Semitic slogans. Noting that "the question before us is not whether Jews are considered to be a separate race by today's standards, but whether, at the time § 1982 was adopted, Jews constituted a group of people that Congress intended to protect," the Court concluded, "Jews and Arabs were among the peoples considered to be distinct races and hence within the protection of the statute."[50] Therefore, it seems clear that Congress could use its section 2 power to remedy a broad range of race-based animus.

It is less clear whether Congress could use the power to remedy other types of discrimination against other classes of people, such as discrimination based on religion, gender, or sexual orientation. Some members of Congress have attempted to use section 2 to remedy religious bigotry in the Local Law Enforcement and Hate Crimes Prevention Act of 2009.[51] In their statement in support of an earlier version of the act, members of Congress indicated they believed that Congress would have the authority under the Thirteenth Amendment to prohibit violence based on religion or national origin "at least to the extent that violence is directed at those religions or national origins that would have been considered races at the time of the adoption of the Thirteenth Amendment."[52] These members of Congress are attempting to conflate race with some religions. As the Court pointed out in *Saint Francis*, the framers of the Thirteenth Amendment also conflated religion with race. Therefore, it is rational for Congress to rely on section 2 to address religious bigotry.

Because the system of slavery subjected female slaves to rape by their masters, some scholars have argued that Congress could use the section 2 power to remedy sex discrimination.[53] Given the systematic subjugation of female slaves, and the fact that some members of the Reconstruction Congress pointed out the damage done to the families of slaves as examples of the harms targeted by the Thirteenth Amendment, it would be rational for Congress to use that power to seek to remedy gender-based violence.[54] After the Court struck down the civil rights provision of the Violence Against Women Act, Congress added "gender" to the classes of people protected by the 2009 Hate Crimes Act, which makes it a federal crime to injure or assault a person based on his or her gender.[55] Members of Congress supporting an earlier version of the bill explained that "although acts of violence committed against women traditionally have been viewed as 'personal attacks' rather than as hate crimes, Congress has come to understand that a significant number of women are exposed to terror, brutality, serious injury, and even death because of their gender."[56] However, enough members of Congress apparently were not convinced that the Thirteenth Amendment alone would be sufficient to justify the protection against gender discrimination, because they amended the statute to limit the coverage of the act's protection against gender-based violence to crimes committed in, or substantially affecting, interstate commerce.[57]

Congress might be more successful at using section 2 to enact other civil rights legislation.[58] Since the *Civil Rights Cases*, the Court has consistently held section 2 is a source of power to remedy civil rights violations by private parties. The Enforcement Act of 1871, which made it a federal crime for private individuals to conspire to deprive a person of their civil rights, creates a strong precedent for such a measure. Since slavery was a system perpetuated by race-based violence, it seems clear that Congress could rationally find that race-based violence was a badge or incident of slavery.[59]

The other issue that members of Congress must confront is the question of what amounts to a "badge or incident of slavery." At the very least, Congress can use section 2 to prohibit forced labor and other "slavery-like" working conditions. Some members of the Reconstruction Congress believed that the Thirteenth Amendment would improve the working conditions of all laborers, not just slaves.[60] In the early twentieth century, leaders of the labor movement seized on this notion and argued that the Thirteenth Amendment granted them the right to organize into unions because working without that right was tantamount to slavery, and members of Congress echoed this view as they enacted the National Labor Relations Act.[61] Although this idea and its accompanying rhetoric have since faded in the labor movement, Congress could seek to revive the idea by enacting laws strengthening the rights of workers just as it strengthened its antipeonage statute.[62]

The need for the most recent amendment to that statute arose when the Court held, in U.S. v. Kozminski, that 18 U.S.C. § 1584, which makes it a crime to knowingly and willingly hold a person "to involuntary servitude," and 18 U.S.C. § 241, which makes it a crime to conspire to interfere with rights secured "by the Constitution or the laws of the United States," were not violated by defendants who used only psychological coercion to keep their employees in exploitative conditions.[63] The Court ruled that both statutes were limited to remedying "cases involving the compulsion of services by the use or threatened use of physical or legal coercion."[64] In 2000, Congress responded by enacting the TVPA, which prohibits the trafficking of persons for sex or other labor or services.[65] With this act, Congress attempted to overrule the Court by providing that "involuntary servitude statutes are intended to reach cases in which persons are held in a condition of servitude through nonviolent coercion."[66]

The TVPA sets up a potential battle between the Court and Congress. The Kozminski decision was based on both statutory and constitutional interpretations.[67] The Court's reading of § 1584 was merely a matter of statutory interpretation, because the Court limited itself to determining what Congress had understood "involuntary servitude" to be when it amended the Anti-Peonage Act in 1948.[68] However, the Court's interpretation of § 241 hinged on the Court's understanding of the meaning of "involuntary servitude" in the Thirteenth Amendment.[69] In the majority opinion, Justice O'Connor took pains to clarify that the ruling was a matter of statutory, not constitutional, interpretation.[70] Nonetheless, it is conceivable that the Court, influenced by Boerne, may find the TVPA to be unconstitutionally inconsistent with its own interpretation of the Thirteenth Amendment, the deferential precedent of *Jones* notwithstanding.[71] If it is upheld, however, the act creates a significant precedent for Congress to use to remedy other coercive working conditions.

In recent years, scholars have suggested that section 2 enables Congress to pass a variety of other statutes. For example, William Carter has argued persuasively that racial profiling by police forces reflects a long-standing equation of race with criminality extending back to the days of slavery and thus might be termed a badge or incident of slavery. Based on this reasoning, Congress might be able to use section 2 to regulate or prohibit the practice of racial profiling.[72] Maria Ontiveros has suggested legislation prohibiting discrimination against immigrants, as a reaction to the Supreme Court's ruling in *Hoffman Plastic Compounds v. National Labor Relations Board*[73] limiting the reach of Title VII's protections for immigrants.[74]

Of course, all these suggested remedies would require factual and legal investigations by Congress before that body could act. What is significant is that, based on Supreme Court precedents and congressional commitment to end any remaining incidents of involuntary servitude, Congress has the autonomous authority to do so. Only the future will tell whether members of Congress are interested in exploring and fulfilling the promise of section 2.

NOTES

1. *City of Boerne v. Flores*, 521 U.S. 507 (1997). For cases applying the *Boerne* test to strike down civil rights provisions, see *Kimel v. Fla. Bd. of Regents*, 528 U.S. 62 (2000) (striking down the provision of the Age Discrimination in Employment Act making rights enforceable against states); *U.S. v. Morrison*, 529 U.S. 598 (2000) (striking down the civil rights remedy in the Violence Against Women Act); *Bd. of Trs. v. Garrett*, 531 U.S. 356 (2001) (striking down the provision of the Americans with Disabilities Act making rights enforceable against states).

2. *U.S. v. Lopez*, 514 U.S. 549 (1995); *U.S. v. Morrison*, 529 U.S. 598 (2000).

3. For a detailed discussion of "rights of belonging," *See* REBECCA E. ZIETLOW, ENFORCING EQUALITY: CONGRESS, THE CONSTITUTION, AND THE PROTECTION OF INDIVIDUAL RIGHTS 6–8 (2006).

4. For further discussion of congressional power to enforce the Thirteenth Amendment, *see* Alexander Tsesis, *A Civil Rights Approach*, 39 U. C. DAVIS L. REV. 1773 (2006), and *Furthering American Freedom: Civil Rights & the Thirteenth Amendment*, 45 B. C. L. REV. 307 (2004).

5. *See* U.S. CONST., amend XIII, § 1 ("Neither slavery nor involuntary servitude . . . shall exist.")

6. Cong. Globe, 39th Cong., 1st Sess. 43.

7. *Id.* at 41.

8. *Id.* at 504.

9. *Id.* at 504.

10. *Id.* at 602.

11. Civil Rights Act of 1866, ch. 31, 14 Stat. 27 (codified at 42 U.S.C. §§ 1981–1983 [2000]).

12. *See* Cong. Globe, 39th Cong., 1st Sess. 476 (1866) (statement of Sen. Saulsbury); *id.* at 498 (statement of Sen. Van Winkle); *id.* at 499 (Sen. Cowan).

13. *See Jones v. Mayer*, 392 U.S. 409, 439 (1968).

14. Cong. Globe, 39th Cong., 1st Sess. 1033 (1866).

15. *Id.* at 1809, 1861.

16. *Dred Scott v. Sandford*, 60 U.S. (19 How.) 393 (1856).

17. *Cong. Globe*, 39th Cong., 1st Sess. 504 (1866) (statement of Sen. Johnson).

18. *Id.* at 43.

19. *Id.* at 1118 (Rep. Wilson); 42d Cong., 1st Sess. 693 (Sen. Thurman); *id.* at 728 (Sen. Sherman).

20. Cong. Globe, 39th Cong., 2d Sess. 345. *See McCulloch v. Maryland*, 17 U.S. (4 Wheat.) 316 (1819) (finding that Congress had the power to enact "appropriate" measures to enforce its enumerated powers, and interpreting "appropriate" broadly).

21. *See* Zietlow, *supra*, at 46–48 (2006); Larry D. Kramer, The People Themselves: Popular Constitutionalism and Judicial Review 212–16 (2004).

22. Anti-Peonage Act, Mar. 2, 1867, ch. 187, 14 Stat. 546, now codified as amended at 18 U.S.C. § 1581 *et seq.* and 42 U.S.C. § 1994.

23. See Peonage, Slavery, and Trafficking in Persons Act, 18 U.S.C. § 1581 [June 25, 1948, c. 645, 62 Stat. 772; Sept. 13, 1994, Pub. L. 103-322, Title XXXIII, § 33016(1)(K), 108 Stat. 2147; Sept. 30, 1996, Pub. L. 104-208, Div. C, Title II, § 218(a), 110 Stat. 3009-573; Oct. 28, 2000, Pub. L. 106-386, Div. A, § 112(a)(1), 114 Stat. 1486].

24. Fair Housing Act, 1968, 42 U.S.C. 3604(e); Hate Crimes Act, 1968, 18 U.S.C. § 245 (the activities protected include attending a school, participating in a government program, applying for or enjoying employment, serving as a state juror, travel in interstate commerce, or using a public accommodation). A lower court has also held that the Public Works Employment Discrimination Act, 42 U.S.C. § 6705(f)(5), which prohibits race discrimination in government contracts, was a valid exercise of the Thirteenth Amendment enforcement power. *See Rhode Island Chapter, Associated General Contractors of America v. Kreps*, 450 F. Supp. 338 (D. Ct. RI 1978). *See also U.S. v. Bob Lawrence Realty*, 474 F.2d 115, 119 (5th Cir. 1973).

25. Now codified as 42 U.S.C. § 1985 (as amended); 18 U.S.C. § 242.

26. *See* Xi Wang, *The Making of Federal Enforcement Laws, 1870–1872*, 70 Chi. Kent L. Rev. 1013, 1049 (1995).

27. *See* Robert K. Carr, Federal Protection of Civil Rights: Quest for a Sword 24–26 (1947).

28. Civil Rights Cases, 109 U.S. 3, 20 (1883).

29. *Id.* at 20–21.

30. *Hodges v. United States*, 203 U.S. 1 (1906).

31. *Id.* at 9–10.

32. *See* Risa L. Goluboff, *The Thirteenth Amendment and the Lost Origins of Civil Rights*, 50 Duke L. J. 1609 (2001); Carr, *supra*, 151.

33. Rebecca E. Zietlow, *To Secure These Rights: Congress, Courts and the 1964 Civil Rights Act*, 57 Rutgers L. Rev. 945 (2005).

34. *See* Rebecca E. Zietlow, *The Judicial Restraint of the Warren Court (and Why It Matters)*, 69 Ohio State L. J. (forthcoming), http://ssrn.com/abstract= 960144.

35. *See, e.g., Heart of Atlanta Motel v. United States*, 379 U.S. 241 (1964) (upholding the 1964 Civil Rights Act); *Katzenbach v. Morgan*, 384 U.S. 641 (1966) (upholding provisions of the 1965 Voting Rights Act); *Monroe v. Pape* (reviving 42 U.S.C. § 1983); *Jones v. Mayer* (reviving 42 U.S.C. § 1982).

36. *Id.* at 423.

37. *Id.* at 440.

38. *Id.* at 441.

39. *Runyon v. McCrary*, 427 US 160, 172 (1976). *See also Patterson v. McClean Credit Union*, 491 U.S. 164 (1989).

40. *Griffin v. Breckenridge*, 403 U.S. 88, 105 (1971). Justice Harlan concurred in the opinion but agreed with the Court's interpretation of the section 2 power. *Id.* at 107 (Harlan, J., concurring).

41. *Id.* at 90.

42. *Id.* at 105.

43. *Id.* at 102.

44.

45. PL-111-84, 2009 Cong. Rec. H10565-11052.

46. An Act to abolish and forever prohibit the System of Peonage in the Territory of New Mexico and other Parts of the United States (March 2, 1867), 187 Stat. 546.

47. *Griffin v. Breckenridge*, 403 U.S. at 102.

48. *Hodges v. United States*, 203 U.S. 1, 8 (1906).

49. *Saint Francis College v. Al-Khazraji*, 481 U.S. 604, 610, 613 (1987).

50. *Shaare Tefila Congregation v. Cobb*, 481 U.S. 615, 617–18 (1987).

51. *See* PL-111-84, 2009 Cong. Rec. H10565-11052.

52. The Local Law Enforcement Enhancement Act of 2001, Report to Accompany S. 625, 107th Cong., 2d Sess., May 9, 2002, Report 107-147, at 17.

53. *See, e.g.,* Pamela D. Bridgewater, *Reproductive Freedom as Civil Freedom: The Thirteenth Amendment's Role in the Struggle for Reproductive Rights*, 3 Gender

RACE & JUST. 401 (2000); Vanessa B. M. Vergara, *Abusive Mail-Order Bride Marriage and the Thirteenth Amendment*, 94 Nw. U. L. REV. 1547 (2000).

54. *See* CONG. GLOBE, 39th[th] Cong., 1st Sess. 42 (1865) (Sen. Sumner citing the right "to be protected in their homes and family" as one of the "natural rights of free men."); *id.* at 504 (Sen. Howard pointing out that slaves had "not the right to become a husband or a father in the eye of the law, he had no child, he was not at liberty to indulge the natural affections of the human heart for children, for wife, or even for friend.").

55. *See* PL-111-84, 2009 Cong. Rec. H10565-11052.

56. The Local Law Enforcement Enhancement Act of 2001, Report to Accompany S. 625 (an earlier, virtually identical version of the 2007 act), 107th Cong., 2d Sess., May 9, 2002, Report 107-147, at 7.

57. See § 249(a)(2) of the Local Law Enforcement Hate Crimes Prevention Act of 2007, H.R. 1592 (Report No. 110-113), 110th Cong., § 1st Sess., March 20, 2007.

58. An example of such a law is the Local Law Enforcement Hate Crimes Prevention Act of 2007, H.R. 1592 (Report No. 110-113), 110th Cong., § 1st Sess., March 20, 2007.

59. See Local Law Enforcement Act of 2001, Report to Accompany S. 625, 107th Cong., 2d Sess., May 9, 2002, Report 107-147, at 17.

60. *See* Lea S. VanderVelde, *The Labor Vision of the Thirteenth Amendment*, 138 U. PA. L. REV. 437 (1989).

61. *See* James Gray Pope, *Labor's Constitution of Freedom*, 106 YALE L.J. 941 (1997); ZIETLOW, *supra*, ENFORCING EQUALITY ch. 4.

62. For example, Congress might want to legislate to improve the rights for immigrant workers who are required to work in sweatshoplike conditions. *See* Maria Ontiveros, *Non-citizen Immigrant Labor and the Thirteenth Amendment: Challenging Guest Worker Programs*, 38 U. TOL. L. REV. 923, 925 (2007); Kathleen Kim, *Psychological Coercion in the Context of Modern-Day Involuntary Labor: Revisiting* United States v. Kozminski *and Understanding Human Trafficking*, 38 U. TOL. L. REV. 941, 962 (2007).

63. *United States v. Kozminski*, 487 U.S. 931, 950 (1988).

64. *Id.* at 949.

65. 22 U.S.C. § 7101 *et seq.* For an excellent discussion of this act and the problem of human trafficking, *see* Kathleen Kim, *Psychological Coercion in the Context of Modern-Day Involuntary Labor: Revisiting* United States v. Kozminski *and Understanding Human Trafficking*, 38 U. TOL. L. REV. 941 (2007).

66. 22 U.S.C. § 7101(b)(13) (2000).

67. Compare *Kozminski*, 487 U.S. at 941 (noting that since the Kozminskis were convicted of conspiracy to violate "the Thirteenth Amendment guarantee against involuntary servitude . . . our task is to ascertain the precise definition of that crime by looking at the scope of the Thirteenth Amendment prohibition of involuntary servi-

tude") with *id.* at 944 ("We draw no conclusions from this historical survey about the potential scope of the Thirteenth Amendment.")

68. *Kozminski*, 487 U.S. at 948.

69. *Id.* at 941.

70. *Kozminski*, 487 U.S. at 944.

71. *But see* William M. Carter, Jr., *Judicial Review of Thirteenth Amendment Legislation: "Congruence and Proportionality" or "Necessary and Proper"?*, 38 U. TOL. L. REV. 973, 982 (2007) (arguing that significant differences between the Thirteenth and Fourteenth amendments justify more judicial deference toward Congress's power to enforce the former amendment).

72. *See* William M. Carter, Jr., *A Thirteenth Amendment Framework for Combating Racial Profiling*, 39 HARV. C.R.C.L. REV. 17, 57 (2004).

73. 535 U.S. 137 (2002)

74. *See* Maria Ontiveros, *Immigrants Workers' Rights in a Post-Hoffman World: Organizing Around the Thirteenth Amendment*, 18 GEO. IMMIGR. L. J. 651 (2004).

11. *Protecting Full and Equal Rights*

THE FLOOR AND MORE

Aviam Soifer

In *Grutter v. Bollinger*,[1] a major recent Supreme Court decision in the realm of affirmative action, Justice Sandra Day O'Connor famously noted for the narrow majority, "Context matters when reviewing race-based governmental action under the Equal Protection Clause."[2] It is perhaps surprising that O'Connor needed to emphasize context at all. Even more sobering is the fact that *Grutter's* contextual approach has become quite controversial, to say the least. In the Court's more recent affirmative action decisions, for example, a new majority appears to have rejected the importance of contextual analysis in favor of more rigid, formalistic reasoning about race.[3]

In even starker contrast to *Grutter's* equal protection contextualism, however, judges generally have not even purported to attend to context as they construe the Thirteenth Amendment. The very existence of the Civil Rights Act of 1866 underscores this ahistoricism, and yet the context of this first federal civil rights act has been ignored and almost entirely forgotten. But context ought to matter. And even those purported textualists who deride context ought to concede that attention should be paid to the text of the first major statute ever passed over a presidential veto.

The core of the 1866 Civil Rights Act remains part of our federal statutes. Most specifically, 42 U.S.C. § 1981 begins: "All persons within the jurisdiction of the United States shall have the same right in every State and Territory to make and enforce contracts, to sue, be parties, give evidence, and to the full and equal benefit of all laws and proceedings for the security of persons and property as is enjoyed by white citizens, and shall be subject to like punishment, pains, penalties, taxes, licenses, and exactions of every kind, and to no other." Neither the words of the statute nor its context have much influenced judicial interpretations. Yet much was and is still at stake in construing this major statute, a crucial national guarantee that emerged directly from the horrors of the Civil War and its tragic aftermath. Recent, even pending decisions simply ignore the text of what remains of the 1866 Civil Rights Act. They also entirely neglect its origins within the promise of the Thirteenth Amendment.[4]

This chapter briefly discusses the fluid political and legal situation from which the 1866 Civil Rights Act emerged. It then argues that even attention to the language alone of this major federal civil rights act can do much to illuminate a number of contemporary controversies. In particular, it focuses on section 1's declaration of a duty to provide the benefit of "full" as well as "equal" legal protection.[5] Throughout the 1866 Civil Rights Act, the Thirty-ninth Congress repeatedly and in various ways underscored the statute's essential effort to "afford reasonable protection to all persons in their constitutional rights of equality before the law."[6]

To be sure, the recent end of slavery and the Civil War, the more recent rise of violent Southern resistance and the Black Codes, and President Andrew Johnson's contemporary bungling all help explain the salience of a basic governmental duty to protect rights and benefits, a theme that pervades the entire statute.[7] But it is also significant that the Thirty-ninth Congress, which sought reasonable protection for "constitutional rights of equality before the law," obviously already believed that there were indeed *constitutional* rights of equality." This was, in fact, several years before Secretary of State William Seward declared, in 1868, the Fourteenth Amendment—drafted by the same Thirty-ninth Congress—to have been ratified. Simply to engage the language of the 1866 Civil Rights Act with seriousness is to realize that the Thirteenth Amendment and the statutes based upon it compel us to rethink the "protection" as well as the "equal" element of the Equal Protection Clause, for example, and other core issues, such as the state-action construct and the provenance of states' rights restrictions on Congress's Enforcement Clause authority.[8]

Necessary rethinking ought to engage the important textual fact that the guarantee of "full and equal" benefits and rights occurs in leading federal civil rights acts all the way from the Civil Rights Act of 1866 through the 1990 Americans with Disabilities Act (ADA).[9] Mercifully, this chapter will serve only as a brief introduction to such basic revisionist thinking. After briefly attempting to situate and to explicate the problematic scope of the Civil Rights Act of 1866, the chapter concludes with several practical suggestions implicit in the recognition that "full" and "equal" are concepts with different meanings—sometimes complementary yet certainly neither always concurrent nor otiose. Analysis of a few recent judicial decisions illustrates some real-life consequences and tensions if we were to recognize the long-standing, explicit, and oft-repeated national commitment to protect "full" as well as "equal" rights.

CONTEXT OR VORTEX?

In *General Building Contractors Association v. Pennsylvania*,[10] the first in a series of modern Supreme Court decisions to significantly narrow the key statutory remnant of the Civil Rights Act of 1866, 42 U.S.C. § 1981, the Court proclaimed that it would follow an interpretive mandate: "We must be mindful of the 'events and passions of the time' in which the law was forged."[11] Yet the Court did no such thing. The context of the Civil Rights Act of 1866 did not even play a cameo role. The majority asked and very restrictively answered two questions remarkably far removed from the issues Congress faced in 1866. The Court had recently determined that discriminatory intent was a prerequisite for equal protection claims, and the justices now extended that anomalous doctrine to § 1981 suits. The Court further held that Judge A. Leon Higginbotham, sitting by designation as a district court judge, had gone much too far in the injunctive remedy he imposed concerning the exclusion of minority workers from the building trades in the Philadelphia area.

As if to underscore a fundamental lack of concern for 1866 and all that, along the way the Court raised strange and shadowy doubts about the origins of the statute it was interpreting. Several analytic moves within the majority opinion by then justice Rehnquist merit close attention. *General Building Contractors* is paradigmatic for the Court's startling disinterest in the context and, as we will see, even in the words of a basic civil rights statute it is construing. As strained as was the holding in *General Building Contractors*,[12] it is the approach and the explanation for its decision that are so painfully illustrative of the longstanding and yet newly revitalized judicial approach to the protection of full and equal rights.

THE BROAD EVOLUTIONARY OUTLINE

Rehnquist first tried to skate right past the statute's origin and text, noting instead that several recent decisions had traced "the evolution of this statute and its companion, 42 U.S.C. § 1982 on more than one occasion [citations omitted], and we will not repeat the narrative again except in broad outline."[13] But close attention to his "broad outline" is illuminating. It will strike some as peculiar, for example, that Rehnquist used "evolution of this statute" as shorthand for statutory sentences and phrases that had not changed for over a century. It is the Court's decisions that evolved—albeit hardly in a linear or evolutionary manner—but not the statute. Ironically, *Jones v. Alfred H. Mayer Co.*,[14] the key decision that triggered a short-lived decade of judicial attention to section 1's language following one hundred years of solitude,[15] clearly has irritated many justices ever since it was handed down in 1968.[16] *General Building Contractors* is a good example of the Court's repeated and subtle—at times almost clandestine— efforts to rein in and/or ignore *Jones* and the statute upon which it is based.

THE SHADOW OF A DOUBT

The "broad narrative outline" in *General Building Contractors* was hardly a mere summary of the past. In fact, Rehnquist introduced several striking new plot twists, beginning with the very start of the story as he chose to tell it for the Court. He wrote: "The operative language of both laws [§§ 1981 and 1982] *apparently* originated in section 1 of the Civil Rights Act of 1866, 14 Stat. 27, enacted by Congress shortly after ratification of the Thirteenth Amendment."[17]

"Apparently"? One would think it possible to look up such an issue. Indeed, the Court itself had done so recently and had found unequivocally on three occasions—as the text compelled them to do—that the key words of what was in the 1980s (and still is today) codified as 42 U.S.C. §§ 1981 and 1982 were lifted directly, verbatim from section 1 of the 1866 Civil Rights Act, where they first appeared in statutory form.[18] Rehnquist's "apparently" might be defended as an attempt to invoke repassage of section 1 of the 1866 Civil Rights Act within the 1870 Enforcement Act.

The majority opinion might mean to suggest that Congress somehow altered the origin of the statutory language when, in 1870, Congress chose to expand the categories of persons protected and the realm of actions that might intrude on the civil rights that were protected. But to consider subsequent expansion as a change in the statutory origin story puts a peculiar spin on what constitutes original statutory language. This position becomes impossible to maintain, however, when one notices that within the same Enforcement Act of 1870, Congress "hereby re-enacted" the 1866 Civil Rights Act, referred to as "the act to protect all persons in the United States in their civil rights."[19] It is clear that an interpretation that tries to limit the reach of § 1981 retroactively is further undermined by language throughout the Enforcement Act of 1870. Congress clearly tried to use the cumulative constitutional enforcement power that it had gained in the

Fourteenth and Fifteenth Amendments, ratified after 1866, and concentrated primarily on the Fifteenth Amendment as it sought to secure the franchise against both public and private interference.[20]

One could ponder why the *General Building Contractors* majority would care to obfuscate the origins of §§ 1981 and 1982 in this way. The main answer, sadly, seems obvious: the Court still has hopes of squeezing section 1 back into the Procrustean bed of state action. Because the Fourteenth Amendment was officially ratified between the 1866 and 1870 statutes—as was the Fifteenth Amendment, the primary concern of the Enforcement Act—the Court invokes the Fourteenth Amendment to give an entirely ahistorical and logically impossible backward legislative intent to what Congress did in 1866. The state-action construct that the Court started to create in the 1870s simply does not fit what either the Thirteenth Amendment or the key 1866 civil rights statute based upon it. Yet these legal changes clearly formed the basis for much of the Fourteenth Amendment. The men of the Thirty-ninth Congress—the authors and adopters of both the statute and the amendment— sought thereby to nationalize and then to constitutionalize what they had wrought. They thereby hoped and expected to make what they regarded as vital legal innovations permanent.[21]

As Rehnquist goes about casting further doubt about the origin story for a broad statute that he seeks to narrow, he takes several distinct further steps. These subtle moves in *General Building Contractors* are noteworthy in themselves, but they are additionally significant because, as we will see, they establish a strategy very much still in use in construing the language of major civil rights statutes. Neither context nor text is allowed to stand in the way of narrowing judicial constructions.

COMBINE AND CONQUER

A few illustrations of the Court's constricting technique should suffice. The first illuminates a striking lack of concern for attention to context. (The others, as we will see in the next section, turn out to be remarkably oblivious to or manipulative of the text of the 1866 Civil Rights Act itself.)

In construing contemporary statutes taken directly from section 1 of the 1866 Civil Rights Act, Rehnquist first quoted from one of the Court's messy 1960s sit-in decisions that construed an entirely different section, one dealing with the tangled and perennially controversial issue of when removal of criminal cases from state to federal court is permissible. Without indicating anything about the jagged federalism context, the majority opinion quoted only the following: "The legislative history of the 1866 Civil Rights Act clearly indicates that Congress intended to protect a limited category of rights, specifically defined in terms of racial equality."[22] The choice of quotation presumably was anchored in the attraction to the majority of the phrase *"limited* category of rights," yet even this particular statement of limit by Justice Potter Stewart was hardly restrictive.[23]

Much historical evidence both before and since *General Building Contractors* indicates quite convincingly that the Thirty-ninth Congress, in enacting the Civil Rights Act of 1866 and thus attempting to secure the fruits of victory after the horrendous and still painfully recent Civil War, understood that it was necessary to do something different to guarantee "practical freedom" throughout the land.[24] In a basic sense, section 1 of the 1866 Civil Rights Act guaranteed only limited rights,[25] of course, but the Thirty-ninth Congress emphasized repeatedly that it considered those rights to be broadly important. Its members included an essential right to national citizenship, the right to be free of any legal disability on the basis of race, and the right to be free of discrimination in a number of significant legal and economic relationships, such as making and enforcing contracts and holding and leasing property. Section 1 also guaranteed the right to "full and equal benefit of all laws and proceedings, as is enjoyed by white citizens" and sought to guarantee that citizens of every race and color "shall be subject to like punishment, pains, and penalties, and to none other, any law, statute, ordinance, regulation, or custom, to the contrary notwithstanding."[26]

The section "Reading the Text" of this essay attends briefly to the most likely meaning of these broad, not to say revolutionary, guarantees and the mechanisms that Congress attempted to establish through the other sections of the Civil Rights Act of 1866 to make them real. For present purposes, it should suffice to say that Congress had used its new authority based on the just-ratified Thirteenth Amendment to attempt to begin to implement the realities for what President Lincoln had called "a King's cure"[27] for the nation's ills, a nation still terribly raw from years of carnage and turmoil. But resistance in the South, both legal and extralegal, quickly and repeatedly compelled Congress to ever more draconian measures to try to protect the former slaves from egregious exploitation, violence, official and unofficial discrimination, and worse.

The Court, in *General Building Contractors*, was uninterested in either the thrum of chaotic everyday life or its social, political, economic, and legal ramifications. In sharp contrast to the earlier Court's attention to detail that helped reveal legislative intent in cases such as *Georgia v. Rachel* and *Price v. United States*,[28] for example, Justice Rehnquist stressed only limits and the close linkage between the 1866 Civil Rights Act and the subsequent passage and ratification of the Fourteenth Amendment. Through a kind of mystical *nunc pro tunc* doctrine, presumed limits that became part of the law two years later could somehow retroactively confine the intent of an earlier statute.

Using a very broad and folksy brush, the Court characterized the 1866 Civil Rights Act and the Enforcement Act of 1870 as "legislative cousins of the

Fourteenth Amendment."[29] It was said to follow that family solidarity indicated that both statutes had to be restricted by means akin to the Court's efforts to narrowly cabin the promise of the Equal Protection Clause. Because the Court a few years earlier had determined (incongruously) that proof of discriminatory motive was a prerequisite to making an equal protection claim, it now somehow had become "incongruous to construe [the Civil Rights Act of 1866] in a manner markedly different from that of the Fourteenth Amendment itself."[30] In the context of his role in the civil rights struggle, the late and great constitutional law scholar Charles L. Black, Jr., once identified "a failure of kinship" as the problematic core of southern resistance to desegregation. But the Court's opinion in *General Building Contractors* showed how one might combine and conquer: "legislative cousins" required the most restrictive common denominator.

A SAMPLER OF HISTORICAL CONTEXT

What would the Court have learned if it had attended to the setting for the 1866 Civil Rights Act?

First, it is difficult to overstate how chaotic the context was when the first session of the Thirty-ninth Congress convened in December 1865. That same month the ratification of the Thirteenth Amendment became official. President Abraham Lincoln had been dead for less than a year, and his little-known successor, Andrew Johnson, was already being quoted as saying that Reconstruction was over and that it was already time to restore the rebel states to the Union. As compelling recent work makes clear, the Thirteenth Amendment was the product of a convoluted process full of political manipulation and compromise, and the Appomattox peace was hardly a clear-cut conclusion to the Civil War itself.

As the Republican-dominated Congress assembled, there was no doubt that it was Reconstruction of the South most of them had in mind. This was not to be a renovation, and certainly not a restoration. It had cost too much blood and treasure to revert to old forms, either of states' rights or of a limited role for the federal government. After mobilizing the Northern war effort through the first-ever federal income tax needed to support a military force that was composed largely of conscripted men by the end of the war, a vast majority of the men of the Thirty-ninth Congress were insistent that so many dead should not have died in vain. It was up to them that the promise of "a new birth of freedom" would be made real for all citizens, and particularly for the former slaves in the South. Not only did they have the opportunity to "turn the artillery of slavery upon itself"[31] but they also now had a new source of congressional power. Section 2, otherwise known as the Enforcement Clause of the Thirteenth Amendment, was something new in the constitutional firmament. At last this Congress had both a terrible Civil War victory and a suitable tool to vindicate it. They now could constitutionalize the Declaration of Independence, a goal long sought by many antislavery leaders and most Republican politicians. They could realize the promise of protection made explicit in the national Republican Party platforms of 1856 and 1860 and insisted upon by the martyred President Lincoln as he promised reciprocal harm to Southerners if Negro soldiers were mistreated.

John Locke had insisted that mankind came in from the state of nature to gain protection, and the Declaration of Independence picked up the theme that the very existence of government was "to secure" certain inalienable rights. Black soldiers sustained terrible losses as they fought valiantly for the Union cause, and it was old learning that allegiance and protection ought to be reciprocals of each other. In addition, *Corfield v. Coryell*[32] was a favorite citation among Republican leaders when asked what fundamental civil rights they intended to secure. In Justice Bushrod Washington's famous *Corfield* elaboration about what the privileges and immunities in Article IV, section 2, ought to be, the first "general head" that Washington listed was "protection by the government," and the rights he specified included "the enjoyment of life and liberty, with the right to acquire and possess property, of every kind, and to pursue and obtain happiness and safety."[33]

Over and over again, leading members of the Thirty-ninth Congress spoke of a national duty to protect the basic rights of the former slaves. They embraced the delicious irony of utilizing federal power that had served the Slave Power to vindicate the rights of its newly freed victims. Now *Dred Scott v. Sandford*[34] and its absolute restrictions on black citizenship might be relegated to the realm of a bad memory, and all persons born in the United States would be declared to be citizens. In addition, there was bittersweet vindication in using the federal Constitution's Privileges And Immunities Clause now for freedom. It had been that Article IV, section 2, provision and its companion language that compelled the return of fugitive slaves, that slaveholders had invoked to trump state power[35] and to claim the right to have their property in slaves protected anywhere in the Union.[36]

The Thirty-ninth Congress's special Joint Committee on Reconstruction soon began hearing horrific testimony about mob rule as well as a myriad of subtle methods that, in practice, restored many of the harsh circumstances of slavery across the South.[37] Bitter and defiant Southern legislators adopted what came to be called the Black Codes, officially restricting the rights of former slaves, and Southern judicial systems were largely in ruin. It soon became tragically clear that the federal military presence, agents of the Freedmen's Bureau, and others could not begin to keep up with the rising tide of Southern resistance.

To the shock of most of the political world and particularly that of Senator Lyman Trumbull, the main sponsor of the Freedmen's Bureau Bill who believed he had assurances of presidential acceptance, President Johnson vetoed that bill in February 1866. Though there had been no tradition whatsoever of Congress's overriding a presidential veto on major legislation, the Thirty-ninth Congress came within a single vote of doing so. Many historians believe that this was the moment when the split between Congress and President Johnson became irreversible.[38]

Yet that same month Johnson also made two startling "extracurricular" blunders. There had been a number of at least symbolic examples of recognition for the new stature of black leaders—for instance, a black minister led the opening prayer in the House of Representatives, a black lawyer was admitted to the Supreme Court Bar, and Frederick Douglass was invited to the White House to confer with Lincoln.[39] But Johnson managed to be patently offensive to Douglass when he came seeking presidential support for black suffrage. Douglass quickly and forcefully told the nation about the president's egregious insults, and he identified that moment as the turning point when the country became aware of Johnson's lack of support for Reconstruction as well as his overt racism.

To add to new awareness of troublesome aspects of a previously obscure politician, Johnson soon thereafter delivered a nearly two-hour harangue to a group of Democratic revelers who came serenading him on Washington's Birthday. In the course of his long oration, he proclaimed that there were traitors in the North as bad if not worse than any in the South. When asked for names, he identified Senator Charles Sumner, Representative Thaddeus Stevens, and abolitionist stalwart Wendell Phillips and even hinted that they were behind Lincoln's assassination.[40] The impact of "one of the most remarkable public speeches ever uttered by an American president"[41] was substantial, with eight states passing resolutions condemning the president and a widely shared sense that, with this speech, Johnson "had accorded official recognition to a split in the government."[42]

Johnson soon added a surprise veto of the Civil Rights Act, against the advice of all but one of his Cabinet members and in the face of messages from around the country. This veto caused "a virtually irreparable breach between the President and the party that elected him,"[43] exacerbated by Johnson's veto message complaining that "a perfect equality of the white and black races is attempted to be fixed by Federal law, in every state of the Union, over the vast field of State jurisdiction covered by these enumerated rights."[44] It was far from easy and some methods used were dubious, but by early April the leaders of the Thirty-ninth Congress had mustered enough votes to override the president's veto—something that had never before happened on any piece of major federal legislation.

READING THE TEXT

As modern justices undertake interpretation of the Civil Rights Act of 1866, they betray an awkward zeal to fit the broad terms of a hard-fought congressional initiative passed in the throes of the Civil War within an abstract, narrowing template developed by the Court itself years later. The modern Court likes to stress the importance of attention to text in interpreting and applying statutes, and some of the justices appear to delight to be known as "textualists," devotees of "original intent," and "strict constructionists." Yet vital words of the 1866 Civil Rights Act still very much on the statute books continue to escape the Court's attention entirely, even as it goes about interpreting what remains of that old statutory text. There is admittedly murkiness concerning some remaining parts of the original 1866 text, because it was revised by a legislative revision commission whose work Congress formally approved in 1874. It seems an extreme version of revisionist history, however, to try to sustain a claim that the authority of the revisers, even as formally approved, somehow trumps the statutory text itself.[45] In any event, the language in what is now § 1981 that most concerns us was not altered at all in the course of the revision.

In particular, section 1's guarantee of "full and equal benefit"[46] of legal protection has never commanded the attention of the Court. Instead in recent years, the justices have used several distinct techniques to undermine Congress's effort affirmatively to nationalize and guarantee fundamental rights. In the words of future president James A. Garfield, of Ohio, the 1866 Civil Rights Act was needed to assure that "personal liberty and personal rights are placed in the keeping of the nation, that the right to life, liberty, and property shall be guaranteed to the citizen in reality . . . We must make American citizenship the shield that protects every citizen, on every foot of our soil."[47]

JURISDICTION OVER JURISDICTION

As with so many difficulties in life, implementation remained a basic conundrum for the Thirty-ninth Congress. With few options and a myriad of distinct, troublesome examples of depredations and forms of resistance at the chaotic ground level, Congress chose to rely primarily on the possibilities of litigation and on radically expanding the jurisdiction of the federal courts. In retrospect, this choice may have been a tragic mistake. Judges and lawyers are probably more inclined than most people to purport to look to the past. In addition, jurisdiction is one of the categories in which the esoteric knowledge of legal initiates is most important and most confusing. Long before the Supreme Court's invention of "Our Federalism" as a doctrine restrictive of federal court jurisdiction,

for example, fear of a flood of cases and of too many issues that properly belonged in state courts helped to motivate restrictions on what Congress seems
plainly to have intended.[48]

For many people trained in law, it seemed too sweeping, for example, that section 2 of the 1866 Civil Rights Act made it a federal misdemeanor for any person
"under color of any law, statute, ordinance, regulation, or custom" to subject
"any inhabitant of any State or Territory to the deprivation of any right secured or
protected by this act."[49] Not surprisingly, federal judges began to resist section 3's
breathtakingly broad provision of federal jurisdiction. Even more upsetting of
long-established norms was section 3's further provision that created what Congress termed a "right to remove" to federal court any suit, civil or criminal, that
had been commenced in state court against any person protected by the act, as
well as any state case involving an officer or Freedmen's Bureau official who
needed federal court protection for carrying out the obligations of the act.

EARLY JUDICIAL INTERPRETATIONS

Quite remarkably, however, initial judicial interpretation of the Civil Rights
Act of 1866 stressed the importance of the rights Congress meant to protect and
acknowledged Congress's new power to do so. Chief Justice Salmon P. Chase's
decision sitting as a circuit judge in In re Turner[50] is the best known, but there
are other significant decisions that similarly proclaimed that the Thirteenth
Amendment "trenches directly upon the power of the states and the people of
the states. It is the first and only instance of a change of this character in the
organic law."[51] As such, said Justice Noah Swayne sitting as a designated circuit
justice and upholding the right of a black woman to testify against a gang of
white men who had invaded her home, the Thirteenth Amendment and the
1866 Civil Rights Act implementing it would "continue to perform its function
throughout the expanding domain of the nation, without limit of time or space"
to afford "protection over every one."[52] In United States v. Hall,[53] Circuit Judge
William B. Woods explained after passage of the Fourteenth Amendment that
federal power protected fundamental rights denied by state action or by "omission to protect."

It is well known that in 1873, in the Slaughterhouse Cases,[54] a sharply divided
Supreme Court chopped away at the Reconstruction-era changes in federal law
and did so in strikingly illogical fashion. This was in many ways the beginning
of the Court's own construction of the "state action" restriction that blossomed
fully in the Civil Rights Cases in 1883 and that has bedeviled clear thinking
about and protection of civil rights ever since.[55] The Court's decision in Blyew
v. United States[56] is considerably less well known, but its technique may turn

out to be eerily familiar. *Blyew* is sometimes celebrated for the recognition by the justices in the majority as well as in the dissent that Congress intended not only to reach the Black Codes but also to guarantee to both races the same modes of trial and the right to jury trials free of discrimination. Justice Strong's majority opinion added: "It is also well known that in many quarters prejudices existed against the colored race, which naturally affected the administration of justice in the State courts, and operated harshly when one of that race was a party accused."[57] But Justice Strong's opinion went on to hold that the Civil Rights Act of 1866 could not trump the following Kentucky statute: "That a slave, negro, or Indian, shall be a competent witness in the case of the commonwealth for or against a slave, negro, or Indian, or in a civil case to which only negroes or Indians are parties, *but in no other case.*"[58]

The facts of *Blyew* are appalling. Lucy Armstrong, a blind black woman who was over ninety years old, was killed with a broad axe. Three other members of her family also were brutally murdered. The dying declaration made by one of the victims, the testimony of two young girls in the family who escaped the killers' notice, and additional evidence plainly established who had committed the unprovoked murders and showed clearly that their motive was extreme racial bigotry.[59] Nonetheless, the Supreme Court reversed the verdict of guilty on the grounds that the federal circuit court did not have jurisdiction. Section 3 of the 1866 Civil Rights Act granted jurisdiction in "all causes, civil and criminal, affecting victims of discrimination who are denied or cannot enforce in the courts or judicial tribunal, of the state or locality where there may be any of the rights secured to them."[60] The Court determined, however, that Lucy Armstrong could not be affected because she was dead and that none of the other witnesses had enough of a legal interest to say that he or she was sufficiently "affected" to fit the case within federal jurisdiction.

This decision, handed down on April 1, 1872, was not a tragic April Fool's joke. It was, in fact, of a piece with a series of extremely formalistic decisions by the Court that began the retrenchment against civil rights that came to dominate the Court and to help enable the rise and maintenance of Jim Crow for many decades.[61] The world might have been different if the Court's extreme foreshadowing of the restrictions of the doctrine of standing had not prevailed. For a variety of doctrinal reasons, the dissenting justices made a strong counterargument, but it failed. The more lasting tragedy may be that there were not then and are not now enough votes on the Supreme Court to recognize the importance of the promise contained within the Civil Rights Act of 1866. As Justice Bradley said in his *Blyew* dissent: "Merely striking off the fetters of the slave, without removing the incidents and consequences of slavery, would hardly have been a boon to the colored race. Hence, also, the amendment abolishing slavery was supplemented by a clause giving Congress power to enforce it by appropriate legislation. No law was necessary to abolish slavery; the amendment did that. The power to enforce the amendment by appropriate legislation must be a power to do away with the incidents and consequences of slavery, and to instate the freedmen in the full enjoyment of that civil liberty and equality which the abolition of slavery meant."[62]

STATUTE, WHAT STATUTE?

As we have seen through some attention to context and a little to text as well, governmental duty to protect vital rights was at the core of the 1866 Civil Rights Act.

It also is sensible to read section 1 of the Fourteenth Amendment through this lens as well, particularly because its authors were the very same members of the Thirty-ninth Congress.

Certainly it is ahistorical in the extreme to assert, as Rehnquist did for the Court in *DeShaney v. Winnebago Cty. Dept. of Social Serv.*,[63] that Fourteenth Amendment guarantees were exclusively about negative rights.[64] But Rehnquist had paved the way earlier through another aspect of his peculiar reading of the 1866 Civil Rights Act in *General Building Contractors*. "The language of the statute," said Rehnquist for the majority, "does not speak in terms of duties."[65] One wonders what statute he read. If the justices or their clerks had read the original 1866 Civil Rights Act, for example, they would have noticed that the words "duty" or "duties" appear nine times. There are numerous additional references to "faithful observance," "color of authority derived from this act," and the like. (Careful readers will remember that earlier in this very case, Rehnquist invoked federal removal jurisdiction from an entirely different section of the 1866 Civil Rights Act to construe the language of section 1.) In any event, the federal guarantee of a right to "full and equal benefit of all laws and proceedings" is still in § 1981. As a matter of logic as well as an issue of history and language, it is hard to interpret this assurance of full benefit and no other pains and penalties without perceiving affirmative governmental duty.

But the pattern of simply ignoring key language within the current § 1981 actually has accelerated recently. In *Domino's Pizza v. McDonald*,[66] for example, the Supreme Court unanimously rejected a black franchisee's rather unsympathetic § 1981 claim to an individual remedy after his company had entered bankruptcy and then settled with the franchisor. Justice Scalia's opinion about agency law and the corporate form may well be correct on the peculiar facts of the case. What is alarming, however, is that § 1981 apparently has now become solely a remedy for what Scalia calls "an impaired 'contractual relationship.'"[67] Scalia simply dropped the full and equal clause from the statute. Lest this seem only a passing point, Scalia stated for the entire Court that the most important response to McDonald's claim was "that nothing in the text of § 1981 suggests that it was meant to provide an omnibus remedy for *all* racial injustice. If so, it would not have been limited to situations involving contracts."[68] But of course the statute was not then and is not now limited to situations involving contracts. Claiming to rely on congressional intent without deigning even to suggest a single reference, Scalia then added a perennial policy argument about burdening the federal courts. "Trying to make [§ 1981] a cure-all not only goes beyond any expression of congressional intent but would produce satellite § 1981 litigation of immense scope." In this, ironically, the Court came full circle and directly echoed President Andrew Johnson's veto message of the 1866 Civil Rights Act.[69]

As we have seen, the Thirty-ninth Congress indeed did seem to seek an omnibus remedy for all racial injustice. A judge is hardly a textualist if he will abruptly jettison language when it does not fit his value system. He surely is anything but an originalist when the origin, structure, and text of the statute being construed matter not at all. It is striking and sad that the current justices unanimously joined in Scalia's opinion and apparently did not object to his total unconcern for the text and context of § 1981—even if they had reason to agree with the result reached.[70]

TAKING FULL AND EQUAL RIGHTS SERIOUSLY

If we were to pay attention to the language of § 1981, what difference would it make? What if we were to accept Justice Rehnquist's point in *General Building Contractors* that the 1866 Civil Rights Act was "a blueprint for the Fourteenth Amendment."[71] The sprawling mansion that the judges wound up building has many rooms but, as we have seen, it has little to do with this blueprint. To use the blueprint to construct an edifice, we would have to take the guarantee of full as well as equal rights seriously. Emboldened by the current Supreme Court, however, the federal judiciary seems to be marching rapidly in the opposite direction. This section of the chapter uses a few recent decisions to illustrate and concludes with a suggestion about some implications if the guarantee of full and equal rights were to be seriously considered.

"LANGUAGE-AND-HISTORY-FREE INTERPRETATION"

It may be difficult to believe, but the degradation of § 1981 may soon get even worse. The Court has accepted a case, *Humphries v. CBOCS West, Inc.*[72] in which the Seventh Circuit held that a black plaintiff could utilize § 1981 to bring a claim of retaliation against his employer. This would seem a minor issue, particularly because in practical terms § 1981 increasingly is only a minor supplement and occasional alternative to Title VII—and retaliation claims still seem to be allowed under Title VII and other modern civil rights statutes. In fact, the Seventh Circuit, by Judge Williams and joined by Judge Richard Posner, mainly tried to bring the checkered record of their own circuit's decisions on the retaliation issue into conformity with decisions in other circuits, particularly after a recent Supreme Court decision[73] had allowed a retaliation claim by the male basketball coach who claimed gender discrimination against the female athletes he coached under Title IX. It seems likely that Judge Frank Easterbrook's vehement dissent was what triggered the Supreme Court's decision to take the *Humphries* case.[74]

Easterbrook donned the mantle of strict constructionist and textualist, vigorously taking potshots at what he calls, for example, "a language-and-history-free interpretation of all federal statutes."[75] For Easterbrook, the *Humpries* case is simple: "(1) The word 'discriminate' does not appear in § 1981. What that statute provides is that all citizens have the same right to make and enforce contracts. How can a decision [*Jackson v. Birmingham Board of Education*] that resolves ambiguity in the word 'discriminate' apply to other statutes with different language? (2) § 1981 was enacted in 1866, long before anti-retaliation norms were created."[76]

Easterbrook claimed that there has been a "sea change in interpretive method" since *Jones v. Mayer* (1968) and *Sullivan v. Little Hunting Park* (1969) and argued specifically that *Sullivan* was a prime example of judges yielding to "the temptation to make any law 'the best it can be'" and "more effective."[77]

ANY CITIZEN?

In *Doe v. Kamehameha Schools/Bishop Estate*,[78] a sharply divided en banc Ninth Circuit Court of Appeals upheld the admissions policy of an iconic private K–12 school in Hawaii that gave preference to Native Hawaiian students to the point of refusing admission to virtually all applicants not Native Hawaiian. Reversing the original panel, Judge Susan Graber's opinion for an eight to seven majority stressed the many statutes in which Congress has itself used Native Hawaiian identity as a criterion for government benefits. A § 1981 attack, therefore, according to the majority, could hardly reflect the will of Congress in dealing with the unique situation of Native Hawaiians and their need for remedial protection, as was intended in the trust that established the Kamehameha School in the late nineteenth century.

The majority did not dwell on the context or text of the 1866 Civil Rights Act, though Judge William Fletcher's concurring opinion began to develop an intriguing distinction between discrimination based on political rather than racial categorization. Fletcher's distinction makes sense against the backdrop of the history of Hawaii. It also resonates with the exclusion of "Indians not taxed" in the original 1866 Civil Rights Act and with the emphasis throughout the statute on protecting those who were vulnerable and discriminated against, as measured by an ideal "white citizen" metric. It seems clear that white citizens who similarly suffered discrimination because of their efforts on behalf of the freedmen were also to be protected. Yet it is a leap to claim that the Thirty-ninth Congress's language or intent was to protect white citizens equally from discrimination perpetrated against them by blacks or by other minorities.

The "full" element of "full and equal" suggests that to treat everyone the same was neither the exclusive nor even the main goal of the sweeping civil rights guarantee enacted by Congress. Rather, the Republican leadership sought to render constitutional the promise of natural rights their party and many anti-slavery activists had long proclaimed, derived in large part from the Declaration of Independence. Such rights, conveniently left vague and subject to case-by-case development in the familiar common law mode of the era, were nonetheless rights that citizens carried with them throughout the United States. The Privileges And Immunities Clause, along with other aspects of Article IV of the federal Constitution, was the most obvious source for such a claim prior to the Civil War. The clause was the floor for basic civil rights, but states could and did afford additional rights to their own citizens. A guarantee of a right to full and equal benefits, as well as of no discriminatory pains or penalties, created an equal floor but offered more. If a state afforded an additional right to a white person beyond the national constitutional rights guaranteed by Article IV, it would be a badge or incident of slavery to deny or fail to protect that same right for former slaves. As William Blake stated centuries ago, "One law for the lion and the ox is oppression."[79]

Recent judicial interpretation of the 1866 Civil Rights Act suggests an upside-down world that is much less Blake and much more Lewis Carroll. One of the most startling examples is to be found in the recent dissent in the *Kamehameha* case. Writing for seven dissenters,[80] Judge Jay S. Bybee began his dissent as follows: "This case involves the application of one of the Republic's oldest and most enduring civil rights statutes, 42 U.S.C. § 1981. That statute—*originally enacted as section sixteen of the Civil Rights Act of 1870*—provides in pertinent part that, 'All persons within the jurisdiction of the United States shall have the same right in every State and Territory to make and enforce contracts . . . as is enjoyed by white citizens.'"[81]

As if to underscore his freedom to disregard text and context, Bybee continued: "Enacted soon after the passage of the Thirteenth and Fourteenth Amendments, § 1981 like—and perhaps more than—most of the reconstruction era civil rights enactments was intended to ensure 'that a dollar in the hands of [any citizen] will purchase the same thing as a dollar in the hands of a white man.' "[82] In addition to the assertion that § 1981 was enacted after the Fourteenth Amendment, this sentence is striking for another reason. The bracketed phrase Bybee supplied inserts "any citizen" where the original phrase in Justice Stewart's opinion in *Jones v. Alfred H. Mayer* was "a Negro."

In a world of the imagination in which race may be said no longer to matter and benign and malign uses of race are claimed to be indistinguishable,[83] it might make sense to render the black man invisible. In a world of text and context, however, Native Hawaiians are not simply fungible with any citizens, and it is more than a happy coincidence that the 1866 Civil Rights Act originated in 1866, prior to the ratification of the Fourteenth Amendment.

The issues raised by the *Kamehameha* case are tangled and important. But it certainly does not make historic or linguistic sense to assert that the Thirty-ninth Congress was or sought to be insistently color-blind.[84] They understood that people came to the starting line of the race of life unequally, and they intended to provide full as well as equal benefits and to disallow differential burdens as much as possible. They would use the law to do so. They sought to guarantee protection as well as equality, and they said as much in the text of the Fourteenth Amendment.

AFFIRMATIVE ACTION FOR PERSONS WITH DISABILITIES?

As Congress passed and President George H. W. Bush enthusiastically endorsed the Americans with Disabilities Act, in 1990, it was often and also formally stated that "people with disabilities, as a group" are "a discrete and insular minority" who have been subjected to "a history of purposeful unequal treatment, and relegated to a position of political powerlessness in our society based on characteristics that are beyond the control of such individuals."[85] In the view of many, this central point has been largely lost as the Supreme Court has for the most part narrowly construed a statute that President Bush initially compared to the Declaration of Independence and declared would, he hoped, "likewise come to be a model for the choices and opportunities of future generations around the world."[86] In a fundamental way, the dominant constricting interpretation of the ADA may be explained as a failure to heed the need for different treatment of those who are unequal. If the "full and equal" rights guaranteed by the ADA[87] were to be realized, judges would have to wrestle with the situational complexity posed when we think clearly about equality.

Treating like cases alike is hardly simple, particularly within a culture that prides itself on individuality.[88] But recognizing differences is also a conundrum.[89] A basic example illustrates the problem: A standard door handle on a standard door does not afford equal access. Some people will not be able to turn the handle or push the door open because of their disabilities. It would be prohibitively expensive, however, if a guarantee of equal access tried to take into account every possible disability. On the other hand, leaving access issues to the marketplace hardly satisfies the aspiration to guarantee the benefits of equality. A cost-benefit analysis is necessary, and a reasonable accommodation seems appropriate, as is recognized by the ADA. We seek to afford both equality and protection. There are some groups whose members have a legitimate claim for special accommodation and for special judicial attention, in part because they have been the victims of past discrimination, in part because they are feared as different. Just as unions owe a duty of fair representation to those who did not prevail in union elections, our legal structure owes a duty of fair representation to our discrete and insular minorities.[90] If we were to attend to the demands posed by the promise of full as well as equal rights, we might help those who are vulnerable to push open a door that on one level is equally open to all but that, on another, may be an impenetrable barrier.

Decisions that construe the ADA illustrate the difficulties of comprehending that sometimes people can and should be treated differently and equally simultaneously. Such situations arise particularly when we are in need of protection, as all of us are at times in our lives. To be sure, protection is often inextricably linked to paternalism, and this helps to explain why protection as a legal concept is underdeveloped. But laws ranging from consumer protection through fiduciary duties to securities regulation unquestionably implicate issues of protection. So should the protection element of equal protection, at least as understood as an edifice built in large measure through use of the blueprint of the 1866 Civil Rights Act.

This is not to assert that the realization of full and equal rights will be untroubled. There are, for example, core tensions involved in determining whether an employer owes a duty to hire a disabled employee for an open position when that employee became disabled on the job, has been transferred, and now is qualified but may not be the best-qualified candidate. The federal courts of appeals are split on the question.[91] But it will not do simply to have faith in employers and the market, as the Seventh Circuit seemed to do in *EEOC v. Humiston-Keeling, Inc.*[92] To decide against the employer, said Judge Richard Posner, would be to "convert a non-discrimination statute into a mandatory preference statute," a result he deemed "both inconsistent with the nondiscriminatory aims of the ADA and an unreasonable imposition on the employers and co-workers of disabled employees."[93] Posner used hypotheticals to bolster his point, arguing that a contrary approach would mean that a twenty-nine-year-old white male with a tennis elbow would get a job over a sixty-two-year-old black woman because of "a hierarchy of protections for groups deemed entitled to protection against discrimination."[94] The very idea of a hierarchy of protections thus is supposed to demolish the very idea of any protection at all.

It is not necessary even to step onto such a slippery slope, of course, and one could wield overblown hypotheticals on the other side to attack blind faith in employers and/or the relative fairness of the market. Neither approach is likely to be productive in wrestling with the tangled issues that surround the commitment made by the nation for more than a century and repeatedly since to guarantee full and equal rights.

CONCLUSION

To be true to the promise embedded in the text and the context of the 1866 Civil Rights Act would require substantial rethinking of legal precedents and popular assumptions alike. It would force us to come to grips with a governmental duty to protect those most vulnerable even from the vagaries of the marketplace. We would have to notice that Congress enacted statute after statute in the decade after the Civil War intended to protect former slaves and their allies from depredations perpetrated by private individuals as well as by state actors. It was no accident, for example, that the Ku Klux Klan Act (1871) took its name from the attempt by Congress to remedy outrages by private individuals hiding their identities behind masks and robes.[95] And, not surprisingly, the Congresses that drafted the Reconstruction amendments—made up of men who established military districts to help govern the South—hardly had states' rights limitations in mind as they wrote and later invoked the Enforcement Clauses of their new constitutional approach.

By ignoring words and the provenance of key federal civil rights statutes in the post–Civil War era, the Court itself helped legitimate the rise of Jim Crow. It remains a bitter irony that even on those rare occasions when the political process works to protect discrete and insular minorities who generally lack political and economic clout,[96] judges tend to intervene to narrow or eliminate the new statutory protections. Paradoxically, lawyers and judges have helped us lose sight of an important legal truth. As Chief Justice John Marshall proclaimed in *Marbury v. Madison*: "The very essence of civil liberty certainly consists in the right of every individual to claim the protection of the laws, whenever he receives an injury. One of the first duties of government is to afford that protection."[97]

This was and still should be among the "constitutional rights of equality" guaranteed in the words of the Thirty-ninth Congress.

NOTES

1. *Grutter v. Bollinger*, 529 U.S. 306 (2003).

2. *Id.* at 327. "Affirmative consideration" actually seems preferable to the phrase "affirmative action" because it is more accurate and less immediately evocative.

3. *Parents Involved in Cmty. Sch. v. Seattle Sch. Dist. No. 1*, 127 S. Ct. 2738 (2007). Writing for the majority in part III-A, Chief Justice Roberts used the context argument in something akin to a judo move. He asserted that because *Grutter* had emphasized "considerations unique to institutions of higher learning" and because the 2007 cases dealt with elementary and high school students, it followed that "the present cases are not governed by *Grutter*." *Id.* at 2754. To Roberts and the plurality for whom he wrote part IV, "when it comes to using race to assign children to schools, history will be heard," citing *Brown v. Bd. of Educ.*, 347 U.S. 483 (1954). *Id.* at 2767.

4. The chapter develops and updates earlier efforts I made to wrestle with the complex context of guaranteeing civil rights during Reconstruction, available at Aviam Soifer, *Review Essay: Protecting Civil Rights; A Critique of Raoul Berger's History*, 54 N.Y.U. L. Rev. 651 (1979), and Aviam Soifer, *Status, Contract, and Promises Unkept*, 96 Yale L.J. 1916 (1987).

5. Civil Rights Act of 1866, ch. 31, § 1, 14 Stat. 27 (1866).

6. Civil Rights Act of 1866 § 4.

7. That the Thirteenth Amendment was the product of rapidly changing ideas and motivations was made wonderfully clear in Michael Vorenberg, Final Freedom: The Civil War, the Abolition of Slavery, and the Thirteenth Amendment (2001). Excellent additional recent studies further illustrate that the period immediately following the Civil War was a time of chaotic and constant change, particularly in regard to extended federal efforts to enforce civil rights in the South. *See, e.g.*, Alexander Tsesis, the Thirteenth Amendment and American Freedom: A Legal History (2004); William S. McFeely, Frederick Douglass (1991); Robert J. Kaczorowski, The Politics of Judicial Interpretation: The Federal Courts, Department of Justice, and Civil Rights, 1866–1876 (1985). Earlier work anticipated similar themes. *See, e.g.*, Harold M. Hyman and William M. Wiecek, Equal Justice under Law: Constitutional Development, 1835–1875 (1982); Leon F. Litwack, Been in the Storm So Long: The Aftermath of Slavery (1979); Michael Les Benedict, A

216 CURRENT LEGAL LANDSCAPES

COMPROMISE OF PRINCIPLE: CONGRESSIONAL REPUBLICANS AND RECON-
STRUCTION, 1863–1869 (1974); JACOBUS TENBROEK, EQUAL UNDER LAW (1965).

8. *See, e.g.,* Civil Rights Cases, 109 U.S. 3 (1883) (state action requirement for Fourteenth Amendment protection); *City of Boerne v. Flores,* 521 U.S. 507 (1997); *Trustees
of Univ. of Alabama v. Garrett,* 531 U.S. 356 (2001) (state sovereignty limitations on
congressional enforcement power under section 5 of the Fourteenth Amendment).
But see Tennessee v. Lane 541 U.S. 509 (2004) (valid use of enforcement power to vindicate fundamental right of access to courts).

9. *See* Civil Rights Act of 1964, 42 U.S.C.A. § 2000a(a) (1964); Americans with Disabilities Act of 1990, 42 U.S.C.A. §§ 2182(a) & 12184(a) (1990).

10. 458 U.S. 375 (1982).

11. *Id.* at 386 (quoting *United States v. Price,* 383 U.S. 787, 803 [1966]).

12. Before *Washington v. Davis,* 426 U.S. 229 (1976), a claim of some discriminatory
intent or motive on the part of a government official appeared sufficient but not necessary for a plaintiff to make out a valid equal protection claim. *Washington v. Davis*
clearly made such proof a necessary precondition. Though the Court nearly extended
this new doctrinal requirement to Thirteenth Amendment claims in *Memphis v. Greene,*
451 U.S. 100 (1981), it was *General Building Contractors* that decided the issue. Even as
a matter of Fourteenth Amendment doctrine, however, the Court has not been consistent recently in applying the discriminatory motive requirement. *See, e.g., Bush v.
Gore,* 531 U.S. 98 (2000) (no allegation of bad motive); *Village of Willowbrook v. Olech,*
528 U.S. 562 (2000) (irrationality sufficient without regard to motive).

13. 458 U.S. at 383–84. His citations were *McDonald v. Santa Fe Trail Transp. Co.,*
427 U.S. 273, 295 (1976); *Runyon v. McCrary,* 427 U.S. 160, 168–69 (1976); *Jones v.
Alfred H. Mayer Co.,* 392 U.S. 409 (1968).

14. 392 U.S. 409 (1968).

15. By the early 1870s, much of the nation was suffering from frustration and fa-
tigue in terms of the stationing of troops in the South. The worsening economic situation culminating in the severe Panic of 1873 compounded the lack of Northern resolve. But the Supreme Court itself had a significant role in narrowing or upending
civil rights guarantees, beginning with decisions such as *Blyew v. United States,* 80
U.S. (13 Wall.) 581 (1872); Slaughterhouse Cases, 83 U.S. (16 Wall.) 36 (1873), discussed
infra at n. 54, and *United States v. Cruikshank,* 92 U.S. 542 (1876), that helped produce
what should be an infamous statement in the *Civil Rights Cases,* 109 U.S. at 25.
Merely eighteen years after the Thirteenth Amendment, the Court held the public
accommodations guarantees of the 1875 Civil Rights Act unconstitutional because:
"When a man has emerged from slavery, and by the aid of beneficent legislation has
shaken off the inseparable concomitants of that state, there must be some stage in the
progress of his elevation when he takes the rank of a mere citizen, and ceases to be the
special favorite of the laws." With the exception of a brief cameo appearance in *Hurd
v. Hodge,* 334 U.S. 24 (1948), parts of the 1866 Civil Rights Act that remained on the

statute books were all but forgotten for nearly a century, and the issue of legal desuetude was a key matter of contention in *Jones.*

16. Application of *Jones* and the language of section 1 of the 1866 Civil Rights Act to overt racial discrimination by a private school enterprise in *Runyon v. McCrary,* 427 U.S. 160 (1976), provoked enough justices so that within a little more than a decade they had asked for additional briefs on the question of whether *Runyon* should be overruled. Ultimately deciding not to go quite so far, a majority in *Patterson v. McLean Credit Union,* 887 F.2d 484 (1989), nonetheless gave § 1981 a remarkably crabbed reading. Congress overrode this interpretation—and may have expanded §§ 1981 and 1982 further—in the Civil Rights Act of 1991. *See* discussion *infra,* at n. 77.

17. 458 U.S. at 384. All three of the decisions Rehnquist cited in the previous sentence unequivocally stated the obvious—section 1 of the Civil Rights Act of 1866 was the core of the origin story for the statutory language subsequently codified as 42 U.S.C. §§ 1981 and 1982.

18. *Id.*

19. Enforcement Act of 1870, ch. 114, § 18, 16 Stat. 140 (1870): "That the act to protect all persons in the United States in their civil rights, and furnish the means of their vindication, passed April nine, eighteen hundred and sixty-six, is hereby re-enacted; and sections sixteen and seventeen hereof shall be enforced according to the provisions of said act."

The 1870 Congress made the broader coverage enacted in sections 16 and 17 enforceable through the mechanisms of the 1866 Civil Rights Act, referred to as "the act *to protect* all persons in the United States in their civil rights" (emphasis added) *Id.*

20. George A. Rutherglen, *The Improbable History of Section 1981: Clio Still Bemused and Confused,* 2003 SUP. CT. REV. 303, 317. Rutherglen's impressive article succinctly discusses the building, increasingly desperate national efforts to protect civil rights in the years just after the Civil War as follows: "From the original enactment of the Civil Rights Act of 1866 through the passage of the Civil Rights Act of 1875, Congress sought in each step that it took to remedy the inadequacies of what it had done before. Freeing the slaves in the Thirteenth Amendment was not enough, nor guaranteeing the capacities of citizenship in the Civil Rights Act of 1866, nor constitutionalizing the equal protection of the laws in the Fourteenth Amendment, nor protecting the right to vote in the Fifteenth Amendment, nor enforcing all of these rights in the Enforcement Act of 1870 and the Civil Rights Act of 1871. These enactments, and many others during Reconstruction, were revolutionary for their times, but they did not produce racial equality. With the end of Reconstruction, this failure became all too apparent, as the Civil Rights Act of 1866 fell into a long period of neglect, along with all the other civil rights legislation passed during this period." *Id.* at 322.

21. *Id. See, e.g.,* Robert J. Kaczorowski, *The Enforcement Provisions of the Civil Rights Act of 1886: A Legislative History in Light of* Runyon v. McCrary, 98 YALE L.J.

565 (1989); Rebecca E. Zietlow, *John Bingham and the Meaning of the Fourteenth Amendment: Congressional Enforcement of Civil Rights and John Bingham's Theory of Citizenship*, 36 AKRON L. REV. 717 (2003); Alexander Tsesis, *Furthering American Freedom: Civil Rights and the Thirteenth Amendment*, 45 B.C. L. REV. 307 (2004); Lea S. VanderVelde, *The Thirteenth Amendment of Our Aspirations*, 38 U. TOL. L. REV. 855 (2007).

22. *Id.* at 384 (quoting *Georgia v. Rachel*, 384 U.S. 780, 791 [1966]).

23. Rehnquist did not choose to quote those parts of Justice Stewart's opinion emphasizing that, for example, "The first section of the 1866 Civil Rights Act secured for all citizens the 'same' rights as were 'enjoyed by white citizens,' in a variety of fundamental areas." *Id.* at 788 (footnote omitted). Nor did he mention that Stewart went on to note that, even within the vexed and always sensitive realm of criminal law removal jurisdiction, "Section 3, the removal section of the 1866 Act, provided for removal by 'persons who are denied or cannot enforce the rights secured them by the first section of this act.'" *Id.* at 788–89 (footnote omitted). Stewart's opinion for a unanimous Court, with only Justice Douglas concurring separately, also noted that within a few months of Congress's veto override to make the Civil Rights Act of 1866 law, Congress established military tribunals through the Freedmen's Bureau Act, of July 16, 1866, ch. 200, 14 Stat. 176 (1866), and combined the recalcitrant rebel states into military districts and instituted martial law, Reconstruction Act of March 2, 1867, ch. 152, 14 Stat. 428 (1967). *Id.*

24. CONG. GLOBE, 39th Cong., 1st Sess. 474 (1866). Senator Lyman Trumbull, the main sponsor in the Senate, frequently returned to a basic theme he stressed from the start of the Thirty-ninth Congress: "Any legislation or any public sentiment which deprived any human being in the land of those great rights of liberty will be in defiance of the Constitution; and if the States and local authorities, by legislation or otherwise, deny these rights, it is incumbent on us to see that they are secured." *Id.* at 77. Even quotations from the Thirty-ninth Congress that Justice Harlan used in his *Jones* dissent, 392 U.S. 409, 468, often emphasized a duty to protect fundamental rights, an issue discussed in detail in Soifer, *Protecting Civil Rights, supra*, at 670–73, 681.

25. A key sticking point was concern that the statute's original broad language might be interpreted to include political rights such as suffrage. The amendment proposed by Representative John Bingham to limit the bill's original language was overwhelmingly defeated, yet when Representative James F. Wilson, chairman of the Judiciary Committee, ultimately agreed to its elimination, Wilson claimed that the change did not materially alter the bill. CONG. GLOBE, 39th Cong., 1st Sess. 1366 (1866).

26. Civil Rights Act of 1866, ch. 31, § 1, 14 Stat. 27 (1866). The only exceptions to section 1's broad sweep of all persons born in the United States into the embrace of its citizenship declaration were those "subject to any foreign power" and "Indians not taxed." *See infra* n. 58.

27. The Collected Works of Abraham Lincoln 254–55 (Roy P. Basler ed., 1946).

28. 458 U.S., at 384, citing 384 U.S. 780, 791 (1966) (Georgia sit-in cases) and 383 U.S. 787, 801, 807 (1966) (Mississippi civil rights murders). For instance, with support from important historical studies by Kenneth Stampp, The Era of Reconstruction, 1865–1877 (1975), and Allan Nevins, The Emergence of Modern America 1865–1878 (1972), Justice Fortas's opinion for a unanimous Court in *Price* noted, "Between 1866–1870, there was much agitated criticism in the Congress and the Nation because of the continued denial of rights to Negroes, sometimes accompanied by violent assaults." *Id.* at 807.

29. 458 U.S. at 389.

30. *Id.*

31. Cong. Globe, 39th Cong., 1st Sess. 1118 (1866).

32. 6 F. Cas. 546 (C.C.E.D. Pa. 1823) (No. 3,230).

33. *Id.* at 551–52.

34. 60 U.S. 393 (1856).

35. *See Prigg v. Pennsylvania*, 41 U.S. 539 (1842). Professor Mark DeWolfe Howe has stated, "If constitutional law had terminated with *Prigg v. Pennsylvania*, scholars and lawyers could confidently assert that there is nothing in the nature of American federalism that disables the Congress from controlling private conduct affecting the civil rights of others." Howe, *Federalism and Civil Rights*, in A. Cox, M.D. Howe & J. Wiggins, Civil Rights, The Constitution, and the Courts 30, 45 (1967).

36. What the North deemed the Slave Power was largely successful in terms of legally requiring the return of fugitive slaves, even in the face of state defiance, *Abelman v. Booth*, 62 U.S. (21 How.) 506 (1859), but the situation was even more complex when masters voluntarily brought slaves into states such as Massachusetts, where Chief Justice Lemuel Shaw followed Lord Mansfield's approach in *Somerset's Case* and declared such slaves to be free. *See generally* Robert M. Cover, Justice Accused: Antislavery and the Judicial Process (1975).

37. Justice Marshall's dissent in *General Building Contractors* used General Charles Schurz's report in S. Exec. Doc. No. 2, 39th Cong., 1st Sess. (1865), to support the point that the majority ignored "a broad congressional scheme intended to work a major revolution in the prevailing social order" and to "eradicate the badges of slavery." 458 U.S. at 408, 411.

38. Johnson's veto message complained that eleven of the thirty-six states were "unrepresented in Congress" and therefore called it "a grave question" as to whether it was "sound policy to make our entire colored population . . . citizens of the United States." Cong. Globe, 39th Cong., 1st Sess. 1679 (1866). Johnson railed against favoritism for former slaves, and he explained that former masters and slaves should be left free to work out their postslavery economic arrangements without government intervention: "Each has equal power in settling the terms, and if left to the laws that

regulate capital and labor . . . they will satisfactorily work out the problem." *Id.* at 1681. Johnson objected even more to what he deemed a radical change in federalism and an unprecedented encroachment of states' rights. *Id.* at 1680–81.

39. Soifer, *Protecting Civil Rights, supra*, at 687.

40. *Id.* at 692–94.

41. JAMES M. MCPHERSON, THE STRUGGLE FOR EQUALITY: ABOLITIONISTS AND THE NEGRO IN THE CIVIL WAR AND RECONSTRUCTION 348 (1964).

42. ERIC L. MCKITRICK, ANDREW JOHNSON AND RECONSTRUCTION 295 (1960).

43. MCPHERSON, *supra*, at 350.

44. CONG. GLOBE, 39th Cong., 1st Sess. 1679–80 (1866). The detailed response by Senator Lyman Trumbull, the main sponsor of the act, could hardly have been clearer about Congress's commitment to protect basic inalienable rights anywhere in the country. *Id.* at 1755–61. Trumbull insisted that "this bill in no manner interferes with the municipal regulations of any State which protects all alike in their rights of person and property." *Id.* at 1761. Trumbull was factually inaccurate about the willingness of Northern states to afford such protection, but the thrust of his remarks throughout the debate—as well as of virtually all the bill's major supporters—was the hope that all states would fulfill their duty to protect fundamental rights, but that the federal government had an obligation to do so if the states did not. The focus was the South, however, and congressional motives certainly were mixed, including a great deal of paternalism as well as the hope among some that the newly freed slaves would not immigrate to the North if they were treated decently in the South.

45. Justice White, joined by Justice Rehnquist, tried a version of this move in his *Runyon* dissent, 427 U.S. 160, 192–214. For an impressive job of carefully taking apart this argument, see Rutherglen, *supra*.

46. Current statute 42 U.S.C. § 1981 provides: "All persons within the jurisdiction of the United States shall have the same right in every State and Territory to make and enforce contracts, to sue, be parties, give evidence, *and to the full and equal benefit of all laws and proceedings for the security of persons and property as is enjoyed by white citizens, and shall be subject to like punishment, pains, penalties, taxes, licenses, and exactions of every kind, and to no other*" (emphasis added). As passed over President Johnson's veto, the scope of section 1 of the 1866 Civil Rights Act was narrower.

The change from "all citizens" (except Indians not taxed) to "all persons" and the inclusion of a few additional legal categories in which full and equal treatment is required—"taxes, licenses, and exactions of every kind"—came about through the Enforcement Act of 1870. The Enforcement Act, passed after the ratification of both the Fourteenth and the Fifteenth amendments, thus expanded the coverage of the 1866 Civil Rights Act. In its section 18, however, the Enforcement Act also explicitly reenacted the entire 1866 Civil Rights Act and proclaimed that the new sections should be enforced through the mechanisms of the older act. See *infra*, at n. 60.

47. CONG. GLOBE, 39th Cong., 1st Sess. app. at 67 (1866).

48. *See generally* Aviam Soifer & Hugh C. Macgill, *The Younger Doctrine: Reconstructing Reconstruction*, 55 TEXAS L. REV. 1141 (1977).

49. Section 2 emphasized the breadth of its coverage as it specified that it meant to criminalize subjecting someone to different punishment, pains, or penalties "on account of such person having at any time been held in a condition of slavery or involuntary servitude . . . *or by reason of his color or race*" (emphasis added). Civil Rights Act of 1866, ch. 31, § 2, 14 Stat. 27 (1866).

50. 24 F. Cas. 337 (C.C.D. Md. 1867) (No. 14, 247).

51. *United States v. Rhodes*, 27 F. Cas. 785, 788 (C.C.D.Ky. 1866) (No. 16,151).

52. *Id.* at 793.

53. 26 F. Cas. 79, 81 (C.C.S.D. Ala. 1871) (No. 15,282). *See also United States v. Mall*, 26 F. Cas. 1147 (C.C.S.D. Ala. 1871) (No. 15, 712). Judge Woods became the first Supreme Court justice from the South after the Civil War when he was appointed in 1869.

54. 83 U.S. 36 (1873). *See, e.g.,* CHARLES L. BLACK, A NEW BIRTH OF FREEDOM: HUMAN RIGHTS, NAMED AND UNNAMED (1999); Richard L. Aynes, *Constricting the Law of Freedom: Justice Miller, the Fourteenth Amendment, and the* Slaughter-House Cases, 70 CHI-KENT L. REV. 627 (1994); Robert J. Kaczorowski, *Reconstructing Reconstruction: The Enforcement Provisions of the Civil Rights Act of 1866; A Legislative History in Light of* Runyon v. McCrary, 98 YALE L.J. 565 (1989).

55. 109 U.S. 3 (1883). Robert Kaczorowski has done an excellent job discussing this throughout much of his work, though I believe we disagree somewhat about the extent of an intended "states' rights" limitation on the power of Congress. George Rutherglen's cogent survey, *supra*, seems to me too willing to accept the state action limitation as if it were intended rather than added through later judicial interpretation.

56. 80 U.S. 581 (1872). *See generally* Robert D. Goldstein, *Blyew: Variations on a Jurisdictional Theme*, 41 STAN. L. REV. 469 (1989).

57. *Id.* at 593. Justices Bradley and Swayne in dissent maintained that section 1 reaches state inaction and "provides a remedy where the State refuses to give one; where the mischief consists in inaction or refusal to act, or refusal to give requisite relief; whereas the second section provides for actual, positive invasion of rights." *Id.* at 597.

58. Ky. Rev. Stat., ch. 107, § 1 (1860).

59. The evidence included the statement made by one of the defendants to the other, for example, that "he [Kennard] thought there would soon be another war about the niggers; that when it did come he intended to go to Killing niggers, and he was not sure that he would not begin his work of killing them before the war should actually commence." *Blyew v. United States*, 80 U.S. at 585.

60. Civil Rights Act of 1866, ch. 31, § 3, 14 Stat. 27 (1866). It is worth noting that the *Blyew* Court, which might be said to have anticipated W. C. Fields in "looking for loopholes," made no mention whatsoever of the Fourteenth Amendment and the repassage of the 1866 Civil Rights Act in the Enforcement Act of 1870. This could be because the federal indictment in the case predated the Enforcement Act, but it seems unlikely that no one would have mentioned an intervening restriction on the scope of the 1866 Civil Rights Act if contemporaries had thought of such a limiting reading.

61. Soifer, *Protecting Civil Rights, supra,* at 1947–48. As Justice Souter recently stated in a different but related context, the judiciary itself has at times been at fault as over time it has used "blunt instruments imposing legal handicaps." *Lane,* 541 U.S. at 535 (Souter concurring, with Justice Ginsburg). Justice Stevens's opinion for the Court held that Tennessee had an obligation to "remove obstacles" to full participation by people with disabilities in the judicial process.

62. 80 U.S. at 601.

63. 489 U.S. 189 (1989).

64. *Id.* at 196. Rehnquist asserted: "[The Fourteenth Amendment's] purpose was to protect the people from the State, not to ensure that the State protected them from each other. The Framers were content to leave the extent of governmental obligation in the latter area to the democratic political processes." *See generally* Aviam Soifer, *Moral Ambition, Formalism, and the 'Free World' of* DeShaney, 57 G.W. L. Rev. 1513 (1989).

65. 458 U.S. 375, 396 (1982). Other aspects of this decision are discussed *supra,* text accompanying nn. 10–13.

66. 546 U.S. 470 (2006).

67. *Id.* at 475. His full statement is: "Any claim brought under § 1981, therefore, must initially identify an impaired 'contractual relationship,' § 1981(b), under which the plaintiff has rights." Perhaps "any" does not mean "any." But there seems an echo here of the Day-Glo markings a homeowner might find on the pavement in front of her house. It turns out to mark the spot for something in the future, such as pending street or sewer work, which will disrupt daily life significantly and also probably be charged to the homeowner.

68. *Id.* at 479. Justice Alito was newly appointed and did not participate.

69. President Johnson complained, "Thus a perfect equality of the white and black races is attempted to be fixed by Federal law, in every State of the Union, over the vast field of State jurisdiction covered by these enumerated rights." Cong. Globe, 39th Cong., 1st Sess. 1679–80 (1866).

70. That the case came from the Ninth Circuit may have influenced some of the justices. The Supreme Court's rate of reversal of Ninth Circuit opinions is notoriously high. *See, e.g.,* Jay S. Bybee & Vik Amar, Supreme Court Statistics, 2007 Ninth Cir-

cuit Judicial Conference (the Ninth Circuit had nineteen cases reversed and only two affirmed during October term 2006).

71. 458 U.S. at 389. Rehnquist said that the 1866 Civil Rights Act "constituted an initial blueprint of the Fourteenth Amendment, which Congress proposed in part as a means of '[incorporating] the guaranties of the Civil Rights Act of 1866 in the organic law of the land.'" *Hurd*, 334 U.S. at 32 (footnote omitted).

72. 474 F.3d 387 (7th Cir. 2007), *cert. granted*, 128 S. Ct. 30 (2007).

73. *Jackson v. Birmingham Bd. of Educ.*, 544 U.S. 167 (2005)

74. The Court's usual practice is not to grant a writ of *certiorari* unless there is a split in the circuit courts on the issue in question. But it may be that a split between Judges Posner and Easterbrook, old comrades-in-arms in the law and economics movement centered at the University of Chicago, carries almost as much weight. (Of course it may be that some antic sense of humor within the Court might have welcomed a case alleging race discrimination in which the defendant operates Cracker Barrel restaurants.)

75. 474 F.3d at 410. After this chapter was completed, the Supreme Court affirmed the Seventh Circuit in an opinion by Justice Breyer, *CBOCS West, Inc. v. Humphries*, 128 S. Ct. 1951 (2008). The majority opinion relied primarily on principles of stare decisis and did not directly confront a strikingly strained discussion of the "true meaning of an Act of Congress" advanced in dissent by Justice Thomas, joined by Justice Scalia., *id.*, at 1961, 1969.

76. *Id.* at 408.

77. *Id.* at 410, 411. According to Easterbrook, *Patterson v. McLean Credit Union*, 491 U.S. 164 (1989), was a prime example of a change to the Court's "current mode of statutory interpretation," and he attempted to distinguish those parts of *Patterson* that Congress specifically overrode in the Civil Rights Act of 1991 from the retaliation issue. *Humphries*, 474 F.3d at 410. (Easterbrook insisted that Congress did not "overrule" *Patterson*, arguing that such a congressional response "adopt[s] new rules but leave in place existing norms that the legislation does not touch." *Id.* at 409.). The majority in *Sullivan v. Little Hunting Park, Inc.*, 396 U.S. 229 (1969), held that a plaintiff in litigation under 42 U.S.C. § 1982 has standing to complain about retaliation, and Jackson concluded that it must have had a substantive component too.

78. 470 F.3d 827 (2006), *cert. dismissed*, 127 S. Ct. 2160 (2007).

79. WILLIAM BLAKE, THE MARRIAGE OF HEAVEN AND HELL (1975).

80. It may be that Judges Reimer and Kleinfeld do not join this section of Bybee's opinion. They specified that they joined only in parts II and III, yet the thrust of their disagreement was with Bybee's analysis in part IV of his dissent. It is not customary for appellate judges to note disagreement with part of an opinion that sets forth the facts and procedural posture of the case.

81. *Kamehameha*, 470 F.3d at 835 (emphasis added). Judge Bybee thus seemed to claim that the 1866 Civil Rights Act actually originated in 1870. If this were a slip of the computer screen, it is a glitch perpetrated in the face of the accurate identification of the origin of the act in 1866 within both the majority and concurring opinions.

82. *Id.* at 857 (quoting *Jones* 392 U.S. at 443 [1968]).

83. *See Parents Involved in Cmty. Sch., supra; Adarand Constructors, Inc. v. Pena,* 515 U.S. 200, 239 (to government, "we are just one race here. It is American." Scalia, J., concurring); *id.* at 241 (benign and malicious prejudice equally noxious, Thomas, J., concurring).

84. The Freedmen's Bureau, for example, clearly utilized race as a criterion for protections it sought to provide. *See generally* Eric Schnapper, *Affirmative Action and the Legislative History of the Fourteenth Amendment,* 71 VA. L. REV. 753 (1985) (race often taken into account in Reconstruction-era protections).

85. 42 U.S.C. § 12101(a)(6)-(7) (1990).

86. Statement of President Bush upon Signing S.933, 101st Cong., 26 Weekly Comp. Pres. Doc. 1165, at 601–2 (July 26, 1990). *See, e.g.,* Symposium, *Disability and Identity,* 44 WM & MARY L. REV. 907-1452 (2003); Michael Ashley Stein, *Same Struggle, Different Difference: ADA Accommodations as Antidiscrimination,"* 153 U. PENN. L. REV. 579 (2004); Samuel R. Bagenstos, *Subordination, Stigma, and "Disability,"* 86 VA. L. REV. 397 (2000); Aviam Soifer, *The Disability Term: Dignity, Default, and Negative Capability,* 47 UCLA L. REV. 1279 (2000).

87. 42 U.S.C.A. §§ 12182(a) & 12184(a) (1990).

88. PETER WESTEN, SPEAKING OF EQUALITY (1990).

89. MARTHA MINOW, MAKING ALL THE DIFFERENCE (1990).

90. *See, e.g., Steele v. Louisville & Nashville R.R. Co.,* 323 U.S. 192 (1944) (union owed minority members duty of fair representation); JOHN HART ELY, DEMOCRACY AND DISTRUST (1980) (theory of constitutional interpretation anchored in representation).

91. The Supreme Court granted *certiorari* to resolve the split in *Huber v. Wal-Mart Stores, Inc.,* 486 F.3d 480, *cert. granted,* 128 S. Ct. 742 (2007), but the case was dismissed before decision. 2008 U.S. Lexis 1095 (Jan. 14, 2008).

92. 227 F.3d 1024 (7th Cir. 2000).

93. *Id.* at 1028.

94. *Id.* at 1027.

95. Congress provided a civil remedy for wrongs brought about by "every person who, under color of any statute, ordinance, regulation, custom, or usage, of any State or Territory, subject, or causes to be subjected, any citizen of the United States or other person within the jurisdiction thereof to the deprivation of any rights, privileges, or immunities secured by the Constitution and laws." *But see Adickes v. S.H. Kress & Co.,* 398 U.S. 144 (1970) (strained reading of "custom" to be congruent with state action restriction).

96. A core concern in U.S. constitutional law courses remains attention to the implications of a famous footnote in *United States v. Carolene Products*, 304 U.S. 144, 152–53 (1938). Footnote 4 described situations such as political vulnerability that might require special judicial concern for "discrete and insular minorities."

97. 5 U.S. (1 Cranch) 137, 163 (1803).

12. *Forced Labor Revisited*

THE THIRTEENTH AMENDMENT AND ABORTION

Andrew Koppelman

> The longer I live the more I see that I am never wrong about anything, and that all the pains I have so humbly taken to verify my notions have only wasted my time.
> —Bernard Shaw, letter to H. G. Wells, 7 December 1916

Dawn Johnsen, who was President Obama's first nominee to head the Office of Legal Counsel (OLC), wrote an amicus brief arguing in passing that restrictions on abortion "are disturbingly suggestive of involuntary servitude, prohibited by the Thirteenth Amendment, in that forced pregnancy requires a woman to provide continuous physical service to the fetus in order to further the state's asserted interest. Indeed, the actual process of delivery demands work of the most intense and physical kind: labor of 12 or more grueling hours of contractions is not uncommon." After she was nominated as the OLC head, Senator Arlen Specter declared that this passage raised "real questions in my mind about her competency to handle this important job." The argument is "to say startling would be a mild characterization," said Specter. "It seems to me pretty hard to say that that's an arguable legal position."[1]

Senator Specter misunderstood Johnsen's position. To say that one thing is "disturbingly suggestive" of another is hardly the same as saying that it is identical to that other thing. Johnsen made this point to support her Fourteenth Amendment claim, by showing the serious nature of the liberty interest at stake. The brief does not argue that the state laws violate the Thirteenth Amendment. She quickly made clear in subsequent statements that she had made no Thirteenth Amendment argument. It did no good, and she withdrew from consideration.[2]

If there was any point of consensus that came out of this sorry episode, it was that if you want to be taken seriously, you had better not make a Thirteenth Amendment argument on behalf of abortion. That is beyond the pale. Senator Specter and his supporters[3] also made it clear that they regarded the position as so clearly wrong that it was not necessary to even give a hint as to what was wrong with it. In this they continued a long tradition of casual dismissal. It is not even clear that they understand the argument.

Most of the essays in this book, I am sure, break new ground, deploying the Thirteenth Amendment in new and creative ways. This is not one of them. I am going to restate an argument I made long ago, in my first article (not counting my law journal note), written in law school and published while I was still a graduate student.[4] I'm going to then consider how the work was received, offer some amendments to the argument, and conclude with some reflections on how, perhaps, it can have more influence in the future.

THE BASIC ARGUMENT

The Thirteenth Amendment reads as follows:

> 1. Neither slavery nor involuntary servitude, except as a punishment for crime whereof the party shall have been duly convicted, shall exist within the United States, or any place subject to their jurisdiction.
>
> 2. Congress shall have power to enforce this article by appropriate legislation.

My claim is that the amendment is violated by laws that prohibit abortion. When women are compelled to carry and bear children, they are subjected to "involuntary servitude" in violation of the amendment. Abortion prohibitions violate the amendment's guarantee of personal liberty, because forced pregnancy and childbirth, by compelling the woman to serve the fetus, creates "that control by which the personal service of one man [*sic*] is disposed of or coerced for another's benefit which is the essence of involuntary servitude."[5] Such laws violate the amendment's guarantee of equality, because forcing women to be mothers makes them into a servant caste, a group which, by virtue of a status of birth, is held subject to a special duty to serve others and not themselves.

This argument makes available two responses to the standard defense of such prohibitions, the claim that the fetus is a person. The first is that even if this is so, its right to the continued aid of the woman does not follow. As Judith Jarvis Thomson observes, "having a right to life does not guarantee having either a right to be given the use of or a right to be allowed continued use of another person's body—even if one needs it for life itself."[6] Giving fetuses a legal right to the continued use of their mothers' bodies would be precisely what the Thirteenth Amendment forbids. The second response is that since abortion prohibitions infringe on the fundamental right to be free of involuntary servitude, the burden is on the state to show that the violation of this right is justified. Since the thesis that the fetus is, or should at least be considered, a person seems impossible to prove (or to refute), this is a burden that the state cannot carry. If we are not certain that the fetus is a person, then the mere possibility that it *might* be is not enough to justify violating women's Thirteenth Amendment rights by forcing them to be mothers.

This is not a purely textual argument. It builds heavily on the Thirteenth Amendment case law, case law that is likely to be unfamiliar to many readers. The unfamiliarity presents a difficulty that I did not see when I wrote the original article. At that time, I naively believed what I had been taught in law school: that, if case law has been laid down by the Supreme Court, repeatedly followed, and never overruled, then it can be relied on as a source of law. The reality isn't that simple. But first, let me describe the argument.

Most of the jurisprudence surrounding the amendment concerns Congress's power under the second section,[7] but I want to begin by focusing on the first, which is self-executing.[8] Although directed primarily against the slavery of the antebellum South, the amendment is broader in scope, as the Court held when it first considered the amendment in the *Slaughterhouse Cases*. "Undoubtedly while negro slavery alone was in the mind of the Congress which proposed the thirteenth article, it forbids any other kind of slavery, now or hereafter. If Mexican peonage or the Chinese coolie labor system shall develop slavery of the Mexican or Chinese race within our territory, this amendment may safely be trusted to make it void."[9] The Court also said that "the word servitude is of larger meaning than slavery, as the latter is popularly understood in this country . . . It was very well understood that . . . the purpose of the article might have been evaded, if only the word slavery had been used."[10]

What, then, does the amendment protect? I said at the outset that the amendment is concerned with both liberty and equality. Each of these concerns is reflected in a different body of case law. Consider them in turn.

LIBERTY

The Court has explained that "involuntary servitude" refers to "the control of the labor and services of one man for the benefit of another, and the absence of a legal right to the disposal of his own *person*, property and *services*";[11] "a condition of enforced compulsory service of one to another,"[12] "that control by which the personal service of one man is disposed of or coerced for another's benefit which is the essence of involuntary servitude."[13]

Thus defined, it follows that "involuntary servitude" includes coerced pregnancy. The pregnant woman may not serve at the fetus's *command*—it is the state that, by outlawing abortion, supplies the element of coercion[14]—but she is serving involuntarily for the fetus's *benefit*, and this is what the Court has said the amendment forbids. If citizens may not be forced to surrender control of their persons and services, then women's persons may not be invaded and their services may not be coerced for the benefit of fetuses. It is as simple as that. The injury inflicted on women by forced motherhood is lesser in degree than that inflicted on blacks by antebellum slavery, since it is temporary and involves less than total control over the body, but it is the same *kind* of injury. When abortion is outlawed, the pregnant woman must serve the fetus, and that servitude is involuntary.

Some of those to whom I've made this argument have responded less with skepticism than with horror. They take it to be a libel on motherhood, which, far from being like slavery, is an exhilarating, awe-inspiring, and joyous experience.[15] It may not be out of place, therefore, to address this concern at the outset. The objection gathers whatever force it has by focusing on the experience of women who *want* to be mothers. But the Thirteenth Amendment doesn't apply to them. The servitude it is concerned with is *involuntary*. The distinction between wanted and unwanted pregnancy is like the difference between wanted and unwanted sex. Can rape be defended on the grounds that sex is an exhilarating, awe-inspiring, joyous experience? Are arguments that focus on the degrading and violative aspects of rape a libel on sex? Plantation slavery cannot be justified on the grounds that many people find gardening deeply satisfying.

Women differ from men in that the services they are capable of performing include the production of human beings. The Thirteenth Amendment, however, draws no distinction between the powers of a man's back and arms and those of a woman's uterus. Both, according to the amendment, belong to the individual who possesses them and cannot be made subject to the command or benefit of another. Indeed, the recent advent of "surrogate motherhood" has shown that women's reproductive powers are as capable as any other of being transacted for in the marketplace, a marketplace that the Thirteenth Amendment establishes as "a system of completely free and voluntary labor throughout the United States."[16]

The compulsion of women to use those reproductive powers for purposes not their own is incompatible with the amendment's strong declaration of universal personal liberty. As the second Justice Harlan observed, the acts of the Reconstruction Congress reflected "the individualistic ethic of their time, which emphasized personal freedom and embodied a distaste for governmental interference which was soon to culminate in the era of laissez-faire . . . Most of these men would have regarded it as a great intrusion on individual liberty for the Government to take from a man [*sic*] the power to refuse for personal reasons to enter into a purely private transaction."[17] Doubtless these men's vision of liberty did not extend to women's control over their childbearing capacities.[18] But the framers did enact that vision in broad language whose scope did not exclude women,[19] and there is no principled reason for excluding women from it today.[20]

The pun on the word "labor" should not distract your attention from the fact that when a woman is forced against her will to carry a child to term, control over her body and its (re)productive capacities is seized from her and directed to a purpose not her own. As Ellen Willis observes, "There is no way a pregnant woman can passively let the fetus live; she must create and nurture it with her own body, in a symbiosis that is often difficult, sometimes dangerous, always uniquely intimate."[21] If there is a difficulty here, it seems to stem from the fact that work is paradigmatically thought of as what *men* do; what women traditionally do is not called work ("My wife doesn't work") except perhaps to the extent that it is performed with the same limbs and muscles that men possess. But what would we call any activity that demanded that a man, in order to produce a tangible result, endure constant exhaustion, loss of appetite, vomiting, sleeplessness, bloatedness, soreness, swelling, uncontrollable mood swings, and, ultimately, hours of agony, often followed by deep depression?[22] (Perhaps one ought also to include the burden of raising the child to maturity, as many women have done when abortions were unavailable to them.)[23]

The germinal case construing the self-executing force of the Thirteenth Amendment is *Bailey v. Alabama*.[24] The case came to the Supreme Court as an appeal from a criminal conviction for fraud. Bailey, a black laborer, had accepted a $15 advance for signing a contract in which he agreed to work for a landholding corporation, the Riverside Company, for a year. Under the contract, he would earn $12 a month, of which $1.25 would be deducted each month to repay the $15 advance. After about a month, Bailey left the job and refused to return to it. He was then prosecuted for defrauding the Riverside Company of $15, convicted, and sentenced to 136 days of hard labor. While there was no evidence that he had intended to defraud the company, an Alabama statute provided that if one breached a service contract without refunding the money paid, fraud would be presumed. Under state rules of evidence, the accused was not permitted to testify about his intentions for the purpose of rebutting the presumption.

In reversing the conviction, Justice Hughes declared that "without imputing any actual motive to oppress, we must consider the natural operation of the statute here in question, and it is apparent that it furnishes a convenient instrument for the coercion which the Constitution . . . forbid[s]."[25] The Thirteenth

Amendment, he concluded, "does not permit slavery or involuntary servitude to be established or maintained through the operation of the criminal law by making it a crime to refuse to submit to the one or to render the service which would constitute the other."[26]

Bailey's definition of involuntary servitude as "that control by which the personal service of one man is disposed of or coerced for another's benefit"[27] encompasses the burden imposed on women by laws against abortion, since the "natural operation" of a statute prohibiting abortion is to make it a crime for a woman to refuse to render service to a fetus. Even had the decision been differently worded, any decision in Bailey's favor would a fortiori protect the woman who seeks to abort, since the servitude to which Bailey was subjected was considerably less—less taxing, less intrusive, and less total in its probable impact on the course of his whole life—than that which forced pregnancy imposes on her.

Bailey also provides an answer to those who would dispute that the servitude is involuntary. Some opponents of abortion think that women should be considered to assume the risk of pregnancy when they consent to have sex.[28] Even if women did deliberately assume such a risk, *Bailey* holds that the right to personal liberty guaranteed by the Thirteenth Amendment is inalienable. "The full intent of the constitutional provision could be defeated with obvious facility if, through the guise of contracts under which advances had been made, debtors could be held to compulsory service. It is the compulsion of the service that the statute [which enforces the amendment] inhibits, for when that occurs the condition of servitude is created, which would not be less involuntary because of the original agreement to work out the indebtedness."[29] So even if the woman is stipulated to have consented to the risk of pregnancy, that does not permit the state to force her to remain pregnant. Rather, the Court has announced a principle of broad application: a contract for service (already a pretty strange characterization of her "consent") is consistent with the Thirteenth Amendment only if the contractor "can elect at any time to break it, and no law or force compels performance or a continuance of the service."[30] Consent to the servitude is simply irrelevant.

EQUALITY

The Thirteenth Amendment is also concerned about the subordination of groups. It is egalitarian as well as libertarian.

This concern about invidious social meanings is most evident in the Court's interpretation of the second section of the amendment, which provides that "Congress shall have power to enforce this article by appropriate legislation."

This provision, the Court has held, "authorizes Congress not only to outlaw all forms of slavery and involuntary servitude but also to eradicate the last vestiges and incidents of a society half slave and half free."[31] On the basis of this interpretation, the Court in *Jones v. Alfred H. Mayer Co.* sustained Congress's authority to outlaw private racial discrimination: "Congress has the power under the Thirteenth Amendment to determine what are the badges and incidents of slavery, and the authority to translate that determination into effective legislation."[32] Tribe thinks that this language, if read literally, grants to Congress a power to protect individual rights "which is as open-ended as its power to regulate interstate commerce."[33] But unlike the Thirteenth Amendment, the Commerce Clause does not specify the evil which Congress is empowered to eliminate.[34] If the Thirteenth Amendment authorizes Congress to eradicate the badges of slavery—even those that, as in *Jones*, do not directly impose involuntary servitude—this can only be because they, too, are among the evils that the amendment forbids.

Why should this be so? Why is it that "the freedom that Congress is empowered to secure under the Thirteenth Amendment includes the freedom to buy whatever a white man can buy, the right to live wherever a white man can live"?[35] The explanation seems to rest on the complex nature of slavery as an institution:

> Although "slavery" as an abstract form does not encompass mere discrimination in the sale of housing, the attention of the congressmen in 1864 and 1865 was not directed simply at an abstract model of slavery, but at a particular instance of that evil which existed in the South. Having flourished for over a century, southern slavery had built up strong interests among those who depended upon it and ingrained habits and attitudes in men of both races. It involved a complex of social and economic as well as legal relationships . . . [The Thirteenth Amendment] appears to have been designed as a full response to the evil perceived. As modern perceptions of that evil grow, the response may take on increasingly broader scope.[36]

Even when slavery is deprived of legal sanction, its imprint on society is not yet wiped out. "When racial discrimination herds men into ghettos and makes their ability to buy property turn on the color of their skin, then it too is a relic of slavery."[37]

The concern about invidious meaning is equally present in the abortion case. If indeed "there can be no doubt that our Nation has had a long and unfortunate history of sex discrimination,"[38] this discrimination has consisted primarily of the systematic use of motherhood to define and limit women's social, economic, and political capacities. Anti-abortion laws would continue and ratify that practice even if they could somehow be restricted to that small subset of women seeking abortions who had contracted not to do so. The issue here is analogous to that of "badges of slavery." Because the subordination of women, like that of blacks, has traditionally been reinforced by a complex pattern of symbols and practices, the amendment's prohibition extends to those symbols and practices.

While the Court reversed Bailey's conviction "without imputing any actual motive to oppress,"[39] and invidious intent is thus not a part of the burden a Thirteenth Amendment challenge to a statute must carry, the pervasive presence of such intent strengthens such a challenge by reinforcing the suspicion that the statute would ratify systematic oppression. Sexism is as pervasive in the anti-abortion worldview as racism was in the Southern peonage system. Just as Southern whites typically assumed that blacks were lazy and irresponsible, anti-abortion arguments in present-day America typically belittle women's capacity for moral agency, often supposing that women who abort simply don't and can't understand what they are doing.[40] Just as the white landowners tended to think that agricultural labor, whether forced or willing, was a suitable role for blacks, so opponents of abortion tend to think that motherhood, whether forced or willing, is a suitable role for women. The view that dismisses a woman's desire to control the course of her life as arising from "convenience, whim, or caprice"[41] is intimately linked to the traditional view that it is ridiculous and inappropriate for women to have or pursue such desires, and that the capacities of women, but not of men, are properly exercised "not for self-development, but for self-renunciation."[42] Laws against abortion place the state's imprimatur on that view by imposing criminal punishment on those who deviate from it. In both cases, the insult is the same: to the extent that either blacks or women are regarded as instruments for satisfying the needs of others rather than as autonomous agents, their dignity as free persons is violated. They are treated as things rather than as persons.

BRINGING THE STRANDS TOGETHER

The injury of compulsory pregnancy, in sum, has both individual and social aspects: forced pregnancy is a deprivation of individual liberty, but that deprivation is selectively imposed on *women*—and women are a group that has traditionally been regarded as a servant caste, whose powers (unlike those of men) are properly directed to the benefit of others rather than themselves. Compulsory motherhood deprives women of both liberty and equality. And the Thirteenth Amendment argument responds to both these injuries.

The Thirteenth Amendment is both libertarian and egalitarian, because the paradigmatic violation deprives its victims of *both* liberty and equality. It compels some private individuals to serve others, and it does so as part of a larger societal pattern of imposing such servitude on a particular caste of persons. If the libertarian and egalitarian rules of decision are both plausible readings of the amendment, it is because each stresses one undeniable aspect of the paradigmatic case. The courts may invalidate laws that impose servitude only on individuals, as it said it was doing in *Bailey*, and Congress may outlaw practices that stigmatize, but do no more than stigmatize, traditionally subjugated groups, as in *Jones*. But if either of *these* cases were paradigmatic of the amendment's prohibition, the other would be inexplicable. While the amendment has been construed broadly to encompass both these injuries, each involves only one of the two main aspects of what the amendment forbids. Compulsory pregnancy involves both. Since the amendment reaches far enough to forbid either of these injuries standing alone, a fortiori it forbids laws that inflict both of them at once.

The argument thus stated is thus open to a number of objections, counterexamples, qualifications, and questions of application. These are addressed in detail in the original article, and I will not repeat these points here.

THE ARGUMENT REVISITED

Plato's Socrates famously noted the limitation of any written argument, that "once a thing is put in writing, the composition, whatever it may be, drifts all over the place, getting into the hands not only of those who understand it, but equally of those who have no business with it; it doesn't know how to address the right people, and not address the wrong. And when it is ill-treated and unfairly abused it always needs its parent to come to its help, being unable to defend or help itself."[43] How well has my offspring managed in the world since I sent it on its way?

ITS RECEPTION

The article has been cited exactly once by a court, as evidence for the proposition that a defense of abortion based on the Thirteenth Amendment was not frivolous.[44] That court pointedly noted that it was not expressing a view on the merits.[45]

In the law reviews, it has been cited eighty-three times.[46] Most of these citations are friendly but brief, sometimes amounting to boilerplate, and do not engage the argument. It has elicited strong objections from three major legal scholars. Judge Richard Posner, describing *Roe* as "the Wandering Jew of constitutional law," noted that commentators have tried to "squeeze" the decision into many different constitutional provisions, including the Thirteenth Amendment. He was dismissive of all such efforts: "I await the day when someone shovels it into the Takings Clause, or the Republican Form of Government Clause (out of which an adventurous judge could excogitate the entire Bill of Rights and the Fourteenth Amendment), or the Privileges and Immunities Clause. It is . . . a desperate search for an adequate textual home, and it has failed."[47] Steven D. Smith described the article as an "ingenious discovery of legal and moral content in a constitutional text beyond what its authors could have contemplated," but then rejected it as a "hatrabbit operation."[48] Neither deems it necessary to explain why the argument is unpersuasive. John McGinnis has offered the fullest and most thoughtful response that has yet been published, albeit packed into a few sentences:

> It is not only that no reasonable person at the time would have thought that unwanted pregnancy was a form of involuntary servitude. Even now such an argument would be treated at best as a pun on labor rather than seriously advanced in a court of law. Servitude, particularly as the context of an amendment that was designed to end slavery relates to economic obligation, not familial obligations. Unwanted pregnancy is no more involuntary servitude than are the other unwanted obligations that may force parents to work for their children, like child support. In fact it is less so because these other obligations may trigger imprisonment if they are not kept. But even assuming the alternative universe in which a Court would apply this clause to the issue of abortion, Professor Koppelman still must make broad political assertions about the subordination of women to counter the obvious point that at least some women voluntarily become pregnant and then, changing their mind, wish to terminate a pregnancy.[49]

McGinnis challenges the thesis on three different grounds: original intent, an analogy with family obligations, and an argument about the force of obligations voluntarily undertaken. But these arguments were already raised and answered in the original article. Specific original intent proves too much, since the framers of the Fourteenth Amendment supported segregated schools and miscegenation prohibitions.[50] Child-support obligations do not raise Thirteenth Amendment concerns because they do not require specific bodily labor from anyone; one can raise the money any way one likes, just like any other contractual obligation. The *Bailey* decision did not relieve Bailey of his debt.[51] And obligations voluntarily undertaken were precisely what was at issue in *Bailey*.[52]

Perhaps you, reading this right now, don't buy the argument. If so, I wish you would write to me and explain why. If there is a defect in the argument, no one has ever stated it in print. Hit me. I want you to.

ITS PHILOSOPHICAL LIMITATIONS

The largest problem with the argument, as I presented it, is that it understates the messiness of the abortion issue and offers too clean a resolution. The article has some of the typical vices of a young person's work: its view of the world is too simple, and it doesn't acknowledge frankly enough the complexity of the issues it takes on.

The boundaries of moral concern are mysterious. No conclusive philosophical account has been offered of where those boundaries are appropriately located.[53] It is a matter of common agreement that late-term abortions are far more morally troubling than early ones, and that infanticide is absolutely prohibited. It is far less clear why this is the case. It is not just that there is no clean, knockdown way to resolve the issue of the fetus's personhood. There is also no clarity about how, as a practical matter, we as a society ought to address these borderlines of status. If the fetus's personhood is conceded for the sake of argument, there is no way to prove that it does not outweigh the Thirteenth Amendment claim. The article's claims were too strong in this regard.[54]

The argument from precedent was similarly too neat. I argued that, given that no one could prove the personhood of the fetus, it was impossible to say that *Roe* is clearly wrong, so it should remain the law. That's not clear, either, because the moral status of a fetus is so uncertain.

What can be shown here is that prohibitions of abortion implicate a constitutional right of great weight, one for which many lives have been sacrificed in the past. This diminishes but does not eliminate the problem of judge-made law. The precedents on which I rely are firmly rooted in the text, and no one seriously questions their validity.

If the claim is thus modified, then it becomes possible to answer the most difficult objection from precedent, one that I addressed too cavalierly in the original article. Parents have a legal duty to render assistance to their children and can be criminally prosecuted if they do not. This duty has never been thought to raise a Thirteenth Amendment issue. But the prohibition of abortion is just an instance of that very duty: the pregnant woman is obligated by law to render needed assistance to her child.

In the article, I tried to answer this objection by arguing that even the obligations of parents would raise a Thirteenth Amendment problem if the parents were not permitted to give their children up for adoption, as in fact they are in every state.[55] I am no longer so certain. Just as we have no conclusive account of the boundaries of moral concern, so we have no conclusive account of the nature and extent of parental obligations to children. I am sure, however, that the opposite claim, that parental obligations *never* raise a Thirteenth Amendment issue, is false. The existence of valid parental duties complicates but does not defeat the Thirteenth Amendment argument for abortion rights.

In the first place, the Thirteenth Amendment case against abortion restrictions rests on more than an analogy. Take another look at the institution of antebellum slavery that the amendment was specifically intended to outlaw. Thus far, in considering what "servitude" means, we have compared forced childbearing only with long days of hard work in the cotton fields. But mandatory motherhood and loss of control over one's reproductive capacities were partially *constitutive* of slavery for most black women of childbearing age, whose principal utility to the slaveholding class lay in their ability to reproduce the labor force.[56] Unlike (unmarried) white women, they had no right even in theory to avoid pregnancy through abstinence; they were often raped with impunity, by their masters and others.[57] Emancipation was intended to free them from such indignities. The effect of abortion prohibitions (whose impact, by the way, has been felt mainly by poor women who are disproportionately black)[58] is thus to consign women to a kind of servitude from which the amendment was supposed to free them.

The most pertinent characteristic of slave mothers was that they were unable to refuse intercourse. But if they had a valid Thirteenth Amendment claim for this reason, then so does any woman who is impregnated as a result of a rape. So the Thirteenth Amendment is relevant to at least a subset of abortion cases. How much further does it extend? That would seem to depend on how voluntary pregnancy is in the full range of other cases. We are back to all the familiar questions of whether a woman who became pregnant after making reasonable efforts to contracept, or a woman too young to be legally competent, has become pregnant voluntarily. The Thirteenth Amendment is at least relevant to these questions. That rebuts the claim that it has no application at all to parental obligations.

ITS RHETORICAL LIMITATIONS

Why didn't the piece have more impact? The Thirteenth Amendment is an unfamiliar idiom. People aren't used to thinking in those terms. Katherine A. Taylor thus observed:

> While feminist theorists have increasingly taken the intriguing approach of challenging abortion restrictions and other coercions of pregnant women as violating the Thirteenth Amendment, equal protection doctrine arguably affords the most appropriate means of challenging statutes that perpetuate women's subordinative status, since "it is the only body of constitutional jurisprudence explicitly skeptical about the rationality of gender-based judgments and specifically

concerned with the justice of gender-based impositions." Thus, it is likely that courts will be more amenable to a (revised) equal protection challenge to the pregnancy restrictions than to a Thirteenth Amendment challenge.[59]

The bounds of legitimate legal argument are not set by rules but by custom and usage. At the time the article was written, not much had been done with the Thirteenth Amendment by anyone in the legal academy. It had been a potent source of law as recently as the 1970s, but it had since gone out of fashion, and arguments that tried to invoke it as a major premise tended to be ruled out of order without a hearing, simply because that kind of thing is not done.[60] This book indicates that that is changing. There is an increasing appreciation that the Thirteenth Amendment has potent current applications.

The abortion issue is not going to be resolved by technical legal argumentation. But lawyers' bad consciences about the poor craftsmanship of *Roe* have certainly had a role in the debate. The Thirteenth Amendment argument can set those at rest. That counts for something.

As Thirteenth Amendment arguments become more familiar, the Thirteenth Amendment case for abortion will become less surprising. At that point, legal argument may once again come into its own, and scholars and judges may once more feel the obligation to answer legal arguments with arguments of their own. The Thirteenth Amendment may again become part of our constitutional conscience. After twenty years, I hope the conversation can begin.

NOTES

Thanks to Ron Allen for comments, and to Marcia Lehr for research assistance.

1. Specter Remarks on Qualifications of Nominee to Head DOJ Office of Legal Counsel, Congressional Documents and Publications, Mar. 19, 2009. Senator Specter also, very unfortunately, cited me as authority for the position that Johnsen had made a Thirteenth Amendment argument. This was based on a misreading both of my article and Johnsen's brief. *See* Andrew Koppelman, Lying About Dawn Johnsen, available at http://balkin.blogspot.com/2009/04/lying-about-dawn-johnsen.html (accessed April 3, 2009).

2. *See* Charles Savage, *Obama Nominee to Legal Office Withdraws*, N.Y. Times, April 10, 2010, at A16.

3. The most prominent of them was the National Review Online columnist Andrew McCarthy, who calls the argument "lunatic" and "farcical" but whose analysis does not proceed beyond the exuberant application of adjectives. *See* Andrew McCarthy, "Lawyer's Lawyer, Radical's Radical," National Review Online, March 9, 2009.

4. Andrew Koppelman, *Forced Labor: A Thirteenth Amendment Defense of Abortion*, 84 Nw. U. L. Rev. 480 (1990).

5. *Bailey v. Alabama*, 219 U.S. 219, 241 (1911).

6. Judith Jarvis Thomson, *A Defense of Abortion*, 1 PHIL. & PUB. AFF. 47, 56 (1971).

7. The major cases are *United States v. Harris*, 106 U.S. 629 (1883) (invalidating conspiracy section of 1871 Ku Klux Klan Act); Civil Rights Cases, 109 U.S. 3 (1883) (invalidating 1875 Civil Rights Act's ban on racial discrimination in public accommodations); *Clyatt v. United States*, 197 U.S. 207 (1905) (sustaining antipeonage statute); *Hodges v. United States*, 203 U.S. 1 (1906) (invalidating law against conspiracies to deprive blacks of their rights); and *Jones v. Alfred H. Mayer Co.*, 392 U.S. 409 (1968) (overruling *Hodges* and holding that Congress has broad power to identify and eliminate "badges of slavery"). Two useful general histories of Thirteenth Amendment jurisprudence are G. SIDNEY BUCHANAN, THE QUEST FOR FREEDOM: A LEGAL HISTORY OF THE THIRTEENTH AMENDMENT (1976), and Howard D. Hamilton, *The Legislative & Judicial History of the Thirteenth Amendment*, 9 NAT'L B.J. 26 (1951).

8. The Court's late twentieth-century decisions have included dicta to the effect that the Court has not yet decided whether the self-executing provision did more than free the slaves. *See City of Memphis v. Greene*, 451 U.S. 100, 125–26 (1981); *Jones v. Alfred H. Mayer Co.*, 392 U.S. 409, 439 (1968); *General Building Contractors Assn. v. Pennsylvania*, 458 U.S. 375, 390 n.17 (1982). This is not accurate. In its early twentieth-century cases invalidating laws that effectively imposed peonage, the Court consistently held those laws to be in conflict with *both* the Thirteenth Amendment and the federal statutes authorized by it. *Bailey v. Alabama*, 219 U.S. 219, 239, 245 (1911); *United States v. Reynolds*, 235 U.S. 133, 150 (1914); *Taylor v. Georgia*, 315 U.S. 25, 31 (1942); *Pollock v. Williams*, 322 U.S. 4, 25 (1944).

9. Slaughterhouse Cases, 83 U.S. (16 Wall.) 36, 72 (1873).

10. *Id.*

11. *Plessy v. Ferguson*, 163 U.S. 537, 542 (1896) (emphases added).

12. *Hodges v. United States*, 203 U.S. 1, 16 (1906).

13. *Bailey v. Alabama*, 219 U.S. 219, 241 (1911).

14. The same is, of course, true of any system of slavery sanctioned by positive law, such as that of the antebellum South: the master did not need to resort to self-help to control his slaves but could rely on the authorities to come to his assistance if necessary.

15. The argument is denounced as "bizarre" on this basis in Wendy Wright, U.N. Meeting on Women Ends in Chaos, Mar. 20, 2003, Concerned Women for America Web site, http://www.cwfa.org/articles/3596/CWA/nation/index.htm (accessed November 20, 2009).

16. *Pollock v. Williams*, 322 U.S. 4, 17 (1944); *cf. Bailey*, 219 U.S. at 245.

17. *Jones v. Alfred H. Mayer Co.*, 392 U.S. 409, 473–74 (1968) (Harlan, J., dissenting).

18. Opponents of the amendment did, however, express fears about its radical egalitarianism, which went unanswered by its proponents. *See, e.g.,* CONG. GLOBE, 38th Cong., 1st Sess. 1488 (1864) (remarks of Sen. Howard: "I suppose before the law a woman would be equal to a man, would be as free as a man. A wife would be equal to her husband and as free as her husband before the law."); CONG. GLOBE, 38th Cong., 2d Sess. 215 (1865) (remarks of Rep. White: "A husband has a right of property in the service of his wife; he has the right to the management of his household affairs . . . All of these rights rest upon the same basis as a man's right of property in the service of slaves.").

19. Unlike, for example, the suffrage provisions of the Fourteenth Amendment. *See* U.S. CONST. amend. XIV, § 2 (reducing congressional representation of a state if "the right to vote . . . is denied to any of the male inhabitants of such State").

20. Whatever reasons justify the extension of Fourteenth Amendment rights to women apply, mutatis mutandis, to the Thirteenth Amendment as well. That the Thirteenth Amendment is not confined to injuries to blacks, or even to those based on race, was suggested by the Court in *Griffin v. Breckenridge,* 403 U.S. 88 (1971), which held that the Ku Klux Klan Act, outlawing private conspiracies to deprive any class of persons of their constitutional rights, was a valid exercise of Congress's Thirteenth Amendment powers. In order to avoid creating a general federal tort law, the Court held that the mental element required for a violation of the statute was "some racial, *or perhaps otherwise class-based,* invidiously discriminatory animus." *Id.* at 102 (emphasis added). In a footnote, the Court added that "we need not decide, given the facts of this case, whether a conspiracy motivated by invidiously discriminatory intent other than racial bias would be actionable." *Id.* at 102 n. 9. A sex-discrimination claim under the statute was held actionable in *Pendrell v. Chatham College,* 370 F. Supp. 494 (W.D. Pa. 1974), in which a college professor alleged a conspiracy to terminate her employment because of, inter alia, her sex. While the court did not cite the Thirteenth Amendment as the constitutional authority for the statute's regulation of private conduct, "no other construction reasonably explains the court's decision," since the facts involved neither state action nor interstate travel. G. Buchanan, *supra,* at 171.

21. Ellen Willis, *Abortion: Is a Woman a Person?* in POWERS OF DESIRE: THE POLITICS OF SEXUALITY 471, 473 (Ann Snitow, Christine Stansell & Sharon Thompson eds. 1983). *Cf.* ROBERT GOLDSTEIN, MOTHER-LOVE AND ABORTION (1988); Motion for Leave to File Brief Amici Curiae on Behalf of Organizations [California Committee to Legalize Abortion et al.] and Named Women in Support of Appellants in Each Case, and Brief Amici Curiae, *Roe v. Wade,* 410 U.S. 113 (1973) (No. 70-18) at 23–24: "Even if the life support services which the woman's body brings into performance for sustenance of the fetus are largely automatic and non-voluntary, they are not non-services or non-actions. They are, according to medical experts, arduous, tiring, and obstructive of other work. The contractions of childbirth are literally 'labor.' They are the most strenuous work of which the human body is capable."

22. This list is considerably abbreviated; the details could (and do, *see* Donald Regan, *Rewriting* Roe v. Wade, 77 MICH. L. REV. 1569, 1579–82 [1979]) fill pages.

23. The coercion involved here is nicely described by Jed Rubenfeld: "From a moral or political view, it seems hardly acceptable to insist that a woman remains perfectly 'free' to do what now would contradict her most elemental feelings of obligation to the child that she has been compelled to bear. The anti-abortionist cannot defend abortion laws on the basis of a woman's abstract freedom to give up the child when the real moral and practical constraints upon this decision have been created by the operation of the very laws in question." *The Right of Privacy*, 102 HARV. L. REV. 737, 790 n. 204 (1989). These constraints would be exacerbated if abortion were illegal and if the laws against it were vigorously enforced (as they were not before *Roe, see* HYMAN RODMAN, BETTY SARVIS & JOY BONAR, THE ABORTION QUESTION 23–24 [1987]), since if all pregnancies now aborted were to come to term, the pool of potential adoptive parents would be exhausted in less than a year. Goldstein, *supra*, at 179–90. In such a world, women who had been forced to bear children would know that the alternative to raising them themselves would be to consign them to state institutions. Such a choice is already faced by mothers of minority or handicapped children, whose chances of adoption are much smaller than those for other children's. *Id.* at 182; U.S. Dept. of Health and Human Services, Children's Bureau, Administration for Children and Families, Children of Color in the Child Welfare System: Perspectives from the Child Welfare Community 8 (Dec. 2003), available at http://www.childwelfare.gov/pubs/otherpubs/children/children.pdf (accessed November 20, 2009) (Caucasian children are five times as likely to be adopted as children from other groups); Claire Baker, *Disabled Children's Experience of Permanency in the Looked After System*, 37 BRIT. J. SOC. WORK 1173 (2007).

24. 219 U.S. 219 (1911).

25. *Id.* at 244–45.

26. *Id.* at 244. For the history of the *Bailey* case, *see* Benno C. Schmidt, Jr., *The Peonage Cases: The Supreme Court and the "Wheel of Servitude," in* ALEXANDER M. BICKEL & BENNO C. SCHMIDT, JR., THE JUDICIARY AND RESPONSIBLE GOVERNMENT, 1910–1921, ch. 9 (1984). The case is likely to be unfamiliar to many readers. "The *Peonage Cases* are a largely forgotten footnote in constitutional law, and not even that in the law of contracts." *Id.* at 906. But this is not because the cases have lost any of their force. Rather, "the free-labor principle of the *Peonage Cases* has become thoroughly embedded in the bedrock of our constitutional and contract law," *id.* at 822, so that no litigant has challenged it in many years. The case for abortion rights is strengthened, not weakened, by relying on a principle so fundamental that it is never questioned.

27. 219 U.S. at 241.

28. This premise is dubious in several different ways. Lifelong sexual abstinence is not a reasonable option for most people, so their decision to decline that option does

not imply consent to anything in particular. Many women lack power in their rela-tionships with specific men. Pressures to have sex are often accompanied by pressures not to use contraception. *See Forced Labor*, 84 Nw. U. L. REV. at 503–5.

29. *Id.* at 242. *Accord Clyatt v. United States*, 197 U.S. 207 (1905); *United States v. Reynolds*, 235 U.S. 133 (1914); *Taylor v. Georgia*, 315 U.S. 25 (1942); *Pollock v. Williams*, 322 U.S. 4 (1944). *Cf.* Peonage Cases, 123 F. 671, 680 (M.D. Ala. 1903): "In the legal sense, whatever they may be in other aspects, such agreements are involuntary in their inception, since the law forbids consent, and therefore treats the agreement as having been made involuntarily—against the will."

30. *Clyatt*, 197 U.S. at 215–16.

31. *Jones v. Alfred H. Mayer Co.*, 392 U.S. 409, 441 n. 78 (1968).

32. *Id.* at 440.

33. LAURENCE H. TRIBE, AMERICAN CONSTITUTIONAL LAW, § 5-13 at 332 (2d ed. 1988).

34. *See* U.S. CONST. art. I, § 8 ("The Congress shall have Power . . . To regulate Commerce . . . among the several States . . .").

35. *Jones*, 392 U.S. at 443.

36. Note, *The "New" Thirteenth Amendment: A Preliminary Analysis*, 82 HARV. L. REV. 1294, 1301–2 (1969).

37. *Jones*, 392 U.S. at 442–43.

38. *Frontiero v. Richardson*, 411 U.S. 677, 684 (1973) (plurality opinion).

39. 219 U.S. at 244. *Cf. Reynolds*, 235 U.S. at 148–49 ("The validity of this system of state laws must be judged by its operation and effect upon rights secured by the Constitution . . ."); *Taylor*, 315 U.S. at 29 (focusing upon statute's "effect" and "neces-sary consequence"); *Pollock*, 322 U.S. at 25 ("We impute to the legislature no intention to oppress . . .").

40. This lamentable tendency recently resurfaced in Justice Kennedy's majority opinion in *Gonzales v. Carhart*, 550 U.S. 124, 159 (2007), which held that abortion meth-ods may be restricted because "some women come to regret their choice to abort the infant life they once created and sustained," possibly resulting in "severe depression and loss of esteem." Justice Ginsburg responded by citing peer-reviewed studies showing that women who abort show no higher rate of psychiatric disorder than those who carry pregnancy to term. *Id.* at 183–84 (Ginsburg, J, dissenting). Kennedy admitted that he had "no reliable data to measure the phenomenon" but deemed it "unexceptionable" that this story is true of "some women." *Id.* at 159 (majority opinion). It is hard to imagine any limits to the proposition that constitutional liberties can be restricted if it sometimes happens that someone regrets exercising the liberty in a given way. Some people who criticize actions of the government later wish that they had kept their mouths shut. Some criminal suspects regret that they didn't confess everything when the police first interrogated them. Some of the slaves freed by the Thirteenth Amendment were old and infirm, and some of them probably regretted leaving the plantation.

41. *Doe v. Bolton*, 410 U.S. 179, 221 (1973) (White, J., dissenting).

42. John Ruskin, *Of Queen's Gardens, in* SESAME AND LILIES 86 (1910; Harold Bloom ed., 1983). Prolife activists tend to believe that "men are best suited to the public world of work, and women are best suited to rear children, manage homes, and love and care for husbands." Kristin Luker, ABORTION AND THE POLITICS OF MOTHERHOOD 160 (1984). *Cf.* FAYE GINSBURG, CONTESTED LIVES: THE ABORTION DEBATE IN AN AMERICAN COMMUNITY (1989).

43. PHAEDRUS, 275d–e (tr. R. Hackforth).

44. *Jane L. v. Bangerter*, 61 F.3d 1505, 1515 n. 9 (10th Cir. 1995)

45. *Id.* at 1515. It was reversing lower-court decisions that had cast scorn on the argument; though those courts did reach the merits, they did so summarily, with little argument. *Jane L. v. Bangerter*, 828 F. Supp. 1544, 1554–55 (D. Utah 1993); *Jane L. v. Bangerter*, 797 F. Supp. 1537, 1548–49 (D. Utah 1992).

46. A Westlaw search of Koppelman/2 "Forced Labor" in the JLR (journals and law reviews) database on April 15, 2009, yielded a list of eighty-eight citations, which I corrected by deleting five articles written by myself.

47. Richard Posner, *Legal Reasoning from the Top Down and from the Bottom Up: The Question of Unenumerated Constitutional Rights*, 59 U. CHI. L. REV. 433, 442 n. 29 (1992).

48. Steven D. Smith, *Idolatry in Constitutional Interpretation*, 79 VA. L. REV. 583, n. 130 (1993).

49. John O. McGinnis, *Decentralizing Constitutional Provisions Versus Judicial Oligarchy: A Reply to Professor Koppelman*, 20 CONST. COMMENTARY 39, 56 (2003).

50. *Forced Labor*, 84 NW. U. L. REV. at 488–89 n. 40.

51. *Id.* at 523.

52. *Id.* at 490–511; for a summary of that argument, *see* part IA *supra*. In fairness to Professor McGinnis, he was responding to the Thirteenth Amendment argument only in passing while conducting a dispute concerned primarily with very different issues. *See* Andrew Koppelman, *How "Decentralization" Rationalizes Oligarchy: John McGinnis and the Rehnquist Court*, 20 CONSTITUTIONAL COMMENTARY 11 (2003).

53. *See* KENT GREENAWALT, RELIGIOUS CONVICTIONS AND POLITICAL CHOICE 98–172 (1988); Jeffrey McMahan, *Cognitive Disability, Misfortune, and Justice*, 25 PHIL. & PUB. AFF. 3 (1996).

54. This obvious issue is only glancingly addressed in the original article. In fact, it's buried inside footnote 155 on pp. 516–17. This is reminiscent of Robert Nozick's description of a certain kind of bad philosophy as "pushing and shoving things to fit into some fixed perimeter of specified shape. All those things are lying out there, and they must be fit in. You push and shove the material into the rigid area getting it into the boundary on one side, and it bulges out on another. You run around and press the protruding bulge, producing yet another in another place. So you push and shove and clip off corners from the things so they'll fit and you press in until finally almost everything

sits unstably more or less in there; what doesn't gets heaved *far* away so that it won't be noticed." Robert Nozick, Anarchy, State, and Utopia xiii (1974).

55. *See Forced Labor*, 84 Nw. U. L. Rev. at 523.

56. *See* Herbert Gutman, The Black Family in Slavery and Freedom, 1750–1925 75–80 (1976).

57. *See* John D'Emilio & Estelle Freedman, Intimate Matters: A History of Sexuality in America 100–104 (1988); E. Genovese, Roll, Jordan, Roll: The World the Slaves Made 413–31 (1976).

58. *See* Brief of Amici National Council of Negro Women et al., *Webster v. Reproductive Health Services*, 492 U.S. 490 (1989) (No. 88-605), and sources cited therein. Black women are also under unusually great pressure to keep and raise their babies, since black babies are relatively unlikely to be adopted. *See supra* n. 23.

59. Katherine A. Taylor, *Compelling Pregnancy at Death's Door*, 85 Colum. J. Gender & L. 85, 146 n. 198 (1997), quoting Reva Siegel, *Reasoning from the Body: A Historical Perspective on Abortion Regulation and Questions of Equal Protection*, 44 Stan. L. Rev. 261, 352 (1992).

60. Thus Larry Kramer observed that even those who offer Thirteenth Amendment arguments "tend to present their ideas somewhat sheepishly, as if slightly embarrassed to offer something so radically at odds with traditional constitutional understandings." *Popular Constitutionalism, Circa 2004*, 92 Calif. L. Rev. 959, 979 (2004). I don't think he was talking about me, since my argument was fairly immune to embarrassment, but the tendency he describes cannot be gainsaid. His description of the reaction is deadly accurate: "Most other commentators, in the meantime, not to mention lawyers, judges, and politicians, dismiss these musings as academic flights of fancy— the kinds of things only law professors, unconnected to reality, would think worth pursuing." *Id.* This reaction illustrates his more general point that "problems come to us framed by a multitude of implicit understandings and assumptions that limit and shape how we reason by defining our sense of how things work." *Id.* at 980.

13. *The Slave Power Undead*

CRIMINAL JUSTICE SUCCESSES AND FAILURES OF THE THIRTEENTH AMENDMENT

Andrew E. Taslitz

From the time of its ratification until today, the Thirteenth Amendment has had a major impact on the American criminal justice system, a matter too often ignored by modern courts. That impact was felt in two ways: first, by section 1's declaration of the nonexistence of slavery or involuntary servitude in the United States; second, and today more important, by section 2's empowering Congress to pass appropriate legislation to enforce the amendment. Such legislation sometimes explicitly acknowledges its roots in the amendment, other times seemingly being merely inspired by it. Yet the criminal justice legislation has largely tended to prohibit acts of violence done to compel the unwilling to labor at hard jobs for little, if any, compensation. I will argue here, however, that pursuant to section 2 Congress has much greater authority to criminalize acts that impose "badges and incidents" of slavery than just those exacting physically coerced labor. I will catalog a few examples of such heightened authority, such as criminalizing racially biased low-level violence interfering with the housing market, or outlawing certain psychological manipulation, devoid of even the threat of physical violence, to compel labor. My goal is to explain briefly why the amendment merits this broader reading—one further enhancing its modern relevance—rather than to detail all the criminal justice implications of that reading.[1]

My basic argument is that section 2 must be understood as not only aiming at slavery and its close cousin, involuntary servitude, but more directly at the Slave Power and the antirepublican culture it spawned. More specifically, I identify four hallmarks of a core concept of chattel slavery, the presence of any one of which was an important prop for the Slave Power and thus an appropriate subject of congressional legislative assault. These props give more meat to the ambiguous "badges and incidents" concept that has defined Congress's section 2 power. The four props are: (1) violence that (2) is expressive of racial subordination (3) used to coerce labor or (4) treat humans more as commodities than as persons. Current doctrine requires the conjunction of props 1 and 3, while I argue that prop 4 can alone be the subject of legislation, as can prop 1 in conjunction with either 2 or 3. Moreover, properly understood, props 2 and 3 significantly broaden the currently accepted scope of section 2's reach. This chapter thus reviews the Northern understanding of the Slave Power, the most useful philosophical conceptions of "slavery" and "chattel slavery," the importance of the contract philosophy underlying the North's opposition to the Slave Power, and a bit of the history of the "badges and incidents" moniker to defend the value of the four props idea, concluding by briefly noting some modern criminal justice implications.[2]

The historical premises that I summarize here have been defended in more depth elsewhere by me and by a number of leading historians. But here I wear the hat not of the historian but of the lawyer/theorist, seeking to blend the plausible lessons of history into a broader philosophical framework that can be a practical guide to modern legal doctrine.[3] Undertaking that task requires that we begin at ground zero: the world of antebellum criminal justice.

ANTEBELLUM CRIMINAL JUSTICE AND ITS DEMISE

SLAVE JUSTICE

Antebellum criminal law provided an important foundation for Southern slavery. The criminal law harnessed the power of state violence to uphold the master's authority while confirming the slave's subjugation and blessing white racism.

Masters, for example, were generally entitled to use force upon their own slaves, even fatal force, without criminal liability, if administered "for the purpose of subduing resistance or imposing discipline." The very rare murder prosecution of a master for killing his slave involved "egregiously cruel" brutality, "even by the highly permissive standards of the slave regime." Whipping was generally accepted as a means for enforcing discipline, some, particularly urban, masters turning to the local jail to administer that punishment publicly on the master's behalf.[4]

Third parties, especially in the later antebellum era, could face criminal punishment, however, for mistreating slaves, largely recognizing the importance of protecting the master against financial loss stemming from injury to his human "property." But whites other than the slave's master or overseer were often nevertheless acting well within the bounds of the law in using violence against slaves that would be an assault were it directed at a white man. For example, in some jurisdictions "any white person" was authorized to stop slaves off-plantation and "correct them" if they refused to submit to questioning. Slave patrollers were likewise frequently permitted to whip slaves outside plantations without a pass or an accompanying white person, though laws might limit the degree of violence (perhaps the number of lashes) allowed. Even when the law criminalized slave abuse, however, prohibitions outlawing slaves' testifying against whites made conviction difficult. The criminal law thus gave slaves but minimal protection.[5]

Yet slaves simultaneously could commit crimes by conduct perfectly acceptable for whites. In urban areas, slaves were arrested for failure to wear badges permitting their unsupervised movement and for unlawful assembly. Slaves also might face charges for murdering or assaulting whites under circumstances where a white defendant would have been seen as acting in self-defense. Criminal laws prohibited slaves' learning to read, engaging in "unbecoming conduct" in the presence of white women, gathering to worship without white supervision, not making way for a white person approaching on a walkway, and even making loud noises. Punishment of convicted slaves could be harsh, including whipping, hanging, and branding, even sometimes ear cropping, maiming, and castration.[6]

Whites aiding slaves in criminal conduct, including assisting runaways, or merely preaching freedom, could face criminal prosecution and the prospect of severe punishment. Indeed, even Northern whites were sometimes expected to aid in the capture of runaways, the Fugitive Slave Act of 1850 authorizing the summoning of bystanders to act as a *posse comitatus* in enforcing the federal law in aid of capture.[7]

In short, the antebellum criminal justice system worked to protect white Southern rule over its slave population. That population had a "double character," treated as property for most purposes but as quasi persons who were culpable for criminal conduct when challenging white rule. The criminal law thus authorized individual white violence, as well as violence by the state, when directed against black slaves, while giving slaves reciprocal protection primarily as necessary to protect the master's investment.[8] Criminal "justice" and Southern racial slavery were thus inseparable.

VICTORS' JUSTICE?

The Thirteenth Amendment eradicated all remnants of masters' justice. If slavery depended on an unequal administration of criminal law, then section 1's absolute bar to slavery in the United States nullified antebellum criminal codes. This nullification applied to any new legislation enforcing a de facto or de jure form of slavery. If states nevertheless failed to accept these prohibitions, section 2, at a minimum, authorized Congress to adopt legislation criminalizing violence akin to that of the masters and compelling state criminal law to comply with the amendment's spirit.[9]

In the short run, the Southern states resisted these implications of the amendment's passage. They first enacted Black Codes, containing criminal provisions substantially tracking those under slavery, and later they relied on racially neutral sounding provisions that were no less oppressive. Congress reacted with criminal statutes meant to address Southern recalcitrance. But the eventual failure of Northern political will and Southern whites' "redemption"—their return to power—doomed these federal statutes. The long-run picture is slightly rosier, and today there is a long list of criminal statutes directed at making real the promised abolition of slavery and involuntary servitude in the United States.[10]

Nevertheless, the criminal justice successes of the Thirteenth Amendment have fallen far short of the amendment's aspirations. In particular, there have been three major criminal justice failures of the amendment. First, it cannot today fairly be understood as having incorporated most of the criminal procedure protections of the Bill of Rights against the states. That failure has, however, been rectified by the modern Court's recognizing that task to have been accomplished by section 1 of the Fourteenth Amendment. Second, the Thirteenth Amendment's exception to the slavery prohibition for those "duly convicted" of crime proved to be a major loophole, long permitting the resurrection of the chain gang and the rise of the convict lease system as de facto ways to re-create aspects of slavery, and still today allowing the flourishing of less-obvious counterparts to those practices. Third, and my focus here, Congress has taken a cramped view of its section 2 powers in designing criminal legislation to battle the Slave Power.[11]

THE SLAVE POWER

The central unifying theme among the diverse supporters of the Thirteenth Amendment was the Union's will to break the Slave Power, sometimes called the "slave interest." Often articulated as a conspiracy by a wealthy, aristocratic planter class to control the nation in furtherance of that class's narrow self-interests, the Slave Power idea came to mean much more. The Slave Power, in the view of many Northerners, had fostered a Southern culture of expressive violence, intolerance, ignorance, and cruelty, inimical to white civil rights as much as black ones. This culture was antirepublican, its unabashed goal being to spread its corruption to the North and throughout the country. The political appeal of the Slave Power idea lay in its contrast with its supposed opposite: Northern free labor ideology.[12]

The Slave Power was linked to the Southern "honor" culture. In this culture, white violence was glorified, particularly as directed at African slaves. Such violence reaffirmed Southern manhood; expressed God's blessing over the "peculiar institution"; marked black-skinned Africans as dependent, unruly inferiors in need of the strong arm of discipline; and enabled white republican equality, for, as leading proslavery theorist T. R. Cobb put it, "every citizen feels that he belongs to an elevated class. It matters not that he is no slaveholder; he is not of the inferior race." While the South thus embraced racial violence as central to virtuous citizen character, the North eventually came (in word, at least) to precisely the opposite conclusion. To the North, the love of racial violence came to represent the essence of the degraded, unvirtuous Southern character. For Northerners, citizen virtue ultimately came to be defined as the opposite of Southern traits. Northerners could not speak of their own virtue other than by contrasting it in the same breath with attitudes and events in the South that Northerners viewed as defining an antirepublican character.[13]

Those events included Southern whites' burning of abolitionist mail, mob assaults on political dissenters, and banishment of Northern whites objecting to Southern policies—most famously of Samuel Hoar, of Massachusetts, who came to South Carolina to challenge in its courts its repeated seizure of Northern free black seamen while their ships were temporarily docked in Southern ports. Actions like these had long linked the Slave Power idea to the crushing of Northern civil liberties. Participants in the Albany convention launching the Liberty Party worried that "the Slave Power is now waging a deliberate and determined war against the liberties of the free states." Senator Thomas Morris, of Ohio, electrified the Senate by declaring, in 1839, the reality of a new power bent on destroying the liberties of the nation, a Slave Power, the "goliath of all monopolies." Liberty Party leaders recognized the rhetorical appeal of the Slave Power as a destroyer of Northern liberties. But the Kansas-Nebraska Act and the *Dred Scott* decision widely convinced Republicans that a newly aggressive Slave Power was at work to nationalize slavery, taint Northern free labor, and crush Northern liberty. Many Republicans now agreed that slavery and liberty were incompatible.[14]

It should thus be no surprise that tirades against the criminality of the Slave Power litter the debates over adoption of the Thirteenth Amendment. In the Senate, Daniel Clarke, of New Hampshire, for example, charged that "she [the Slave

Power] sent assassins to murder the Chief Magistrate . . . She shot down Union soldiers in the streets of Baltimore; she has sent armies in the field, and she now seeks the nation's life and the destruction of her government." Clarke feminized the Slave Power to brand it as cowardly. Legislation would not be enough to kill her, said Clark, but rather a constitutional amendment was needed. Absent that solution, the witch's hands would be left "unlopped, to clutch again such unfortunate creatures as it could lay hold upon." James Ashley, of Ohio, similarly claimed that the Slave Power had "silenced every free pulpit within its control, and debauched thousands which ought to have been independent," while Congressman William D. Kelley, of Pennsylvania, thundered, using "slavery" as a metaphor for the Slave Power, that it was slavery that "expelled that venerable scholar, jurist and statesman [Samuel Hoar] from the limits of South Carolina" and that "by threats and demonstrations of violence twice banished that friend of the Union and of mankind, George Thompson, from the limits of our country."[15]

While Kelley and Ashley focused on the Slave Power's deprivations of white freedoms, many Republicans sought to end attacks against blacks' freedoms. Some Republicans went so far as expressly to state that emancipation per se vested each freed slave with important basic rights, "inalienable rights . . . to live and live in a state of freedom . . . to breathe the free air and enjoy God's free sunshine . . . to till the soil, to earn his bread by the sweat of his brow . . . to the endearment and enjoyment of family ties." In the view of many historians, Republicans linked the protection of blacks from racial and political violence with defeat of the Slave Power. Although other historians have argued for a narrow reading of what the framers and ratifiers of the Thirteenth Amendment meant it to mean, for my purposes the central point—one rarely, if ever, challenged—is that the Slave Power idea was central to understanding the events that led to that amendment.[16]

But if one function of the Thirteenth Amendment was to destroy the Slave Power, how could the amendment further that goal? Debates over the Confiscation acts, precursors to the Thirteenth Amendment, help to answer this question. One theme repeatedly struck in Northern pamphlets, letters, and newspaper editorials during these debates was this: confiscating the masters' land and their slaves would consume the wealth that sustained them and break the back of antirepublican rule. The *New York Times* captured this sentiment when it described the war as one "of the aristocracy of the South, nominally against the working people of the North, but really against the whole people, and against Democracy itself." The Union thus had to "strike at the higher classes," a blow best struck both out of military necessity and to "depress the traitorous aristocracy who hated the Union and Democracy and will always hate them." By emancipating the slaves and confiscating the rebels' estates and dividing or cheaply selling their land among Union soldiers and poor Southern whites, these advocates railed, the Slave Power could be forever buried. For many Northerners, therefore, confiscation of planters' slaves and land would mean "bringing the North physically and morally into the South, thus creating a more truly unified and virtuous nation."[17]

The calls during these debates for the confiscation of all slaveholders' land ultimately did not win the day. But the theory that ending slavery—in the sense of depriving the masters of the wealth from physically coerced labor—was necessary to putting a stake through the heart of the Slave Power remained vibrant and is one fair way to understand the minimum scope of section 1 of the Thirteenth Amendment. But what if that measure proved insufficient to do the job? Section 2 authorized Congress, within limits discussed below, to drain the Slave Power of other sources of its vitality *if* denying it the human wealth that was its life's blood failed to kill it. Understanding the wisdom of this reading requires some ruminations about the meanings of "slavery," "chattel slavery," and freedom of contract in a republic.[18]

SLAVERY, CHATTEL SLAVERY, AND THEIR CORE PROPS

Philosophers, historians, and law professors heatedly debate the meaning of slavery. Rather than tediously examining these varied definitions, I simply offer my own, drawing in part on other commentators' work, to offer a definition most consistent with American history and the underlying assumptions of America's constitutional structure and culture.[19]

SLAVERY VERSUS CHATTEL SLAVERY

SLAVERY

Slavery is foremost an extreme lack of control over one's work, including lacking any voice in the conditions under which that labor takes place. Part of what makes the lack of control extreme is that it is enforced by the master's power to exercise physical force or its threat to attain obedience. Even if that power is not exercised (the "benign" master), it is the existence of that power that matters. Legal recognition of the master-slave relationship adds the state's power to use force to that of the master but is not a necessary condition for the existence of the relationship. Were it otherwise, the slave could be emancipated by law but with his life thoroughly unchanged. Any effort to combat slavery must, therefore, involve criminalizing private as well as public efforts to subject individuals to a "master's" will.[20]

Maintaining a system of such subjection requires the loss of specific forms of freedom. The ancient Greeks saw slaves as necessarily lacking four freedoms: (1) to be legally recognized by the community, thereby conferring a right of access to the courts; (2) to be protected against what would otherwise be illegal seizure, detention, or other violation of the person; (3) to be able to go where one wants; and (4) to work as one pleases. At least two of these lost freedoms—lost access to courts and lost protection against unjustified seizure—implicate the criminal justice system. A person who lacks access to the criminal courts as a complainant has no recourse when subjected to private violence. Seizure and detention by private parties would likewise be criminal—in modern terminology, being a form of kidnapping or false imprisonment—were it directed at free persons. Seizure and detention of individuals by the state, on the other hand, is also a way of starting a criminal prosecution and, in modern terms, limits the state's power to investigate crime, most notably via the Fourth Amendment's prohibition against "unreasonable searches and seizures."

Anti-Slavery International (ASI), an organization dedicated to ending slavery throughout the world, defines slavery as having four characteristics that in significant ways mirror the ancient Greeks' definition of the four missing freedoms. A slave, declares ASI, is (1) forced to work through physical or mental threat; (2) while being owned or controlled by an employer, usually through actual or threatened mental or physical abuse; (3) who is "dehumanized, treated as a commodity, or bought and sold as 'property'"; and (4) is "physically constrained or has restrictions placed on his/her freedom of movement."[21] ASI's definition seems to expand upon that of the ancient Greeks in two important ways: first, by including in the definition of the necessary means for compelling work the actual or threatened use of "mental," not merely physical, abuse; and, second, by emphasizing the treatment of the slave as a commodity, to be bought and sold. ASI's definition is consistent with much of the American experience of slavery and would permit criminalizing forms of mental abuse generally not adequately reached by current antislavery criminal legislation.

The most controversial portion of both the Greek and ASI definitions is their limited focus on the labor relationship. Both Southern slavery apologists and Northern free-labor proponents indeed understood the moral status of slavery as linked to conceptions of the proper function of labor relations in a republican society. The Greek definition is even narrower, moreover, by its limitation to using only actual or threatened physical force rather than "mental abuse." But, once again, the role of physical force or its threat was important in the debate over whether slavery should expand, be contained, or die. Yet there is a cognate concept, "chattel slavery," rather than the idea of "slavery" simpliciter, that better encompasses the psychological component of the oppression of bondage in a way that more clearly justifies the extension of anti-slavery criminal legislation to addressing that component; expands such legislation's reach beyond solely the labor relationship; and better explains the proper role of section two of the Thirteenth Amendment in regulating criminal justice . . . [22]

CHATTEL SLAVERY

Chattel Slavery Defined

With *chattel* slavery, servants are treated as property, thus lacking control "not just over work but over their lives as a whole."[23] Property exists as an extension of the master's will.[24] Property lacks human rights, may be bought and sold, cannot itself own property, and exists as a mere instrument for fulfilling the owner's (the master's) desires. Human property, of course, is not quite like other property, for it has a mind of its own, legs with which to flee, and a nature that responds to motivations other than force or its threat, the first and last of these qualities not being shared by most other living property, such as livestock. Southern law, ideology, and culture recognized this unique status of human property but considered it property just the same. Indeed, these unique qualities made human property particularly subject to loss, requiring special efforts, such as slave patrols and fugitive slave warrants, to protect the masters' interests. This conception of a subset of humanity as a special form of property thus helps to explain the South's complex system of criminal justice.[25]

But even this description fails to capture the extreme loss of control that defines chattel slavery, for to be a chattel slave is to be,

> in the first instance, someone lacking in the power to dispose of his/her physical and mental powers, including both the capacity to produce and control of the body generally (extending to sexuality and reproduction); . . . to dispose of the means of production; . . . to select a place of residence; . . . to associate with others and establish stable bonds; . . . to decide on the manner in which one's children will be raised; and . . . to fix the rules governing the affairs of the states in which one resides. Slaves are distinguished from other groups— helots, serfs, sharecroppers, poor but propertied peasants, and propertyless proletarians—by the combination of the breadth and depth to the powers that others have over them.[26]

This extreme loss of freedom thus specifies a wider potential (though not unlimited) zone of criminal justice system concerns—from forced sexual activity to compelled isolation from friends and family to forced sale of children—designed to undermine the supports on which *chattel* slavery stands.

Chattel Slavery Versus Freedom of Contract

Chattel slavery, particularly as it existed in the antebellum United States, is thus best understood as a wholesale rejection of a contract philosophy widely embraced by nineteenth-century Northerners. Southerners used the threat of physical coercion to bar blacks from entering into enforceable agreements. But an examination of the Northern contract philosophy in which Southerners saw slaves as playing no part also reveals the extent to which the psychological manipulation and cultural deprivation needed to turn humans into chattel can be so brutal as to merit the attention of the criminal justice system.

Contract Philosophy

William Graham Sumner, in the postbellum period, captured the near-sacred status of contract. Said Sumner, "A society based on contract is a society of free and independent men." Contract imposed transitory obligations based upon competitive bargaining between equal, autonomous persons, thus being thoroughly inconsistent with chattel slavery.[27] Contract made "a man . . . a source of power over himself"[28] and "marked the difference between freedom and coercion."[29]

There were three central elements to contract philosophy: consent, exchange, and self-ownership.[30]

Consent required the absence of compulsion and knowledge of the obligations incurred and of their consequences. Exchange implied reciprocity, incurring a burden in return for a benefit. Knowledgeable, formally equal parties would presumably each agree to accept burdens only when the benefits of doing so exceeded the cost. Self-ownership was rooted in the Lockean idea that each person is "master of himself, the proprietor of his own person, and the actions or labour of it." Self-ownership implied an entitlement to the fruits of one's own labor. Although many seventeenth- and eighteenth-century commentators saw wage labor as inconsistent with true autonomy—independence lying primarily in owning the means of production—wage labor gained increasing acceptance in the nineteenth century. Labor thus came to be seen as the one part of one's self that could be sold in the market for a price, entitling the purchaser to keep some portion of that labor's fruits pursuant to the terms of a freely negotiated contract. But, though at first disputed, the eventual widespread understanding was that persons could not otherwise contract away the ownership of the rest of what made them what they were. Any contrary rule would deny them the autonomy to make future freely chosen agreements upon which the legitimacy of a contract-based society depends.[31]

Southern Rejection

Slave codes offended all these principles of contract. Slaves could not engage in contracts, own property, leave the plantation without the master's permission, lay claim to wages, or resist corporal punishment. Slaves were often forbidden to read or write, partly to prevent them from forging passes or reading abolitionist literature, but also because their status as property meant that they were seen as lacking the ability to benefit from, or the need for, the independence of mind that an education was meant to foster. The Louisiana code recited the bottom line bluntly: "All that a slave possesses belongs to his master; he possesses nothing of his own," for he is, by definition, "one who is in the power of a master to whom he belongs." If some Southern thinkers quibbled with these characterizations, James Henley Thornwell, for example, insisting that slaves still owned themselves and their souls, lacking only the ability to contract, law and practice belied such sophistry.[32]

Force alone was too often insufficient to maintain the master's rule. Slaves might flee, hide, retaliate, thieve, feign illness, slow work's pace, or resist in myriad ways, both large and small. Psychological coercion was thus necessary to maintaining the slave system, and it was slaves' status as property that rendered them vulnerable to such coercion. A master might threaten to sell a recalcitrant slave far from his family or to life in more brutal conditions "down South." Alternatively, the master might threaten to sell the slave's wife or children or, if they lived on other nearby plantations, to deny the slave weekend passes to see them. The slave's enforced illiteracy and ignorance made it hard for him to flee or to imagine a life independent of his master as a realistic option. Masters sought to buttress these mental limits by having white clergy preaching sermons of obedience to masters lest the slave face hellfire. Psychological manipulation's power was thus inextricably linked to the slave's status as a chattel. Moreover, it was that status that ultimately made the Slave Power an abomination to the North, for a thing that can be traded like boots or oxen cannot be the man on which the free-labor society of freely contracting individuals depends. The South's rejection of the North's version of contract philosophy helps to explain why it was the death of the *Slave Power*, not solely of forced labor, that must be understood as a central concern of the Thirteenth Amendment.[33]

EXPRESSIVE RACIAL VIOLENCE

There is one final aspect of American slavery's nature to keep in mind: the expressive nature of racial violence. Some theorists have argued that slavery can involve three types of force, only one of which—"productive force"—is definitional to slavery. Productive force is used to compel slaves to produce at all and to do so in the amounts that the master wants. Distributive force is used to ensure that the master's share of the benefits of labor (often all but what was needed for the slave's subsistence went to the master) is greater than what he could obtain by contractual bargaining. Symbolic force is used to express the public understanding of the slave as abjectly subordinate to the master.[34]

Whether or not these theorists are right to say that symbolic force is not part of slavery's essence, it was part of *American chattel slavery's* essence. Moreover, the message was not simply one of subordination but of *racial* subordination. White violence marked slaves as dishonorable, a dishonor already branded on their skin by its color. White violence reaffirmed not merely the slave's inferiority and dependence but also that of his entire racial group. Moreover, black skin color was a mark of God's punishment on these supposed descendants of Ham, the biblical son of Noah cursed for seeing his father's nakedness. Blackness implied a stunted mind and a simple heart in need of white care and guidance, "care" that could be administered only with the whip, for "tangible punishments and rewards, which act at once on their senses, are the only sort most [slaves] can appreciate." White wrath wreaked on black skin joined even poor whites with rich ones in a fraternity of the skin, making Southern republican civilization possible, argued the masters' apologists. So deep is the curse of race that the few "free" blacks of the antebellum South were thus granted only the most impoverished sort of freedom.[35]

PROPS REDUX

In sum, therefore, American chattel slavery is best defined as labor coerced by expressive racial violence (or its threat) directed at human property. Perhaps this definition is better described as the "core" concept of slavery, remembering that slavery is but one extreme end of a spectrum of labor relations, an end whose boundaries may be fuzzy at the margins. This core requires the conjunction of all four elements noted above: slavery is (1) violent, (2) meant to express racial subordination (3) in order to coerce labor (4) from human property. Furthermore, all these elements must be informed by contract philosophy and free-labor ideology. But the Thirteenth Amendment extends beyond this core. For example, it prohibits "involuntary servitude," such as peonage. Such servitude likely only embraces elements 1 and 3, though it is often accompanied in our history by element 2 and perhaps "property-like" treatment akin to, without completely embracing, element 4. If state or private violence to obtain labor is thus sufficient to implicate the amendment, then surely any relationship between this minimum and the full four-element core also "shall [not] exist within the United States." Of importance, involuntary servitude, like true slavery, contradicts key aspects of the nineteenth-century Northern contract doctrine, thus justifying the extension of the Thirteenth Amendment's core prohibition beyond American chattel slavery.[36]

If section 1 of the amendment bars relationships falling well short of the core idea of American chattel slavery, however, why bother with this idea of the core at all? My answer: because the core gives meaning to section 2. Section 1 is best understood as expressing the hope that ending slavery *and* involuntary servitude would kill the Slave Power and the corrupt culture it fostered. But if those steps proved to be inadequate—if one element ("chattelhood") or certain combinations of other elements of the core concept of American chattel slavery survived—then congressional legislation might be needed to drive the Slave Power back to the grave. The Slave Power can be undead—neither fully alive nor fully dead, stalking the republic to feed on freedom's blood, unseen in the darkness. Truly killing the undead, I argue, is what section 2 is all about.[37]

This interpretation of section 2 makes sense for three reasons. First, if section 2 merely prohibits what section 1 has already declared a nullity, it is hard to see what of substance section 2 adds, other than perhaps clarifying a power already inherent in section 1 Second, and more important, the ambiguity and breadth of section 2's language invites this reading, for the Northern victors' goal (and I here embrace victors' justice) in enacting the amendment was to drive a stake through the Slave Power's heart. The four humors that kept that heart beating are what I have called the four "props" of American chattel slavery. These props make the best philosophical sense of section 2's meaning when read in light of the American revolutionary project. The props idea, although admittedly not part of the framers' "original meaning," is consistent with the Northern contract and free-labor ideologies of the time, with the amendment's underlying goals, with the implicit (sometimes explicit) fears that lead to the ratification of the amendment, and with the logic of an antislavery "living constitutionalism." The four props idea also has the virtue of placing sensible limits on congressional power under section 2.[38]

Section 1, as I have read it, bars certain practices rooted in actual or threatened physical violence. Violence cannot, in section 2, however, be prohibited in itself or the amendment would absurdly become the wellspring authority for prohibiting all violent crimes, from fistfights to everyday purse snatchings. Nor can the amendment fairly be read as prohibiting all forms of expressive racial subordination or of coerced labor that are devoid of even threatened violence, for that would render other constitutional provisions governing those subjects redundant. Thus, violence must still be linked to racial subordination or to labor coercion to fall within section 2's scope. But no such problem arises with the fourth prop. A person can still be treated much like a chattel (see the discussion of the *Kozminski* case that follows) even absent physical violence, though some measure of psychological "violence" is likely necessary. The implications of viewing section 2 as aimed at killing the remnants of, or central supports for, the Slave Power thus include authority for criminalizing expressive racial violence divorced from the labor setting, physically or psychologically coerced labor divorced from racial bias, and any de facto or de jure efforts to treat persons as property.

But what if the Slave Power survives, albeit in weakened form, even if none of the four core elements still exist; would Congress have power to do anything it deems necessary to finish the job? No. The core idea of American chattel slavery imposes limits on congressional power under the Thirteenth Amendment as well. If freedom is slavery's opposite, then ending slavery would mean ensuring *all* freedom, a concept so capacious that it would be hard to give it limits, an uncontrolled legislative discretion that usually troubles the courts. Even the story I have told here might arguably support an interpretation requiring giving slaves political rights to ensure them voice, as well as all the basic civil rights contained in the Bill of Rights to give them robust protections against abuses of their persons and property. But I reject that interpretation, for it would render section 1 of the Fourteenth Amendment, which, among other things, does incorporate most of the Bill of Rights against the states, and all of the Fifteenth Amendment, which guarantees political rights such as voting, pointlessly repetitive. The concept of the core avoids these problems while rooting section 2 of the Thirteenth Amendment's scope in fundamental principles that make the best sense of our history.[39]

Nor do I mean to suggest, on the other hand, that the Thirteenth Amendment can reach only certain forms of *racial* expression. Rather, expressive racial violence, by being part of the core, is a "paradigm case" from which extensions may be made to "racelike" animus, such as may be involved in ethnic or religious violence, through an analogical process well defended and developed elsewhere. This paradigm case form of reasoning is not, however, an invitation to unduly roving judicial power, both because extensions of doctrine must be rooted in the core elements defining the paradigm case and because it is in the first instance for Congress, not the courts, to formulate section 2 remedies. But Congress must itself use a sound reasoning process, for my concept of the core requires identifying whether one of the four core elements still exists, whether its existence is so egregious as to be capable of fostering a culture in important ways reminiscent of the Slave Power, and what means are required to remedy the problem. These are matters fraught with ambiguity and normative judgments and requiring the collection and analysis of empirical data to which the legislature, rather than the courts, seems institutionally best suited. If this observation is not always correct, it is certainly most apt in the area of criminal justice, which is modernly nearly entirely statutory in nature and reflective of moral judgments held to be fundamental to our republican society by the American people.[40]

BADGES AND INCIDENTS REDUX

The Supreme Court's modern precedent firmly establishes that the Thirteenth Amendment reaches beyond the simple prohibitions against slavery and involuntary servitude, reaching, at least via section 2, its "badges and incidents." The amendment's strongest supporters embraced this view. Senator James Harlan, of Iowa, roared that the amendment would be a "battle axe" against any "incidents of slavery." Such incidents, said Harlan, included interfering with family relationships, jury participation, and property ownership.[41] Senator Henry Wilson suggested a perhaps broader scope to the prohibition of "incidents":

> If this amendment shall be incorporated by the will of the nation into the Constitution of the United States, it will obliterate the last lingering vestiges of the slave system; its chattelizing, degrading, and bloody codes; its dark, malignant, barbarizing spirit; all it was and is, everything connected with it or pertaining to it, from the face of the nation it has scarred with moral desolation, from the bosom of the country it has reddened with the blood and strewn with the graves of patriotism. The incorporation of this amendment into the organic law of the nation will make impossible forevermore the reappearing of the discarded slave system, and the returning of the despotism of the slavemasters' domination.[42]

Opponents of the amendment seemed implicitly to embrace Wilson's characterization of its purpose as rooting out the vestiges of the Slave Power. For many opponents, especially in the South, section 1 was far less troubling than section 2. A delegate to the Mississippi constitutional convention captured these concerns well, declaring that "the second section confers extraordinary power upon Congress," power that the delegate feared would be "unlimited." He was unwilling "to trust to men who know nothing of slavery the power to frame a code for the freedmen of the State of Mississippi."[43]

Even in the face of the impending amendment, the South, of course, tried to re-create de facto, if not de jure, slavery in the Black Codes, "a set of vagrancy laws, legal apprenticeships, and broad local police powers that forced ex-slaves to enter into labor contracts against their will." Simultaneously, to fend off challenges to the codes and related measures, South Carolina and other Southern states declared in their resolutions ratifying the amendment that Congress could not use its second clause to legislate on ex-slaves' civil rights.[44]

Congressional Republicans recoiled at this turn of events in the South, moving to adopt a series of measures, most important the Civil Rights Act of 1866 and the Freedmen's Bureau Act, to turn the tide.[45] The Civil Rights Act clearly reflected the contract philosophy of the age, recognizing the rights to "make and enforce contracts, to sue, be parties, and give evidence, to inherit, purchase, lease, sell, hold, and convey real and personal property, and to full and equal benefit of all laws and proceedings for the security of persons and property, as is enjoyed by white citizens, and shall be subject to like punishment, pains, and penalties, and to none other, any law, statute, ordinance, regulation, or custom, to the contrary notwithstanding."[46]

In Senate debates on January 19, 1866, Senator Lyman Trumball insisted that if the amendment ended only forced labor, then the "promised freedom is a delusion . . . With the destruction of slavery necessarily follows the destruction of the incidents of slavery." Section 2, Trumbull stressed, gave Congress the power to prohibit practices associated with slavery and its "badges." Trumbull continued: "If in order to prevent slavery Congress deem it necessary to declare null and void all laws which will not permit the colored man to contract, which will not permit him to testify, which will not permit him to buy and sell, and to go where he pleases, it has the power to do so, and not only the power, but it becomes its duty to do so." The amendment was thus, in Trumbull's view, meant to abolish not only slavery but also "all provisions of State or local law" infringing on rights to property, free movement, and education. Comments by other legislators during debates over the Civil Rights Act and related Reconstruction-era legislation echoed these sentiments, though Senator Howard went further, claiming that the amendment was always intended to guarantee "to persons who are of different races and colors the same civil rights."[47]

A number of these comments, some coming after the amendment's ratification, may have been revisionist history, and there were ample dissenters from these claims. Moreover, it is likely that there was no single, fixed meaning of this broad and ambiguous amendment in the eyes of the various framers and ratifiers, who had "competing motivations as well as disparate notions about freedom, many of which were not fully formed or, for political purposes, not explicitly stated." Nevertheless, the history does suggest that section 2 may plausibly be read as extending to "badges" (best read as "symbols") and "incidents" (accompanying features) of slavery, not solely to the prohibition of slavery itself. Yet no clear definition of the "badges and incidents" idea is reflected in the debates over the amendment or its implementing legislation. But the comments made, when put in the context of the broader history of slavery, the Civil War, and Reconstruction, do support a reading empowering Congress to address the key elements necessary to supporting a political culture rooted in freedom of contract—including access to the courts, juries, and other legal institutions needed to enforce contractual rights and the conditions, such as personal safety, that make such rights possible—while continuing to wage war on the contract culture's opposite, the Slave Power.[48]

MODERN IMPLICATIONS

The four props approach to defining the "badges and incidents" of slavery suggests that congressional power to criminalize conduct supportive of the Slave Power's remnants extends well beyond physically violent coercion of labor. Violence designed to send a message of racial subordination, two of the four props, for example, could be outlawed via federal hate crimes statutes reaching purely intrastate, local acts having nothing to do with compelling work. Similar legislation could be crafted to focus on even minor "move-in" and other "anti-integrationist" violence aimed at limiting racial minorities' access to the housing market because of its special power to mark racial groups as subordinate pseudocitizens. Court decisions, such as *United States v. Kozminski*, unwisely suggesting in dicta that federal criminalizing of even the most brutal psychological terror used to coerce labor from two vulnerable, mentally retarded persons would not be within the scope of congressional statutory power pursuant to section 2, should be overturned, for subjection to psychological coercion of a similar nature was part of what made slaves into mere chattel, the fourth of the props. The bottom line is that section 2, soundly read, grants Congress far more criminal justice system power than it has chosen to use to kill the modern Slave Powers of our time. Fear of exceeding its constitutional authority should thus not hamstring Congress. Only the lack of political will can do so.[49]

NOTES

1. *See generally* DANIEL J. FLANIGAN, THE CRIMINAL LAW OF SLAVERY AND FREEDOM 1800–1868 (1987); EDWARD L. AYERS, VENGEANCE AND JUSTICE CRIME AND PUNISHMENT IN THE 19TH CENTURY AMERICAN SOUTH (1984); *Jones v. Alfred H. Mayer Co.*, 392 U.S. 409, 439 (1968) ("badges and incidents"); Jennifer Chacon, *Misery and Myopia: Understanding the Failures of US Efforts to Stop Human*

Trafficking, 74 FORDHAM L. REV. 2977, 2990–96 (2006) (summarizing modern legislation); U.S. CONST. amend. XIII.

2. For background on my approach here to constitutional interpretation, *see*, *e.g.*, ROBIN WEST, PROGRESSIVE CONSTITUTIONALISM: RECONSTRUCTING THE FOURTEENTH AMENDMENT 192–98 (1994) (constitutional history as normative guidance); LAURA KALMAN, THE STRANGE CAREER OF LEGAL LIBERALISM 174–206, 237–39 (1998) (lawyer's history).

3. I have defended this blending of history and philosophy to spark practical ideas about the Constitution's modern meaning in Andrew E. Taslitz, *Search and Seizure History as Conversation: A Reply to Bruce P. Smith*, 6 OHIO ST. J. CRIM. L.765 (2009) (hereafter *Conversation*). For citations to my own and others' historical work in this area, *see* parts II–III *infra*.

4. *See* RANDALL KENNEDY, RACE, CRIME, AND THE LAW 30–31 (1997) (generally and source of quotes); AYERS, *supra*, at 102, 133 (forms of punishment).

5. *See id.* at 31–33 (slave mistreatment); AYERS, *supra*, at 135 (similar); THOMAS D. MORRIS, SOUTHERN SLAVERY AND THE LAW, 1619–1860 197 (1996) (bounds of law, correction, patrollers); DAVID J. McCORD & THOMAS COOPER, THE STATUTES AT LARGE OF SOUTH CAROLINA 99 (A.S. Johnston 1836–41).

6. *See* AYERS, *supra*, at 103–4, 132–33, 136 (urban areas, punishment, murder, assault); KENNEDY, *supra*, at 76–77 (reading, worshipping, insubordination).

7. *See* ANDREW E. TASLITZ, RECONSTRUCTING THE FOURTH AMENDMENT: A HISTORY OF SEARCH AND SEIZURE, 1789–1868 127–28 (2006) (fugitive slave law); GEORGE M. STROUD, A SKETCH OF THE LAWS RELATING TO SLAVERY IN THE SEVERAL STATES OF THE UNITED STATES OF AMERICA 178 (2d ed. 1856).

8. *See* ARIELA J. GROSS, DOUBLE CHARACTER: SLAVERY AND MASTERY IN THE ANTEBELLUM SOUTHERN COURTROOM 3–5 (2000) ("double character" as property and persons); MORRIS, *supra*, at 2 (slaves' quasi personhood especially evident in criminal cases).

9. U.S. CONST. amend. XIII; *see* FREDERICK M. LAWRENCE, PUNISHING HATE: BIAS CRIMES UNDER AMERICAN LAW 154 (1999).

10. *See* TASLITZ, *supra*, at 248–50 (Black Codes); AYERS, *supra*, at 151 (later, more covert substitutes for Black Codes); FLANIGAN, *supra*, at 318–24 (criminal provisions of Civil Rights Act of 1866), 351–78 (fitful, ineffective enforcement of early criminal laws).

11. *See* TASLITZ, *supra*, at 254, 284 n. 40 (Fourteenth Amendment incorporation of the Bill of Rights); AYERS, *supra*, at 177–222 (rise of chain gangs and convict lease system); William Carter, Jr., *Race, Rights, and the Thirteenth Amendment: Defining the Badges and Incidents of Slavery*, 40 U.C. DAVIS L. REV. 1311 (2007) (cramped view of section 2 authority generally).

12. *See* GARRETT EPPS, DEMOCRACY REBORN: THE FOURTEENTH AMENDMENT AND THE FIGHT FOR EQUAL RIGHTS IN POST–CIVIL WAR AMERICA 10, 57,

73, 102–3, 151, 157, 230, 266 (2006); Andrew E. Taslitz, *Hate Crimes, Free Speech, and the Contract of Mutual Indifference*, 80 B.U. L. Rev. 1283, 1374–79 (2000) (hereafter *Mutual Indifference*); Andrew E. Taslitz, *Condemning the Racist Personality: Why the Critics of Hate Crimes Legislation Are Wrong*, 40 B.C.L. Rev. 739, 767–77 (1999) (hereafter *Racist Personality*); Eric Foner, Free Soil, Free Labor, Free Men: The Ideology of the Republican Party Before the Civil War 11–18, 39, 42 (1995); James Brewer Stewart, Holy Warriors: The Abolitionists and American Slavery 78–79 (1996).

13. Taslitz, *Mutual Indifference, supra*, at 1316–37 (honor culture); Taslitz, *Racist Personality, supra*, at 767–76; Earl J. Hess, Liberty, Virtue, and Progress: Northerners and Their War for the Union 78 (2d ed. 1997); Thomas R. R. Cobb, An Inquiry into the Law of Negro Slavery in the United States of America, to Which Is Prefixed, an Historical Sketch of Slavery ccxiii (1858) (quote).

14. Taslitz, *supra*, at 104, 143–49, 158, 172, 206, 246–47, 254–55 (Hoar, mail, assaults, banishment, dissenters, Kansas-Nebraska Act, *Dred Scott*); Foner, Free Soil, *supra*, at 88–97, 101; Russell B. Nye, Fettered Freedom: Civil Liberties and the Slavery Controversy, 1830–1860 225 (1949) (Albany convention quote); Hess, *supra*, at 10–17; B. F. Morris, The Life of Thomas Morris: Pioneer and Long a Legislator of Ohio 32–34, 119–20, 181, 217 (1856); Silvana R. Siddali, From Property to Person: Slavery and the Confiscation Acts, 1861–1862 (2005) (Slave Power as "guilty authors of the rebellion"); Stewart, *supra*, at 185, 197, 201.

15. Cong. Globe, 38th Cong., 1st Sess. 1369 (March 31, 1864) (Daniel Clarke quote); Cong. Globe, 38th Cong., 2d Sess. 138 (1865) (James Ashley); Cong. Globe, 38th Cong., 1st Sess. 2984 (1864); Michael Vorenberg, Final Freedom: The Civil War, the Abolition of Slavery, and the Thirteenth Amendment 94 (2001) (feminization).

16. Cong. Globe, 38th Cong., 1st Sess. 2990 (1864) (quotes); Michael Kent Curtis, No State Shall Abridge: The Fourteenth Amendment and the Bill of Rights 29 (1986) (Republicans and necessity Slave Power's defeat); Earl Maltz, Civil Rights, the Constitution and Congress, 1863–1869 24 (1990).

17. See Taslitz, *supra*, at 241; Siddali, *supra*, at 201–12 (2005); N.Y. Times, July 25, 1862.

18. See Siddali, *supra*, at 201–12 (wealth deprivation and killing Slave Power); Daniel W. Hamilton, The Limits of Sovereignty: Property Confiscation in the Union and the Confederacy during the Civil War 78–81 (2007) (describing the sad end of attempted policy of rebel land confiscation).

19. See generally Subjugation & Bondage: Critical Essays on Slavery and Social Philosophy (Tommy L. Lott ed. 1998) (essays debating slavery's meaning) (hereafter Subjugation & Bondage).

20. *See* RICHARD ENNALS, FROM SLAVERY TO CITIZENSHIP 11 (2007); *cf.* Gloria Steinem, *Foreword, in* ENSLAVED: TRUE STORIES OF MODERN DAY SLAVERY xi (Jesse Sage & Liora Kasten eds., 2006) ("Yes, most forms of slavery are now illegal, at least on paper. But some cultures normalize them by caste or debt servitude or sexual practice . . .").

21. *See* R. M. Hare, *What Is Wrong with Slavery, in* SUBJUGATION & BONDAGE, *supra*, at 209, 211–12 (Greeks); W. L. WESTERMANN, THE SLAVE SYSTEMS OF GREEK AND ROMAN ANTIQUITY 35 (1955); ENNALS, *supra*, at 258 (ASI).

22. *See* TASLITZ, *supra*, at 102–4, 131–32, 138–39 178–86, 198–204.

23. ENNALS, *supra*, at 11.

24. *See* Joshua Cohen, *The Arc of the Moral Universe, in* SUBJUGATION & BOND-AGE, *supra*, at 281, 285–86.

25. *See* TASLITZ, *supra*, at 106–30, 207–15.

26. *See* Cohen, *supra*, at 285–86 (using word "slave" but clearly describing "chattel slave").

27. *See* AMY DRU STANLEY, FROM BONDAGE TO CONTRACT: WAGE LABOR, MARRIAGE, AND THE MARKET IN THE AGE OF SLAVE EMANCIPATION 1–3 (1998); WILLIAM GRAHAM SUMNER, WHAT SOCIAL CLASSES OWE TO EACH OTHER 24, 118, 124 (1972; orig. pub. 1883).

28. 1 THEODORE DWIGHT WOOLSEY, POLITICAL SCIENCE; OR, THE STATE THEORETICALLY AND PRACTICALLY CONSIDERED 74–76 (1877).

29. STANLEY, *supra*, at 2.

30. *See id.* at 1–3.

31. *See id.* at 1–11; *see also* JOHN LOCKE, SECOND TREATISE OF GOVERNMENT 19, 27 (C. B. Macpherson ed., 1980; orig. pub. 1690); STANLEY, *supra*, at 11, 16–18 (discussing some protected forms of contract in nineteenth-century Northern thought).

32. *See* STANLEY, *supra*, at 17–20; GEORGE STROUD, A SKETCH OF THE LAWS RELATING TO SLAVERY 10, 31 (1968; orig. pub. 1856); JAMES H. THORNWELL, THE RIGHTS AND DUTIES OF MASTERS: A SERMON PREACHED AT THE DEDICATION OF A CHURCH, ERECTED IN CHARLESTON, SC, FOR THE BENEFIT AND INSTRUC-TION OF THE COLOURED POPULATION 22, 24 (1850).

33. *See* TASLITZ, *supra*, at 98–104, 111–24, 131–37, 149–51, 210–21.

34. *See id.* at 95–101; Cohen, *supra*, at 288–90.

35. *See* TASLITZ, *supra*, at 95–101; JAMES OAKES, SLAVERY AND FREEDOM: AN INTERPRETATION OF THE OLD SOUTH 153–54 (1st ed. 1998) (quoting 1 COTTON PLANTER AND SOIL OF THE SOUTH 233 [1857]).

36. *See* ENNALS, *supra*, at 11 (spectrum); RISA GOLUBOFF, THE LOST PROMISE OF CIVIL RIGHTS 135–37, 143–45 (2007) (modern "involuntary servitude," including peonage). Baher Azmy, *Unshackling the Thirteenth Amendment: Modern Slavery and a Reconstructed Civil Rights Agenda,* 71 FORDHAM L. REV. 981 (2002).

37. *Cf.* Carter, *supra*, at 1351–53; THE UNDEAD AND PHILOSOPHY: CHICKEN SOUP FOR THE SOULLESS (Richard Green & K. Silem Mohammed eds., 2006).

38. On the significance of original meaning versus intention, "living constitution-alism," and the "American constitutional project" to constitutional interpretation, *see generally* Taslitz, *Conversation*, *supra*.

39. *Cf.* Carter, *supra*, at 1353–55 (arguing that history must, and institutional com-petencies may, limit the Thirteenth Amendment's otherwise capacious meaning); TASLITZ, *supra*, at 11–12, 284 n. 40, 304 n. 28 (incorporation); AKHIL REED AMAR, AMERICA'S CONSTITUTION: A BIOGRAPHY 18–29, 396–401, 442–45 (2006) (Fif-teenth Amendment).

40. *See* Carter, *supra*, at 1357–61 (protected groups and activities); JED RUBEN-FELD, A THEORY OF CONSTITUTIONAL SELF-GOVERNMENT: FREEDOM AND TIME 196–207 (paradigm case reasoning); ELLEN PODGOR ET AL., CRIMINAL LAW: CONCEPTS AND PRACTICE 51–55 (2005) (statutory nature criminal law); JOHN BRAITHWAITE & PHILIP PETTIT, NOT JUST DESERTS: A REPUBLICAN THEORY OF CRIMINAL JUSTICE 54–85 (1990).

41. *See Jones*, 392 U.S. 409 (1968); ALEXANDER TSESIS, THE THIRTEENTH AMENDMENT AND AMERICAN FREEDOM: A LEGAL HISTORY 42 (2004); CONG. GLOBE, 38th Cong., 1st Sess. 1439–40 (Apr. 6, 1864).

42. CONG. GLOBE, 38th Cong., 1st Sess. 1324 (1864); *see* TSESIS, *supra*, at 174.

43. *See* TSESIS, *supra*, at 48; JOURNAL OF THE PROCEEDINGS AND DEBATES IN THE CONSTITUTIONAL CONVENTION OF THE STATE OF MISSISSIPPI 137–38 (1865) (*quoted in* Howard D. Hamilton, *The Legislative & Judicial History of the Thir-teenth Amendment*, 9 NAT'L B.J. 26, 45–46 [1951]).

44. *See* VORENBERG, *supra*, at 230–31.

45. *See id.* at 233–34.

46. CONG. GLOBE, 39th Cong., 1st Sess. 211–12 (Jan. 12, 1866); Civil Rights Act, 14 Stat. 27 (1866).

47. CONG. GLOBE, 39th Cong., 1st Sess. 211–12 (Jan. 12, 1866); CONG. GLOBE, 39th Cong., 1st Sess. 503–4 (Jan. 30, 1866); *see also* TSESIS, *supra*, at 53–54; VOREN-BERG, *supra*, at 236.

48. *See* VORENBERG, *supra*, at 236–37.

49. *See* TSESIS, *supra*, at 137–60; Jeannine Bell, *Hate Thy Neighbor: Violent Racial Exclusion & the Persistence of Segregation*, 5 OHIO ST. J. CRIM. L 47 (2007); *Kozmin-ski*, 487 U.S. 931 (1988).

14. Toward a Thirteenth Amendment Exclusionary Rule as a Remedy for Racial Profiling

William M. Carter, Jr.

This chapter addresses a particular remedy for a specific type of Thirteenth Amendment violation: namely, the exclusion from criminal trial of evidence obtained by racial profiling. As a matter of constitutional interpretation and historical context, racial profiling should be treated as a badge or incident of slavery prohibited by the Thirteenth Amendment. The victims of racial profiling should both be able to sue violators and to prevent evidence obtained by racial profiling from being used against them in criminal proceedings.

The exclusionary rule bars the use of evidence in a criminal trial where that evidence was unconstitutionally obtained. Whatever the abstract merits of current arguments surrounding the efficacy or wisdom of the exclusionary rule generally or in other contexts,[1] the Thirteenth Amendment does not countenance the government's obtaining criminal convictions based upon evidence gathered by police practices that amount to a badge or incident of slavery. While the exclusion of evidence that is relevant to the defendant's guilt potentially carries social costs, those costs are justified in cases of racial profiling because the practice is abhorrent to the Thirteenth Amendment and the rule of law.

RACIAL PROFILING AS A THIRTEENTH
AMENDMENT VIOLATION

Racial profiling occurs when law enforcement officials use an individual's race or ethnicity as an *ex ante* basis for criminal suspicion. A racial "profile" is made up of factors, including race, that law enforcement officials believe are predictive of criminal behavior. For example, a narcotics-trafficking profile used in an airport might include factors such as the purchase of one-way tickets shortly before flight time, persons leaving the airplane who do not ask for directions, certain clothing, a hurried appearance, and the fact that the suspect is African American or Latino.[2] Law enforcement officials then investigate those individuals who meet the profile's elements.[3]

Racial profiling is a badge or incident of slavery prohibited by the Thirteenth Amendment because it both reflects and perpetuates deeply rooted cultural biases concerning the supposed connection between race and criminality. The myth of blacks' inherent propensity for crime was essential to the system of slavery in the United States. Stereotypes about blacks' alleged congenital predisposition for crime and violence served several purposes that were critical to maintaining the institution of slavery and the subordinate legal, social, and economic status of the freedmen after the end of de jure enslavement.

The enslavement of human beings presented an inherent contradiction in a country that was philosophically premised upon Enlightenment ideals of individual liberty, equality, and inherent human worth but that was also an agrarian aristocracy willing to exploit slave labor. This dissonance was lessened by the purposeful and systematic dehumanization of the enslaved. If the enslaved were deemed not to be full human beings, then they were not entitled to the agency and freedom human beings were presumed to have as a matter of natural rights. In the context of Enlightenment ideals, rationality was the key defining factor of humanity. By subverting the idea of Africans' rationality, slaveholders—as well as nonslaveholders who supported or at least failed to oppose slavery—could more easily justify slavery in a putatively free society. One such dehumanizing stereotype depicted blacks as savage "Black Beasts" predisposed by nature toward savagery, larceny, and criminality in general.[4] This stereotype was not only used to justify blacks' enslavement but also meant that their supposedly reprobate nature justified constant suspicion and monitoring.

The Thirteenth Amendment's abolition of chattel slavery also included the abolition of the badges and incidents of slavery. The amendment, in the words of one of its primary advocates, was designed to "obliterate the last lingering vestiges of the slave system . . . all it was and is, everything connected with it or pertaining to it . . ."[5] The Supreme Court has also recognized that the

Thirteenth Amendment reaches beyond forced labor and encompasses conditions that have sufficient historical connection to the institution of chattel slavery or the lingering effects thereof.[6] Racial profiling is a continuation of the historical stigmatization of minority groups as inherently predisposed toward crime. As such, it is precisely the type of lingering effect of the slave system that the Thirteenth Amendment prohibits.[7] I do not suggest that police officers necessarily intend to act upon such stereotypes when they use racial profiling. Rather, I contend that many law enforcement officials, like the rest of society, have unconscious biases about the supposed connection between race and crime and may act upon those biases in deciding whom to investigate.

THE ORIGINS AND DEVELOPMENT OF
THE EXCLUSIONARY RULE

The Supreme Court has never addressed whether the exclusionary rule applies in cases of racial profiling. While a person who proves a Thirteenth Amendment violation is certainly entitled to bring a civil action,[8] it remains unsettled whether that same person would be entitled to have evidence obtained in violation of the Thirteenth Amendment suppressed if she were subject to criminal prosecution. In this section, I briefly discuss the origin of and policies underlying the exclusionary rule and describe several cases that have considered whether the exclusionary rule should be applied in cases of racial profiling.

The Supreme Court has long held that suppression of evidence is an appropriate remedy where the evidence has been obtained via unconstitutional police practices.[9] The exclusionary rule has been characterized as serving multiple purposes. While the rule functions to ensure "that no man is to be convicted [based upon] unconstitutional evidence,"[10] it is primarily designed to safeguard constitutional rights as to society generally and to avoid erosion of those rights.[11] In order to accomplish these purposes, the exclusionary rule is designed "to compel respect for the constitutional guaranty in the only effective available way—by removing the incentive to disregard it."[12] The rule also protects judicial integrity by "ensuring that the judiciary does not tacitly condone, and thus become an accomplice to, law enforcement misconduct by accepting its proceeds."[13]

To date, the Supreme Court has applied the exclusionary rule only to Fourth, Fifth, and Sixth Amendment violations. The Court first applied the exclusionary rule to federal cases involving Fourth Amendment violations in *Weeks v. United States*.[14] *Mapp v. Ohio*[15] extended the rule's application to state prosecutions.

The Supreme Court's recent decision in *Hudson v. Michigan*, while not overruling its earlier cases,[16] demonstrates the Court's increasing discomfort regarding the exclusionary rule. *Hudson* involved a violation of the Fourth Amendment's "knock and announce" rule, which generally requires police officers to announce their presence and wait a reasonable time after announcement before entering a dwelling to execute a search warrant.[17] Because it was conceded that the police had violated the knock and announce rule, the question presented in *Hudson* was whether suppression of the evidence obtained in the unconstitutional search was an appropriate remedy for this Fourth Amendment violation. The Court held that it was not. The *Hudson* Court stated that "suppression of evidence has always been [a] last resort" for Fourth Amendment violations since the exclusionary rule "generates substantial social costs, which sometimes include setting the guilty free and the dangerous at large."[18]

The Court stated that the exclusionary rule is to be applied only where its deterrence benefits clearly outweigh its social costs.[19] In *Hudson*, the Court believed that the costs of applying the exclusionary rule to knock and announce violations would include not only the suppression of incriminating evidence in a particular case but also the proliferation of complicated litigation over whether a knock and announce violation had occurred and an increased delay between police officers' announcing their presence and entering a dwelling to execute a warrant, which could in turn lead to violence against them or destruction of evidence.[20] The Court held that these costs outweighed any deterrence benefits that would flow from application of the exclusionary rule to knock and announce violations.[21] Accordingly, the Court held that applying the exclusionary rule to knock and announce violations was unwarranted.

The Court continued to narrow the scope of the exclusionary rule in its recent decision in *Herring v. United States*.[22] In *Herring*, the defendant sought to suppress evidence obtained as the result of a search pursuant to an arrest under a warrant that had previously been withdrawn. The Court assumed for the sake of argument that such an arrest would violate the Fourth Amendment as an arrest without probable cause but nonetheless held that the exclusionary rule would not apply. The Court, citing *Hudson*, held that "the fact that a Fourth Amendment violation occurred—*i.e.*, that a search or arrest was unreasonable—does not necessarily mean that the exclusionary rule applies . . . Indeed, exclusion has always been our last resort, not our first impulse."[23] As in *Hudson*, the Court focused exclusively on the deterrence rationale for the exclusionary rule.

THE EXCLUSIONARY RULE IN RACIAL PROFILING CASES

Hudson and *Herring* provide reason to doubt the current Supreme Court's enthusiasm for the exclusionary rule, even in the traditional criminal procedure context. Nonetheless, both *Hudson* and *Herring* acknowledged that suppression of evidence remains a viable remedy for constitutional violations. It remains unclear whether the rule applies to other constitutional violations. In this section, I briefly review cases considering whether to apply the exclusionary rule to evidence obtained by racial profiling.

Courts that have considered the issue have generally concluded that suppression of evidence obtained by racial profiling may be justified in an appropriate case.[24] Most courts, however, never reach the issue of whether the exclusionary rule should be applied because a combination of Supreme Court and lower court decisions have made it difficult to prove racial profiling in the first place. If racial profiling were considered a Fourth Amendment violation, suppressing the unconstitutionally obtained evidence would be an obvious remedy since it is clear that the exclusionary rule applies to evidence obtained in violation of the Fourth Amendment. In *Whren v. United States*, however, the Court held that a police officer's "subjective intentions play no role in ordinary, probable-cause Fourth Amendment analysis."[25] Under *Whren*, as long as the police officer had an objectively reasonable motivation for making the search or seizure, such as the existence of a minor traffic violation, the Fourth Amendment inquiry ends. Thus, a court will deem a search and seizure "reasonable" under the Fourth Amendment even if the "objectively reasonable" grounds were no more than a pretext for racial profiling. Racial profiling is therefore immunized from serious Fourth Amendment scrutiny except in cases where a police officer has *no* basis for a search or seizure other than racist policing.

The *Whren* Court stated that "the constitutional basis for objecting to the intentionally discriminatory application of the laws is the Equal Protection Clause, not the Fourth Amendment."[26] Most lower courts, however, have adopted an unduly grudging approach to equal protection claims alleging racial profiling, holding that racial profiling does not violate the Equal Protection Clause unless race was the *sole* motive for the officer's action. In *United States v. Avery*,[27] for example, the defendant moved to suppress evidence of cocaine found in his carry-on bag at an airport. Despite testimony by one of the arresting officers that race was one of the factors used in drug courier profiles, the court found no equal protection violation. The court held that although the Equal Protection Clause prohibits law enforcement officials from targeting an individual because of his race, "because of" in this context means that the decision is based *solely* on racial considerations. The defendant's equal protection challenge therefore failed since he could not prove that his race was the *only* reason he had been selected for investigation. Given that the defendant could not meet this "sole motive" standard, the question of whether the exclusionary rule would be an appropriate remedy was moot.[28]

Read together, these cases mean that a person seeking to suppress evidence garnered by racial profiling stands little chance of success under the current state of the law. While the exclusionary rule clearly applies to Fourth Amendment violations, racial profiling is largely immunized from any serious Fourth Amendment scrutiny under *Whren*. And although racially selective law enforcement presumptively raises equal protection concerns, most courts that have considered the issue have held that racial profiling violates the Equal Protection Clause only when race is the officer's sole motive, which is seldom the case, since a racial profile, by definition, includes factors other than race. Therefore, under both the Fourth Amendment and the Equal Protection Clause, the difficulty of proving the substantive violation means that the question of the appropriate remedy is never reached.

There is some precedent for applying the exclusionary rule to racial profiling. In *United States v. Laymon*,[29] the court granted the defendant's motion to suppress evidence obtained by racial profiling. In *Laymon*, the court concluded that the officer's allegedly legitimate reason for stopping the defendant's car for a traffic violation was a pretext for the use of racial profiling to catch suspected drug couriers. The court concluded that "profile stops may not be predicated on unconstitutional discrimination based on race [or] ethnicity"[30] and granted the motion to suppress.

While *Laymon* is one of the few cases to directly reach the question of whether the exclusionary rule applies in cases of racial profiling, it is likely only of limited value. *Laymon* was decided before the Supreme Court's pronouncement in *Whren* that courts may not under the Fourth Amendment examine a police officer's subjective motivation for a search or seizure. The *Laymon* court granted suppression pursuant to the pre-*Whren* Fourth Amendment case law regarding pretextual stops, which asked "not whether the officer *could* validly have made the stop, but whether under the same circumstances a reasonable officer *would* have made the stop in the absence of the invalid purposes."[31] Thus, in *Laymon*, the court found a substantive Fourth Amendment violation by virtue of the pretextual stop and therefore ordered suppression of evidence as a remedy. After *Whren*, however, if the officer *could* have undertaken the search or seizure for a legitimate purpose, then the officer's actual subjective motivation—even if constitutionally invalid—is immunized from scrutiny. After *Whren*, a court presented with the facts in *Laymon* would therefore be unlikely to find a Fourth Amendment violation.[32]

The dissenting opinion in *United States v. Taylor*[33] also analyzed the applicability of the exclusionary rule to evidence obtained by racial profiling. In rejecting the defendant's motion to suppress evidence of cocaine found in his bag, the majority concluded that the search did not raise Fourth Amendment concerns because it was consensual and therefore not a "seizure" under the Fourth Amendment. The majority acknowledged that equal protection concerns would exist if the defendant had proven that he had "been selected for a consensual interview because he was an African-American, that the law enforcement officers . . . implemented a general practice or pattern that primarily targeted minorities for consensual interview, or that they had incorporated a racial component into the drug courier profile."[34] The majority believed, however, that such issues were unsupported by any evidence in the record.

The dissenting judges in *Taylor* took a very different view of what the record proved and the consequences that should flow from the officers' conduct in the case. The dissenters began by noting that the Equal Protection Clause applies to consensual encounters between the police and citizens and that the police therefore may not rely upon a person's race in deciding whether to initiate a consensual encounter.[35] Their review of the record convinced the dissenting judges that law enforcement officials had "singled out the defendant and stopped him solely because he was an African-American male"[36] and that the defendant's subsequent consent to the search could not legitimize the decision to target him in the first place because of his race. The dissenting judges charged that the majority had "abdicat[ed] [its] judicial responsibility by endorsing a racist law enforcement policy . . ."[37] Because of the invalidity of the initial decision to question and detain the defendant, the dissenting judges would have ordered suppression of the evidence seized.

In *United States v. Jennings*,[38] the defendant, an African American man, was stopped and detained by the police at an airport. A search of the defendant revealed evidence of drugs, which the defendant moved to suppress at his trial. The defendant predicated his motion to suppress on the Equal Protection Clause, arguing that the decision to stop him was racially motivated.

On the particular facts in *Jennings*, the court refused to apply the exclusionary rule because the defendant failed to show by a preponderance of the evidence that racial profiling had in fact occurred.[39] However, in examining the defendant's motion to suppress, the court stated that "a law enforcement officer would be acting unconstitutionally were he to approach and consensually interview a person of color solely because of that person's color, absent a compelling justification. Further, evidence seized in violation of the Equal Protection Clause should be suppressed." In concluding that the exclusionary rule applies to equal protection violations, the court quoted the Supreme Court's decision in *Elkins v. United States*, which stated that "no distinction can logically be drawn between evidence obtained in violation of the Fourth Amendment and that obtained in violation of the Fourteenth. The Constitution is flouted in either case."[40]

In sum, the Supreme Court has drastically limited the availability of the Fourth Amendment as a remedy for racial profiling. Litigants have therefore turned to the Equal Protection Clause with limited success. Nonetheless, most courts that have directly considered the issue have concluded that suppression of evidence may, in an appropriate case, be a proper remedy when the evidence was obtained in violation of the Equal Protection Clause.

TOWARD A THIRTEENTH AMENDMENT EXCLUSIONARY RULE FOR RACIAL PROFILING

While the cases discussed in the preceding provide some guidance, they have not engaged in the type of comprehensive analysis necessary to justify extension of the exclusionary rule to Thirteenth Amendment violations, particularly after the Supreme Court's recent decisions in *Hudson* and *Herring*, which indicate the Court's skepticism toward the exclusionary rule generally. In this final section, I provide that analysis. Particularly when viewing racial profiling through the prism of the Thirteenth Amendment, I conclude that suppression of evidence obtained though racial profiling is not only justified but essential.

To begin with, I reject *Hudson*'s assertion that justification for the exclusionary rule can be found only with reference to the goal of deterrence and, even then, only when the deterrent effect is overwhelmingly apparent on the facts of a given case. While deterrence is one of the reasons to suppress evidence obtained in violation of the Constitution, it is only one reason. As Justice Breyer noted in his dissent in *Hudson*, suppression of illegally obtained evidence was, prior to *Hudson*, thought to be the rule rather than the exception.[41] In the absence of an applicable exception, "a court will simply look to see if the unconstitutional search produced the evidence."[42] If so, the evidence is to be excluded from trial, even without proof of the deterrent effect of suppression in the context of the specific constitutional violation that occurred in the case.

Even accepting *Hudson* on its own terms, however, there is an even greater need for deterrence in cases of racial profiling than in most Fourth Amendment cases. Although violations of the Fourth Amendment's knock and announce requirement are not trivial matters, they are unlikely to cause the type of reductive dehumanization that occurs when law enforcement officials stigmatize all persons of color as potential criminals. The Thirteenth Amendment's framers intended that blacks would enjoy full civil equality, which would include at an absolute minimum the destruction of vestiges of the Slaves Codes and Black Codes that constrained blacks' freedom of movement based upon their supposed predisposition to criminality.[43]

A strong deterrent is also necessary in light of the widespread nature of racial profiling. Justice Kennedy, who provided the crucial fifth vote for the *Hudson* majority, noted that *Hudson* did not involve a proven pattern or practice of Fourth Amendment violations. Justice Kennedy noted that "if a widespread pattern were shown, and particularly if those violations were committed against persons who lacked the means or voice to mount an effective protest, there would be reason for grave concern."[44] Racial profiling is widespread, in the form of both formal profiles and unarticulated "hunches" about which types of persons are more likely to be engaged in criminal behavior.[45] The pervasiveness of racial profiling presumably indicates that the police have a strong incentive to commit this constitutional violation, which requires a strong disincentive if they are to be deterred from doing so. Indeed, defenders of racial profiling argue that it is the most effective means of detecting certain types of crimes.[46] While this is untrue,[47] a strong deterrent against racial profiling is needed if police officers widely *believe* it to be true and therefore formally use race as part of criminal profiles. Additionally, the pervasiveness of racial profiling is also a product of ingrained historical and cultural biases regarding race and criminality. A strong deterrent is therefore also needed to force police officers to stop and think before acting on a "hunch" that may be more a reflection of unconscious bias than of behavioral observation.[48]

Moreover, the exclusionary rule has traditionally been thought to serve purposes beyond deterrence, and it is here that understanding racial profiling as imposing a badge or incident of slavery proves most powerful. Protecting judicial integrity is also one of the traditional rationales for suppressing unconstitutionally obtained evidence. The Supreme Court has long cautioned that the judiciary cannot be complicit in racial discrimination by other state actors or private persons.[49] Because racial profiling represents the "repetition of our not-too-distant history when only *some* members of our society were able to travel without fear of unwarranted governmental intrusion,"[50] it amounts to the imposition of a badge or incident of slavery in violation of the Thirteenth Amendment.

The various states' Slave Codes that existed before the Civil War cemented in American law and culture a presumed connection between race and criminal propensity. In many states, certain acts were crimes only when committed by enslaved persons of African descent.[51] The Slave Codes also explicitly made race a basis for criminal suspicion. The Black Codes, which were enacted after constitutional emancipation, continued this practice.[52] The sciences and popular culture also came to embrace the stereotype of greater black propensity for crime.[53] The judiciary should refuse to be complicit in the continuation of this legacy of slavery and the continued stigmatization of African Americans as congenital criminals.

Finally, in considering the social costs of excluding evidence obtained by racial profiling, one must also consider the social costs of allowing convictions based even in part upon evidence gathered via this abhorrent practice. As Justice Thurgood Marshall noted in a similar context, "because the strongest advocates of Fourth Amendment rights are frequently criminals, it is easy to forget that our interpretations of such rights apply to the innocent and the guilty alike."[54] Focusing solely on the possibility that suppressing evidence in a particular case may result in "setting the guilty free and the dangerous at large"[55] both minimizes the societal damage caused by racial profiling and misses the larger point of the exclusionary rule. Racial profiling undermines the rule of law by creating a system in which race is functionally equated with criminality and criminal suspicion is based upon who you are rather than what you do. Racial profiling is an inefficient law enforcement tactic because, by definition, it arbitrarily sweeps in large number of persons who are *not* criminals but happen to meet the racial element of a criminal profile. This practice causes injury and humiliation to innocent persons who are treated as presumptive criminals. Race-based policing also damages police-community relations, which makes members of minority communities less likely to cooperate with the police in investigations. In short, the costs of racial profiling far outweigh any conceivable benefits and the damage it does justifies excluding from criminal trials evidence obtained by racial profiling.

NOTES

1. *See, e.g., Hudson v. Michigan,* 547 U.S. ____, 126 S. Ct. 2159 (2006).

2. *See, e.g., United States v. Avery,* 137 F.3d 343, 347 (6th Cir. 1997).

3. Although supporters of racial profiling contend that it is more efficient than reliance upon purely behavioral observations, most of the relevant empirical evidence indicates that any efficiency gains are largely illusory and to the extent they exist at all, they are outweighed by the substantial harms racial profiling causes. *See generally* DAVID A. HARRIS, PROFILES IN INJUSTICE: WHY RACIAL PROFILING CANNOT WORK (2002); William M. Carter, Jr., *A Thirteenth Amendment Framework for Combating Racial Profiling,* 39 HARV. C.R.-C.L. L. REV. 17 (2004).

4. *See, e.g.,* A. LEON HIGGINBOTHAM, JR., IN THE MATTER OF COLOR, RACE AND THE AMERICAN LEGAL PROCESS: THE COLONIAL PERIOD 41–47 (1978); Carter, *supra*; Paul Finkelman, *The Crime of Color,* 67 TUL. L. REV. 2063, 2093 (1993); Douglas L. Colbert, *Challenging the Challenge: The Thirteenth Amendment as a Prohibition Against the Racial Use of Peremptory Challenges,* 76 CORNELL L. REV. 1, 13–32 (1990).

5. Jacobus tenBroek, *Thirteenth Amendment to the Constitution of the United States: Consummation to Abolition and Key to the Fourteenth Amendment,* 39 CAL. L. REV. 171, 175 (1951), citing CONG. GLOBE, 38th Cong., 1st Sess. 2941 (1864) (statement of Senator Wilson).

6. *See Jones v. Alfred H. Mayer Co.,* 392 U.S. 409 (1968).

7. For a more detailed discussion of racial profiling as a Thirteenth Amendment violation, *see* Carter, *supra*.

8. For example, 42 U.S.C. § 1983 provides a federal civil cause of action for the deprivation of "any rights, privileges, or immunities secured by the Constitution and laws" by persons acting under color of state law.

9. *See, e.g., Weeks v. United States,* 232 U.S. 383 (1914), *Mapp v. Ohio,* 367 U.S. 643 (1961).

10. *Mapp,* 367 U.S. at 657.

11. *See, e.g., Elkins v. United States,* 364 U.S. 206, 217 (1960) ("The rule is calculated to prevent, not to repair [constitutional violations].")

12. *Mapp,* 367 U.S. at 656.

13. Brooks Holland, *Safeguarding Equal Protection Rights: The Search for an Exclusionary Rule under the Equal Protection Clause,* 37 AM. CRIM. L. REV. 1107, 1119–20 (2000), citing *Mapp* and *Elkins.*

14. *Weeks v. United States,* 232 U.S. 383 (1914).

15. *Mapp v. Ohio,* 367 U.S. 643 (1961).

16. 547 U.S. ____, 126 S. Ct. 2159 (2006). Justice Kennedy specifically noted in his concurrence that "the continued operation of the exclusionary rule, as settled and defined by our precedents, is not in doubt" despite the skeptical language regarding the rule in the majority opinion. *Id.* at 2170.

17. For a discussion of the "knock and announce" rule, *see Wilson v. Arkansas,* 514 U.S. 927 (1995).

18. *Hudson,* 547 U.S. ____, 126 S. Ct. at 2163 (citations and internal quotation marks omitted).

19. *Id.* at 2163.

20. *Id.* at 2165–66.

21. *Id.* at 2166.

22. ____ U.S.____, 129 S. Ct. 695 (2009).

23. *Id.* at 700.

24. *See, e.g., United States v. Laymon,* 730 F. Supp. 332 (D. Colo. 1990) (granting motion to suppress where the traffic stop was based upon racial profiling); *United States v. Jennings,* 985 F.2d 562, 1993 WL 5927, *4 (6th Cir. 1993) (unpublished) (stating in dicta that "evidence seized in violation of the Equal Protection Clause should be suppressed" but holding that defendant failed to prove that racial profiling had occurred). *But see United States v. Cuevas-Ceja,* 58 F. Supp. 2d 1175, 1183 (1999) (stating, in a racial profiling case, that "suppression of evidence pursuant to the exclusionary rule is normally a remedy for violations of the Fourth Amendment [and not the Equal Protection Clause]").

25. *Whren v. United States,* 517 U.S. 806, 813 (1996).

26. 517 U.S. at 813.

27. 137 F.3d 343 (6th Cir. 1997).

28. *Avery,* 137 F.3d at 352–58. *See also United States v. Travis,* 62 F.3d 170, 174 (6th Cir. 1995) ("We have no need to reach [the question of whether the exclusionary rule

applies to Fourteenth Amendment violations] because the detectives in this case did not choose to interview the defendant solely because of her race."). For other cases discussing the "sole motive" standard in racial profiling cases under the Equal Protection Clause, *see* Carter, *supra* at 36–44.

29. 730 F. Supp. 332 (D. Colo. 1990).

30. *Id.* at 339.

31. *Id.* (internal quotation marks omitted and emphasis in original).

32. A second problem with *Laymon*'s holding is that the court assumed that suppression of evidence is always required when that evidence was obtained in violation of the Fourth Amendment. *But see Hudson*, 126 S. Ct. at 2164 ("Identification of a Fourth Amendment violation [is not] synonymous with application of the exclusionary rule to evidence secured incident to that violation.").

33. 956 F.2d 572 (6th Cir. 1992) (en banc).

34. *Id.* at 578–79.

35. *Id.* at 581.

36. *Id.* at 582.

37. *Id.* at 583.

38. 985 F.2d 562, 1993 WL 5927, *4 (6th Cir. 1993) (unpublished).

39. *Id.* at *5.

40. *Id.* at *4, quoting *Elkins v. United States*, 364 U.S. at 215 (internal quotation marks omitted). As Judge Batchelder noted in her concurrence in *Jennings*, the quote from *Elkins* refers not to the Fourteenth Amendment's Equal Protection Clause but to its Due Process Clause and dealt with the applicability of federal constitutional rights to the states via the Due Process Clause. *Jennings*, 1993 WL 5927 at *7. The particular quote from *Elkins* that the *Jennings* majority cited is therefore not directly on point with regard to applying the exclusionary rule to equal protection violations.

41. *Hudson*, 126 S. Ct. at 2175 (Breyer, J., dissenting) (stating that the Court had previously refused to apply the exclusionary rule in criminal trials only "where there [was] a specific reason to believe that application of the rule would *not* result in appreciable deterrence [of the constitutional violation at issue].") *Id.* at 2175 (Breyer, J., dissenting) (emphasis added).

42. *Id.* at 2181.

43. *See generally* Carter, *supra* at 60–64.

44. *Id.* at 2171 (Kennedy, J., concurring).

45. *See* HARRIS, supra.

46. *See* Carter, *supra* at 17–19, 27–29 (discussing the arguments for and against racial profiling).

47. *See generally* Carter, *supra*.

48. It has been argued that only intentional behavior is subject to deterrence. *See* Holland, *supra* at 1119–24. While it is of course true that behavior that is literally reflexive cannot easily be deterred, there is a difference between reflex and unconscious

bias. If a police officer sees two men, one white and one black, leaving an airplane together and believes both are acting equally suspicious, he has to decide which to follow. The decision to follow the black man may be driven by the officer's unconscious biases, but undertaking the surveillance is still a conscious decision.

49. *See, e.g., Shelley v. Kramer*, 334 U.S. 1 (1948) (finding state action in judicial enforcement of private individuals' racially restrictive covenants). *See also Taylor*, 956 F.2d at 583 (dissenting opinion of Judge Keith) (arguing that failing to suppress evidence gained by racial profiling amounts to the judiciary's "endorsing a racist law enforcement policy . . .").

50. *Taylor*, 956 F.2d at 591 (Martin, J., dissenting).

51. *See, e.g.,* KATHERYN K. RUSSELL, THE COLOR OF CRIME: RACIAL HOAXES, WHITE FEAR, BLACK PROTECTIONISM, POLICE HARASSMENT, AND OTHER MACROAGGRESSIONS 15 (1998) (noting that "race was the most important variable in determining [criminal] punishment under the slave codes"); Finkelman, *supra* at 2093 (1993) ("In colonial and early national America, color became associated with inherently criminal behavior in almost every area of law. Following Virginia's lead, most of the British mainland colonies began to create a legal system that made race a *prima facie* indication of criminality.").

52. *See* Carter, *supra* at 64–70.

53. *Id.* at 66–70.

54. *United States v. Sokolow*, 490 U.S. 1, 11 (1989) (Marshall, J., dissenting).

55. *Hudson*, 547 U.S. ___, 126 S. Ct. at 2163 (citations and internal quotation marks omitted).

15. *Immigrant Workers and the Thirteenth Amendment*

Maria L. Ontiveros

Imagine a group of nonwhite workers laboring in fields, slaughtering livestock, tending children, and cleaning houses. Some are controlled by guns, chains, and overt threats of beatings; others by psychological coercion and fear. Imagine that the state can separate them from their children. Churches that shelter or hide them to prevent separation are prosecuted for breaking the law. Imagine these workers are systematically denied access to the courts and remedies for violations of workplace rights. Imagine a group of workers being smuggled or running to freedom, pursued by dogs and armed guards. Imagine that these workers are excluded from the rights and privileges of citizenship. These images, reminiscent of chattel slavery before the Civil War, are also the images of some of today's undocumented immigrant workers.

This chapter examines the world of immigrant workers through the lens of the Thirteenth Amendment. It begins by describing how the lives of immigrant workers are shaped by their legal status. It argues that the combination of current U.S. labor and immigration laws have created a caste of workers of color, laboring beneath the floor created for free labor, denied the rights of citizenship, and subject to human rights abuses that arguably violate the Thirteenth Amendment. Immigrant workers, in general, do not receive the same level of workplace protection as nonimmigrant workers; thus, they can be considered a caste of workers laboring below the floor set for free labor. "Guest workers" labor in something akin to "involuntary servitude" because their ability to quit is substantially circumscribed and because they are unable to become citizens. Finally, undocumented immigrants lack many of the basic human, civil, and labor rights afforded others in the United States. This chapter concludes by arguing that Thirteenth Amendment theory (and decent treatment of immigrant workers) can be advanced by recognizing the treatment of immigrant workers as a violation of the amendment.

Immigrant workers can be divided into two groups: those with legal authorization to be in the United States (either as citizens or as holders of valid immigration documents) and those without authorization. Although the laws, as written, differentiate between these two groups, in reality, it is difficult to analyze them separately. Their realities are intertwined for many reasons. About one-third of the 6.6 million unauthorized families are "mixed," containing a combination of citizens (for instance, minor children born in the United States), documented immigrants (perhaps someone on a work visa), and undocumented family members (someone who entered the country illegally or overstayed a visa).[1] In addition, people often conceal their undocumented status, and others change status (for instance, becoming documented by marrying or going through naturalization or, to the contrary, becoming unauthorized by staying in the United States after a visa has expired). Finally, when someone like an employer, customer, coworker, or community worker looks at an immigrant worker, he or she may not understand the different legal rights afforded different people or may harbor prejudices based more on race or national origin than immigration status. Thus, the treatment immigrants experience does not always reflect their legal status. Analytically, even though different legal regimes regulate each group, the legal structures for both groups create disadvantaged castes whose treatment arguably violates the language and/or purpose of the Thirteenth Amendment.

As a result of these factors, the number of undocumented versus documented immigrants is difficult to determine. One thing is clear, however. Authorized or not, immigrants are part of our communities and workforce. As of 2000, there were almost 30 million immigrants in the United States, over 10 percent of the population.[2] The number of unauthorized immigrants entering the United States has exceeded the number of authorized immigrant entrants every year since 1995.[3] From best estimates, approximately 10.3 million unauthorized immigrants live in the United States.[4] One out of every twenty-three workers in the United States (4.3 percent) is an undocumented worker.[5] Today's undocumented immigrants come primarily from the south—approximately 50 percent come from Mexico and 25 percent from other Latin American countries.[6]

The proportion of undocumented workers is higher in certain regions of the country and in certain industries. One out of every four private household workers, for example, lacks proper work authorization,[7] and 60 to 70 percent of California's farmworkers do not have the legal right to work in the United States.[8] Undocumented workers are concentrated in food manufacturing, agriculture, private household/domestic service, hotels, food preparation, construction, and textiles.[9]

THE LEGALLY CONSTRUCTED WORLD OF IMMIGRANT WORKERS

The laws of the United States seek to protect a variety of rights, including workers' rights, human rights, civil rights, and citizenship rights. For workers, this group of laws can be viewed as the floor created for "free labor" in America. Unfortunately, the laws have been applied and interpreted in such a way as to systematically exclude immigrant workers. At some point, this systematic exclusion creates a group of workers who labor below the floor, in a situation akin to slavery and one that should be prohibited by the Thirteenth Amendment.

IMMIGRANT WORKERS IN GENERAL

Generally speaking, workers in the United States rely on a combination of free market forces, government regulation, and collective bargaining to ensure decent treatment. Under free market theory, an employee who is being treated badly or being paid too little will leave a job and move to a different employer, thereby giving all employers an incentive to pay fair wages and treat workers decently. In addition, the government restricts free market forces through a series of laws that create a floor for treatment of workers in the United States. Employers and employees may not negotiate for terms and conditions that fall below this floor. This floor ensures, among other things, a minimum wage and overtime premium; prohibits discrimination on the basis of race, sex, and other factors; and protects health and safety. Finally, in certain workplaces, unions represent workers and collectively bargain with employers to establish the terms and conditions of employment. Employees in unionized workplaces generally fare better than those in the unorganized free market.[10]

Immigrant workers fall outside the umbrella of these protections for several reasons. First, many of the occupations/industries in which they work are not covered by government regulations protecting minimum wage or the right to organize. Agriculture and domestic work, for example, are either excluded from protection or treated differently. These exclusions arose, in part, because these jobs were performed initially by slaves and then later by other disempowered groups.[11] Second, most protective regulations cover only larger employers, and immigrant workers tend to work for smaller enterprises.[12] Finally, the laws cover those workers in a traditional employer-employee relationship only. Many immigrant workers, on the other hand, find themselves excluded because they work for subcontractors (especially in janitorial, agricultural, and textile work) or are categorized as independent contractors (especially domestic and home-care workers).[13]

More subtle factors also inhibit immigrant workers from receiving important protections. Language barriers, lack of knowledge about rights, and cultural power imbalances make it difficult for immigrant workers to insist on being treated fairly. On a more basic level, U.S. domestic law simply does not prohibit discrimination based on immigrant or immigration status. Although the federal antidiscrimination law known as Title VII prohibits discrimination based on "national origin," the U.S. Supreme Court ruled that discrimination based on citizenship is distinct from discrimination based on national origin.[14] Thus, an employer is free to refuse to hire immigrants, even those with proper work authorization, simply because they prefer citizens. Unlike many other countries and international treaties to which the United States is a signatory, our domestic law does not address discrimination based on migrant status. Thus, the systematic exclusion of all immigrant workers creates a caste of workers laboring below the floor set for free labor. Although these factors affect all immigrant workers, in general, certain subgroups face additional hurtles.

GUEST WORKERS

A guest worker or temporary worker is a person from a foreign country who arrives on a restricted visa to work in the United States. Examples of this type of worker include engineers from India working in California's Silicon Valley on an H-1B visa; farmworkers in North Carolina on an H-1A visa, and construction laborers in Oregon on an H-2B visa. Although the terms of the visas vary, they typically tie the worker to a particular employer. The employer generally has to "prove" that it needs the employee and get authorization to hire a specific visa holder. If the worker quits or is fired, the visa is revoked, and the person must return to his or her country of origin. The visas may limit the ability of the worker's family to come to the United States, to work in the country, or to fully participate in society. The visas last for a limited period of time, and they contemplate the employee's returning home rather than staying in the United States and becoming a citizen. Part of the continuing immigration debate in the U.S.

Congress covers exactly what the parameters of a temporary or guest worker program should be.

These limitations create a variety of problems for guest workers that have Thirteenth Amendment implications. Without visa portability, free market checks on low wages or poor treatment do not work because employees are not free to leave and find better employment elsewhere.[15] They are also deterred from complaining about workplace treatment, wages, hours, or other terms and conditions of employment, for fear of discharge. For guest workers, discharge means visa revocation, followed by deportation or a transition into the status of an undocumented worker. As a result of this fear, agricultural visa workers (holders of H-2A) have been deterred from filing claims, often relying instead on worker advocate and church groups to bring claims on their behalf.[16] In addition, administrative regulations have specifically limited the ability of legal services corporation attorneys (legal services for the poor) to represent holders of the H-2B visa, thereby denying them access to the courts.[17] This situation offends the Thirteenth Amendment because its prohibition of involuntary servitude seeks to eliminate those situations where workers are not free to leave abusive employment. Further, one of the defining elements of a slave's status was the inability to have his or her rights adjudicated in court.

A larger problem with guest worker programs stems from their basic premise that workers should be in the United States as temporary, noncitizen labor. When people are brought to the country without any expectation or ability for them to become permanent members of the community, they remain outsiders throughout their stay. Without the ability to become connected to the community, it is far more difficult for them to develop the type of capacity necessary to advocate for their rights or to put themselves forward as the fully realized individuals that they are. When they are brought here, under those conditions, for their *labor*, they run the risk of being viewed and treated as strictly commodities and not as human beings. The commodification of human labor, in many ways, defined slavery.

The history of guest or temporary workers shows how this dynamic has played out in the past. California's agricultural industry has used a series of guest workers for over two centuries, and, for the most part, they have labored in conditions that are suspect under the Thirteenth Amendment.[18] When Spanish missionaries arrived to "settle" California, they brought indigenous Mexican slaves with them to tend the fields and work in the missions. As chattel slaves, they were afforded no labor, human, civil, or citizenship rights. When that population perished, the missionaries replaced them with native Californians, who were kept in a situation akin to slavery. Families were separated and housed separately by age and gender. They were prohibited from leaving the missions and required to work. If they escaped, they were forcibly returned.

The native Californians legally received freedom from slavery in 1826, but they continued to work in different versions of involuntary servitude until mid-century. Some were arrested for petty "crimes," such as drunkenness, and forced to work on missions to serve out their sentences. Others were put to work under the terms of statutes, such as the Indian Indenture Act, which allowed local farmers to petition courts and indenture Indians if they needed labor. The Act for the Government and Protection of Indians compelled Indian labor, created a vagrancy law (which included the ability of citizens to apprehend and auction off Indians for labor), and prohibited native Californians from making legal claims to their land. These brutal labor and human rights conditions took their toll on the native population. It fell from a high of 700,000 before Spanish occupation to a mere 15,000.

Without a sufficient native population to meet its needs, California agriculture turned to Asia for guest workers. Chinese agricultural workers, arriving in the mid-1800s through early in the next century, faced a variety of restrictions on their labor, human, civil, and citizenship rights. Many arrived with a huge amount of debt owed to labor brokers, leaving them unable to quit oppressive jobs, much as slaves were unable to leave exploitative conditions. Immigration policy restricted the ability of Chinese women to arrive and stay, thus preventing family formation. When Chinese laborers started to demand labor and civil rights, the government responded by prohibiting future Chinese immigration (under the Chinese Exclusion Act [1882]) and by prohibiting all Asians from becoming citizens through naturalization. Asians, as a racial group, were prohibited from naturalizing until 1952. After 1893, Chinese laborers were required to register with the government and carry identification papers. If they failed to do so, they were arrested, sentenced to hard labor, and then deported.

Workers from Japan, who tended the fields from approximately 1900 until World War II, experienced a similar fate. At first, agricultural employers welcomed them as an easily exploitable workforce. Families formed, and many Japanese became citizens through either naturalization or birth. When these workers reacted to their exploitation by asserting labor and civil rights, however, their human, civil, and citizenship rights were stripped away. Immigration laws were amended to prohibit any more of the existing Japanese immigrants from naturalizing and to prohibit further immigration from Japan. Once the Japanese became people "ineligible for citizenship," California's Alien Land Act (1913) prevented Japanese agricultural workers from owning agricultural land and from leasing it for more than three years. This restriction on property ownership parallels the conditions of slaves, who also could not own property. During World War II, these same Japanese workers were imprisoned in internment camps, stripped of their property, and those holding U.S. citizenship were forced to denounce their citizenship.

During and following World War II, California agriculture turned to Mexico for its next group of temporary, noncitizen workers. Under the Bracero Program, more than 5 million workers would come to work the fields. These workers, mainly unaccompanied men, lived in ramshackle housing and worked for subsistence wages. Employers took excessive deductions from their meager paychecks to cover room, board, and travel expenses. Many workers never saw their employment contracts and later found themselves unable to quit. They were segregated from society, labored in oppressive conditions, and prohibited from becoming members of the political community. The U.S. Labor Department official in charge of the Bracero Program, Lee G. Williams, described the program as "legalized slavery."[19]

Each of these historical uses of noncitizen, immigrant labor created a segregated group of workers of color laboring in substandard conditions that often violated their basic human rights. Each group was limited in its ability to become citizens and full members of the political community. Members were targeted, in part, because of their race. As a group, they experienced a deprivation of their labor rights, their human rights, their civil rights, and their citizenship rights, echoing the deprivations of those in chattel slavery. Arguably, today's visa programs represent yet another version of this deprivation.

UNDOCUMENTED WORKERS

The treatment of undocumented workers also raises a variety of concerns under the Thirteenth Amendment. Undocumented workers are workers who do not have the legal right to be present in or to work in the United States and are subject to deportation upon discovery. They may have entered the country illegally or overstayed a visa, not leaving when they were legally required to do so. Although our de jure immigration policy prohibits undocumented workers, our de facto economic system relies heavily upon their labor, especially in some sectors of the economy. Workers lacking legal authorization to work routinely manage to become employees. Although employers have a legal obligation to verify that each new employee is authorized to work in the United States, the law makes it easy for employers to nonetheless employ unauthorized workers. Some employers simply ignore their obligation and do not check the immigration status of new employees. Others may check for status at the time of hire but do not recheck when a work visa expires. Other employers check documentation and are given false documents by the prospective employees.

The law facilitates the employment of undocumented workers because, instead of actually prohibiting the employment of undocumented workers, the law requires only that employers check for authorization. The law, in essence, sets up a paperwork requirement for employers. As long as employers are presented with and record documents that look reasonably genuine, the employer is in compliance with the law. In this way, employers can hire employees that they suspect (or know) are undocumented and still comply with the law. In addition, employers are given several days' notice to make sure they have their paperwork in order. Once notice of an inspection is given, an employer can fire unauthorized workers. Finally, the penalties for paperwork violations are fairly low, thus giving many employers no incentive to comply with the law. As a result of this structure, the law can claim to prohibit the employment of undocumented workers while in practice allowing many employers to utilize them.

Many employers favor undocumented workers because they are easily exploitable, willing to do difficult work for wages and in work conditions below those required for legally authorized workers. The unauthorized represent 36 percent of all insulation workers; 29 percent of all roofers, drywall installers, and miscellaneous agricultural workers; and 27 percent of all butchers, food processing workers, and construction helpers. They are over 20 percent of all dishwashers, maids, and housekeepers.[20] As a group, these jobs are extremely dangerous[21] and/or low paying.[22] As a practical matter, many undocumented workers feel they have little or no recourse if they are abused in the workplace. If they complain and their status is discovered and/or reported, the law requires that they be fired and then deported. Physically, deportation is a difficult process that begins with incarceration in an immigration detention facility and then transport across the border. Deportation often results in psychological and emotional hardships as deportees leave family members behind in the United States. Many deportees try to reenter the United States illegally, a dangerous process that results, on average, in one death a day. Many workers will not complain about abusive work conditions and risk these consequences.

In addition, the legal system has specifically held that undocumented workers are entitled to fewer remedies when their workplace rights are violated than workers with proper authorization. In the case of *Hoffman Plastic Compounds v. Nat'l Labor Relations Board*[23] (hereafter *Hoffman*), the U.S. Supreme Court ruled in a case where an undocumented worker was fired because of his activity in supporting and organizing a union, in violation of the National Labor Relations Act. Normally, the National Labor Relations Board (NLRB) would order that such an employee be reinstated and given compensation for the wages (or back pay) he lost because of his unlawful discharge. In *Hoffman*, however, the Court said that the NLRB did not have authority to give the undocumented worker his job back because of his immigration status and could not be given back pay because such a remedy would conflict with national immigration policy.

As a result of *Hoffman*, undocumented workers as a group are legally excluded from receiving the same remedies as documented workers. This two-tier remedy system, legally created and sanctioned by the state, reinforces the two-tier labor system created by immigration policy and market forces. Undocumented workers thus become a caste of people laboring, without legal protection or recourse, below the floor created for fee labor in the United States.[24] This situation replicates, at least to some extent, the status of slave laborers.

Undocumented workers are disadvantaged in ways outside the workplace as well. They are excluded from participation in a variety of social services, such as driver's licenses, legal aid, or welfare. They may not become citizens. Although the Supreme Court ruled, in 1982[25] that undocumented children must be allowed to attend public school for free, even that decision has recently come under attack. As a group, they are verbally attacked and demonized by conservative commentators and politicians. Thus, as with chattel slaves, their deprivations affect more than just their labor rights.

As a result, undocumented workers constitute a group of workers who are excluded from basic workers' rights, human rights, citizenship rights, and civil rights protection. They can be viewed as this century's peculiar institution. On the one hand, the United States has brought them in for their labor and continues to benefit from it. The labor and immigration laws facilitate their subordination. On the other, their continued presence in an "illegal" status conflicts with the country's stated law and political philosophies of equality and decency. Some wish they would simply go away or be deported, but, like the slaves of the Old South, 10 million people, many of whom are the parents or relatives of U.S. citizens, cannot simply be wished away. Immigrant rights advocates suggesting a program to transition undocumented workers into legal status are often strongly opposed by those who see this as rewarding lawbreakers and forever changing the racial composition of the Untied States.

IMMIGRANT WORKERS AND THE REINVIGORATION OF THE THIRTEENTH AMENDMENT

From a Thirteenth Amendment perspective, immigrant workers provide a tremendous opportunity to reengineer the amendment in ways that help all workers. Considering the possibility that the Thirteenth Amendment could protect immigrant workers in general because they constitute a class of workers laboring beneath the floor for free labor reinforces the use of the amendment as a guarantor of labor rights. Viewing poorly crafted guest worker programs as potential violations of the Thirteenth Amendment provides an opportunity to unpack the definition of "involuntary servitude" and also focuses on the racialized nature of labor oppression and commodification. Examining the treatment of undocumented labor as this century's peculiar institution emphasizes the human rights, civil rights, and citizenship rights dimensions of the amendment.

In addition to these analytical insights, the inclusion of immigrant workers in Thirteenth Amendment discourse offers a variety of practical advantages. For those who wish to use the Thirteenth Amendment as a legislative tool, immigrant rights groups focusing on the rights of "trafficked workers" have been successful in passing legislation based on the Thirteenth Amendment to provide new, civil remedies for trafficked workers; to expand the definition of "involuntary"; and to relax some immigration restrictions. For those who seek redress in domestic courts, attorneys have brought a variety of challenges grounded in the Thirteenth Amendment to protect the rights of immigrant workers. In addition, advocates have been active and successful in international forums challenging various U.S. policies regarding immigrant workers. Finally, from an organizational perspective, immigrant rights groups have been gaining political power and moral traction through their use of public campaigns for human rights, citizenship rights, and labor rights.

The fight to end chattel slavery was long and difficult. Ultimately, it required political and moral strength. The fight to provide decent treatment for immigrant workers in the United States, especially undocumented workers, seems equally arduous and intractable at times. Using the constitutional amendment that ended chattel slavery to address the problem makes sense—legally, politically, and morally.

NOTES

1. A family is a "family unit," defined to include a couple living together (with or without children) or a solo individual living on his or her own. An unauthorized family is one where the head or spouse is an unauthorized migrant. In 2005, there were approximately 14.6 million people living in 6.6 million unauthorized families. Jeffrey S. Passel, Unauthorized Migrants: Numbers and Characteristics, 2005, http://www.pewhispanic.org (accessed Dec. 5, 2007).

2. Steven A. Camarota, Immigrants in the United States: 2000, Center for Immigration Studies, 2001, http://www.cis.org/articles/2001/back101.html/.

3. Passel, *supra.*

4. *Id.*

5. *Id.*

6. Michael Fix & Jeffrey S. Passel, Immigration and Immigrants: Setting the Record Straight (The Urban Inst.), May 1, 1994, http://www.urban.org/pubs/immig/immig.htm. Another 12 percent come from countries in Asia. Thus most undocumented workers are people of color.

7. B. Lindsay Lowell & Robert Suro, How Many Undocumented: The Numbers Behind the U.S.-Mexico Migration Talks (Mar. 21, 2002), http://www.pewhispanic.org/site/docs/pdf/howmanyundocumented.pdf, at 7–8.

8. Phillip Martin, Labor Relations in California Agriculture: 1975–2000 (2000), http://migration.ucdavis.edu/rmn/changingface/cf_alra25/9_2000_martin.html.

9. Passel, *supra.*

10. BARRY T. HIRSCH & DAVID A. MACPHERSON, UNION MEMBERSHIP AND EARNINGS DATA BOOK: COMPILATIONS FROM THE CURRENT POPULATION SURVEY (Washington, D.C.: Bureau of National Affairs, 2005).

11. Maria L. Ontiveros, *Female Immigrant Workers and the Law, in* THE SEX OF CLASS (Dorothy Sue Cobble ed., 2007).

12. *Id.*

13. *Id.*

14. *Espinoza v. Farah Mfg. Co., Inc.,* 414 U.S. 86 (1973).

15. This, in turn, creates problems for domestic workers unencumbered by visa restrictions because they must compete against the visa workers for the same jobs.

16. Michael Holley, *Disadvantaged by Design: How the Law Inhibits Agricultural Guest Workers from Enforcing Their Rights,* 18 HOFSTRA LAB. & EMP. L. J. 575 (2001); Kimi Jackson, *Farmworkers, Nonimmigration Policy, Involuntary Servitude, and a Look at the Sheepherding Industry,* 76 CHI-KENT L. REV. 1271 (2000).

17. D. Michael Dale, Maria Andrade, and Laura K. Abel, Memorandum in Support of Petition on Labor Law Matters Arising in the United States, Mexican NAO Submission 2005-1 (H-2B Visa Workers) (Apr. 13, 2005), http://www.dol.gov/ilab/media/reports/nao/submissions/2005-01memo.htm (accessed Dec. 8, 2009).

18. California agriculture provides a particularly good example, because the agricultural industry is large and important to the economy. In addition, agricultural work was at the heart of chattel slavery. For a fuller analysis of these issues, *see* Maria L. Ontiveros, *Noncitizen Immigrant Labor and the Thirteenth Amendment: Challenging Guest Worker Programs,* 38 U. TOLEDO L. REV. 923 (2007).

19. LINDA C. MAJKA & THEO J. MAJKA, FARM WORKERS, AGRIBUSINESS, AND THE STATE 136 (1982).

20. Passel, *supra.*

21. Sarah Cleveland et. al., *Inter-American Court of Human Rights Amicus Curiae Brief: The United States Violates International Law When Labor Law Remedies Are Restricted Based on Workers' Migrant Status,* 1 SEATTLE J. SOC. JUST. 795, 805–7 (2003). *See also* Justin Pritchard, *Mexican-Born Workers More Likely to Die on Job,*

L.A. Times, Mar. 14, 2004, at A1 (Associated Press study finds that approximately one Mexican dies each day in a job-related incident).

22. Cleveland, *id.* at 805–6.

23. 535 U.S. 137 (2002)

24. Maria L. Ontiveros, *Immigrant Workers' Rights in a Post-Hoffman World: Organizing Around the Thirteenth Amendment*, 18 Geo. Immigr. L. J. 651, 658 (2004).

25. *Plyler v. Doe*, 457 U.S. 202 (1982)

16. A Thirteenth Amendment Agenda for the Twenty-first Century

OF PROMISES, POWER, AND PRECAUTION

Darrell A. H. Miller

Over forty years ago, in *Jones v. Alfred H. Mayer Co.*,[1] the Supreme Court recognized that the Thirteenth Amendment empowers Congress to proscribe private racial discrimination in the sale of property. Even sympathetic readers were surprised by the Court's apparent abandonment of the Fourteenth Amendment state-action civil rights paradigm in favor of direct regulation of private behavior under a Thirteenth Amendment "badge and incident" of slavery analysis. Perhaps most revolutionary was the Court's conclusion that a right to own property "can be impaired as effectively by those who place property on the market as by the State itself."[2] According to *Jones*, Congress may prohibit such discrimination through its Thirteenth Amendment enforcement power, even in the absence of state action, "for, even if the State and its agents lend no support to those who wish to exclude persons from their communities on racial grounds, the fact remains that, whenever property is placed on the market for whites only, whites have a right denied to Negroes."[3] The majority concluded that the nation had made a promise with the Thirteenth Amendment, and "if Congress were powerless to assure that a dollar in the hands of a Negro will purchase the same thing as a dollar in the hands of a white man . . . then the Thirteenth Amendment made a promise the Nation cannot keep."[4]

This chapter explains how *Jones*'s recognition of Congress's power to regulate certain private preferences under its Thirteenth Amendment enforcement power is consonant with congressional purpose during the Reconstruction era. It also suggests how this recognition helps to establish a framework for understanding the Thirteenth Amendment's applicability to current forms of discrimination, which are often the product of unconscious bias, systematically faulty heuristics, and disparate impacts rather than express bigotry.[5]

Jones's proposition that the Thirteenth Amendment authorizes direct regulation of private preferences when those preferences help perpetuate a badge or incident of slavery may seem revolutionary, but it is, in fact, historically indicated. In 1865, the states ratified the Thirteenth Amendment. Shortly thereafter, Congress set to work to tear up slavery "root and branch."[6] As I have written elsewhere,[7] Congress debated the Civil Rights Act of 1866 amid numerous reports of Southern attempts to replicate slavery through both positive law and private collective action.

For example, white Southerners used strategies that modern antitrust scholars would recognize as anticompetitive. Whites used form labor contracts for freedmen, conspired to fix wages, used labor market division strategies, and tied services. Representative William Windom, of Minnesota, complained that "planters combine together to compel [the freedmen] to work for such wages as their former masters may dictate, and deny them the privilege of hiring to any one without the consent of the master."[8] An Alabama planter pledged that freedmen would be made serfs through private restraints alone: "It won't need any law for that. Planters will have an understanding among themselves: 'You won't hire my niggers, and I won't hire yours'; then what's left for them? They're attached to the soil, and we're as much their masters as ever."[9]

Southern whites—even those with no property interest in slaves themselves—used public pressure, social ostracism, community customs, and physical violence to intimidate those individuals, black or white, who challenged white supremacist entrenchment.[10] Often the public and private discriminations worked together. Southern governments used facially neutral vagrancy or licensing laws to imprison or fine freedmen who, because of private prejudice, found it impossible to comply with the law. For example, freedmen were arrested and charged as vagrants for having no home or employment, despite the fact that private discrimination kept many of them from obtaining housing or a job—except according to the terms dictated by their former masters.[11] In this way, Southern whites, working through express agreements, tacit understandings, and racial norms acted as a kind of cartel whose purpose and effect was to stymie black equality.[12]

In response, Reconstruction opponents, including President Andrew Johnson himself, deferred to the market. Among his reasons for vetoing the Civil

Rights Act of 1866, Johnson referenced his faith in the invisible hand of supply and demand. According to Johnson, the Civil Rights bill "frustrate[d]" the inevitable "adjustment" by former slaves and former masters to a new economic model. If only "left to the laws that regulate capital and labor," a "harmonious" new equilibrium would arise between the two.[13]

Congress rejected this free market faith by overriding Johnson's veto.

Instead, as *Jones* confirmed, Congress regarded the Thirteenth Amendment as a tool empowering it to adjust private economic relationships in order to counter these collective action problems. Although Southern intransigence and Northern passivity frustrated Reconstruction for close to a century,[14] the fact that Congress acted to regulate in the area of private economic choice has profound implications today for the meaning of the amendment and for congressional power under its authority.

Certainly, at a minimum, the amendment authorizes Congress to prohibit private parties from compelling service in a way that functionally replicates African slavery. In fact, the Thirteenth Amendment arguably should be self-implementing in that specific circumstance and should authorize injured parties to bring private lawsuits for coercive compelled service, even against other private parties.[15] But *Jones* and the history of the 1866 Civil Rights Act also suggest a broader authority. Congress may regulate certain public and private behavior that arises from personal and individual preferences when that behavior, if aggregated, would lead to a similar type of cartel behavior or disparate impact as manifested during Reconstruction.[16]

In advancing this argument, I do not propose that the entire doctrinal structure of antitrust law should be engrafted onto the Thirteenth Amendment.[17] But I do suggest that Congress is permitted to take into account the potential economic and social effects of aggregated personal preferences, hidden biases, or racial heuristics when legislating under the Thirteenth Amendment.

Neither do I suggest that all personal preferences, conscious or unconscious, may properly be regarded as evidence of, or leading to, a "badge" or "incident" of slavery. Other constitutional values, like privacy and religious freedom, temper what Congress may be able to regulate under its otherwise broad authority.

Further, any appropriate congressional legislation would need to be historically contextualized. As suggested by William Carter and Mark Rosen, among others, a preliminary model for what may constitute "appropriate" Thirteenth Amendment legislation would look something like figure 16.1, where the *x* axis represents a nonexclusive list of those types of behaviors that have some historical indicia or close analogue in American slavery. The *y* axis represents those group members who could have historically suffered a "badge" of slavery in America. Congressional Thirteenth Amendment power is at its most puissant where the *x* and *y* axes meet; those portions of the graph where the shading becomes lighter

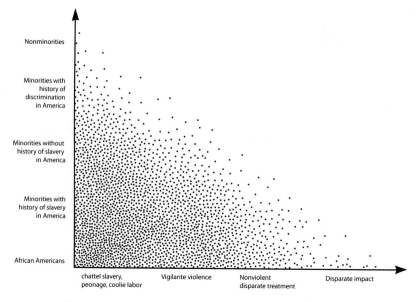

FIGURE 16.1

represents congressional Thirteenth Amendment authority to legislate as a prophylactic; and, finally, where the graph shows little to no shading reflects areas
in which Congress would have little or no power to legislate under a Thirteenth
Amendment rationale.[18] Instead, Congress would have to turn to other constitutional authority such as the Commerce Power or spending power to address these
instances of discrimination or disparate impact.

A policy agenda based on this model could touch on several areas in which
private or public preferences, whether conscious or unconscious, lead specifically
to systematic disadvantage of minorities. Further, a Thirteenth Amendment policy agenda may empower Congress to act in areas that it currently cannot reach—
either because of constitutional limitations on its Commerce Clause power[19]
or because of similar restrictions on its Fourteenth Amendment enforcement
authority.[20]

For example, a number of states have felon disenfranchisement laws. However, courts have stated that race-neutral felon disenfranchisement, untainted
by discriminatory intent, is not an equal protection violation, even if it results in
widespread disparate impacts.[21] Under the Thirteenth Amendment Congress
could use its enforcement authority to abrogate these laws based on their disparate impact. As evidence for its action, Congress could find systematic disparate
impact based on these laws, take testimony that the acts systematically disadvantage a population most closely tied with chattel slavery—namely African

Americans—and recognize that the Southern states historically used criminality as a proxy for race in perpetuating slave culture.[22]

Congress could legislate in the area of the death penalty as well. In *McCleskey v. Kemp*,[23] the defendant presented statistical evidence that proved that black defendants in Georgia were systematically more likely to be sentenced to death for killing whites than for killing blacks. However, the Court concluded that these disparate impacts alone could not lead to an equal protection violation. Absent some proof of discriminatory purpose, disparate impacts were not enough.[24] Congress could use its Thirteenth Amendment power to conclude that these disparate impacts fall disproportionately on a group with a historical link to American slavery, that disparate use of capital punishment was an aspect of the slave-owning culture, and that some remedial or prophylactic legislation (perhaps through a mandatory DNA exoneration regime, for example) is required to address these disparate impacts.

Voluntary race-conscious affirmative action plans in schools—limited under the Fourteenth Amendment[25]—may be authorized by Congress under its Thirteenth Amendment enforcement power. Congress could, for example, find that racial minorities are systematically disadvantaged by private preferences in municipal residency, acknowledge that these private preferences systematically disadvantage a population with a history intimately tied to chattel slavery, and recognize that restrictions on the type and availability of education among slaves were an essential component of maintaining the slave-owning culture.

Finally, the advent of unprecedented choice in human offspring due to advances in reproductive technology warrants congressional attention under this Thirteenth Amendment model. Specifically, Congress could conclude that certain types of reproductive services (for example, in vitro selection for specific racial phenotypes) pose a threat of systematic private preferences for a certain racial phenotype (for example, light-skinned children over dark-skinned children); Congress could recognize that dark-skinned individuals are a population that have a historical connection to American chattel slavery[26] and that the process of valuing and selecting humans based on certain desirable physical traits was an important component of the slave-owning culture and economy.[27]

The Thirteenth Amendment power to legislate in response to individual discriminatory preferences is a powerful tool. *Jones* states that Congress need only articulate some "rational basis" to define a phenomenon as a "badge of slavery" and legislate against it.[28] Laurence Tribe has stated: "Congress possesses an almost unlimited power to protect individual rights under the Thirteenth Amendment. Seemingly, Congress is free within the broad limits of reason, to recognize whatever rights it wishes, define the infringement of those rights as a form of domination or subordination and thus an aspect of slavery, and proscribe such infringement as a violation of the Thirteenth Amendment."[29]

Such a generous interpretation of Thirteenth Amendment enforcement power would restore Congress's prestige in civil rights policy, prestige lost since the Rehnquist Court began to impose a "proportionality" and "congruence" test on Congress's exercise of its Fourteenth Amendment enforcement power.[30]

However, as the old saw goes, we must be careful what we wish for. Congressional Thirteenth Amendment enforcement power operates in ways "direct and primary, operating upon the acts of individuals"[31] unmediated by state action, interstate commerce, or, as I have argued, by evidence of discriminatory intent. One can easily imagine Congress's wielding its Thirteenth Amendment power in ways that are not just hostile to individual freedom but are positively despotic.[32]

And so, any new Thirteenth Amendment agenda must be tempered by prudence and precaution. Congress must have broad license to construct remedial or preventative legislation, especially in light of new technology and persistent racial inequality. But the Court must retain authority to tell Congress, when it exceeds its broad mandate, that its legislation is not "appropriate." Some of the grounds for Court authority will be on the basis of other, conflicting constitutional values, such as privacy or freedom of speech. Others will flow from the proposed historical framework outlined in this chapter.[33] While the result would be to prevent Congress from using the Thirteenth Amendment to legislate in areas that may be popular or even practical, American democracy, American liberty, and the very integrity of the Thirteenth Amendment itself cannot tolerate unchecked congressional power in this area. Only by achieving the correct balance of legislative innovation versus judicial oversight may we, to paraphrase James Baldwin, turn the great shame of American slavery into America's greatest opportunity.

NOTES

My thanks to the Thirteenth Amendment conference participants at the University of Chicago Law School, held April 17–18, 2009, as well as special gratitude to Paul Finkelman, Amy Dru Stanley, Alex Tsesis, Taunya Banks, and Sherrilyn Ifill. Some material in this chapter originally appeared in Darrell A. H. Miller, *White Cartels, the Civil Rights Act of 1866 and the History of* Jones v. Alfred H. Mayer Co., 77 FORDHAM L. REV. 999 (2008).

1. 392 U.S. 409 (1968) (holding that 42 U.S.C. § 1982, the modern codification of the Civil Rights Act of 1866, forbids private racial discrimination in sale of real estate and that the Thirteenth Amendment authorizes such legislation).

2. *Id.* at 420–21 (internal quotation marks and citation omitted).

3. *Id.* at 421 (internal quotation marks and citation omitted).

4. *Id.* at 443.

5. For a discussion of unconscious bias, *see* Charles Lawrence III, *The Id, the Ego, and Equal Protection: Reckoning with Unconscious Racism*, 39 STAN. L. REV. 317 (1987); *see also* Charles Lawrence III, *Unconscious Racism Revisited: Reflections on the Impact and Origins of "The Id, the Ego, and Equal Protection,"* 40 CONN. L. REV. 931 (2008).

6. CONG. GLOBE, 42d Cong., 2d Sess. 728 (1872) (statement of Sen. Sumner).

7. *See* Darrell A. H. Miller, *White Cartels, the Civil Rights Act of 1866 and the History of* Jones v. Alfred H. Mayer Co., 77 FORDHAM L. REV. 999 (2008).

8. CONG. GLOBE, 39th Cong., 1st Sess. 1160 (1866) (statement of Rep. Windom).

9. LEON F. LITWACK, BEEN IN THE STORM SO LONG: THE AFTERMATH OF SLAVERY 415 (1980) (quoting J. T. TROWBRIDGE, THE SOUTH: A TOUR OF ITS BATTLE-FIELDS AND RUINED CITIES 427 [1866; repr. Arno Press 1969]).

10. For a discussion of the use of violence and its legitimization on the basis of "self defense" in the Reconstruction South, *see* Darrell A. H. Miller, *Guns as Smut: Defending the Home-Bound Second Amendment*, 109 COLUM. L. REV. 1278, 1329–34, 1347–49 (2009).

11. *See* Miller, *White Cartels, supra*, at 1028–31.

12. For a sustained discussion of this type of cartel behavior, *see* Richard H. Mc-Adams, *Cooperation and Conflict: The Economics of Group Status Production and Race Discrimination*, 108 HARV. L. REV. 1003 (1995).

13. Veto Message of President Andrew Johnson, Mar. 27, 1866, *reprinted in* 8 A COMPILATION OF THE MESSAGES AND PAPERS OF THE PRESIDENTS 3610 (James D. Richardson ed., 1897).

14. Reconstruction efforts fizzled during the latter half of the nineteenth century; however, congressional regulation of other, nonracial, private economic relationships did not. The lessons of Reconstruction gave intellectual support for antitrust laws of late 1800s and early 1900s. *See* Miller, *White Cartels, supra*, at 1036–38.

15. *Compare* Baher Azmy, *Unshackling the Thirteenth Amendment: Modern Slavery and a Reconstructed Civil Rights Agenda*, 71 FORDHAM L. REV. 981, 1060 (2002) (arguing that a *Bivens*-style action should be recognized under the Thirteenth Amendment) *with John Roe I v. Bridgestone Corp.*, 492 F. Supp. 2d 988, 997 (S.D. Ind. 2007) and *Bhagwanani v. Howard Univ.*, 355 F. Supp. 2d 294, 301 n. 5 (D.D.C. 2005) (rejecting a *Bivens*-style Thirteenth Amendment remedy).

16. Congress may have this authority to legislate, even though the Thirteenth Amendment of its own force may require a far higher showing of disparate impact. *See City of Memphis v. Greene*, 451 U.S. 100, 124–29 (1981) (disparate impact caused by closing of street in predominantly black neighborhood did not suffice to raise a Thirteenth Amendment claim).

17. For example, I do not believe that evidence of specific discriminatory agreements is required for Congress to recognize a custom, convention, or heuristic that potentially leads to cartel-like behavior or disparate impacts.

18. This graph does not capture a potential power under the Thirteenth Amendment to punish or remedy retaliation against nonminorities who do not toe the white supremacist line. *Sullivan v. Little Hunting Park, Inc.*, 396 U.S. 229 (1969). Nor does this graph express the Court's interpretation of section 2 power to proscribe racially disparate treatment of whites under 42 U.S.C § 1981. *See McDonald v. Santa Fe Trail Transp. Co.*, 427 U.S. 273 (1976).

19. *See United States v. Morrison*, 529 U.S. 598, 616–17 (2000) (striking down provisions of the Violence Against Women Act [VAWA] of 1994, 42 U.S.C. § 13981, as an invalid exercise of Commerce Power).

20. *Id.* at 623–27(provisions of VAWA applicable to private parties not a proper exercise of Congress's Fourteenth Amendment power).

21. *See Johnson v. Gov. of Fla.*, 405 F.3d 1214, 1222 n. 17 (11th Cir. 2005); *Cotton v. Fordice*, 157 F.3d 388 (5th Cir. 1998); *Wesley v. Collins*, 791 F.2d 1255, 1262–63 (6th Cir. 1986). For a discussion of potential limits of the Fifteenth Amendment to accomplish this goal, *see* Richard L. Hasen, *The Uncertain Congressional Power to Ban Felon Disenfranchisement Laws*, 49 HOW. L. J. 767, 781–83 (2006).

22. *See* Paul Finkelman, *The Crime of Color*, 67 TUL. L. REV. 2063 (1993).

23. 481 U.S. 279 (1987).

24. *Id.* at 298–99.

25. *Parents Involved in Cmty. Schs. v. Seattle Sch. Dist. No. 1*, 551 U.S. 701 (2007).

26. Using the Thirteenth Amendment to address gender selection poses a more difficult question. On the one hand, the historical connection between gender and slavery is not nearly as tight as between skin color and slavery. Nevertheless, a case can be made that females of whatever color have suffered disabilities that mirror the type of disabilities placed upon slaves in the South, that they are a minority and in certain situations can suffer a "badge or incident" of slavery, and that the pernicious effect of choosing boys over girls in vitro is close enough to selective valuation of slaves to warrant its proscription under the Thirteenth Amendment enforcement power. For a discussion of how women have suffered legal disabilities analogous to slaves, *see* Marcellene Elizabeth Hearn, Comment, A *Thirteenth Amendment Defense of the Violence Against Women Act*, 146 U. PA. L. REV. 1097, 1163–68 (1998); *see also* Lawrence G. Sager, A *Letter to the Supreme Court Regarding the Missing Argument in Brzonkala v. Morrison*, 75 N.Y.U. L. REV. 150, 152–54 (2000).

27. *See* Taunya Lovell Banks, *Colorism: A Darker Shade of Pale*, 47 UCLA L. REV. 1705, 1714 n. 32 (2000) ("Some slave owners placed a higher economic value on slaves of mixed ancestry."); *see also* HENRY WIENCEK: AN IMPERFECT GOD; GEORGE WASHINGTON, HIS SLAVES AND THE CREATION OF AMERICA 130–31 (2004) (noting Washington's payment of a premium for "mulatto" over "Negro" slaves). In making this point, I do not suggest that Congress could, or should, be able to regulate the racial characteristics of a person's potential mate in order to control the natural offspring of such a union. Neither do I address the perilous and difficult issue of whether

Congress could use the Thirteenth Amendment to proscribe selective abortions motivated by gender or race preferences.

28. *Jones*, at 440.

29. 1 LAURENCE H. TRIBE, AMERICAN CONSTITUTIONAL LAW 927 (3d ed. 2000).

30. Under current Fourteenth Amendment jurisprudence, congressional legislation under section 5 of the Fourteenth Amendment must be both congruent and proportional to the injury sought to be prevented or remedied. *See, e.g., Kimel v. Fla. Bd. of Regents*, 528 U.S. 62, 83–84 (2000); *City of Boerne v. Flores*, 521 U.S. 507, 520 (1997).

31. *Jones*, at 438 (quoting Civil Rights Cases, 109 U.S. 3, 23 [1883] [citations and internal quotation marks omitted]).

32. For example, one can imagine a scenario in which Congress, using its Thirteenth Amendment enforcement power, would define the terminally ill as a "subordinated class" with a right to life and forbid family members from making end-of-life decisions for their spouses or relatives, any state constitution and domestic relation law notwithstanding.

33. In addition, the process of political participation and accountability could put a check on the most egregious examples of congressional excess.

Epilogue
The Enduring Legacy of the Thirteenth Amendment

Robert J. Kaczorowski

This extraordinary collection of essays on the Thirteenth Amendment shows how it encompasses the sweep of U.S. history. These essays demonstrate that the Thirteenth Amendment connects the promise of liberty that spawned and justified the American Revolution with our current struggles to protect individual liberties in the areas of personal rights, criminal justice, and immigration reform.

Several scholars explore the Thirteenth Amendment's antecedents in the American Revolution and the antebellum abolitionist movement and the nation's failure to achieve the amendment's promise of freedom. Alexander Tsesis persuasively argues that the Thirteenth Amendment, interpreted in light of its revolutionary and abolitionist foundations, provided the constitutional authority "to translate the principles of the Declaration of Independence and the preamble [to the Constitution] into enforceable laws," establishing for the first time in the nation's history that "the national government had a constitutional mechanism for guaranteeing the fundamental rights of life, liberty, and property to its citizenry." Pulitzer Prize–winning historian James McPherson agrees and elaborates the Thirteenth Amendment's foundation in the abolitionist movement during the Civil War, which achieved the abolition of slavery and made this promise of freedom and racial equality secured by the national government a central goal of the Republican Party during the Civil War and Reconstruction. Sadly, the nation moved away from these objectives in the 1870s, and, by the end of the nineteenth century, McPherson laments, "African Americans found themselves disfranchised, segregated, and suppressed into a second-class citizenship in which economic exploitation reinforced caste discrimination." William Wiecek explains the processes and strategies Southerners used to transform the status of African Americans from that of freemen and citizens protected in their equal civil and political rights under federal law to virtual reenslavement. He shows that, by 1900, the South had rejected the North's "abolitionist/Republican vision" of a regime of racially equal rights secured by federal law and replaced it with nominal racial equality in law and "apartheid and rightslessness" in fact.

Two scholars place the failure to secure true freedom and racial equality under the Thirteenth Amendment in national institutions. George Rutherglen places primary responsibility for the regression of black Americans on the Supreme Court. He argues that it curtailed the scope of federal authority to enforce the Thirteenth Amendment and its guarantee of civil rights and racial equality when it reduced the amendment to a guarantee against the "badges and incidents of slavery" and then narrowly defined "badges and incidents of slavery." Michael Vorenberg attributes the nation's failure in the Civil War era to secure the full rights of freemen for black Americans to the congressional Republican supporters of the Civil Rights Act of 1866 and the Fourteenth Amendment. He argues that they narrowed the Thirteenth Amendment's universal guarantee of the rights of freemen in the "illiberal move of tangling . . . freedom rights, once regarded as expansive, . . . with the [narrower] ascriptive qualities of citizenship." His point is that since the state determines what are the rights of citizens and which citizens may enjoy which rights, the framers' "tangling" of freedom rights and citizenship rights permitted the states to deny black Americans the full rights of freemen.

Several scholars discuss the Thirteenth Amendment's applications to issues of workers' rights in the twentieth and twenty-first centuries. James Gray Pope traces the rise and fall of organized labor's interpretation of the Thirteenth Amendment, which it persuaded the Supreme Court to adopt in 1911 as a constitutional guarantee of workers' rights to organize, to bargain collectively, and to strike as rights that are essential to establish and maintain free labor. Although labor's interpretation of the Thirteenth Amendment has slipped into desuetude, Pope argues that "labor's Thirteenth Amendment idea—that labor freedom necessarily includes the rights to organize and strike" fits well with the present-day doctrine of freedom of association and "is now embodied in international labor standards." This leads him to believe that labor's interpretation of the Thirteenth Amendment can be revived as a constitutional theory to overturn the current system of labor law established by the antilabor provisions of the Taft-Hartley Act (1947), which he views as establishing a law of slave labor. Risa Goluboff is not so optimistic. Risa Goluboff analyzes the Thirteenth Amendment's transformation from a *Lochner*-era guarantee of contractual freedom to a New Deal conception of an affirmative and ongoing governmental duty to protect the economic security and personal safety of each person through a commitment to free labor and a guarantee of a minimum standard of living. This transformation entailed a new model for the government's role in protecting civil rights. However, by the end of the Warren Court era in the late 1960s, the Fourteenth Amendment's equal protection guarantee "had become the dominant way of thinking about civil rights," and "it was difficult to envision the Thirteenth Amendment as anything but an equal protection guarantee without a state-action requirement." But, Maria Ontiveros sees the Thirteenth Amendment as a source of legal protection for immigrant workers, both documented and undocumented, even within an equal protection theory. These workers are excluded from the various protections citizen workers enjoy, including the right to be a citizen, and "the systematic exclusion of all immigrant workers creates a caste of workers laboring below the floor set for free labor," a caste akin to slave labor, which offers fertile grounds to use the Thirteenth Amendment "as a guarantor of labor rights."

Other contributors to this volume view the Thirteenth Amendment as a constitutional guarantee of rights beyond the rights of workers. Andrew Taslitz argues that, in abolishing the badges and incidents of slavery, the Thirteenth Amendment authorizes Congress to criminalize "expressive racial violence divorced from the labor setting, physically or psychologically coerced labor divorced from racial bias, and any de facto or de jure efforts to treat persons as property." He cautions that the Thirteenth Amendment does not authorize Congress to prohibit all violent crimes or all forms of racial subordination or labor coercion devoid of violence. The limiting principle is that violence must be linked either to "racial subordination or labor coercion." Rebecca Zietlow maintains that the Supreme Court's interpretations of the Thirteenth Amendment support her view that it authorizes Congress to punish crimes committed against individuals because of their race, national origin, and religion. She also argues that a broad understanding of "badges and incidents of slavery" similarly supports this interpretation, reasoning that, "since slavery was a system perpetuated by race-based violence, it seems clear that Congress could rationally find that race-based violence was a badge or incident of slavery." She further argues that, because slavery often involved sexual assaults, rape, and other acts of violence committed against women, the Thirteenth Amendment could be interpreted to authorize Congress to remedy acts of sexual discrimination on the theory that the subordination of women as women was a common feature of slavery.

Several authors want to extend the Thirteenth Amendment even further. William Carter argues that the exclusionary rule should be applied to bar the introduction of "evidence gathered by police practices that amount to a badge or incident of slavery," such as racial profiling. He maintains that racial profiling should be treated as a badge or incident of slavery because "it both reflects and perpetuates deeply rooted cultural biases concerning the supposed connection between race and criminality." Suppressing unconstitutionally obtained evidence in these situations would help eliminate police practices that equated race with criminality and based criminal suspicion "upon who you are rather than what you do," both of which are elements of the system of caste and racial subordination inherent in slavery. Laws prohibiting abortion violate the Thirteenth Amendment, argues Andrew Koppelman. Without the legal right to abortion, a pregnant woman who does not want to give birth would be coerced into a "forced pregnancy and childbirth, by compelling the woman to serve the fetus," a condition that fits squarely within the U.S. Supreme Court's definition of involuntary servitude: "'that control by which the personal service of one man [*sic*] is disposed of or coerced for another's benefit which is the essence of involuntary servitude.'"[1]

Aviam Soifer's discussion of recent Supreme Court decisions interpreting the Civil Rights Act of 1866 does not present much hope for the Court's recognition of the Thirteenth Amendment as a broad guarantee of civil rights. He accuses the Rehnquist Court of "a striking lack of concern for attention to context" in interpreting the Civil Rights Act and the Fourteenth Amendment. The framers spoke repeatedly "of a national duty to protect the basic rights of the former slaves," and they expressed this duty in the words of the Civil Rights Act, which reveal that a "governmental duty to protect vital rights was at [its] core." The Supreme Court "began the retrenchment against civil rights" in the nineteenth century, and this retrenchment "came to dominate the [Supreme] Court and to help enable the rise and maintenance of Jim Crow for many decades." The Rehnquist Court has continued this retreat by holding that "Fourteenth Amendment guarantees were exclusively about negative rights," ignoring the words of the Civil Rights Act, which repeatedly imposes affirmative duties on the federal government to protect and enforce the full and equal rights of all Americans. Soifer acknowledges that implementing this core guarantee of the Civil Rights Act of 1866 will "require substantial rethinking of legal precedents and popular assumptions alike." His discussion of recent court decisions does not hold out much hope that this rethinking will occur.

Although I share many of the views of the Thirteenth Amendment expressed in this volume, my understanding of its historical background and the scope of legislative authority it confers on Congress to enforce constitutional rights is somewhat different and broader than that expressed by the other scholars. I have presented these views elsewhere, so I will simply summarize some of them here in order to suggest alternative theories one might use to deal with some of the current issues raised in this collection of essays. In short, my view is that the framers of the Civil Rights Act of 1866 and the Fourteenth Amendment interpreted the Thirteenth Amendment as an affirmative constitutional guarantee of liberty that delegated to Congress plenary power to enforce the rights of freemen, which they equated to the privileges and immunities of U.S. citizens.[2]

In my view, perhaps the most important sources of the framers' understanding of Congress's plenary legislative authority to enforce constitutional rights of freemen, ironically, were the Fugitive Slave acts, the statutes Congress enacted in 1793 and 1850 to enforce the Fugitive Slave Clause, and the Supreme Court's interpretation of the Fugitive Slave Clause affirming Congress's plenary power to enforce it. The text of the clause provided congressional Republicans with a model for the language of the Thirteenth, Fourteenth, and Fifteenth amendments. Congressional Republicans modeled the civil remedies, the criminal penalties and the federal enforcement structure they adopted in the Civil Rights Act of 1866, the Enforcement Act of 1870, and the Ku Klux Klan Act (1871) on the provisions of the 1793 and 1850 Fugitive Slave acts. Republicans based their understanding of the Thirteenth and Fourteenth amendments as delegations of plenary constitutional authority to enforce Americans' fundamental rights on the U.S. Supreme Court's interpretation of the Fugitive Slave Clause in *Prigg v. Pennsylvania* and, more generally, the Court's theory of implied powers affirmed in *McCulloch v. Maryland*. A brief review will clarify.

On its face, the Fugitive Slave Clause prohibited the states into which a fugitive slave escaped from enacting any laws that interfered with the service or labor the slave owed in the slave state from which s/he fled. It provided that "no Person held to Service or Labour in one State, under the laws thereof, escaping into another, shall, in Consequence of any Law or Regulation therein, be discharged from such Service or Labour, but shall be delivered up on Claim of the Party to whom such Service or Labour may be due."[3]

Remarkably, the second Congress of the United States enacted a statute, in 1793, to enforce the Fugitive Slave Clause, the first statute enacted by Congress to enforce a constitutional right. Congress's action was remarkable because the Fugitive Slave Clause was located in Article IV, and it did not expressly delegate enforcement authority to Congress. Nevertheless, acting at the behest of President George Washington, President Washington's secretary of state, Thomas Jefferson, and Attorney General Edmund Randolph, Congress enacted three federal causes of action to assist owners of slaves who fled into another state to recapture them and to sue anyone who assisted in the slaves' escape or interfered with their recapture for tort damages and a civil fine.[4]

Slaveholders availed themselves of the remedies the 1793 Fugitive Slave Act afforded them. Every constitutional challenge to the statute in state and federal courts was rejected, and claimants successfully sued for certificates of removal, the civil fine, and tort damages. This contributed to the emergence of a class of professional slave catchers and the abuse of kidnapping free blacks on the claim that they were fugitive slaves. Free states enacted antikidnapping statutes, which provided due process rights for those accused of being fugitive slaves. State antikidnapping laws directly conflicted with the Fugitive Slave Act. State and federal courts uniformly upheld the 1793 act, but interested parties sought the final authority of the U.S. Supreme Court to resolve the legal issues these cases presented.[5]

In a test case agreed to by the states of Maryland and Pennsylvania, the U.S. Supreme Court unanimously struck down the Pennsylvania Anti-Kidnapping Act (1825) and upheld the constitutionality of the 1793 Fugitive Slave Act. Speaking through Justice Joseph Story in the 1842 decision of *Prigg v. Pennsylvania*, the Supreme Court interpreted the Fugitive Slave Clause's prohibition on the states from discharging the fugitive slave from the service or labor owed in another state as a constitutional guarantee "of a positive, unqualified right on the part of the owner of the slave, which no state law or regulation can in any way qualify, regulate, control or restrain."[6]

More important, the Court interpreted the prohibition on the states as "a positive and unqualified recognition" of the slave owner's "positive and absolute right" of property in the slave, which the owner could enforce against anyone who interfered with it. Speaking through Justice Story, the Court declared that this constitutional recognition of the slaveholder's property right in his slave "puts the right to the service or labor upon the same ground, and to the same extent, in every other state as in the state from which the slave escaped." Moreover, "all the incidents to that right attach also." The Court based its interpretation of the Fugitive Slave Clause on its wording and on Chief Justice John Marshall's theory of broad implied powers in *McCulloch v. Maryland*.[7]

Story further explained that whenever a slave owner judicially enforced his property right pursuant to the Fugitive Slave Clause, his action was a case or controversy arising under the Constitution of the United States. Since the slave owner's right to reclaim the slave "is a right of property," it was "capable of being recognized and asserted by proceedings before a court of justice, between parties adverse to each other," which "constitutes, in the strictest sense, a controversy between parties, and a case 'arising under the constitution of the United States,' within the express delegation of judicial power given by [the Constitution]." Story concluded that "Congress . . . may call that power into activity, for the very purpose of giving effect to that right; . . . it may prescribe the mode and extent in which it shall be applied, and how, and under what circumstances, the proceedings shall afford a complete protection and guarantee to the right." Story asserted that "Congress has taken this very view of the power and duty of the national government" when it enacted the Fugitive Slave Act of 1793, which

conferred on the owner the right to seize the fugitive slave and to secure a warrant of removal, the right to sue for the civil penalty, and the "right of action for
or on account of such injuries."[8]

Congress enacted an even more sweeping and effective statute in 1850. The
Fugitive Slave Act of 1850 created a federal enforcement structure to discharge
the duty the act imposed on federal officials to enforce the slaveholders' property right, under penalty of a civil fine payable to the slave owner if the officials
failed to discharge their duty to enforce the statute. It also made it a federal
crime to assist a fugitive slave to escape or to interfere with her/his recapture,
and it created an additional federal tort remedy with statutory damages in cases
where the slave could not be recovered. The federal government enforced this
statute, and the Supreme Court upheld its constitutionality in the 1850s.[9]

During the Civil War, Congress repealed the Fugitive Slave acts of 1793 and
1850. The Thirty-eighth Congress adopted and sent to the states for ratification
in 1864 its proposal for an amendment abolishing slavery. The Thirteenth Amendment was ratified in December 1865 as the Thirty-ninth Congress convened.
Many of the framers and supporters of the Thirteenth Amendment who served
in the new Congress expressed their belief that it revolutionized the Constitution of the United States by transforming it from a fundamental guarantee of
slavery to a universal guarantee of liberty. These legislators were the framers of
the Civil Rights Act of 1866 and the Fourteenth Amendment.[10]

In the debates leading to the enactment of the Civil Rights Act of 1866, the
framers of the Fourteenth Amendment interpreted the Thirteenth Amendment
as a universal guarantee of liberty delegating to the Thirty-ninth Congress as
much constitutional authority to protect and enforce the natural rights and equality of all American citizens as earlier Congresses had exercised to protect and enforce the property right of slaveholders in their slaves. The "badges and incidents
of slavery" interpretation the Supreme Court engrafted onto the Thirteenth
Amendment in 1883 was hardly mentioned in the Civil Rights Act debates in
1866. Republican leaders affirmed the theory of broad implied powers the Marshall Court adopted in *McCulloch v. Maryland* and the Taney Court applied in
Prigg v. Pennsylvania. Just as Justice Story interpreted the Fugitive Slave Clause's
prohibition against the states from interfering with the master's right to the service
or labor of his slave as a positive and absolute constitutionally secured property
right, so the framers of the Civil Rights Act, quoting from Story's *Prigg* opinion,
interpreted the Thirteenth Amendment's prohibition against slavery as an affirmative guarantee of liberty, which delegated to Congress the same plenary authority
to define and enforce the civil rights of all Americans, not just the civil rights of the
former slaves.[11]

Thus, the principal author of the Civil Rights Act, Senator Lyman Trumbull,
of Illinois, proclaimed that "liberty and slavery are opposite terms; one is op-

posed to the other." In prohibiting slavery, "the Constitution secures freedom to all Americans," he insisted. The Thirteenth "amendment declared that all persons in the United States should be free. This [civil rights] measure is intended to give effect to that declaration and secure to all persons within the United States practical freedom." With the Thirteenth Amendment in the Constitution, Trumbull opined, "I hold that we have a right to pass any law which, in our judgment, is deemed appropriate, and which will accomplish the end in view, secure freedom to all people in the United States." The floor manager of the Civil Rights bill in the House of Representatives, Representative James Wilson, of Iowa, quoted from *McCulloch v. Maryland* and *Prigg v. Pennsylvania* to support the same conclusion. Representative Wilson proclaimed that "the end" of the Thirteenth Amendment "is the maintenance of freedom to the citizen." Wilson thus asserted that the enforcement of the constitutionally secured rights of freedom is one of the ends for which Congress possesses plenary power.[12]

The Republican leaders' theory of plenary congressional power was also premised on their belief that equality and the natural rights of life, liberty, and property proclaimed in the Declaration of Independence constituted the civil rights of all Americans as citizens of the United States. Thus, Senator Trumbull declared that "the liberty which a person enjoys in society" is "the liberty to which a citizen is entitled; that is the liberty which was intended to be secured by the Declaration of Independence and the Constitution of the United States originally, and more especially by the amendment which has recently been adopted." Many of the framers reasoned that the social contract between the national government and the people of the United States not only empowered Congress but also obligated it to secure citizens' inalienable natural rights in return for their allegiance. Equating the Thirteenth Amendment's guarantee of liberty to the principles of the Declaration of Independence, Trumbull declared that the Thirteenth Amendment put the principles of the Declaration of Independence into the Constitution by establishing the status of all Americans as that of freemen, that is, as citizens, and thereby imposed on Congress the duty to secure to them "as United States citizens the rights that all free men enjoy, namely, the inalienable rights to life, liberty, property and equality before the law."[13]

Representative Wilson expressed the same views in the House. He declared that the rights of U.S. citizens are "the absolute rights of individuals" and include "the right of personal security, the right of personal liberty, and the right to acquire and enjoy property. These rights have been justly considered, and frequently declared, by the people of this country, to be natural, inherent, and inalienable." Asserting the social contract principle of Congress's power to enact the Civil Rights bill, Wilson declared: "Now, sir, I reassert that the possession of these rights by the citizen raises by necessary implication the power in Congress to protect them."[14]

Wilson based Congress's power to enact the Civil Rights Act on two premises: that the civil rights it secured constitute some of the natural rights of U.S. citizenship and that the sovereign nature of the national government encompassed not only the power but also the duty proclaimed in the Declaration of Independence to protect the rights of its citizens. He declared that he based his "justification of this bill" on the "broad principle" that *we possess the power to do those things which Governments are organized to do*," namely, "to protect a citizen of the United States against a violation of his rights," even if the violation is attributable to "the law of a single State." Consequently, the people of the United States, "being entitled to certain rights as citizens of the United States, were entitled to protection in those rights, and [Congress's] power to protect them [in their inalienable rights] is necessarily implied from the entire body of the Constitution, which was made for the protection of these rights, and upon the duty of the Government to enforce and protect all those rights."[15]

The Republicans' theory of Congress's civil rights enforcement power was grounded on their theory of U.S. citizenship. The power to "intervene" by "our laws and our courts" to "maintain the proud character of American citizenship . . . ," Wilson proclaimed, "permeates our whole system, is a part of it, . . . *the right to exercise this power depends upon no express delegation, but runs with the rights it is designed to protect*." Wilson insisted that Congress possessed "the same latitude in respect to the selection of means through which to exercise this power that belongs to us when a power rests upon express delegation; and that the [judicial] decisions which support the latter maintain the former." Congress also possessed the power "to select the means in accordance with the doctrines laid down in the case of McCulloch vs. The State of Maryland."[16]

Many of the framers and supporters of the Civil Rights Act of 1866 applied the broad theory of Congress's implied powers articulated by Chief Justice John Marshall in *McCulloch v. Maryland* and Justice Story in *Prigg v. Pennsylvania* and argued not only that the Thirteenth Amendment delegated to Congress the constitutional authority to enforce the natural rights of United States citizens, but also that the Privileges and Immunities Clause of Article IV, § 2, cl. 1, the Bill of Rights, and especially the Fifth Amendment's explicit guarantee of life, liberty, and property delegated this authority. Thus, Wilson declared: "Now, sir, in relation to the great fundamental rights embraced in the bill of rights, the citizen being possessed of them is entitled to a remedy." Referring to *McCulloch* and *Prigg*, Wilson admonished: "That is the doctrine . . . as laid down by the courts. There can be no dispute about this. The possession of the rights by the citizen raises by implication the power in Congress to provide appropriate means for their protection; in other words, to supply the needed remedy." Since "the citizen is entitled to the right [sic] of life, liberty, and property," Wilson admonished, "the power is with us to provide the necessary protective remedies." In a resounding assertion of the social contract, Wilson proclaimed that these remedies "must be provided by the government of the United States, whose duty it is to protect the citizen in return for the allegiance he owes to the Government." Other participants in the Civil Rights bill debates acknowledged the supporters' intent to enforce rights guaranteed in the Bill of Rights.[17]

More probative of the framers' understanding of Congress's legislative authority to secure Americans' constitutional rights than what they said is the legislative action they took to secure these rights. In enacting the Civil Rights Act of 1866 into law, not only did the framers of the Fourteenth Amendment say they were exercising the plenary power to enforce the constitutional rights of American citizens that earlier Congresses had exercised to protect the property right of slave owners, but they also demonstrated, through the Civil Rights Act, their exercise of this plenary power. The framers modeled the Civil Rights Act's civil and criminal remedies and enforcement structure on the Fugitive Slave acts, and incorporated into the Civil Rights Act sections of the Fugitive Slave Act of 1850.[18]

In introducing the Civil Rights bill in the House of Representatives, Representative Wilson proclaimed that the Civil Rights bill was intended to enforce the constitutionally secured right of freedom through the power Congress had previously exercised to enforce the constitutionally secured right of slavery, and he noted that the enforcement provisions of the Civil Rights bill "are made up of the several sections of the old fugitive slave law," "the constitutionality of which has been affirmed over and over again by the courts." Declaring that he was "not willing that all of these precedents, legislative and judicial, which aided slavery so long, shall now be brushed into oblivion when freedom needs theirs assistance," Wilson was determined to use them to "work out a proper measure of retributive justice by making freedom as secure as they once made slavery hateful." Underscoring the irony here, Wilson asserted: "I cannot yield up the weapons which slavery has placed in our hands now that they may be wielded in the holy cause of liberty and just government. We will turn the artillery of slavery upon itself."[19]

Congress exercised plenary civil rights enforcement power in enacting the Civil Rights Act and supplanted the states' police power over civil rights in several ways. First, Congress supplanted the states' power to determine the status of inhabitants of the United States when it defined and conferred citizenship on all Americans in every state and territory of the United States; second, Congress supplanted the states' power to determine the rights individuals shall enjoy when it defined some of the civil rights all Americans were to enjoy as U.S. citizens; and third, Congress supplanted the states' power to discriminate on the basis of race when it guaranteed that all U.S. citizens were to enjoy these civil rights on the same bases as the most-favored class of citizens enjoyed them, that is, as whites enjoyed them.[20]

Although Congress supplanted the states' police power in the ways just described, it nevertheless preserved concurrent state jurisdiction over civil rights to regulate the extent to which different classes of citizens enjoyed these rights and the manner in which they exercised them. For example, the states were still empowered to determine that married women, minors, and the insane would not have the same right to make and enforce contracts or to hold property that adult men and unmarried adult women enjoyed. The framers' understanding of equal rights was grounded in a class-based theory of equality. However, the Civil Rights Act rendered illegal racially discriminatory denials of the civil rights it secured. The Civil Rights Act demonstrates that the framers expressed in law their view that race, color, or previous condition of servitude were no longer legal classes or legitimate bases for excluding individuals from the enjoyment of these civil rights. But the statute also secured the civil rights of whites against unreasonable civil rights infringements and denials, such as infringements based on religion, country of origin, and political affiliation.[21]

Like the framers of the Fugitive Slave Act of 1850, the framers of the Civil Rights Act of 1866 and the Fourteenth Amendment exercised plenary power to enforce citizens' civil rights by enacting civil and criminal remedies for violations. They made it a federal crime to violate a citizen's civil rights. However, they limited federal criminal penalties to civil rights violations committed by individuals acting under color of law or custom and motivated by racial animus in order to preserve state jurisdiction over ordinary crimes and to impose criminal penalties on state and local executive and judicial officials in the Southern states who were failing or refusing to enforce or were denying the civil rights of black Americans. Through this criminal provision, Republicans sought to compel state judges and law-enforcement personnel to enforce the civil rights of all Americans regardless of race. They also intended to punish Southerners who, acting in their private capacities as landowners and employers of black laborers, violated the civil rights of blacks when they engaged in practices formerly used by slave owners to control and discipline their slaves authorized by state Black Codes and local ordinances and customs for subordinating and subjecting free blacks to the economic and social control of whites.[22]

The framers of the Civil Rights Act conferred exclusive jurisdiction on federal courts to remedy violations of the civil rights the statute conferred and secured. Because the act secured civil rights on the same bases as whites enjoyed them, rather than the absolute enjoyment of these rights, federal civil jurisdiction was limited to violations motivated by some animus the framers considered impermissible, such as racial, religious, or ethnic prejudice or political partisanship. Federal *criminal jurisdiction* under section 2 of the act was limited to violations motivated by racial animus and committed under color of law or custom.

Nevertheless, within these limitations, the framers conferred on the federal courts jurisdiction directly to remedy violations of substantive rights.[23]

The framers created a radical remedy for civil rights violations caused by state action or state inaction: they conferred on federal courts, to the exclusion of the states, jurisdiction to try civil actions and criminal prosecutions arising under state law. Whenever a party in a civil action, a victim of a crime, or a defendant in a criminal prosecution arising under state law was unable to enforce within state law enforcement institutions or was denied by the state any of the rights secured by the Civil Rights Act, the framers conferred on the federal courts original jurisdiction to try the civil action or criminal prosecution. Section 3 of the act authorized federal courts and federal legal officers to supplant state courts and state legal officers and to administer civil and criminal justice to remedy civil rights violations caused by state action or inaction. This section demonstrates that the framers of this statute, like those of the Fugitive Slave Act of 1850, exercised plenary remedial power and authorized the displacement of state systems of justice whenever the federal government was required to enforce citizens' civil rights because of the state's failure to do so. In addition, the framers authorized the removal to a federal court of any civil or criminal action commenced against any officer or other person for any actions "committed by virtue or under color of authority derived from" the Civil Rights Act or the Freedmen's Bureau Acts or for refusing to do any act because it would be inconsistent with the Civil Rights Act.[24]

From 1866 to 1871, the federal district court in Louisville, Kentucky, exercised this jurisdiction and administered criminal justice in cases involving blacks, either as defendants or as the victims of crimes committed by whites who would have otherwise gone unpunished. Black Kentuckians could not get civil or criminal justice in Kentucky's courts because the state's rules of evidence prohibited blacks from testifying in any case in which a white person was a party. Consequently, the U.S. attorney in Louisville, Benjamin H. Bristow, asserted jurisdiction in cases involving blacks and prosecuted whites accused by blacks of having committed crimes against them. The federal court upheld the constitutionality of this provision and dispensed criminal justice in these cases until 1871. In that year, the U.S. Supreme Court affirmed the constitutionality of this jurisdiction but interpreted the language of section 3 as authorizing federal criminal prosecutions only against black defendants, and the Kentucky legislature repealed the racially discriminatory testimony statute and permitted black witnesses to testify on the same basis as white witnesses. Section 3 also authorized the federal courts to protect the civil rights of white unionists and Union soldiers in the South from civil rights violations committed by private individuals motivated by political animus. Former Confederates persecuted unionists and Union soldiers with violence, economic harassment, and with vexatious lawsuits and criminal prosecutions for actions they had taken during and after the Civil War and under the authority of federal law.[25]

Not only did the framers of the Civil Rights Act and Fourteenth Amendment incorporate the kind of civil and criminal remedies earlier Congresses had adopted in the Fugitive Slave acts, but they also incorporated the enforcement structure from the Fugitive Slave Act of 1850. Like the 1850 act, the 1866 statute authorized federal judges to appoint U.S. commissioners to enforce the act and the rights it secured, and it imposed a duty on federal officers "to institute proceedings against all and every person" who violated the act, enforcing the duty by requiring federal officials to pay a fine of $1,000 to the victim of a civil rights violation on their failure diligently to enforce the statute. Again like the 1850 act, the Civil Rights Act authorized federal commissioners to summon to their aid "the bystanders or posse comitatus of the county" as they thought necessary to perform their duties under the act and "to insure a faithful observance of" the Thirteenth Amendment. As the Fugitive Slave Act of 1850 imposed criminal penalties of a fine and imprisonment against anyone who prevented the arrest or harbored, concealed, rescued, or assisted the escape of fugitive slaves, the Civil Rights Act imposed analogous criminal penalties against anyone who hindered or prevented a federal officer from executing a warrant or process issued pursuant to the act or prevented the arrest or harbored, concealed, rescued, or assisted the escape of anyone subject to arrest under the act. The 1866 act authorized the president of the United States to reassign federal judges and legal officers to where they were most needed to redress violations of the statute and to deploy the armed services or state militia "as shall be necessary to prevent the violation and enforce the execution of this act."[26]

The Civil Rights Act of 1866 represents, at the very least, the constitutional power the framers of the Fourteenth Amendment understood the Thirteenth Amendment delegated to Congress to enforce constitutional rights and they actually exercised to enforce constitutional rights, since they were the legislators who enacted the Civil Rights Act. Furthermore, the framers repeatedly expressed their intention to incorporate the provisions of the Civil Rights Act into the Fourteenth Amendment to ensure the statute's constitutionality and to put the statute's rights guarantees into the Constitution to protect against their possible repeal by a future Congress. The framers thus intended to incorporate into the Fourteenth Amendment their interpretation of the Thirteenth Amendment's plenary power to secure and protect "the [natural] rights that all free men enjoy" as promised by the Declaration of Independence. Opponents of the Civil Rights Act and the proposed Fourteenth Amendment repeatedly acknowledged this connection between the statute and the amendment. The framers necessarily intended the Fourteenth Amendment to delegate to Congress the plenary power to define and enforce in the federal courts the substantive constitutional rights of U.S. citizens they had just exercised in enacting the Civil Rights Act. The Fourteenth Amendment is therefore an amplification of the rights enforcement authority the framers exercised when they enacted the Civil Rights Act of 1866 to implement the Thirteenth Amendment.[27]

Congress's power to enforce individuals' rights pursuant to the Thirteenth Amendment is much broader according to this interpretation than the "badges and incidents of slavery" interpretation. It offers a potentially more efficacious approach to enforcing the rights this volume's scholars argue the Thirteenth Amendment secures, or should secure today. On this view, the Thirteenth Amendment's guarantee of liberty necessarily encompasses all the rights the Supreme Court has decided are protected by the right to liberty guaranteed in the Fourteenth Amendment's Due Process Clause under the substantive due process doctrine. Furthermore, because these fundamental rights are secured as rights of U.S. citizenship, the federal government's authority to secure these rights is plenary and not limited to correcting state violations. Congress is authorized to legislate to enforce these rights directly against any violation.

It has long been my view that the framers of the Civil Rights Act of 1866 and the Fourteenth Amendment intended to make more explicit the nationalization of civil rights achieved by the Thirteenth Amendment, albeit while also preserving concurrent state jurisdiction. Although the historical evidence supports this interpretation, it presents a problem. Even though the framers supplanted the states' police power over civil rights only to the extent they deemed necessary to protect them and sought to preserve state jurisdiction over ordinary civil and criminal civil rights violations, their theory of civil rights as constitutionally secured rights of U.S. citizenship gives to Congress the authority to supplant the states' police power completely.[28]

In its 1873 decision in the *Slaughterhouse Cases*, the Supreme Court recognized that this interpretation of the Thirteenth and Fourteenth amendments entailed the recognition of Congress's plenary power to enforce constitutional rights. The Court rejected the petitioners' argument that the Thirteenth and Fourteenth amendments secured the fundamental rights in which liberty consists as rights of U.S. citizenship precisely because it would have recognized plenary congressional authority to secure fundamental constitutional rights. In this five-to-four decision that liberal and conservative legal scholars agree was inconsistent with the framers' intent, Justice Samuel Miller declared that this understanding would "transfer the security and protection" of "nearly every civil right for the establishment and protection of which organized government is instituted" "from the States to the federal government." It would "bring within the power of Congress the entire domain of civil rights heretofore belonging exclusively to the States." It "would constitute this court a perpetual censor upon all legislation of the States, on the civil rights of their own citizens," which would "fetter and degrade the State governments by subjecting them to the control of Congress" in the exercise of their powers of the "most ordinary and fundamental character." In short, this view of federal constitutional rights would change "the whole theory of the relations of the State and Federal governments to each other and of both these governments to the people." The Court rejected such far-reaching changes "in the absence of language which expresses such a purpose too clearly to admit of doubt." Even a Court dominated by justices committed to interpreting the text of the Constitution according to the understanding of its framers is not likely to adopt such a far-reaching interpretation of the Thirteenth Amendment.[29]

Later Reconstruction Congresses continued the approach to constitutional rights enforcement adopted in the Fugitive Slave acts of 1793 and 1850 and the Civil Rights Act of 1866. They exercised plenary power to enforce Fourteenth Amendment and Fifteenth Amendment rights when they enacted the Enforcement Act of 1870 and the 1871 Ku Klux Klan Act. These statutes explicitly imposed civil liability and criminal penalties on state officials and private individuals who interfered with or prevented citizens from exercising their constitutionally secured rights, such as the right to vote in state and federal elections and the First Amendment rights to freedom of speech and freedom of assembly for political purposes, the right to life and the right to the equal protection of the law. These statutes went beyond the 1866 act by establishing federal criminal jurisdiction to punish constitutional rights violations committed by private individuals without regard to state action or inaction. Furthermore, the 1870 Enforcement Act reenacted the Civil Rights of 1866 pursuant to the recently ratified Fourteenth Amendment, to ensure its constitutionality, and it also extended to all persons in the United States the same specific civil rights as are enjoyed by white citizens that the Civil Rights Act of 1866 originally conferred on U.S. citizens. The 1870 Enforcement Act extended to all persons the federal remedies and processes the 1866 act secured to U.S. citizens to enforce their civil rights, and it expressly criminalized deprivations of these civil rights under color of law or custom and because of "such person being an alien, or by reason of his color or race." Thus, Congress expressly declared that, in addition to race, color, and previous condition of servitude, alienage was no longer a legitimate basis for denying or infringing civil rights.[30]

The federal attorneys and federal judges who were charged with enforcing the 1866, 1870, and 1871 statutes accepted their charge and enforced them. The Department of Justice directed U.S. attorneys to prosecute all violators, and government attorneys followed the attorney general's directives and vigorously enforced these statutes and brought prosecutions against thousands of defendants with surprising success. Federal judges uniformly upheld the constitutionality of these statutes against constitutional challenges filed by defendants' attorneys. All three branches of the federal government shared a common understanding that the government of the United States possessed plenary power to fulfill its duty to enforce the fundamental constitutional rights of all Americans, and they joined together in a heroic effort to protect American citizens by prosecuting violators of these statutes.[31]

The intertwined history of slavery and freedom reveals a profound moral anomaly in U.S. constitutionalism. Whereas the U.S. Supreme Court affirmed the plenary power that Congress, the federal executive, and the federal courts exercised before the Civil War to secure and enforce the constitutionally secured property right of slave owners in their slaves, the Court refused to affirm the same plenary power that Congress, the federal executive, and the lower federal courts exercised to secure the fundamental rights of freemen after the Civil War. In its interpretations of the Thirteenth Amendment as a guarantee against the badges and incidents of slavery and of the Fourteenth Amendment as a guarantee against state action, the Supreme Court perpetuates the morally problematic principle that these amendments do not authorize as much constitutional authority to protect the human rights and equality of all Americans as the original Constitution authorized to protect the property rights of slave owners. Aware of this history, we are confronted as a society with the moral dilemma the framers of the Thirteenth and Fourteenth amendments confronted and resolved in 1866 when they acted to secure fundamental individual rights. The question is whether the Supreme Court is willing to confront and resolve this troubling moral question as did the framers of the Thirteenth and Fourteenth amendments, or will choose to ignore it and thereby perpetuate this moral anomaly of U.S. constitutionalism.

NOTES

1. *Bailey v. Alabama*, 219 U.S. 219, 241 (1911).

2. *See, e.g.*, Robert J. Kaczorowski, *Congress's Power to Enforce Fourteenth Amendment Rights: Lessons from Federal Remedies the Framers Enacted*, 42 HARV. J. ON LEGIS. 187 (2005) (hereafter Kaczorowski, 42 HARV. J. ON LEGIS.); Kaczorowski, *The Supreme Court and Congress's Power to Enforce Constitutional Rights: An Overlooked Moral Anomaly*, 73 FORDHAM L. REV. 153 (2004) (hereafter Kaczorowski, 73 FORDHAM L. REV.); Kaczorowski, *Revolutionary Constitutionalism in the Era of the Civil War and Reconstruction*, 61 N.Y.U. L. REV. 863 (1986) (hereafter Kaczorowski, 61 N.Y.U. L. REV.); Kaczorowski, THE POLITICS OF JUDICIAL INTERPRETATION: THE FEDERAL COURTS, DEPARTMENT OF JUSTICE AND CIVIL RIGHTS, 1866–1876 (1985) (hereafter, Kaczorowski, THE POLITICS OF JUDICIAL INTERPRETATION).

3. U.S. CONST. art. IV, § 2, cl. 3.

4. Act of Feb. 12, 1793, ch. 7, 1 Stat. 302. §§ 3, 4. The legislative history of the 1793 Fugitive Slave Act is recounted in William R. Leslie, *A Study in the Origins of Interstate Rendition: The Big Beaver Creek Murders*, 57 AM. HIST. REV. 63 (1952); Paul Finkelman, *The Kidnapping of John Davis and the Adoption of the Fugitive Slave Law of 1793*, 56 J.S. HIST. 411 (1990).

5. Robert J. Kaczorowski, *Fidelity Through History and to It: An Impossible Dream?* 65 FORDHAM L. REV. 1663, 1673–85.

6. *Prigg v. Pennsylvania*, 41 U.S. (16 Pet.) 539, 612 (1842).

7. *Id.* at 613; *McCulloch v. Maryland*, 17 U.S. (4 Wheat.) 316 (1819) and its relationship to Justice Story's opinion in *Prigg* is analyzed in Kaczorowski, 73 FORDHAM L. REV. 168–81.

8. *Prigg*, 41 U.S. (16 Pet.) At 616–17.

9. Act of Sept. 18, 1850, ch. 60, 9 Stat. 462. *Ableman v. Booth*, 62 U.S. (21 How.) 506, 526 (1858); *see* Kaczorowski, 73 FORDHAM L. REV. 191–204.

10. Kaczorowski, 73 FORDHAM L. REV. 204–5; Kaczorowski, 42 HARV. J. ON LEGIS. 199.

11. Kaczorowski, 42 HARV. J. ON LEGIS. 200–202; Kaczorowski, 73 FORDHAM L. REV. 209–16. CONG. GLOBE, 39th Cong., 1st Sess. 474–75, 1118, 1294 (1866) (hereafter CONG. GLOBE).

12. CONG. GLOBE at 474–75, 504, 1118, 1294 (1866). *See* Kaczorowski, 73 FORDHAM L. REV. 211–15.

13. CONG. GLOBE at 474; *see* Kaczorowski, 73 FORDHAM L. REV. 223–30.

14. CONG. GLOBE at 1118.

15. CONG. GLOBE at 1119; *id.* app at 157.

16. *Id.* at 1119; *id.* app at 157; *see also id.* at 570, 1151–53,1293–95, 1832–33.

17. *Id.* at 1294; *see also id.* at 1291–92, 1152,1153, 1270, 1833, 476, 500, 1120, 1156–57, app 158–59; Kaczorowski, 73 FORDHAM L. REV. 216–30.

18. Kaczorowski, 73 FORDHAM L. REV. 205–9.

19. CONG. GLOBE at 1118.

20. Civil Rights Act of 1866, ch. 31, 14 Stat. 27; Kaczorowski, 42 HARV. J. ON LEGIS. 204–30.

21. Civil Rights Act of 1866, ch. 31, 14 Stat. 27 §§ 1–3; Kaczorowski, 42 HARV. J. ON LEGIS. 216–19, 250–54.

22. Civil Rights Act of 1866, ch. 31, 14 Stat. 27 § 2; Kaczorowski, 42 HARV. J. ON LEGIS. 230–46.

23. Civil Rights Act of 1866, ch. 31, 14 Stat. 27 §§ 2, 3; Kaczorowski, 42 HARV. J. ON LEGIS. 230–60, 281–82.

24. Civil Rights Act of 1866, ch. 31, 14 Stat. 27 § 3; Kaczorowski, 42 HARV. J. ON LEGIS. 246–49.

25. *United States v. Rhodes*, 27 F. Cas. 785 (C.C.D. Ky. 1866) (No. 16,151); *Blyew v. United States*, 80 U.S. (13 Wall.) 581, 592–93; Kaczorowski, 42 HARV. J. ON LEGIS.

248–49, 250–60; Kaczorowski, THE POLITICS OF JUDICIAL INTERPRETATION 8–13, 108–16; ROSS A. WEBB, BENJAMIN HELM BRISTOW: BORDER STATE POLITICIAN 51–58 (1969); Ross A. Webb, *Benjamin Helm Bristow: Civil Rights Champion, 1866–1872*, 15 CIVIL WAR HIST. 39, 39–42 (1969); Victor B. Howard, *The Black Testimony Controversy in Kentucky, 1866–1872*, 58 J. NEGRO HIST. 140, 146–53 (1973).

26. Civil Rights Act of 1866, ch. 31, 14 Stat. 27, 28–29, §§ 4–9; Kaczorowski, 42 HARV. J. ON LEGIS. 260–63.

27. CONG. GLOBE at 474; Kaczorowski, 42 HARV. J. ON LEGIS. 263–80.

28. Robert J. Kaczorowski, THE NATIONALIZATION OF CIVIL RIGHTS: CONSTITUTIONAL THEORY AND PRACTICE IN A RACIST SOCIETY, 1866–1883 (1987) (submitted as a doctoral dissertation to the University of Minnesota [1971]); Kaczorowski, 61 N.Y.U. L. REV. 863.

29. Slaughterhouse Cases, 83 U.S. (16 Wall.) 36, 76, 77, 78 (1873).

30. Act of May 31, 1870, ch. 114, 16 Stat. 140; Act of Apr. 20, 1871, ch. 22, 17 Stat. 13. The Civil Rights Act of 1866 was reenacted in the Act of May 31, 1870, ch. 114, 16 Stat. 140, 144, § 18; civil rights were extended to "all persons within the jurisdiction of the United States," *in id.*, § 16, and criminal penalties were imposed on persons acting under color of law or custom who deprived aliens of their civil rights, in *id.* § 17.

31. Kaczorowski, THE POLITICS OF JUDICIAL INTERPRETATION is a systematic history of the federal government's enforcement of these federal civil rights statutes during Reconstruction.

ACKNOWLEDGMENTS

Along the trek of completing of this project I received a wealth of help and support. Without the concern of many mentors this collection would have been impossible. I am particularly grateful for the advice and encouragement of Mark Tushnet, Sanford Levinson, Alfred L. Brophy, Daniel W. Hamilton, Jack Rakove, Harold Hyman, Richard Delgado, and Mary Frances Berry. I have also benefitted from the editorial excellence of Peter Dimock, Philip Leventhal, and Anne Routon at Columbia University Press.

As with all that I do, my family is an unending wellspring of joy. During the course of writing and editing, my son Ariel learned how to recognize letters and ride a two-wheel bicycle—at three years of age no less!—and my daughter began to read and play the piano, at five. My wife, Alexandra Roginsky Tsesis, continues to reach new heights as a surgeon and to be a source of inspiration for me.

For the depth of all their guidance, generous expenditure of time, patient correction, timely criticism, courteousness, and overall understanding I am forever grateful.

CONTRIBUTORS

WILLIAM M. M. CARTER, JR., is a professor of law at the Temple University Beasley School of Law. He specializes in constitutional law, civil rights, critical race theory, and international human rights law. His articles include "A Thirteenth Amendment Framework for Combating Racial Profiling," in the *Harvard Civil Rights–Civil Liberties Law Review*.

DAVID BRION DAVIS has been elected a member of the American Academy of Arts and Sciences and the American Philosophical Association. He is the Sterling Professor of History Emeritus at Yale University and director emeritus of Yale's Gilder Lehrman Center. His book *The Problem of Slavery in Western Culture* won several prestigious awards, including the Pulitzer Prize. Davis won the Bancroft Prize and National Book Award for *The Problem of Slavery in the Age of Revolution*.

PAUL FINKELMAN is President William McKinley Distinguished Professor of Law and Public Policy and Senior Fellow, Government Law Center, Albany Law School. He specializes in American legal history, race, and the law. His books include *Imperfect Union: Slavery, Federalism, and Comity*.

Risa L. Goluboff is professor of law, professor of history, and Caddell and Chapman Research Professor at the University of Virginia. Her book *The Lost Promise of Civil Rights* won the 2008 James Willard Hurst Prize, given by the Law and Society Association for the best work in sociolegal history published in 2007. She was a 2009 recipient of a Guggenheim Foundation Fellowship.

Robert J. Kaczorowski, professor of law and director of the Condon Institute in Legal History at Fordham University School of Law, is author of *The Politics of Judicial Interpretation: The Federal Courts, Department of Justice, and Civil Rights, 1866–1876* and coeditor of *Constitutionalism in American Culture: Writing the New Constitutional History*.

Andrew Koppelman is John Paul Stevens Professor of Law and professor of political science at Northwestern University. His latest book is *Same Sex, Different States: When Same-Sex Marriages Cross State Lines*.

James M. McPherson is the George Henry Davis '86 Professor of American History at Princeton University, where he taught for forty-two years before retiring in 2004. He is the author of more than a dozen books on the era of the American Civil War, including his first book, *The Struggle for Equality: Abolitionists and the Negro in the Civil War and Reconstruction* (1964), and his Pulitzer Prize–winning *Battle Cry of Freedom: The Civil War Era*.

Darrell A. H. Miller is an assistant professor at the University of Cincinnati College of Law. He received his J.D. from Harvard Law School and is also a graduate of Oxford University and Anderson University.

Maria L. Ontiveros is a professor at the University of San Francisco School of Law. Her research focuses on the Thirteenth Amendment and workplace issues affecting immigrant workers, especially immigrant women. She coauthors a leading casebook on employment discrimination.

David M. Oshinsky is the Jack S. Blanton Chair in History, Distinguished Teaching Professor at the University of Texas at Austin. His books include *Polio: An American Story*, which won the 2006 Pulitzer Prize for history of the United States, and *A Conspiracy So Immense: The World of Joe McCarthy*, which won the Hardeman Prize as the best book about the U.S. Congress.

James Gray Pope is professor of law and Sidney Reitman Scholar at the Rutgers University School of Law. His writings on workers' rights have appeared in a variety of publications, including the *Columbia Law Review*, *Labor History*, *Law and History Review*, *New Labor Forum*, and the *Yale Law Journal*.

GEORGE A. RUTHERGLEN is the John Barbee Minor Distinguished Professor of Law and Edward F. Howrey Research Professor at the University of Virginia. He has written numerous articles on civil rights and employment discrimination and authored or coauthored several books, most recently *Civil Rights Actions: Enforcing the Constitution* and *Employment Discrimination: Visions of Equality in Theory and Doctrine*.

AVIAM SOIFER is the dean and professor at the University of Hawai'i School of Law. His book, *Law and the Company We Keep*, was awarded the triennial Alpha Sigma Nu National Jesuit Book Prize. He serves on several boards of trustees and advisory committees of public interest organizations dealing with medical care, human rights, and judicial and legal education in the United States and abroad.

ANDREW E. TASLITZ, Welsh S. White Distinguished Visiting Professor of Law, University of Pittsburgh School of Law, 2008–2009, and professor of law, Howard University School of Law, specializes in criminal procedure and its history and is the author of *Reconstructing the Fourth Amendment: A History of Search and Seizure, 1789–1868*.

ALEXANDER TSESIS'S most recent book is *We Shall Overcome: A History of Civil Rights and the Law*. His other books include *The Thirteenth Amendment and American Freedom: A Legal History*. Since 2007, he has been on the Loyola University School of Law (Chicago) faculty.

MICHAEL VORENBERG is associate professor of history in the Brown University History Department. His first book, *Final Freedom: The Civil War, the Abolition of Slavery, and the Thirteenth Amendment*, dealt with the making and meaning of the Thirteenth Amendment and the development of a new constitutional order after the Civil War.

WILLIAM M. WIECEK is the Congdon Professor of Public Law at the College of Law and a professor of history at the Maxwell School of Syracuse University. He took his LL.B. at the Harvard Law School and his Ph.D. in history at the University of Wisconsin–Madison. He is the author of *The Birth of the Modern Constitution: The United States Supreme Court, 1941–1953*, vol. 12 of

The Oliver Wendell Holmes Devise History of the Supreme Court of the United States.

REBECCA E. ZIETLOW is the Charles W. Fornoff Professor of Law and Values at the University of Toledo College of Law. She is the author of *Enforcing Equality: Congress, the Constitution, and the Protection of Individual Rights.*

INDEX

326   *Index*